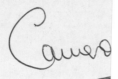

Discovery Guide to
Yemen

Chris Bradley

IMMEL
Publishing

Discovery Guide to Yemen, first edition

Published by Immel Publishing Ltd.,
20 Berkeley St., London W1X 5AE.
Tel: 0171 491 1799; fax: 0171 493 5524.

General Series Editor Paula Casey-Vine
Commissioning Editor Peter Vine
Layout, cover design and typesetting by Johan Hofsteenge
Printed by Paramount Printing Co. Ltd Hong Kong

A CIP catalogue record for this book is available from the British Library

ISBN 1 898162 15 8

To help with the next edition, the reader is asked to send information and comments to the General Editor, *Discovery Guide to Yemen,* Immel Publishing Ltd., 20 Berkeley St., London W1X 5AE.

ACKNOWLEDGEMENTS

Unlike earlier eras, when travellers had months or even years for journeys in south Arabia, everything in the 1990s is usually done at breakneck speed. I would like to thank the following people who have helped me through this project. Some of whom I already knew, and others who have become new friends. I covered most of the ground myself, but there are times when I got too close to the project and needed some fresh input.

Jack Jackson is an expert on the Yemen who very kindly agreed to oversee the information contained within the book – and to add pieces where necessary. Matt Dickinson has cast his eyes over the desert sections. Similarly Brian Wood has checked the mountain and Tihama sections. Dave Farrow passed on his considerable knowledge of the birds of southern Arabia. My thanks to you all. At an official level I greatly appreciate the help of Mr Idrees al-Shammam and Mr Fadhl al-Maghafi of the Yemen Embassy in London, who handled all my documentation and permissions efficiently.

Arrangements on the ground were made through the Yemen Arab Tourism Agency (YATA) and I must acknowledge all the hard work and effort put into the project by Abdulkarim Abu Taleb and Yahya Abu Taleb at the office in Sana'a. Of the many YATA drivers who accompanied me around the country I would especially like to thank Mohammed Saleh, who had as much of an adventure as I did; my good friend Abdul Warith alKateeb, who explained many of the mysteries of the Yemen; Yahya al-Housini, who introduced me to the Mahweet region; Massad Ali, who struggled through the mud to get me to Shahara; and Ahmed Shathan and Ali Abdullah al-Reim who were helpful in Sana'a.

At the General Tourism Authority office of the Ministry of Culture and Tourism, I am grateful for the time and effort offered by Abdullah Hizam and Yahya al-Olfi. The Tourist Officer in Seiyun, Hassan Ali Sheikh Bahumaid was extremely helpful with information about the Hadramaut.

My gratitude also goes to the staff of the Yemenia office in London, especially Captain al-Othary, for their help and assistance with flights from London. I would like to thank the proprietors and staff of the Taj Sheba in Sana'a (in particular the extremely helpful and capable Mathew Kurian and Hureen Advani); the Aden Movenpick Hotel (special thanks to manager Robert Fierz and resident manager Alaa Hamid); the Ambassador Hotel in Hodeidah (proprietor Saleh Ahmed Al-Shami and general manager Ahmed Al-Akhrash); and the staff of the Bilquis Hotel in Marib. Fuad al-Futaih has kindly allowed me to reproduce one of his fine prints in the book.

Finally, my gratitude goes to Tim Mackintosh-Smith who helped to unravel some of the intricacies of social and tribal Yemen – I hope more people get to know and love the country as much as he does.

CONTENTS

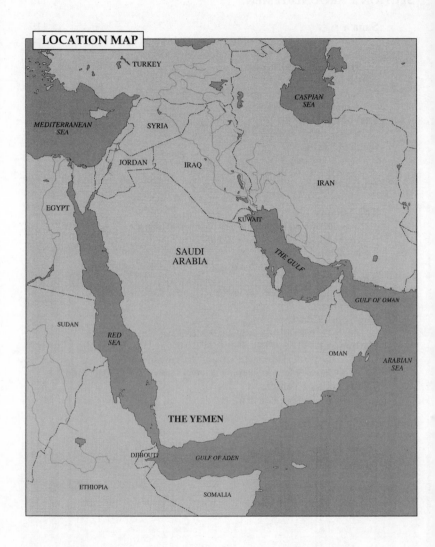

LOCATION MAP

INTRODUCTION

I am sure that most people intending to visit the Yemen have bemused friends and relatives who wonder why on earth anyone would wish to travel there. Such questions are usually posed by those who know little of the Middle East and nothing about the Yemen. In fact the only image most people can evoke is one of arid desert areas crossed by camel tracks. This type of scene can of course be found, but it is only one aspect of a country that has infinitely more to offer.

The main attraction for travellers to Yemen is the fascinating history of the region and the discovery that there is life after Egypt. Inevitably the overriding and lasting impression is of the phenomenal variety in scenery, which surprises everyone. The friendliness of the Yemenis themselves is also a great bonus.

I first became interested in the Yemen whilst working in Saudi Arabia in the 1970s, and could not believe that there was a 'green and wonderful land' further south. I travelled to the Yemen Arab Republic (YAR) – North Yemen – in the 1980s. After unification I visited places in the former People's Democratic Republic of Yemen (PDRY) as best I could – but found I needed a good guidebook – eventually I realised I would have to write it myself! In this Discovery Guide to Yemen I have omitted prices since they are constantly changing. In any case, within twenty-four hours of arrival travellers will become aware of local costs and operations, which are similar to those in other Middle Eastern countries. I have also standardised many local words and names in an effort to make them easier to understand. For example, I use Mokha not al-Mukha, Hodeidah not al-Hudaydah. The hoped-for smooth unification of North and South Yemen was interrupted by the Gulf War, an influx of returnees and internal friction. This led to a short outbreak of hostilities between rival Northern and Southern troops in May 1994, the effects of which will be felt for quite some time especially in the south. Like many countries, the Yemen is in a state of change – better to see it now, before it alters too much.

The Yemen will be many things to many people. For me, it is the dramatic view north from Kahail; eating local food at the Suq al-Hubz in Sana'a Old City; looking across Wadi Hadramaut from the top of Husn al-Urr; and watching the sun go down at Bir Ali. May you also return with treasured memories from this special country.

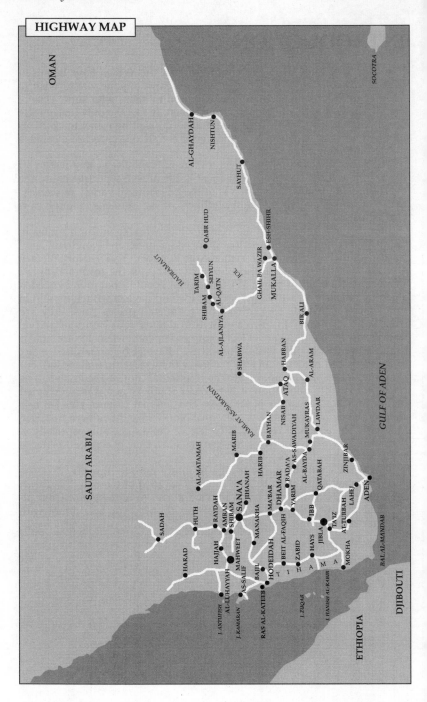

Husn al-Guwayzi, near Mukalla.

SECTION 1:
BACKGROUND

Travel Facts

Country File

TRAVEL FACTS

TRAVELLING TO YEMEN

By Road

There is an excellent road link with **Saudi Arabia** along the Tihama coastal plain. While this is the major entry and exit point for Yemenis and Saudis, there is a basic problem for other visitors coming from Saudi Arabia into Yemen – how to get into Saudi Arabia in the first place! With no international tourist industry as such the only visitors likely to arrive by this route will be foreign workers who have a Saudi sponsor, but they will still require a Yemen visa. An added problem is that the Yemen government do not recognise Saudi control over this border region, claiming that it was seized illegally in 1934.

The latest and most interesting development is on the **Omani** border, roughly midway along the Arabian peninsula's Indian Ocean coastline. At the end of 1992 the two governments finally signed a border agreement, fixing the boundary and facilitating immigration and customs posts. This makes it possible to enter Yemen overland from Oman.

By Sea

The expected rise in trade through the port of **Aden** should increase the possibilities of arriving by sea. It will take several years for this to become a serious option, as the average traveller would find it much easier, quicker and probably cheaper to fly from Djibouti. If you do arrive by ship there are immigration facilities at Aden, Hodeidah and Mokha.

By Air

The cost of flying to the Yemen is not unreasonable, but there is little choice of how and when you go. Several factors have affected the frequency of flights and the cost of tickets: the limited number of carriers; the minimal tourist industry; the high percentage of business travellers; and the fact that there are few through routes for international carriers (it is a destination in itself).

In London, Paris, Frankfurt and Rome it is easiest to contact the local **Yemenia** (Yemen Airways) office. Most of these offices also double as tourist information centres whether it is individual or group travel that you are looking for. These flights are popular and almost always full, so it is important to make your bookings well in advance especially during holiday periods such as Christmas and Easter. It is particularly important when making your return flight reservation, as many of the aircraft can only take off in the rarefied air of Sana'a (2,200m above sea level) at less than maximum load.

Yemenia is a small airline that is hoping to merge with the state airline of the old PDRY, al-Yemda. The combined airline will serve the unified country internationally and domestically allowing you to make easy connections within the country. The main advantage of travelling with Yemenia is that there is no change of aircraft *en route* and no transit at a foreign airport, now using Airbus A310s. In late 1993 al-Yemda started their own non-stop weekly service between London and Aden. British Airways also inaugurated a twice weekly London–Aden–Sana'a– London service, but this was suspended in May 1994. Lufthansa, Air France and KLM can offer connections through their respective countries. Egyptair and Royal Jordanian also offer transfer flights, but the length of transit stops is sometimes prohibitive.

If you start your flight to the Yemen from outside Europe there are many more possibilities, even to Aden. In the **Middle East** there are direct flights by Yemenia from Cairo, Amman, Damascus, Dubai, Abu Dhabi and Bahrain. National airlines flying to Sana'a include Royal Jordanian, Egyptair, Syrian Arab Airlines, Gulf Air and Saudia. From **Africa** Yemenia fly out of Khartoum, Addis Ababa, Asmara and Djibouti, and there are flights by Ethiopian Airlines, Sudan Airways and Air Djibouti. From **Asia** Yemenia fly from Karachi and Bombay. Pakistan International Airlines also serves Sana'a.

Yemenia has its own offices in all major cities in Yemen, whereas other airlines are handled by numerous tour and general selling agencies with offices usually only in Sana'a.

Yemenia	*Al-Yemda*	*British Airways*
52, Stratton St.,	33, Heddon St.,	Tel: 0181-759 5511
London W1X 5FF	London W1R 7LL	
Tel: 0171-491 7186.	Tel: 0171-287 9993.	

Yemenia 737 at Seiyun Airport.

Arriving in Yemen

The arrivals hall at the airport still has some old signs about filling in currency declaration forms, dating from the days when it was necessary to exchange US$150 upon arriving. The bank is usually staffed by a man with a briefcase, who unfortunately does not issue exchange receipts (see Money). You will need to get some local cash if you intend paying for a taxi to the city centre (or pay in US dollars).

Passport control is reasonably quick (see Documentation) but the baggage usually beats you into the customs hall.

Unlike many main airports, Sana'a International is still very relaxed and sleeps for most of the day. If you are with a group, the agency representatives will meet, assist and transfer you with the minimum of fuss. If you are arriving alone, try to find other new arrivees to split the cost of a taxi to the centre. Above the taxi rank is a sign giving the cost for a journey to Tahrir Square, about 20 minutes' journey.

The luxury **Taj Sheba Hotel** is ideally placed in the centre and a good place to aim for even if you are not staying there. Other top class hotels are some way out beyond the ring road. One of the best developments in accommodation over the last two years has been the conversion of some tower houses in the old city into small hotels (see Accommodation).

Before leaving Sana'a to tour the country it is better to reconfirm your return flight out of Yemen. This can be done through the tour agent responsible for your travel arrangements or direct with any Yemenia office or the agency that represents your particular airline.

Departing from Yemen

Always allow plenty of time for getting to the airport and checking in. All luggage has to go through an X-ray machine before it even gets near to the check-in desks. You can take out of the country anything bought as a souvenir, except items thought to be of historic interest over 40 years old. Be sure to put any *jambias* (the traditional Yemeni curved dagger), knives or swords into your check-in luggage, rather than taking them as hand luggage.

You may have to pay airport departure tax; it depends on whether it is already included in your ticket. Nobody seems to know in advance whether it is included or not, so I suggest that you arrive with US$10 cash in case you do have to pay.

You have to fill in a departure card before passing through passport control. The departure lounge has a cafeteria and some souvenir shops that accept rials. The duty-free shops only take hard currencies, there is no alcohol available, only cigarettes, perfumes and electronics.

When called to the gate there is another X-ray machine for your hand luggage. Transfer to the plane is by bus.

TRAVELLING WITHIN YEMEN

Agency tours use 4x4 (four-wheel drive) vehicles suited to off-road tracks as well as asphalt roads. Public transport around the country is limited to express buses and shared taxis. In the town centres there are private taxis, collective taxis (known as *dababs)* and route buses. There is no railway system and only limited internal flights.

During the preparation of this book I have tried to cover most of the sites which tourists will wish to see. In most cases I have dealt with visits as if you have a vehicle. In the case of tour groups – which tend to be adventure tours – the drivers and leaders will know how to get to the various sites, but I have added items of useful information.

Individual tourists who have decided to arrange everything through an agency have the advantage of going where and when they like. For independent travellers I have included most of the practical information which is likely to remain unchanged.

Car Hire

International car hire companies are not fully represented in the Yemen. Tourist sites are best visited using 4x4 vehicles, which most Yemenis are quite rightly reluctant to entrust to tourists with little or no knowledge of off-road driving. Most 4x4 vehicles are thus hired with a driver, which can help your trip considerably, as he will know the route (there are few signposts and the maps are poor) and be able to get through checkpoints. These vehicles and drivers can be organised through tour agencies.

Some companies do allow cars, including 4x4 vehicles, to be hired and driven by tourists. If you have friends in the country who will travel with you this is a good idea, but before you plan on doing it, consider the following: Do you know where you are going? Is your Arabic good enough to get through the checkpoints (there is sometimes a suspicion of foreigners travelling without a Yemeni guide)? Are you competent at driving a 4x4 in sand, mud etc.? Do you have enough basic provisions and equipment for what you intend to do? Remember that many of the roads are poor quality, especially in the south. Two companies that hire vehicles without drivers are al-Mamoon and Hadda Car Hire (see Travel Agencies).

Express Buses

Fast daily bus services connect most of the major towns and cities and this is a good way to travel as long as you do not want to visit anything *en route*. Once you buy a ticket there is a guaranteed seat, a definite departure time and a virtually assured arrival time. There are usually video films playing on board with a halfway stop for meals and drinks.

These expresses are operated by the **General Transport Corporation** and tickets must be bought in advance, often the evening before. Bus stations and ticket offices are not always in the town centre and you might need to take a taxi there if you are carrying luggage. As a tourist the main problem is the amount of time it takes to get a ticket and the inflexibility of the departure time and stops *en route*. Often you will be told at what time you can get a ticket, but upon returning, another time will be given or the bus will already be full!

Departures tend to be early in the morning around 7 o'clock and in the afternoon at 2 o'clock. From **Sana'a** there are services to and from Aden, Ta'iz, Hodeidah, Qatabah, Rada'a and al-Bayda (all departing from Bab al Yemen) and Sadah, Hajjah and Marib (departing from Bab Shu'ab). From Aden (Sheikh Othman bus station) you can get to Ta'iz, Mukalla and Ataq. There are also services from Ta'iz to Hodeidah, from Hodeidah to Harad and from Mukalla to Seiyun. Buses only travel on tarred roads, but the network is expanding quite rapidly.

Personally I do not use these buses for general sightseeing but rather as an efficient and economical way of getting between the main centres instead of flying internally. For tourist purposes it is better to use the highly developed system of shared taxis.

VEHICLE NUMBER PLATES

One thing that puzzles a lot of visitors is the great variety of vehicle registration plates. In case you are not certain what sort of vehicle it is that you are just about to step into, this list may help:

Blue – private cars from the old YAR
Yellow – taxis
Red – private vans and trucks
Black – private vehicles from the old PDRY
Green – government vehicles
Dark blue – police vehicles
White with red numbers – military vehicles
White with red square – diplomatic vehicles
White – Temporary imports (duty free) usually belonging to oil companies and aid agencies, much sought-after by the hijacking bedouins of the desert regions!

Shared Taxis

On all the express bus routes and to many more destinations reached by dirt tracks there is a good network of shared taxis that charge a set fee for the journey. The main advantage of these is that they depart throughout the day and leave when full. If you are travelling independently or making daily excursions this is an economical way of getting from town to town.

As an example of how they can be used, consider a half day tour to Kawkaban, Shibam and Thulla. This would be quite expensive if hiring a Sana'a taxi for half a day. But you can get a shared taxi to Shibam and then hitch a lift or get a private taxi up to Kawkaban. You could walk up, but I think it is better to go by taxi and walk back down to Shibam. You could then get another lift or private taxi to Thulla and then a shared taxi back to the capital.

There are several advantages in travelling in this way. You get to meet more people *en route* (and tend to be offered lifts by locals who speak a European language); you do not have to worry about keeping the private taxi driver waiting if you decide to spend longer at a particular place, and it tends to be cheaper.

On longer journeys the cost of a shared taxi is about 25 per cent more than the express bus, but they are much faster especially on mountain roads. For the major routes there are coloured stripes that indicate which taxi goes where:

Sana'a (Bab al-Yemen) – Hodeidah (blue)
Sana'a (Bab al-Yemen) – Ta'iz and Aden (green)
Sana'a (Bab Shu'ab) – Marib (yellow)

Sana'a (Bab Shu'ab) – Hajjah (brown)
Hodeidah (near Hotel Ambassador) – Ta'iz (red)
Hodeidah (Jizan Road) – Jizan (red)

Taxis depart from many different places in the city depending on the destination (and sometimes on the time of day) with temporary changes such as local road works. Ask at your hotel.

Shared taxis are also more flexible than buses in that they allow you to break your journey where you want to; the taxi can soon pick up another passenger. There is always a friendly atmosphere when travelling like this, as cigarettes, water and *qat* (a mildly narcotic leaf which is chewed) are offered around and the locals will appreciate your efforts to communicate. They usually want to know which country you are from and what you have seen in the Yemen. It is never difficult to say that you think the Yemen is a beautiful country – and you will have friends for life.

There should be fixed fares per person, but as with taxi drivers world-wide you will sometimes be asked to pay a bit more. All you can do is to ask a fellow passenger (or even at your hotel) how much it should be and try to watch how much the others hand over. Always agree the fare before setting off. One of the considerations is the number of tourists involved. If there are fewer than three people in your group, the shared taxis are good value, but for larger numbers it may be worthwhile to hire a private taxi.

Private Taxis

In the cities private taxis can be identified by their black stripes, but they are not limited to the city boundaries and often head out to surrounding villages. They are more expensive than shared taxis, but offer speed, flexibility and personal service. As always, agree a price at the beginning of the journey.

In addition to being used to get from A to B, you can also hire them for half a day, a full day or for sightseeing tours. Always make sure that the driver knows that he has to wait for a certain length of time if you want to visit a place. If the driver does more than expected, a tip would be a good idea, especially if he spent more time than anticipated just hanging around.

Never expect a taxi driver to know anything about the town in which he is working. Even major hotels are sometimes a complete mystery. A hand-written note will often not be much use either, but at least you will be able to stop and between you ask directions from pedestrians.

Collective Taxis (*Dababs*)

These busy little minibuses traverse the main streets of Sana'a, Ta'iz and Hodeidah and stick to fixed routes at fixed prices. The main problem is working out exactly where they are going, but once you have cracked it, the service is fast, friendly and excellent value. If they are empty, you can also treat them as private taxis and pay them to go where you want.

This is an efficient urban transport system run by private individuals, but is common only in the northern cities. In the south they still have a poorer bus service.

Town Buses
There are inner city bus routes in all towns, but *dababs* are popular in the northern cities because of their frequency. Aden and Mukalla have good cheap bus services, but again the problem is finding out how and when and where.

Hitch-hiking
There is no tradition of hitching for fun in the Yemen and it is only really resorted to by people too poor to pay for a shared taxi. Travelling alone, you do sometimes find yourself waving down a passing vehicle to give you a ride to some obscure desert site or ruin, but even so you would be expected to offer some money for the lift.

Internal Flights
Yemenia and al-Yemda are the airlines of the two former republics, which are scheduled to merge. Unfortunately this merger has been delayed, which has led to confusion and duplication of internal routes. Yemenia has flights from Sana'a to Aden, Hodeidah, Ta'iz, Seiyun, Riyan (Mukalla), al-Ghaydah, Ataq and al-Buqe (on the Saudi border). Al-Yemda flies from Aden to Sana'a, Seiyun, Riyan, al-Ghaydah and Ataq.

Internal flights are unfortunately not a priority for the airlines and they can sometimes be cancelled in favour of international flights or for maintenance. Tourists must pay for tickets in hard currency and refunds for a cancelled flight can be a problem unless handled through a tour agency.

My advice is to fly if time and distance is a problem; for example the Seiyun–Sana'a service is good, taking less than two hours compared to two days by road. For closer destinations think about buses or shared taxis. With delays, it once took me all day to fly from Sana'a to Aden, which I could have done by bus in half the time. With the air ticket and the taxis to and from the airports it also worked out at four times the cost!

Trekking and Cycling
Both these activities require specific planning. See p. 45-6.

Out of Bounds Areas
The country has opened up tremendously since unification. However there are still areas which are sensitive for various reasons, and where tourists are not allowed. **Checkpoints** on roads and tracks will prohibit entry to certain areas and it is always better to obey the soldiers rather than to argue or try to find another way around.

For strategic and military reasons there are many hill and mountain tops that cannot be reached because of installations. Some places are always forbidden, such as Hodeidah port, Ras al-Kateeb, the Kamaran Islands, Perim Island and the area around the coast in the south-west. Others, like as-Salif, are sometimes open if you apply for special permission.

Some regions are closed to tourists because of a security threat, where tourist safety cannot be assured. These include areas like Wadi al-Jawf, Sirwah, Wadi Idim and some places to the north and south of Wadi Hadramaut.

You should not need to worry about these areas, however, as your driver

Walking to Jibla.

will never take you anywhere known to be unsafe, and the soldiers will not let you through a checkpoint into an insecure zone.

ACCOMMODATION

The unification of North and South Yemen has highlighted one particular problem more than any other: the chronic shortage and general poor quality of accommodation in the south. Having said that, there are some excellent hotels and *fonduqs* (guest houses), but generally not enough to look after all the visitors.

Now that the south is more accessible – especially Wadi Hadramaut almost every tourist wants to include it in their visit. The problem is how to cater for all these foreigners, most of whom expect certain standards of comfort. During this transitional period there will be many heated arguments and disappointed people as too many visitors scramble for too few beds. But the picture is changing already and some new clean accommodation is emerging, although it will take time to cater for all standards.

If you are travelling without reservations, be prepared to sleep rough, as hotels and *fonduqs* can fill to overflowing with just a couple of tour groups, who always take preference. Some groups have decided to camp rather than risk the hotels being overbooked, especially in the Hadramaut.

Even though the word *fonduq* means 'hotel' it has come to mean a local guest house usually in some sort of traditional building, while 'hotel' means a more modern Western style of accommodation. However, the locals often still call any hotel a *fonduq*, even the Taj Sheba. When I use the word here, I generally refer to an older building with large rooms, mattresses on the floor, and shared bathrooms.

In almost every town and village you visit, you will see a gloomy room, known as a *lokanda*, crammed with string beds. These serve many purposes: tea shops, *qat* venues, smoking dens and sleeping quarters. If all else fails you can usually arrange to unroll your sleeping bag and sleep with the locals.

Whatever the class of accommodation, there are good and bad standards, with corresponding value for money. My comments are based on my experiences and observations. In my rating system, I would gladly spend a night in anything which I have marked as low as two stars, but some of the comments may mean that a nearby place is better value for money. Anything with one star I have put in for reference and emergency, but would advise middle-of-the-road tourists to look elsewhere. Some travellers, of course, may prefer to live with the locals and would only choose to stay in the lower standard places. Some establishments may be temporarily or permanently closed due to the unstable tourist industry.

MONEY

Currency

Before unification, the two countries had separate central banks and currencies the **rial** (YR) in the YAR and the **dinar** (YD) in the PDRY. Since 1990 there has been a fixed exchange rate between them (one dinar is equal to 26 rials) and both can be used around the entire country, even though rials are more widespread and will probably take over completely.

Until the revolution against the Imam in 1962, the north used the old Maria Theresa thaler (dollar), which had been introduced in Ottoman times. This heavy silver coin had outlived its purpose in most other countries and been replaced by paper money. With the YAR came Yemeni rial notes.

In British-ruled Aden, which was administered from Bombay until 1937, the major currency was the Indian rupee. This was replaced in 1951 by the East African shilling which was widely circulated through the Protectorates, together with many other foreign coins. In 1964 the Federation of South Arabia issued the South Arabian dinar, which became the Southern Yemen dinar in 1967. With the formation of the PDRY came the Yemeni dinar in 1971.

The Yemeni rial is divided into 100 fils. There are coins of 25 fils, 50 fils and 1 YR in circulation, but you will normally find everything expressed in multiples of whole rial. There are bank notes of 1, 5, 10, 20, 50, and 100 YR, all with Arabic script on the front and English on the reverse.

The I YR note seems to be disappearing in favour of the coin, so if you get a good example, keep it if only for the picture of coffee trees (not *qat*) on the reverse. There are two types of 5 and 50 YR notes, three kinds of 10, 20 and 100 YR.

The Yemeni dinar is slowly being replaced in the south, but since the locals still use the word 'shilling' as well, the situation can be somewhat confused. There are 1,000 fils in one dinar, also referred to as 20 shillings. Thus one shilling is 50 fils. There are coins of 5, 10, 25, 50, 100 and 250 fils, with large notes for 250 and 500 fils, 1, 5 and 10 YD. All the notes have a picture of a *sambook* (dhow) in Aden harbour.

> **MONEY**
>
> The word *rial* comes from *real*, the Spanish coin which flooded the country during the great coffee-trading years of the seventeenth and eighteenth centuries. The word dinar is taken from the Latin word for money, *denarius*.

Money Exchange

Cash and travellers' cheques of all major currencies can be exchanged at the airport (if the bank is open), most banks and larger hotels. Try to insist on a receipt as you will need one if you want to pay your hotel bills in local currency (many only accept US$ anyway), and for exchanging back at the end of the trip (which is a virtual impossibility).

The dollar exchange rate is artificially low. It is imposed by the government and used for all 'official' tourist and business dealings, including transport costs, agency fees and hotel accommodation – which can often not be paid in rials anyway, only in hard currency.

The most useful hard currency is US dollars, as they are now accepted everywhere. You will find rates for other currencies but I would advise you to stick with dollars for both cash and travellers' cheques. If you also have a small wad of lower-denomination dollar notes they can be helpful for emergencies, such as paying for the taxi from the airport, if you have no rials.

However, for your own 'unofficial' spending money, for food, drinks and souvenirs for example, it is sometimes (but not always) possible to obtain a better exchange rate for both cash and travellers' cheques. This 'open rate' exists to supply those who would otherwise not get access to hard currencies: businessmen travelling abroad (the YR is almost useless outside Yemen), foreign bank account holders and people wishing to buy expensive imported goods for which payment is only accepted in dollars.

Unofficial money changers surrounded by bricks of bank notes operate quite openly in the *suq* in Sana'a. The main problem is that the rate can sometimes get out of hand, or the government may decide to crack down on these illegal dealings. Either way, there are regular purges by the police, who raid the shops and arrest the dealers (and any unfortunate tourist that happens to be there), and the 'open rate' market disappears. However, this causes a shortage of hard currency which can only be satisfied by offering a better rate and so it gradually starts up again.

The best rates are obtainable in Sana'a. There is less need for foreign currency, and thus lower rates, in Hodeidah, Ta'iz and Aden. Outside of these cities you will only be able to exchange officially.

The system might sound chaotic, and it is. Until the situation changes (which it could do at any time, with, for example, the re-introduction of an official exchange upon entering the country), you should make all official payments in hard currency (which is also a good bargaining tool). If the 'open rate' is operating you can get some spending money, but I must stress that this market is illegal. Otherwise change a small amount officially, but make your more expensive souvenir purchases in dollars, for which you will definitely get a better rate, as the shop-owners also want dollars.

It is almost impossible to get any sort of cash against a credit card, but all

Wadi al-Khun, eastern Wadi Hadramaut.

large hotels and souvenir shops will accept payment by this method – at the official rate of course. The number of acceptable credit cards is very limited.

DOCUMENTATION

Regulations for entry into Yemen are now fairly standard, and certainly much easier than before unification, particularly in the former PDRY.

Visas

Every visitor to the Republic must hold a valid passport and obtain a visa before arriving in the country. Visas will not be issued to anyone who has an entry stamp for Israel. Applications, to any Yemeni Embassy or Consulate, must be made in duplicate accompanied by two passport photographs. You can contact the Embassy visa section and arrange things yourself by post (or personal visit), or use specialist companies who can get the visas for you – and do all the running around. One such is Travcour, 9, Chester Mews, London SW1X 7AJ. Tel: 0171-223 7662.

After the visa has been issued you usually have three months in which to enter the country. Passports and visas are usually inspected whilst checking in for a flight to the Yemen.

Tourist visas are issued as a matter of course (it is better not to state that you are a journalist), but business visas require a letter from your Yemeni contact, sponsor or agent.

Immigration

Immigration cards (issued on the aircraft or available at the airport) must be filled in before going through passport control. If you are travelling independently just choose the name of a hotel that you like the look of for your address in the Yemen.

Your passport will normally be stamped 'Leave to enter for one month' with another stamp saying 'Entry' and the date of arrival in Arabic. If you need to extend your stay beyond a month for whatever reasons, simply go to the nearest Immigration Office in Sana'a, Aden, Ta'iz or Hodeidah. You must do this a few days before the month is up, and they will grant you an extension of two or four weeks at no cost.

If you are planning to leave the Yemen and then re-enter, then as a tourist you would need to reapply for a second visa outside the country. If you are on business, your Yemeni agent can arrange for an exit and re-entry visa from the Immigration Office.

Customs

Beyond luggage reclamation are the customs desks where Westerners seem to get off lightly compared to others, with usually just a quick rummage inside bags and cases.

One litre of alcohol is allowed for personal consumption. The proliferation of modern video equipment seems to be causing some concern; the main worry is the importation of tapes that might not be as blank as they seem. Video and film cameras should be declared and are likely to be entered into your passport to ensure that they leave when you do, and some tapes may be taken for a quick inspection. Magazines may be confiscated.

Make sure you have a chalk mark made on every piece of baggage, or the soldier at the gate will send you back.

EMBASSIES

Most Republic of Yemen embassies are only concerned with issuing visas. Tourist information must be obtained elsewhere.

When applying for a visa allow plenty of time for processing.

Republic of Yemen embassies around the world include:

United Kingdom
57, Cromwell Road
London SW7 2ED
Tel: 0171-584 6607
Fax: 0171-589 3350

United States
Suite 840
600 New Hampshire
Ave NW
Washington DC
20037
Tel: 202-965
4760/1/81
Fax: 202-337 2017

France
25, Rue Georges Bizet
75016 Paris
Tel: 472 36176
Fax: 472 36941

Germany
Adenaueralle 77
5300 Bonn 1
Tel: 0228-
220273/451/261490
Fax: 0228-229364

Netherlands
Surinamestraat 9
2585 GC
The Hague
Tel: 070-653936

Italy
Via Le Regina
Margherita
Code 00198 Rome
Tel: 841 6735/7611
Fax: 841 0801

Canada
Suite 1100
350 Sparks St
Ottawa
Ontario KIT 7S8
Tel: 613-232 8583/25
Fax: 613-232 8276

Switzerland
19, Ch Du Jonc
1216 Cointrin
Tel: 798 5333/4/5
Fax: 798 0465

Some foreign embassies in the Republic of Yemen, all in Sana'a, include:

United Kingdom
PO Box 1287
Hadda St
Tel: 215630-3

United States
PO Box 22347
Saawan St
Tel: 238842-5

France
PO Box 1286
Al-Bawnia Area
Tel: 275995/201958

Germany
PO Box 41
Street 22 (off Djibouti
St)
Tel: 216756-8

Netherlands
PO Box 463
Hadda St
Tel: 215626-8

Italy
PO Box 1152
Building no 9, Street
no 29
Tel: 265616/78846

A few countries have representatives in Aden:

UK: Tel. 32711-3

France:
Tel. 32129/090

Italy: Tel. 31848

Germany:
Tel. 32162/011

The newly formed **British-Yemeni Society** can be a great source of information with regular monthly meetings and lectures in London to promote friendship between the two countries. For details contact the Yemen Embassy in London.

TIME

Yemen is three hours ahead of Greenwich Mean Time.

ELECTRICITY

The voltage hovers around 220V, but can sometimes drop below this. Power failures are not unusual, but the larger hotels and buildings have standby generators ready to kick in. In smaller towns and villages the electricity supply is somewhat erratic, and a whole mountainside can be plunged into darkness for hours in the evenings. It is always a good idea to keep a torch handy as soon as the sun goes down.

If you have electrical equipment that needs to be plugged in, plugs are available in Sana'a.

COMMUNICATIONS

Considering that until the 1950s there was only one telephone in North Yemen, and that belonged to the Imam (I wonder who he called!) the country has made great strides in getting a telephone system organised. Unfortunately the systems in the two parts of the country do not yet seem to be compatible, with the result that it is almost impossible to call Aden from anywhere in the north. The north has by far the better system, both internally and internationally.

Internal Telephone Calls

Most internal public phone boxes take only coins, but there are a certain number that take **phonecards.** The most important is in the telephone office next door to the post office in Tahrir Square in Sana'a. These PTC cards can also be used at the airport, but there is no guarantee of getting through. Do not forget that they can be used for calls inside the old YAR only.

Internal dialling codes:

Sana'a	01
Aden	02
Hodeidah	03
Ta'iz + Ibb	04
Sadah	051
Marib	063
Hajjah	07
Mukalla	0952

International Telephone Calls

To call the Yemen from the U.K., the international code is 010967, but it is almost impossible to reach the former PDRY. International calls are handled by the Yemen International Telecommunications Company system (TeleYemen). Ringing out is a quick and efficient service run by Cable and Wireless at several locations, and phonecards are available for 80 and 160 units. These cards are different from those for internal calls. The rate is the same throughout the day and night, an 80 unit card will give you about a minute to the UK. For phonecard collectors there are some rare picture cards to be found.

The main international telephone offices in Sana'a are at the Ministry of Telecommunications building (the tall square building on the northern side of Tahrir Square) and opposite the Chinese Embassy ten minutes' walk west of Tahrir Square up az-Zubeiry Street. There are similar offices in Hodeidah, Ta'iz and Ibb, and they are generally open from 8.00 until 20.00.

A private company has also set up business on the street between Tahrir Square and the Taj Sheba Hotel, about 100m down on the right. They do not issue cards but take a deposit against the call, the difference being settled at the end.

International codes from the Yemen are:

UK	0044
USA/Canada	001
Australia	0061
New Zealand	0064
Germany	0049
Netherlands	0031
France	0033
Spain	0034
Italy	0039

Many offices also now have fax machines.

Postal System

There are standard postal facilities around the country, with offices in some relatively small communities. Post is not delivered in the Yemen but is deposited at post office boxes for people to collect. All international mail goes from Sana'a or Aden, so for speed it would always be better to post from these cities. The main post offices in all cities and towns are easy to find in the centres.

Stamps of both the two former countries are still being used, so it can get a bit confusing, but the counter staff are usually extremely helpful and patient. For stamp collectors there is a vast choice of designs as some offices seem to keep sheets for years. There is also a numismatic counter at the main office in Sana'a.

OPENING HOURS AND PUBLIC HOLIDAYS

Generally all offices, public buildings and shops are open in the mornings and then close for the afternoon *qat* sessions. Most **shops** will then reopen in the evenings. All business ceases on Fridays and in some cases on Thursdays as well. Opening hours are as follows:

Ministries and public buildings	08.00-14.00
	(officially, but usually nearer 12.00)
Banks	08.00-12.00
Post offices	08.00-13.00 + 16.00-20.00
Private companies, travel and tour agencies	08.00-12.00 + 16.00-19.00

Holidays

National holidays are split between those that are celebrated on the same day each year and those of the Islamic calendar that creep forward by about 11 days every year. The exact date of these depends on the new moon.

The fasting month of **Ramadan** tends to slow things down drastically (see Islam), and it can be difficult to get things organised. The end of the fast is celebrated by the 'small' feast of **Id al-Fitr**, which lasts a few days, when no business is done at all. The 'big' feast of **Id al-Kabir** starts on 10 Dhu al-Haj in the Islamic calendar, and also lasts for some days. The Islamic New Year (1 Muharram) is also a holiday, as is the Prophet Mohammed's birthday on 12 Rabi al-Awal (the third month). From 1998 Ramadan will fall for a few years over the Christmas period which will be interesting for the tourist industry.

The holidays which fall on the same date each year are: **Labour Day** (1 May), the **Day of National Unity** (22 May), **Revolution Day** (of the old YAR) (26 September), and **National Day** (of the old PDRY) (14 October).

CLOTHING
The code of dress is quite simple for visitors – keep yourself covered and you will be accepted everywhere. Loose and light **trousers and shirts** are the best option for both men and women, and baggy trousers with many pockets are ideal.

Women should cover their arms and legs at all times so as not to cause offence when walking around in public. For men, brief running shorts are not acceptable anywhere and it is probably better to avoid shorts altogether. The looser your clothing, the more comfortable and less conspicuous you will be.

Beaches and hotel pools are the only places for revealing swimwear, and nudity is not permitted anywhere. Tourists wearing Yemeni clothing with a *jambia* are humoured.

Warmer clothing is needed in winter in the **highlands,** when it can get very cold at night (the temperature sometimes drops to freezing point). Sweatshirts and jackets will be needed between November and February. Take a light waterproof jacket if you intend trekking in the mountains, where it can rain throughout the year, or if you are visiting the country in the rainy seasons of July-September and March-April.

As protection against the sun, I always recommend taking a **sun hat,** or buy a local head cloth in the *suq*.

WHAT TO TAKE
Try to keep your personal luggage to a minimum. This will make your journey infinitely more enjoyable than if you carry around things that you 'might need'. In addition to casual and smarter clothing, I always take swimwear and light training shoes, with stronger walking shoes for trekking, a small first aid kit and toiletries, a Swiss Army knife, sunglasses, sun cream, a small towel, a small alarm clock (for those early starts) and a torch (preferably a head torch if camping).

Do not forget to take a camera and films (see Photography) and of course travellers' cheques and various amounts of cash (see Money). A driving licence and credit card might be useful for emergencies.

In other countries I always carry a drinking water bottle but I find that in the Yemen the plastic mineral water bottles are sufficiently strong and light. Most other everyday travel items which you might need can be bought from shops or street traders in the cities.

I am not a great believer in tourists bringing small gifts of pens and sweets for the children, as this usually creates a mini-riot, and sometimes generates more ill will than good. However a few small coins or postcards

The Citadel at Umm Layla in north Yemen.

from your own country can be an added expression of gratitude to a family who have just let you look around their house in the mountains or hut in the desert.

HEALTH AND SAFETY

The only compulsory health requirement is that visitors should have a **yellow fever** injection if they are coming from an infected area. However the regulations are subject to change, so do check with your tour operator, travel agent or the Yemen Embassy.

Most people take **malaria** tablets if they are travelling in the Tihama or the south. **Hepatitis** injections are also generally advised and it would be worth enquiring about **cholera, tetanus and typhoid.** Most medical centres have lists of recommended inoculations for all countries.

Try to plan ahead and take any medical supplies you might need as some things may not be available locally. This also applies to such things as high factor **sun cream** or spare **contact lenses or glasses.** Always carry a basic first aid kit to cover minor accidents in remote places, as well as any specific medications you might need.

When you arrive in Sana'a, you might initially feel short of breath and dizzy. This is due to the altitude and you will acclimatise quickly, but avoid expending large amounts of energy. The **sun** can be a serious problem in the mountains, on the coast and in the desert and I always carry a sun hat, sun cream and sunglasses. In summer avoid being out in the sun too much at midday and always remember to drink lots of fluid.

On the coast **humidity** is a problem which can lead to dehydration, sweat sores and infections of broken and tender skin. The local pharmacy will normally have something to treat it with. Otherwise consult a doctor.

Water

Avoid **dehydration** by drinking large amounts of water daily, even if the climate is dry and you are not perspiring very much. Bottled mineral water is available everywhere at low prices, and you should always carry some when walking and trekking, even for relatively short distances. Most tap water is theoretically safe, but people generally drink bottled water. Try to avoid untreated water in villages, especially in the mountains, where it often comes from open cisterns. (Green weed lying on cistern water is supposed to bring prosperity – but it might bring you a lot more as well!).

Even if a restaurant only has tap water to drink, they will usually send out to the local shop for bottled water (*ma* or *moya*) or soft drink (*barid* meaning 'cold') for tourists.

Avoid drinking from streams and bathing or wading in stagnant pools or rivers as there is a risk of **bilharzia**.

Hygiene

One could give a mass of advice about what to do and what not to do concerning food hygiene. But it all depends on the situation in which you find yourself. Advising you always to eat hot food and no salads in a clean restaurant is not much help if you are in a village with one grimy establishment serving lukewarm chicken, rice and vegetables. Common sense is always the best guide – if you do not like the look of a place, then do not eat there. There are always tea and biscuits to keep you going until the next decent restaurant, or you can carry your own supplies.

There is some delicious food to be bought from streetside vendors (see Yemeni Food), and the risks are no greater than in restaurants. Some people do advise against this but higher prices do not necessarily guarantee higher hygiene standards, and I know many people who eat from the dirtiest places and are never sick!

Sickness

Sickness can strike anywhere, at any time. It might be caused by fatigue, sun, water, food, flies or even poor personal hygiene, but in most cases it lasts 24 hours and then leaves you to recover. I always carry **diarrhoea** tablets and **antibiotics**, but you can usually sort it out by starving yourself for 24 hours with plenty of water and tea (no milk). If the problem persists then consult an English-speaking doctor (a phone number is usually available through the larger hotels).

Exotic medical problems like snake bites, scorpion stings or stone-fish wounds are so unlikely that the best advice is not to put your hands under rocks or walk bare footed on the coral. For serious accidents go straight to a clinic or hospital, regardless of the expense or time. If it is serious enough for an operation, consider whether it would be better to travel home first.

Most of the **medical facilities** are in the main towns but efforts are being made to spread clinics into the countryside. Primary health care is one of the major projects for the government, which is currently assessing the strengths and weaknesses of the northern and southern systems. The two will then combine as a single unified plan aimed at immunising all children against the major diseases.

Hospitals

If you need to go to hospital **(mustashfa)** you might be pleasantly surprised by the standards of equipment and personnel in the cities. If you go to a clinic in the remote regions you could equally be persuaded that you were not as ill as you thought.

Good foreign doctors and medical staff are assisting around the country and treat foreigners well.

The main hospitals are:

Sana'a:
Republican **(al-Jumhuri)**, Bab Shu'ab Tel: 202192/3
Revolution **(al-Thawra)**, Bab as-Salaam: 246971-5
Kuwait General (near ring road to Wadi Dhahr): 203282/4
Military **(al-Askari)**, Bab al-Balqua: 203131/3
Aden:
Republican **(al-Jumhuri)** Khormaksar
People's **(ash-Shaab)**, Crater
Ta'iz:
Republican **(al-Jumhuri)**, Harat al-Mustashfa: 74467
Revolution **(al-Thawra)**, ash-Shamasi: 210842-4
Military **(al-Askari)**, Salah Road: 74800
Hodeidah:
Revolution **(al-Thawra)**, Corniche Road: 252127/9
Al-Olfi, al-Mustashfa St: 74558
Jibla:
Jibla American Baptist Hospital
Hajjah:
Republican **(al-Jumhuri)**: 40252

There are also smaller clinics in Sadah, Rada'a and Ibb. In case of serious accident it would be better to have Air Ambulance Insurance.

Safety

Assuming that you are not trying to bypass checkpoints and heading into insecure areas like Wadi al-Jawf, you will normally have no personal security problems in the Yemen. Tourists generally find the Yemenis helpful and trustworthy. There is a much greater chance of someone finding your wallet and returning it, than of someone trying to take it from your pocket. However, common sense should obviously be used in dealing with people who you do not know, and you should look after your money and property. With a few simple precautions you should not have any problems.

I always keep my **cash, travellers' cheques, passport and airline ticket** on me all the time, usually in a money belt; I have never lost anything from a hotel room, but I take the view that it would be easier for someone to steal anonymously from a room than directly from me. Street crime is almost unknown.

The source of potential violence you are most likely to meet is the **stone-throwing** children in many mountain (and now some southern) villages and towns. Shahara has a bad reputation in this respect, the children, even small girls, seem to be actively encouraged by their parents. It is difficult to know why they do it – distrust between East and West, Muslim and *nazrani* ('Nazarene' – Christian), Third World and First World – but the best way to deal with it is to wave for as long as possible (while they are waving, they cannot throw!), keep your eyes on them and move out as quickly as possible. Never pick up a stone and threaten to throw it back, but keep smiling and curse them under your breath. This is just the sort of situation that could lead to a bad accident which might result in the closing of the area to tourists. Perhaps this is what the locals want?

Try to avoid any sort of confrontation as the communication barrier can lead to misunderstandings. Do not forget that if you step outside the bounds of decent tourist behaviour, it is the locals who have the upper hand. As long as Yemeni traditions on dress, alcohol and behaviour are observed, however, you should experience few problems and will be surprised by the people's friendliness and hospitality. However, it is wise to be cautious in all tribal areas.

The influx of so many **refugees** over the last few years (Ethiopians, Somalis) has brought some changes in the cities. Now there are regular lines of women, crippled men and children begging at traffic lights and on pavements outside tourist hotels and restaurants.

Children in Manakha.

WHAT TO BUY

Many items that visitors would normally buy as souvenirs or gifts are actually made in other countries. The *futah* (a type of male wrap-around skirt) and *mashadda* (headcloth) are more likely to come from Bangalore or Sumatra than from Beit al-Faqih or Sana'a. Nevertheless, they are what the local people wear and are useful pieces of clothing as well as keepsakes ideal for the odd fancy dress party!

If you are buying clothing or material at an ordinary shop, you can try bargaining but will probably not get very far. However, in a recognised tourist or souvenir shop all the rules of Middle Eastern haggling apply – start at about half the offered price, settle for three-quarters and then ask for more off for buying in bulk or for paying in dollars.

Items possibly made in the Yemen include *jambias,* jewellery, worked leather, carved wood and some fabrics and rugs in the Tihama. The main reason for all the imports is that they are much cheaper than the local versions, which tend to be produced for quality rather than quantity.

Jambias

The *jambia* is one of the unique Yemeni institutions. It is a curved dagger consisting of three sections: blade, handle and sheath. The main value is in the handle, which is sometimes passed down through many generations and can be worth thousands of dollars. There is much international concern over the use of rhino and giraffe horn for very expensive *jambias,* although new handles tend to be made from cattle horn, wood, bone, plastic and even artificial amber.

Blades imported from the Far East cost about 10 per cent of the price of locally produced ones, but sheaths are usually made locally and vary from wood wrapped in leather strips to highly ornate silver scabbards beautifully inscribed. Some of the more ornate ones have a small container in the upturned end, used for keeping *kohl,* an eyelid cosmetic. The sheaths are sown onto decorated belts, the better ones being hand woven.

You will notice some well dressed men wearing a type of dagger that has a more slender curve. Traditionally these *thuma* daggers are carried by the *qadis* and *sayyids* of religious nobility.

You can buy some second hand daggers for around US$10, and they look good, even though the handle is plastic. New ones start at around double that price. The *jambia* is seldom worn in south Yemen.

Jewellery

For hundreds of years **silver jewellery** has played an important part in Yemeni life. It has traditionally formed the greater part of a bride's dowry, which is paid to the woman and kept by her for personal use in case of divorce or abandonment. It is also a tradition for new silver objects to be added to an existing piece to mark the arrival of each child.

Some of the more valuable silverware is stamped or signed by the workman, and could bear a Jewish name if it dates from before 1948. Very old pieces seldom reach the market, however, as there has always been a tradition of melting down unfashionable items and reworking them into newer pieces.

There are many items to choose from in the souvenir shops but not all will have the amount of silver quoted by the seller. Even with gold and silver being mined in the country, it was easier to obtain much of the original silver by melting down Maria Theresa dollar coins and then sometimes adding other metals such as tin.

The jewellery comes in many forms: necklaces, bracelets, anklets, earrings, bangles and chains sometimes decorated with ornate containers for Koranic verses. Some of the necklaces have complete Maria Theresa dollars and other coins as decorations themselves.

Today there is a move away from silver towards **gold** and you will see a great deal of gold for sale in the sparkling jewellery shops. Modern gold and silver designs are good value as generally the cost of the workmanship is not included. Prices in Ta'iz are usually better than in Sana'a.

There are also some fine (and bulky) examples of beads, necklaces and ornaments made from other precious and semi-precious materials such as **agate, opal, turquoise, amethyst, jasper and red coral.** Yemeni traders are no less cunning than anyone else in the jewellery and gem business, so beware of claims that you can sell the items for a profit back home – you would need very specific knowledge, a thick wallet and a steady nerve for going through customs.

Following the departure of many Jewish silversmiths to Israel in the late 1940s, with few Muslims skilled enough to replace them, there was some concern about the future of the local jewellery-producing industry. Jews still make most of the silver jewellery in the north.

Some very clever (and cheap) strings of beads are sold by children in many places. Some look like red coral but are in fact tiny fragments of ordinary coral, ground up and added to plastic. Buy a couple and keep the children happy.

Weapons and Guns
In addition to *jambias* there are many other metal weapons that you can buy. Swords, knives and spears can all be found in dusty corners of shops, as can old Bedouin rifles and pistols. With the correct documentation and the agreement of your airline you can bring these items back with you.

Metalwork
Engraved trays and coffee pots with little cups originate from a variety of countries and are probably more representative of North Africa and the Indian subcontinent than of southern Arabia. The same applies to the various *mada'ah* (hubble-bubble) water pipes, introduced by the Turks.

Tihama Products
Some of the most specific Yemeni items are the **pots, baskets** and **material** from the Tihama. The pots especially are excellent cheap and colourful souvenirs, and are unique to this region. The small incense burners are strange enough to keep your visitors guessing for ages. The main problems are their weight and fragility.

Baskets and containers made from straw and palm fronds are also produced here, but tend you be squashed during the rigours of travel. Straw hats are useful items to buy for travelling. Weaving is still done at certain places along the coast, and Beit al-Faqih is probably the most likely place to find it.

Print by Fuad al-Futaih.

The material is expensive but unique. There is no tradition of carpet weaving in the Yemen, but rough goat-hair or sheep-wool rugs can be found.

Hadrami Products

The handicrafts market in Seiyun and other local shops in Wadi Hadramaut can offer **everyday agricultural items.** The strange conical **straw hats** for women are good value whatever you decide to do with them. Hadrami honey is very expensive but famous throughout Arabia for its superb taste and quality. The main problem is finding someone who is prepared to sell you some, as it is in such demand.

Prints and Paintings

Other unique souvenirs are the prints and paintings being produced by a new wave of Yemeni artists. Both originals and copies can be bought, although many of the originals are being snapped up by local dealers as investments for the future. Some are faithful views of towns, cities and villages, whilst others are interpretations of folkloric tales and strange stories. They are good value, easy to carry, highly original and better than a framed Egyptian papyrus!

Every tourist centre now seems to have a print and picture shop, so you can afford to look around and bargain. The best-known artist is Fuad al-Futaih, originally from Aden but now working in Sana'a. His range of pen and ink drawings and prints can be found in Gallery No. 1 at the top of the Samsarat al-Nahas in the Sana'a *suq.* There is another Gallery No. 1 in Khartoum Street (also known as Mogahed Street) south of az-Zubeiry Street, midway between Ali Abdul Mogni Street and Hadda Road.

Other Items

In addition to the items featured above there are many other products worth taking back. As this is southern Arabia it might be a good idea to take small gifts of **incense** and **spices.** There are hundreds of traders dealing in all the spices you need for the kitchen. Many already come prepacked. Like the spices, the incense is mainly imported from India (or sometimes Somalia) and can be bought in small cakes or as a gum resin at reasonable prices. You could buy some locally grown 'coffee Arabica'. *Kahwa* is the general word for coffee, but *bunn* is the uncooked bean, whereas *qishr* is a hot infusion of the coffee husks including cardamon and ginger. Brightly painted metal cases are becoming popular, but all these are produced in India or Pakistan.

Music cassettes are also good value. Most shops offer a range of local, Egyptian, Middle Eastern and Western music. You can normally buy a cassette outright, but some of the more popular local songs are only on a single master tape. If you want to buy a copy you may have to come back an hour or so later when it has been duplicated. Hadrami music is popular in the south, as is that from the Heraz region, Tihama and Sana'a songs in the north .

One souvenir shop of note in Sana'a is the old General Tourism Corporation building which used to be the official tourist office, but is now relegated to selling a few souvenirs. It is at the far western end of Tahrir Square and usually has a good supply of posters, prints, paintings, postcards, pots, rugs, jewellery and silverware all at fixed prices. It is open 8.00–13.00 but not Fridays.

In Aden there is the remarkable Lax Emporium with a wealth of distinctive souvenirs for sale (see Aden).

YEMENI FOOD AND DRINK

While it does not have an international reputation, Yemeni food tends to be very good, and can be excellent. A basic diet of cereals, rice, vegetables and meat keeps dishes simple and wholesome, and you will seldom see any Yemenis who look undernourished.

Breakfast in a Yemeni home would tend to be *biard ma'tomat* (scrambled eggs and tomato) *or fool* (natural beans). Eggs also come alone *(biard sada)* or with the yolk separated *biard ayoun* ('eggs of the eyes'). In restaurants, *fool* is the most popular breakfast dish and is served with oil, onions or chilli as preferred, and scooped up with fresh bread, as is *kibda*, a delicious mixture of liver, onions and tomato. *Lahm sihar* are small pieces of cooked meat, and *degga* is ground meat with garlic, tomatoes, onions and chilli – just what you need to get the day (and your bowels) moving!

Lunch rather than dinner is the main meal, probably because of the loss of appetite after chewing *qat* in the afternoons. The favourite dish in the highlands is *selta*, which is made with whatever ingredients are available and thus varies greatly in taste and appearance around the country. The most common contents are eggs, tomatoes, onions, beans, potatoes, and okra all cooked up into a broth. To this is added *helba* (fenugreek) after it has been ground, soaked and whipped. Some *seltas* come without meat (ask for *selta bidoon lahma)*, others have lamb or ground meat. It is cooked and served in the same dish, a blackened soapstone or red earthenware pot that still continues to cook the food long after it has been served. Local variations include the Sana'a green *selta*, the colour of which is provided by the addition of a locally grown small type of leek.

Side dishes would include *sahawiq*, a spicy dip of tomatoes, garlic and chilli; *humus* (sesame seeds and chick peas); *ruz* (rice), sometimes with nuts and raisins; *tabikh* or *moushakl* (cooked vegetables); and *salata* (salad). *Maraq* is a spicy meat soup which, like *selta*, is easy to prepare in a restaurant. Other local dishes such as *aseed* (a type of corn porridge) require a lot of preparation and are impractical to make outside of the home. This is also true of *bint al-Sahn*, a hot sweet pastry with ghee and honey, which is served after the main course, as a dessert. For the latter, you are likely to have fruit in season or the universal creme caramel to choose from. Occasionally you come across odd desserts like *fateh bil mohz*, a sweetened bread with bananas.

In the Tihama and on the south coast, **fish** and **seafood** play an important part in the local diet. *Sayd* is whole grilled fresh fish, and *harees* are smaller pieces of fish. If you see Yemeni-style prawns on a menu, particularly in Aden and Hodeidah, treat yourself to a very tasty dish indeed. A speciality of Aden is *zurbiyan*, meat or fish with an interesting style of rice.

An experience never to be forgotten is to watch a local eater in a *mikhbaza* restaurant literally attacking *aseed ma'aruz*, a special dish containing the head of an animal. To reach the tender bits requires the use of the eater's fingers, fists, jaw and any other handy implements. The resultant mess leaves the restaurant looking as though it has just been ram-raided!

The evening meal is generally a light affair, consisting of much the same dishes as breakfast.

Restaurants

As a visitor you will usually use three types of local restaurant. A *matam selta* is a specialist restaurant serving only one quality dish at a time, normally *fool* for breakfast, *selta* for lunch and *fool* again for dinner. A more general *matam* will also change fare throughout the day, but will have more choices such as eggs and meat. A *mikhbaza* specialises in one particular food, such as *samak* (fish) and serves it throughout the day, possibly with *fatta* (pounded breadcrumbs) mixed with dates or bananas and soup or broth.

Many of the better hotels serve good international cuisine, while a local *fonduq* in the mountains can provide the same simple meal that the family are having. As the Yemen becomes more international, outlets for **fast food** are being established, from *dijaj mashwi* (spit-grilled chicken) and *showarma* (a sort of doner kebab) to hamburgers, fries and stuffed peppers. Even on the streets you will not go hungry, with tasty kebabs, *felafel*, chips, *m'tahak* (thin pancakes fried on a large circular hot plate) and even corn on the cob ingeniously cooked on old car wheels!

In the cities, especially in Sana'a, there are specialist restaurants offering **international food** including Chinese, Italian, Vietnamese, Ethiopian and many more. Most of the newer establishments in the capital are situated on or around the ring road.

Bread

Bread accompanies every meal in the Yemen, and comes in a wonderful variety of shapes, sizes and tastes.

The most basic type, called *hubz*, is about the size of a gramophone record, and is baked commercially in large ovens. In most towns you can find the baker shovelling dozens of these at a time into a large furnace. Also commercially produced are the long mini loaves called *ruti*, served in many local restaurants and sold in shops.

The *tannur* is the open topped oven that can be found in some restaurants and many houses, where the women bake bread in the early morning. A roadside lunch stop will normally be at a place baking its own bread called *temeez*. The baker deftly kneads and rolls the blobs of dough, punctures the surface with a multi-spiked metal brush, stretches it over the handled implement called the *makhbezah*, before slapping it onto the inner wall of the *tannur*. After about a minute, the baked bread is hooked out with a metal stick ready for immediate consumption. Also fresh from the *tannur* is the huge, thin and crispy *rashoosh*, served for example with grilled fish in the Tihama. The *melooj* variety is like a large *temeez* but without the holes.

For a good *lahuh* bread, best *dhurra* sorghum should be used, which produces a thicker spongy type of large pancake. This will often be prepared with *leban* (sour milk) plus some spicy additives to give the dish a bitter taste. Around the Bab al-Yemen and Bab as-Salaam in Sana'a you can sometimes see traders selling boxes of bread rolls that look more like brown bars of soap. This is *kidma*, traditionally bread for soldiers, but now surprisingly enjoying a wider appeal.

Drinks

Bunn (coffee beans) is only drunk in the mornings, whereas *chai* (tea) and *qishr* are available in most places throughout the day. Proper **qishr** should be boiled for at least half an hour and spiced with cinnamon, cardamom and ginger.

Apart from the hotels and restaurants which regularly serve tourists, hot drinks always come with sugar, but you can try to get it *bidoon suker* (without sugar). If you want tea with milk, which is common in the mornings, ask for *chai haleeb*, otherwise it will always arrive black – *chai ahmer*.

Yemen produces a whole range of **teeth-rotting fizzy drinks**, many produced under licence such as Sinalco and Seven-Up. With the amount of fruit grown in the country there are now many healthier **fruit drinks** in small individual containers. Like many Arab countries, reconstituted powdered milk is readily available in bags, cartons and boxes. Yemen also has an indigenous milk-producing industry. Yoghurt is also widely available.

Alcohol

It is interesting to reflect that the word 'alcohol' is taken from the Arabic *al-kohl* – a particular irony. It is the same word as is used for the cosmetic powder which stains the eyelids (used by women, old men and children), and means 'essence' or 'spirit'.

Despite its origins you must remember that the Yemen is a strict Muslim country where the drinking of alcohol by locals is not permitted, although the rules are generally flexible for non-Muslim tourists. You can bring alcohol into the country for personal use, but you must not drink in public or offer it to Yemenis.

The government realises that becoming a totally dry country would make it harder for companies to recruit non-Muslim engineers and technicians for the new industries, so despite continual objections by the fundamentalists, alcohol is tolerated and available throughout the south and in certain outlets in the north. In the highlands it cannot be found outside some major hotels in Sana'a and Ta'iz.

In the Tihama and the south, where there has been greater outside influence, the situation is more tolerant. A legacy of British rule was the Seera brewery in Aden which continued to produce a passable **local beer**, until it was closed in 1993. Imported canned beers together with bottles of **spirits** can be bought at most hotels in Aden and even in some bars.

One curiosity of all this is the massive but illegal trade in alcohol across the Red Sea and Gulf of Aden. The coastal smugglers bury the cases and boxes all over the desert around Mafraq, inland from Mokha. Incredibly the prices are probably lower than you would pay in your local off-licence at home. The authorities sometimes have a crackdown and invite the press to public displays of bottle smashing, while, just up the road, the better hotels in Hodeidah continue to sell beer and spirits.

Alcohol can be bought with rials, but if you go to the Victory Duty Free Shop in Aden (about 500m behind the Aden Hotel) you can buy cases of beer and bottles of spirits only with hard currency. Prices are slightly higher than at Mafraq but lower than in the hotels.

MUSEUMS

There are some excellent objects on show in the museums around the country. The highlights are the National Museums in Sana'a and Ta'iz, closely followed by Aden and Seiyun. The more important museums are usually open during the official hours, but that is not always the case with minor ones. The main problem is that the museum staff are government employees and get paid whether or not they have any visitors. Unless they are chased by superiors some museum staff, especially those off the main tourist routes, do not even open the doors.

The south has a number of smaller museums, some of which you will never find open if you arrive unannounced. Communication and numbers of visitors are the key, but there is a long way to go before you can turn up at Ataq, for example, and go straight into the museum.

There are descriptions of the museums in the relevant travel sections, and all **should** be open at least every morning from 09.00 to 12.00 except Friday. The following is a brief overview.

Sana'a:	National	– excellent
	Military	– well worth a visit
	University	– interesting if you have time to spare
Ta'iz:	National	– excellent in a strange way
	Salah	– interesting if you have enough time
Aden:	National	– very good if you can get in
	Military	– well worth a visit
Dhafar:	Himyar capital site	– the only real thing to see when you get there
Zabid:	Nasr Citadel	– very small but interesting
Seiyun:	Sultan's Palace	– very interesting
Mukalla:	Sultan's Palace	– interesting if open
Ataq:	Shabwa	– interesting but never open!
Beyhan:	Timna	– four interesting rooms but never open!
Ad-Dhala:	Military	– small
Habilayn:	Military	– small

PHOTOGRAPHY AND FILMING

Opportunities for stunning photography abound in such a dramatic country, but there are certain unwritten rules that need to be observed. There is no problem in bringing a normal **stills camera** into the country, and I would hope that every visitor would do just that. A **video camera** should be declared at customs upon arrival, when its details may be entered into your passport, to ensure that it leaves when you do. Video tapes, blank or not, may be required for inspection. **Larger cinecameras** would need authority from the Ministry of Information and Culture.

As you travel around you will notice that most Yemeni **males** are not exactly camera-shy, which tends to result in a large number of 'staged' shots with children and adults alike putting on ridiculous grins and theatrical poses. What you should not do however is to try taking photographs of men who do *not* want their picture taken. It is always worth indicating that you intend taking their photograph (*soora*), and if they object, simply leave them alone – that is, after all, only good manners. The alternative is to use a long lens so that it is not so obvious whom you are shooting. With videos, the locals in many places are quite used to seeing themselves on playback by squinting through the viewfinder. Instant pictures are a great way of striking up a relationship, but only if you never want to see the picture again.

Photographing women is not acceptable, and their privacy should be respected at all times. Some people bend the rules by taking long shots from a distance, or general shots, such as in a crowded *suq*, when a woman just happens to be passing. But be very careful, as heated arguments can arise if people think you are overstepping the mark. Mountain women in the north and those in the ten-gallon straw hats of the Hadramaut are the most vociferous objectors. The strong, unveiled women of Jebel Sabr near Ta'iz and those in the Tihama are more co-operative. Very occasionally a more modern man and his wife will allow you take her picture if you ask, but this might only happen after a long and friendly conversation. Some women travellers are invited to join groups of local women, and sometimes this provides an opportunity to take photographs in a privileged situation, but again beware of the fragile friendship that has sprung up.

It is forbidden *(memnur)*, to **photograph military** or **police personnel,** or any official buildings that they come out of. Buildings with an aerial on top or a guard outside are best avoided. Even a distant shot of the citadel in Sana'a can get you into trouble with the guards, who assume that you then have enough information to overthrow the government. Airports and harbours are considered to be of strategic importance, as are major factories and power stations. If you are caught, the very least that is likely to happen is that you will be taken away for questioning, so beware. But strangely enough there are no restrictions on taking pictures of the new dam at Marib.

Try to calculate how much **film** you will use, and then double it. It is always better to return with unused film, which you can use at a later date, than hope to buy exactly what you want. Standard print film is usually available in most large towns, but there are no guarantees as to how well it has been stored. Transparency film is almost impossible to obtain, except in Sana'a, so make sure you take enough.

Try to keep your camera protected from the sun and dust, although this is almost impossible. The heat of the Tihama and the south is a real problem during the summer. I don't think I have ever had my camera as hot as it became in the Hadramaut in August; I could only just hold it!

ENTERTAINMENT

Most Yemeni entertainment is connected with family celebrations such as marriages and births, and these last for many days. As a visitor you should accept any invitation you may get to a **wedding.** Sometimes you will be attracted by the noise and lights of the **Thursday night celebrations.** This is a good opportunity to observe the smartly dressed locals enjoying themselves to the accompaniment of music and dancing. In the daytime the hill

The bridegroom at a wedding celebration, Wadi Dhahr.

overlooking Wadi Dhahr is a good place to see music and dancing on a Friday morning.

If you are staying in a *fonduq* in the mountains you will sometimes get the chance to hear **music**. It is not played professionally but just the locals enjoying themselves. You would probably be expected to pay a small amount, but it is not a performance just for your benefit; you will be simply the catalyst to get it going. Often the men will get up to dance and wave their *jambias* around.

The rapid spread of television is consuming most of the population's attention in the evenings, even in the remotest villages. In the main towns there has been a dramatic rise in video machine ownership and tape rental from local shops. In the cities cinemas are popular, and they show high action 'blood and guts' movies to full houses throughout the day. Boys are also getting a taste for newly introduced **video games** to accompany the slightly older table football and pool.

The top hotels in Sana'a and Aden are the only places where you will find such things as **live bands** and **discos** and entry is normally dependent on you having an evening meal. See the local press for details. Cultural events are sometimes organised by the various embassies and councils; details are available from them or on supermarket notice boards, or sometimes in the *Yemen Times*.

It is not exactly entertainment, but for relaxation try a visit to a *hammam* for a soak, bathe and cleansing; it is an invigorating experience!

SPORT

Many of the younger Yemeni men are great sportsmen, but they lack the facilities to develop their interest further. Since 1984 the two Yemens have sent a team to every summer Olympics, but as yet with no success. Events covered are **football, judo, boxing** and **athletics,** but there is no great history of distance running, unlike in the country's Red Sea neighbours Ethiopia and Somalia.

For spectators there are usually league football matches to be seen on Thursdays and Fridays in the major towns. Sports clubs tend to be more abundant in the south and on the coast where you can find table tennis, chess and *carob,* an Indian boardgame played with draughts pieces.

Visitors who enjoy **running** can join the Hash House Harriers who organise runs in the Sana'a region every Monday afternoon. Contact them at the British Council or the Embassy Club. Some embassies also organise sporting competitions for expatriates, details can be obtained direct from them. **Swimming** and **tennis** are popular activities in residential compounds and at top hotels, where there is generally a fitness centre and sauna.

Adventure sports such as **hang-gliding, mountain biking** and **scuba diving** are available, but not on any sort of organised basis. Permission might be required to do certain activities, especially scuba diving. This might be very difficult to obtain. Some expatriates living and working in Hodeidah and Aden have managed to get some scuba dives in both the Red Sea and Gulf of Aden, but this is very much a private undertaking with personal equipment. Some people are bringing bicycles to the Yemen both for sport and for transport.

MEDIA

It is estimated that over 90 per cent of the population have access to a **television** set which makes it an excellent medium of communication, in a country with a relatively poor infrastructure. There are two television stations, essentially the old government networks of the YAR and the PDRY, which broadcast from Sana'a and Aden. From Sana'a you can receive daily news in English at 19.30 for 15 minutes, but international coverage is limited. For the most part the hours are taken up by imported Egyptian feature films and soap operas, interviews, educational programmes and government debates.

Private satellite dishes are springing up all over the city skylines to keep local businessmen in contact with world events. All major hotels now offer a selection of satellite channels, including Cable News Network (CNN).

At present all **radio** broadcasts from inside the Yemen are in Arabic. The Asian service of the BBC World Service and Voice of America can be picked up with a short-wave radio.

Several **newspapers** are available, mainly, of course, in Arabic. Before unification all newspapers in both countries were government controlled. With the push towards democracy since 1990, however, opposition publications have emerged.

The only English language newspaper is the **Yemen Times,** edited by Abdulaziz al-Saqqaf, a respected scholar and publisher. This weekly Sana'a publication presents the basic facts of government policy and comments on what effect this has on the general public, together with interesting interviews of prominent people. I strongly recommend that you buy a copy as it is one of the few ways to actually find out what is going on.

For international coverage of the Arab world you can sometimes find copies of the Yemen edition of the Middle East Times, which is published in Cairo. Bookshops in the cities and at large hotels often sell Time and Newsweek.

TRAVEL AGENCIES AND TOUR OPERATORS

Since permits are no longer required for travelling around the country, the need for a central tourist office has vanished, according to the Ministry of Culture and Tourism. This has left the promotion and operation of the entire tourist industry in the hands of private tour operators and the airline Yemenia. Between them they provide what information is available for the visitor. Yemenia offices abroad act as unofficial tourist offices and help as much as they can with promotional brochures, details of operators and agencies etc.

The old General Tourism Corporation building, which used to issue permits and acted as a tourist office, is still at the western end of Tahrir Square, but now only exists as an official souvenir outlet. The individual traveller will find it difficult to obtain even basic up-to-date travel information. There are three choices for visits: group travel, individual tours and independent travel; for the first two you would need to use the facilities of a tour agency based in Yemen.

Group travel has the advantage that you know exactly what itinerary you will be following and what you will see. Most reputable tour operators are experienced in what they offer in their brochures and usually include all the major highlights. Variations can offer specialised tours dealing with specific aspects of the country (historical tours, trekking, bird watching etc.). All the practical details are taken care of, leaving you to travel, see and experience. All tour groups in the Yemen must be handled by a recognised tour agency, which deals with all the arrangements for transport, accommodation reservations (an important point) and security.

Alternatively, you can have a purpose made itinerary to suit your specific requirements. Agencies both outside and inside the Yemen offer these, but the operation will be done by a recognised Yemen tour agency. The advantage of an **individual tour** is that you can arrange to see exactly what you want, when you want; the disadvantage is that they do not come cheap. As with group travel, you have the satisfaction of knowing that your hotel or *fonduq* will be reserved, which can be critical outside of Sana'a or over holiday periods.

If you are not joining a group, it is worthwhile considering hiring a vehicle and driver through a tour agency, even for just a day to get to a particularly remote place. YATA prefers people to make their arrangements before arriving so as to ensure that everything is organised. However, they are also happy to discuss itineraries on the ground. You will see their fleet of 4x4s and buses all over the country.

Going alone or with friends and making your own arrangements gives you flexibility of choice, at the lowest cost; no agent or operator takes a percentage. For experienced travellers (especially those who have been to other Arab countries), it is possible – and enjoyable – to get around on your own, but this is not the place to start learning.

Problems the independent traveller is likely to face are: no national tourist office and a general lack of information and maps; few people speak anything other than Arabic outside the towns; many of the sites are difficult to reach and are not served by public transport; and it will take about twice as long to do the same itinerary as it would on an organised tour. But the advantages are: you will get to see exactly what you want; you will have closer contact with the locals; it will hopefully cost less. Another fact to bear in mind is the general lack of accommodation throughout the country which can be a problem without reservations.

For a first visit on your own it is worthwhile spending two or three days in Sana'a before heading out, as it tends to be the only place to track down elusive maps, books and information.

If you decide on an organised tour, you will find that, although they are still relatively rare, there are some **travel companies** which have the experience and knowledge to get the best out of the country. Most itineraries are similar and include all the major highlights, but vary in standards of accommodation (some include camping), price, duration and departure dates. Experienced tour operators are:

Explore Worldwide
1 Frederick St
Aldershot
Hampshire GU11 1LQ
Tel: 01252-319448
Fax: 01252-343170

Exodus
9, Weir Rd
London SW12 OLT
Tel: 0181-675 5550
Fax: 0181-673 0779

Jasmin Tours
Tel: 01628-531121

Voyages Jules Verne
Tel: 0171-723 5066

British Museum Tours
Tel: 0171-323 8895

Abercrombie & Kent
Tel: 0171-730 9600

Every overseas tour operator selling trips to the Yemen, however, must contract a **local agency** to operate the tours on their behalf. This ensures the highest degree of local knowledge is employed in arranging tours. The major local tour companies are:

Yemen Arab Tourism Agency (YATA)
Airport Road, PO Box 1153 Sana'a
Tel: 224236 or 224277
Fax: 251597

The most established and respected agency in the country, YATA has dealt with tourists from the very beginning of the industry in 1972. A fleet of 4x4 vehicles are driven by experienced drivers many of whom can speak English, French, German and Italian. Everyone working in the office speaks English so contact them in advance with your requirements for details of individual tours. YATA has offices, representatives and agents throughout the country.

Universal Travel
Saif Dhi Yazeen St
PO Box 10473, Sana'a
Tel: 275028/9/30
Fax: 275134

Another large company which deals with many overseas groups and provides good transport and service.

Many other agencies of differing size, cost and quality offer tours around the country. All the following are based in Sana'a:

ABM Tours
PO Box 10420
Tel: 270856/7
Fax: 274106

Al-Mamoon Travel and Tourism
PO Box 10127
Tel: 242008/79261

Bazara Travel and Tourism
Az-Zubeiry St
PO Box 2616
Tel: 205925/865
Fax: 209568

Arabian Horizons
Tel: 275366/414
Fax: 275415

Marib Travel and Tourism
PO Box 161
Tel: 272432/5/6
Fax: 274199

Hadda Car Hire
Tel: 240237

If you arrive in Aden, most of the major agencies listed above have their own representatives, usually in the larger hotels. Otherwise you could try the former PDRY national agency:

Arabia Felix Tourist
Ma'alla Main Rd
P0 Box 6233
Tel: 41913/43124

WHEN TO GO TO YEMEN

It is possible to travel around the country at any time of the year, but some seasons are more pleasant than others.

Most people tend to avoid the **heavy summer** rains, which occur roughly from July to September, when some of the roads and tracks in the mountains can be flooded. The humidity on the coast and the heat in the Hadramaut can also make it an exhausting time, but you do get the most daylight. Personally I enjoy travelling in the summer as there are very few other tourists and accommodation is easy to obtain. Both day and night temperatures are comfortable in the mountains, but you must be able to cope with temperatures around 40°C on the coast.

The **small rains** occur during March and April, which is often a popular time to visit, owing to the Easter holiday. The rest of the year is usually dry but you would certainly see rain in the mountains around Ibb. **September** and **October** are my favourite months as the fields are green with crops

Mountains near Mahweet.

from the summer rains and there are few other visitors on the roads and in the hotels.

By far the busiest time for tourism is from **November to March,** particularly over Christmas and New Year when almost every hotel bed is booked (many times over). The daytime temperatures in the highlands are near perfect, but it does become cold at night. On the coast it is still hot through the day, but very pleasant in the evenings.

Religious events and holidays play a major part throughout the year. The holidays can often be a bonus for the traveller, enabling you to see unusual aspects of everyday life. The fasting month of **Ramadan** is a difficult time to get things organised but not impossible. You might experience problems finding places to eat and drink through the day (restaurants tend to open at about 15.00 and stay open through the night), and some drivers and guides can get irritable. The evenings are lively and you might have problems sleeping while everyone else is up. On the positive side there will be fewer tourists around during Ramadan and thus less strain on the agents and hotels.

TREKKING

The highlands of the Yemen are surely one of the greatest undiscovered trekking regions in the world. The very idea of trekking in Arabia seems strange to many people, but on seeing photographs they can understand the attraction, even though it is not actually encouraged by the government.

Obviously trekking or even just walking around the mountains is the best way to appreciate the beauty and grandeur of this 'Roof of Arabia'. But the activity is still in its infancy and you must plan and organise almost everything yourself. Routes are unmarked, directions vague and destinations unfamiliar, but with a sense of adventure such trekking is unique. It is best to plan on walking in the mornings, as after about 14.00 the mountains are often covered in mist, usually with rain.

If there is such a thing as an established trek area then it is in the Heraz mountains based on Manakha, within easy reach of both Sana'a and Hodeidah. There are several basic treks that can be undertaken with the minimum of planning and equipment (see West of Sana'a in Section 2). For treks lasting more than a day you would need to plan fully what equipment you require. This can really only be judged by your trekking experience in other countries.

Basic essentials include food, water, warm and waterproof clothing, good footwear, a medical kit, a torch and a compass. Outside Manakha it is difficult to arrange accommodation unless you know the area and speak good Yemeni Arabic, so it would be advisable to carry a tent and be independent.

Other areas that I strongly recommend for mountain walking are Hajjah, Mahweet, Jebel Bura, Ibb/Jibla and at-Turbah. In fact it is possible to walk the whole way from the Wadi Sharas area of Hajjah down the central range of mountains to the Hujjariya region south of Ta'iz. Half-day and full-day treks are mentioned in the relevant sections. However, always be aware of local conditions and note that some trekkers have recently had trouble with the local people at Mawheet and around Hajjah.

Some tour operators are starting to offer **itineraries** with more than just the half-day walk around Manakha, and I think that trekking will really take off in the future.

CYCLING

This may seem an odd way of getting around, but it is becoming more popular. A tour operator in Holland has tried the idea and run several successful tours using **mountain bikes** with a back-up vehicle. As an individual arriving with your own bike you can be independent of the agencies and go virtually where you want. Some cyclists have had hassles in the mountains, usually in the form of stone-throwing, but this would mainly stem from them wearing brief cycling shorts.

A strong mountain bike is recommended as the dirt roads (and even some of the real ones) are in a poor state. You would also need very low gears to get up some of the incredible mountain passes. Even the thought of cycling up the 33km hill between Hajjah and Amran is enough to make the limbs ache, but one mountain bike ride that I would love to make is down the old road between Dhamar and Hammam Ali. I have measured one section of 31km of fast dirt track, almost all of it downhill!

MAPS

The first tourist map of the new Republic was published in 1993 by the General Tourism Authority, PO Box 129, Sana'a and is a useful 1:1,500,000 travel aid. There are still some old General Tourism Corporation 1:1,000,000 **tourist maps** of the YAR available locally with useful, if outdated, plans of the major cities. There is a 1: 4,000,000 map issued by the Ministry of Construction which indicates the general state of the roads (paved, gravel or feeder), but is useless for sightseeing.

YAR tourist brochures with small maps of Sana'a, Ta'iz, Hodeidah and Marib were issued free, but can now sometimes be found for sale in shops. Accurate large scale town plans are for sale in Sana'a.

Several maps can be bought outside the country but they mainly cover the old YAR, and do so with varying degrees of inaccuracy. For my own travels I use a combination of half a dozen old and very old maps – some of the best date from the 1930s and 1950s and are now almost impossible to obtain, but you can try.

Some of the following maps can be obtained or ordered from specialist travel and book shops:

Yemen Arabic Republic 1:1,000,000, available from:
Cordee Book Distributors,
3a De Montfort St
Leicester
LE1 7HD
Tel: 01533 543579

Tactical Pilotage Charts 1:500,000. Map TPC K-6A covers most of the country, but for north of Huth you need TPC J-6C, and for east of Mukalla TPC K-6B. Usually available from:
Stanfords Map and Travel Retailers,
· 12 Long Acre,
London
WC2E 9LP
Tel: 0171-836 1321

Yemen 1:700,000 Road Map. Road map produced by Astrolabe Productions Editions, also sometimes available from Stanfords, or direct from:
Editions Astrolabe
46 Rue de Provence
75009 Paris

Yemen Arab Republic 1:1,000,000 published by:
Deutsch-Jemenitische Gesellschaft e.V.
D-7800
Kronenstrasse 11
Freiburg
Germany

The YAR was mapped to a high standard by the Ordnance Survey, but many single sheets were needed for the whole country. These were previously on sale at Stanfords but have since been withdrawn and occasionally you can find them decorating walls in tour agency offices. If you can get hold of them, these would be ideal maps for planning treks in the Heraz mountains around Manakha.

No maps of the former PDRY are available apart from two that date from the late 1950s. The Royal Geographical Society commissioned two 1:500,000 South Arabia maps based on information from travellers over the previous 25 years. Their reference numbers are 8000/7/57/SPC/RE and 8000/8/58/3818/R. If you can find them they are excellent.

The highly detailed sketch map of the Hadramaut which accompanies the book by D. van der Meulen and H. von Wissman, published in the 1930s, *Hadramaut: Some of its Mysteries Unveiled* is also very useful.

Towerhouse in Wadi Dhahr.

COUNTRY FILE

BRIEF HISTORY

In an attempt to make the history more relevant to particular places, the main historical information is provided in the travel sections. However I include below a brief chronological list of the major historical events and indicate where more details can be found.

Southern Arabia is said to be one of the oldest inhabited regions in the world, a fact which, even if not substantiated by archaeological evidence, is certainly backed up by traditional stories which reach back to Noah. Many of the early dates and periods given below should be considered as indications only; precise dating is at present not possible.

	5000 BC	Early village settlements in the highlands.
	1300 BC	Domestication of the camel aids trade development.
	1200 BC	Start of the early frankincense trade routes through the desert edge communities to supply the Egyptian Empire (see Gold and Incense Road).
Ancient Kingdoms	**1000 BC**	Urban settlements identified on trade route. Emerging southern Arabian kingdoms of Awsan, Saba, Hadramaut, Ma'in and Qataban (see East of Sana'a).
	950 BC	Possible visit of Queen of Sheba to King Solomon.
	700 BC	Construction of dam at Marib?
	500 BC	Sirwah temples built? Start of Sabaean prosperity and rule. Awsan Kingdom falls to Sabaeans?
	400 BC	Ma'in rises against Saba. Baraqish becomes Ma'in capital for short time.
	300 BC	Greek Empire gives way to emerging Romans.
Rise of the Himyars	**115 BC**	Himyarite Kingdom rivals Saba (see Dhamar Ibb).
	100 BC	Sana'a rises at centre of inland trade route (see Sana'a).
	24 BC	Romans attempt to conquer Arabia Felix under Aelius Gallus but fail.
	100 AD	Hadramaut Kingdom defeats Qataban. Sabaeans take control of Ma'in Kingdom. Discovery of monsoon winds allows Roman traders to bypass overland trade routes.
	200	Ghumdan Palace built in Sana'a?
	260	Himyarite Kingdom defeats Sabaeans?
	300	Himyars control southern Arabia.

400	Roman Empire gives way to Byzantium. Demand for incense drops.
525	Ethiopians defeat Yusuf Dhu Nuwas and occupy Himyarite Kingdom.
570	So-called 'Year of the Elephant': Axumite leader Abraha tries to capture Mecca using elephants; the dam at Marib collapses for the last time; the Prophet Mohammed is born in Mecca (see Islam).
575	Persians defeat Ethiopians and set up their kingdom.
628	Badhan the Persian Governor of Yemen embraces Islam. Great mosques in Sana'a and al-Janad built.
632	Death of Prophet Mohammed in Medina.
660	Yemen falls under Umayyid control from Damascus.
750	Abbasid caliphs rule Yemen from Baghdad.
819	Ziad dynasty starts in the Tihama (see Zabid).
847	The Beni Yufir dynasty rules from Sana'a.
897	Yahya al-Hadi arrives in Sadah and starts the Zaidi dynasty that lasts until 1962 (see Sadah).
1021	The Ethiopian Najahids take control from the Beni Ziad at Zabid.
1046	Ali as-Sulayhi starts the Sulayhid state (see Manakha).
1069	The Sulaymanids control the northern Tihama.
1080	The Beni Zuray control Aden (see Aden).
1087	Queen Arwa moves the capital of the Sulayhids from Sana'a to Jibla (see Ibb).
1099	Hamdanid Sultans take Sana'a.
1159	The Mahdids take control from the Najahids in Zabid.
1173	Turanshah al-Ayyubi takes the Tihama for his brother Saladin and sets up an Ayyubid dynasty with the capital at Ta'iz (see Ta'iz).
1228	Rasulid rule replaces the Ayyubids. Famous mosques built in Ta'iz.
1324	Zaidi Imams eventually rule from Sana'a.
1454	The Tahirids from Rada'a rule most of the south (see Dhamar–Lawdar). The Kathiris establish themselves in Wadi Hadramaut (see Seiyun).
1497	Vasco da Gama finds sea route to India.
1507	Affonso d'Albuquerque occupies Socotra for the Portuguese (see Socotra).
1515	Mamelukes of Egypt take Sana'a.
1517	Zaidi Imams control most of country by default as rising Ottomans claim Hijaz.
1538	The fleet of Suleiman the Magnificent takes the Tlhama and Aden. Start of first Turkish Ottoman occupation.

Beginning of Islam

Rise of the Imams

Europeans arrive

	1547	Turks take Sana'a from Zaidi Imams. Start of coffee industry.
	1623	Ottoman Turks driven out of Sana'a by Zaidi Imams.
	1635	Turks expelled completely from southern Arabia. Period of powerful Imams based in Sana'a. Coffee trade booming.
	1658	Imam Mu'ayyid reunites Yemen.
	1729	Sultan of Lahej takes Aden and south from Zaidis.
British in	1798	Start of British interest as they take Perim Island.
the South	1839	British take Aden from Sultan of Lahej.
	1849	Start of second period of Ottoman rule in the Tihama. Maria Theresa dollar widely used for currency.
	1857	British take Lahej.
	1882	Turks occupy most of the north, British the south.
	1904	Imam Yahya takes over from his father Imam Mohammed.
	1905	Border agreed between Turks and British, until 1990.
	1911	Treaty of Da'an signed by Turks giving Imam Yahya autonomy in highland regions.
	1918	Turks leave Yemen after defeat in First World War. Imam Yahya in control of North Yemen.
	1925	Imam Yahya takes Hodeidah from Idrisi Emirs (see Hodeidah).
	1934	Saudi Arabia takes province of Asir in northern Tihama settled by Treaty of Ta'if.
	1937	Aden becomes British Crown Colony.
	1948	Imam Ahmed takes over after Yahya's assassination. Majority of Jews leave Yemen for new State of Israel (see Jewish Yemenis).
Civil Wars and	1962	Death of Imam Ahmed followed by revolution
Independence		and civil war in the north (see Politics).
	1963	Declaration of independence from British control in the south (see Politics).
	1967	Last British troops leave Aden.
	1969	Establishment of the Yemen Arab Republic in north.
	1970	People's Democratic Republic of Yemen formed in south.
	1978	Lt Col Ali Abdullah Saleh becomes president of YAR.
	1986	Civil war in PDRY, Aden wrecked.
	1990	Unification of YAR and PDRY to become the Republic of Yemen.
	1993	First democratic General Election.
	1994	Northern forces defeat southern troops attempting to secede from union.

EARLY TRAVELLERS

Southern Arabia has always been an exotic destination even for the early travellers, mainly because the area was thought to be rich in luxurious items famous throughout the known world. Some of the accounts of these travellers are highly imaginative and fanciful, and were written by people who knew that their claims could never be challenged (at least not in their lifetimes). Some of these books are still available (see Further Reading).

Bible stories   The Bible is arguably the first source of written information we have about the area, assuming that the flowery stories of Noah and his descendants, the travels of the Queen of the South (Sheba) and the details of the 'Magi bearing gifts' are all based on real events.

The earliest descriptions which can be historically verified, however, come from the scholars of the ancient world, and deal with the shipping and trade routes. Herodotus, Pliny and Ptolemy all mention Arabia as being rich in goods, but the best description from pre-Islamic times is by an unknown writer describing the sea trade between Egypt and India from around the first century AD. His work *Periplus Maris Erithraei* ('Circumnavigation of the Erythrean Sea') gives valuable details of the ports *en route*. Of particular interest are his descriptions of the now lost port of Muza, which point to it being north of Mokha.

Around 1230 **Marco Polo** gave the names of all the ports along the Indian Ocean coastline and told weird and wonderful tales of the islands and their inhabitants, who could weave magic spells on passing sailors. A century later came the tremendous account of an amazing adventurer called **Ibn Battuta** who sailed around and travelled over much of what was then the known world. He visited Arabia and East Africa around 1328 and travelled overland from a port he calls al-Ahwab to Zabid, Jibla, Ta'iz and Aden. Unfortunately there is little detail in his accounts but much of his information and reported history are good.

Colonial   The next reliable accounts were by Portuguese
expansion   navigators looking for a route to the Indies. **Pero de Couilha** visited Aden in 1487 and a decade later **Vasco da Gama** succeeded in sailing around the tip of Africa. Almost certainly the first European to venture inland was the Italian **Ludovico di Varthema** in 1503. He was taken under guard from Aden to Sana'a but then escaped and incredibly made his way back to Aden.

The first Europeans into Wadi Hadramaut were a couple of unlikely Portuguese Jesuit priests towards the end of the sixteenth century. **Father Antonio de Montserrat** and **Father Pedro Paez** were on their way from Goa to

**Into the
Hadramaut 'by
mistake'**

Ethiopia and decided to try an inland 'shortcut'. This was
not a good idea as it took them over five years to get
through, but fortunately for them it was during the first
Turkish occupation rather than the Zaidi Imamate. They
were the first westerners to enter northern Yemen from
the east, and the last for another three centuries!

Ancient carved blocks, re-used in a modern house in Dhafar.

**The British
arrive**

In 1609 there was the first account of a British ship
trading in the area, courtesy of a merchant by the name of
John Jourdain who described all the details of Mokha
port and his journey to Sana'a. A year later **Sir Henry
Middleton** arrived. He was the sort of traveller who
gives the British a bad name abroad; he looted, plundered
and threatened to blow up Mokha. In much the same
mould was **Affonso d'Albuquerque,** a Portuguese
colonialist of the early seventeenth century, who sailed in
and out of Aden trying to take the port, which he
described as 'containing many beautiful houses . . . every
peak crowned by a castle'. He failed, and so set about
another of his plans: to steal the body of the Prophet
Mohammed from Medina and then hand it back in
exchange for the city of Jerusalem!

A few years later **Pieter van den Broecke** gave us an
insight to Sana'a at that time, and described seeing the
relic of Noah's Ark kept in the Great Mosque. By 1620

there were many European businessmen setting up trading posts in Mokha in order to participate in the new and profitable coffee trade, but few ventured inland. Mokha rose and fell and Aden became the next great centre of interest.

First scientific expedition

One of the great names among early travellers in southern Arabia was **Carsten Niebuhr**, a German surveyor on a scientific mission sponsored by King Frederick V of Denmark. The journey was a monumental task of research, in which he visited the Near and Far East; only Niebuhr himself survived from the six that started out. In 1762-4 the team visited the Yemen, where two of them died: **Peter Forsskal** the brilliant botanist aged only 31 succumbed to fever in Yarim; and the academic **Friedrich von Haven** died of malaria in Mokha. The descriptions, measurements and samples that they obtained are invaluable sources of information.

The British in Aden

British agents of the Indian forces regularly called at Aden, which was developing into the great supply station of the East. **Lt J. R. Wellsted** of the survey ship *Palinurus* copied the ancient inscriptions at Husn al-Ghurab and started the rush for further examples for the experts to decode. In the meantime two Frenchmen had succeeded in reaching the ancient sites of the area for the first time. In 1843 **Joseph-Thomas Arnaud** arrived in Marib, describing the old city in a way which indicates that little has changed since then. **Joseph Halevy** travelled to Marib and Ma'in in the 1870s disguised as a Jew and so had to endure the ridiculous impositions which were placed on the local Jewish communities. Between them they brought back over 700 examples of carved inscriptions.

Everyone heads for the desert

In the same year as Arnaud reached Marib, a German soldier was approaching the desert wastes from the other end. **Baron Adolf von Wrede** travelled as a tribesman, calling himself Abdul Hud and set out from Mukalla. His disguise was probably not very good as he generally had a terrible time and was often threatened with death for being a spy, but he did get across the *jol* into the upper reaches of Wadi Do'an.

By the end of the nineteenth century there was a new breed of serious traveller who wanted to visit, investigate, observe and report. In 1882 the Austrian scholar **Eduard Glaser** started the first of his four visits over twelve years and collected 2,000 inscriptions under the protection of the Ottomans. In 1892 **Walter Harris** reached Sana'a in disguise by camel caravan, only to be promptly arrested and thrown out. But he does write enthusiastically about the ruins of the Ghumdan Palace and the area around Manakha on his way out. In the

same year the German **Leo Hirsch** got into Wadi
Hadramaut and reached Tarim. His companion was
Imam Sherif Khan Bahadur, who was acting as surveyor
for **Theodore and Mabel Bent,** a British couple who
followed the same route the following year, when she
became the first European woman into the Hadramaut.

**The British in
South Arabia**

The ousting of the Turks in 1904 brought Imam Yahya
to Sana'a and initiated his isolationist regime, when
foreigners were simply not allowed to enter. Special
mention should be made here of **Hugh Scott,** who visited
the north on an official expedition with **Everard Britton**
in the 1930s to gather specimens and information on the
flora and fauna for the British Museum. His book *In the
High Yemen* is an excellent reference point and general
travel guide with unique photographs and accounts of
the people met, including Imam Yahya.

With the closing on the north to foreigners, and easier
access through British Aden, many travellers chose to
visit the south, with Wadi Hadramaut and the capitals of
the ancient kingdoms as their goals.

A contemporary of Harris was **Wyman Bury,** who
travelled widely as a native adopting the name Abdullah
Mansur. His wanderings took him to places never before
visited by Europeans and his book *The Land of Uz* is a
Boy's Own adventure that captures an age of heroic
innocence.

The 1930s was a time when the penetration of the
hinterland really took off with a new breed of British
officer who wanted to explore and report. **R. A. B.
Hamilton** (later Lord Belhaven) walked many miles,
often with only a guide. He summed up his feelings on
clambering over endless miles of lava fields: 'You feel like
an ant climbing over the cinders of a boiler room'.

German interest

The most complete survey at the time was undertaken
by the Dutch consul from Jeddah, **Colonel Daniel van
der Meulen** and the German **Hermann von Wissman.**
The descriptions of their two journeys at the beginning
and end of the 1930s are classics which are well worth
reading. In complete contrast is another German **Hans
Helfritz,** who seemed to get himself into some
remarkable scrapes. He claims to have got to Shabwa but
was certainly arrested in Harib and taken to Sana'a where
he was deported through Hodeidah. In the process, he
became the first European since those distant Jesuit
priests to travel from east to west across northern Yemen.

The story of the early travellers really ends with the
outbreak of the Second World War, by which time the
opportunities for further pioneering work had gone
(except for some of the journeys of **Wilfred Thesiger,**
who concentrated mainly on the Rub al-Khali and Oman

Palace at Seiyun, Wadi Hadramaut.

Travellers in the 1930's

desert regions). The romance had already been lifted when **Harry St John Philby** motored along the edge of the Rub al-Khali between Najran and Wadi Hadramaut in two heavy vehicles while acting as advisor to the Saudi ruler. But there are still two names that must be mentioned, which sum up the classic British traveller in South Arabia before the war – Ingrams and Stark.

Harold Ingrams was the Resident Political Officer in Aden and put the amazing 'Ingrams Peace' into effect. This required visiting, cajoling and satisfying all the tribal chiefs in the Aden Protectorate throughout the 1930s. In all, over 1,200 signatures were required. His travels with his wife Doreen are well documented in several books spread over many journeys and many years.

In and out of Aden

Freya Stark has been an inspiration to many who might never have travelled beyond their armchair had she not written so many books about her travels. Although she travelled widely in the Arab world it is probably her books on southern Arabia for which she will best be remembered. Her minute descriptions of everyday life, sometimes in diary form, are the last reminders of a way of life that was about to change rapidly and radically.

THE GOLD AND INCENSE ROAD

During the Neolithic and Bronze Ages, early agricultural settlements established themselves in the fertile wadis flowing into the Rub al-Khali or Empty Quarter. By retaining the seasonal flow of water down the wadis it was possible for a most unlikely trading route, the Gold and Incense Road, to be supplied with fresh food and water.

The **sea trade** of the area was initially intended to supply the wealthy Egyptian civilisations with incense and gold, perfumes and spices. The uses were threefold: to burn as sweet smelling incense in temples and homes as offerings to the gods; to purify and embalm dead bodies during the mummification process; and for medicine. Incense was thought to be an essential part of everyday life (and death) for the ancient Egyptians and to keep up with demand, the people of what was then called Punt set up a supply route that was well protected.

Trading with Ancient Egypt

Queen Hatshepsut describes the 'expedition to Punt' in relief carvings on her funerary temple at Deir al-Bahari near Luxor. All the imported exotic goods and spices are shown in detail and it is thought that the name 'Punt' may have been given to both sides of the southern Red Sea including southern Arabia.

Despite the domestication of the camel around 1300 BC there is no evidence to suggest that there were any major **overland trade routes** until around 1000 BC. A safe route then developed which meandered along the desert edge, where supplies of food and water could be obtained from the communities. These new routes linked the Mediterranean directly to the areas of production of the valuable incense, particularly frankincense.

But the traders did not restrict themselves to what they could produce locally along the southern coast or Socotra (incense, frankincense, myrrh and gold), but sailed annually with the monsoons to India and East Africa. Precious woods, spices, silk, feathers and valuable skins were imported to Qana, and then sent north, while the locals retained the secret of where these luxury items originated.

Great wealth from South Arabia

The trade appears to have centred on a kingdom called **Saba,** the earliest mention of which is the Bible, when the Queen of Saba (Sheba) travelled to meet King Solomon (see Marib History). The exotic goods of southern Arabia were in demand throughout the Mediterranean and the Levant, creating vast wealth which was spent on improving the route and the towns through which it passed. The most ambitious project was at the Sabaean capital

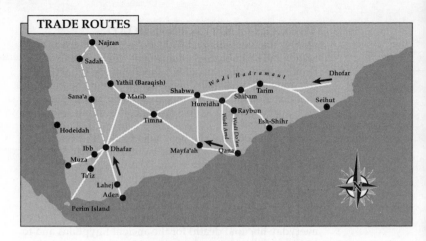

itself with the building of the Marib dam during the eight century BC, which is mentioned in the Koran.

Wealthy desert kingdoms

Even as late as the fifth century BC mystery still surrounded the production of the luxury goods; Herodotus wrote about the 'winged serpents' that protected the frankincense tree. But the incredible wealth of the trade had also allowed other towns on the route to rise up and proclaim their independence of Marib and the Kingdom of Saba. Ma'in to the north and Qataban and Hadramaut to the south, all set up their own minor kingdoms.

The Greeks and Romans conquered Egypt and inherited the local taste for the precious goods that came from Arabia. When they named the known regions of the world, Arabia was divided into three; **Arabia Petraea** ('stony' Arabia) based on the Nabatean capital Petra; **Arabia Deserta** ('desert' Arabia) covering most of the central Syrian desert; and **Arabia Felix** ('happy' Arabia) the prosperous peninsula from which all the luxury items came. It can also mean 'green' or 'fortunate' Arabia referring to the well-watered mountains or irrigated land around the Marib dam.

Romans attempt to conquer

The **Romans** under Emperor Augustus tried to conquer the trade route, with an expedition under Aelius Gallus in 24 BC. The popular belief is that they failed upon reaching the walls of Marib, but some scholars think that the army might have reached as far as Shabwa. Whatever happened, the stranglehold on the trade was already loosening as new factors affected the situation in the first 300 years of Christianity.

Greek sailors managed to sail with the monsoon winds to India and Africa, so breaking the monopoly of the Sabaeans and allowing the Romans to trade by sea. Meanwhile the northerly 'Silk Road' through Asia was

Trade decreases

carrying many of these wonderful items direct from India and the Far East at lower cost. The rise of **Christianity** around the Mediterranean virtually halted the call for incense as it was no longer needed in religious or funerary ceremonies. Finally there were momentous internal struggles for control of the Saba Kingdom, which eventually ended when the Himyars defeated the Sabaeans and moved their capital to Dhafar (near Yarim).

The **Himyars** took what was left of the overland trade and shifted the routes into the mountains through Sana'a and Sadah. The final nail in Marib's coffin was the total collapse of the dam, which ended any possible hope of keeping the desert route going. The Bedouins who had been employed to protect the caravans turned on their employers and regularly attacked the declining desert towns. With the mysteries of the trade solved and the dam collapsed beyond repair, the cities became ruins and the inhabitants left to settle in many regions of the Arab world.

All that we know of this fascinating period of history are some vague stories with a few names and approximate dates. Hopefully excavations can be carried out to gather more information from the desert areas around Marib and along the full length of the route, which will fill the gaps of our knowledge. There really is buried treasure out there somewhere!

However, the government's current emphasis is on researching and maintaining Islamic sites and monuments, not pre-Islamic ones. The greatness of Sheba may take some time to be revealed as it takes bold decisions to advance the knowledge of what the Prophet referred to as a 'pagan land'.

GEOGRAPHY

Between Africa and Asia

The Republic of Yemen lies at the southern tip of the Arabian Peninsula and has **borders** with only two Arab countries: Saudi Arabia to the north and Oman in the east. Ethiopia lies across the Red Sea and Somalia is on the other side of the Gulf of Aden, both giving Yemeni coastal areas a strong African influence. The Red Sea and Indian Ocean coastlines meet at the strategic Bab al-Mandab ('Gateway of Tears') directly opposite Djibouti. A look at a world map shows clearly how the peninsula is a bridge between Africa and Asia and thus has aspects of both, but it has had time to develop it's own unique identity.

The **southern and northern extents** of Yemen's territory are approximately $12\frac{1}{2}°$ and $19°$ N, placing it well inside the Tropic of Cancer. The **eastern and western limits** are $42\frac{1}{2}°$ and $53°$ E. The total area is 530,000sq km, making it larger than California but smaller than Texas. It is about the same size as France, and about twice the size of the UK. The capital, Sana'a, is roughly on the same latitude as Bangkok, Dakar and Guatemala City and shares a longitude with Baghdad and Mogadishu.

A rich coastline

The Red Sea coast is a flat plain varying in width from 20 to 50km and is the continuation of the Tihamat ash-Sham. The Tihama begins north of Jeddah and runs the length of the lower half of the eastern coast. Inland from this rise the western mountains which generally run parallel to the coast and contain several high altitude plateaus that are extremely fertile owing to deposited silt. Sana'a lies on the edge of one of these productive basins. The surrounding mountains form a watershed between the seasonal rivers that flow into the Tihama and those draining into the vast wastes of the Rub al-Khali. This desert area forms a natural barrier along the northern border of the country, stretching all the way to Oman.

The **Gulf of Aden** offers an opportunity for land access from the east, but is interrupted by mountains and large wadis running into the sea. This eastern region is largely a semi-desert wilderness that accounts for about half of all the land area, but it is penetrated by a fabled geographical feature, Wadi Hadramaut.

The true origin of the **name** 'Yemen' has been lost through the millennia, but there are several possibilities. The Roman name Arabia Felix ('happy' Arabia) could be linked with the Arabic word *yumn* meaning 'happiness'. Alternatively, it could derive from the Arabic word *yameen,* which means 'to the right'. If you are in Mecca, looking in the direction of the sunrise, Yemen is to the right. (The right hand of the body is also regarded as 'clean' or good, whereas the left is not).

There is another tradition, according to which ancient Arabia was split into two, with southern Arabia being referred to as al-Yaman, and the most northerly region called ash-Sham, a name used locally for Syria and it's capital Damascus.

The Yemen

Many Arab names (people, countries and towns etc.) are prefixed by the definite article: al-Hamdani, al-Yemen and al-Luhayyah. The English word 'Yemen' is prefixed by the word 'the', because of the translation from the Arabic 'al-Yemen'. Personal and town names tend to drop this prefix in translation, but some Arab countries retain it: the Sudan and the Lebanon are other examples. It is said by some that this is the case when the word originally refers to a geographical region which later becomes a political entity.

GEOLOGY

The Arabian peninsula is tilted along the edge of the Red Sea, part of the great scar on the earth's surface running from Russia to southern Africa. The Yemen coastline takes in both the narrowest and widest points of the Red Sea (29km at the Bab al-Mandab and 354km in the northern Tihama). As Arabia continues to drift away from Africa (at about 4cm per year), tremendous upheavals in the land mass have given the Yemen many peaks over 3,000m, including the highest on the peninsula, Jebel Nabi Shu'ayb at 3,660m.

Unstable landmass

Associated with these land movements are relatively frequent **earthquakes** (one on 13 December 1982, 80kms south of Sana'a, measuring 5.7 on the Richter Scale, caused 3,000 deaths), **hot springs** (Hammam Damt and

Hammam Ali) and evidence of **volcanic activity** (north of Sana'a and Aden). The underlying granite only occasionally shows itself, the general landscape being formed by weathered sandstone (at-Tawila and Kawkaban) and limestone (Amran region).

Travelling around the country you will see an amazing variety of geology, from perfectly flat, untouched sedimentary layers (the plateaux surrounding Wadi Hadramaut) to some that have been heavily folded, sometimes through 90° to form vertical strata, due to associated volcanic activity (between Shuqra and al-Aram). Outcrops of dark basalt, extinct volcano cones, black lava flows, shining traces of quartz and marble, and red and green tuffs, continually reveal themselves in the most surprising places.

Shahara Bridge in the Highlands

The **mineral wealth** of the region has long been known and exploited, including silver, alabaster, copper and salt. To these can be added new discoveries of iron, zinc and manganese, all in the north and the oil and gas reserves on the Rub al-Khali perimeter. Semi-precious gemstones, mainly agate, opal, turquoise and amethyst, have also been mined and polished here. **Fossils** dating from when large areas were under the sea can be found in great abundance in the exposed layers of limestone at heights of up to 2,800m, especially those surrounding Amran.

Precious minerals

CLIMATE

Broadly speaking there are four main climatic types, all corresponding to the main geographical regions and determined by their altitude and the effect of the seasonal monsoons: the Tihama and the south coast (up to 300m above sea level); the foothills (300m–2,200m), the central highlands (2,200m–3,600m); and the eastern desert (2,200m–1,100m).

Altitude levels

THE MONSOONS

The monsoon winds were one of the reasons why the southern Arabian kingdoms prospered in pre-Islamic times with early sea traders sailing annually to and from India and East Africa. Essentially there are two monsoon seasons, summer and winter, but unlike the more powerful Indian summer monsoon the winds here are less predictable.

In the summer months the south-west monsoon winds blow from the Indian Ocean towards the Asian land mass and are associated with the heavy summer rains. These saturated winds are pushed up and over the mountain barrier of southern Arabia depositing huge amounts of water. On the coast this is a period of high humidity throughout the summer months from May to September. During the winter months the winds reverse and blow from Central Asia in the north-east, giving dry, clear and cold conditions. The lighter rains occur in April and May.

The Tihama and the South Coast
(e.g. Hodeidah and Aden)

Extreme conditions

The majority of the 2,000km of coastline is backed by a flat humid plain with very high temperatures which can rise to 50°C in the summer. Winds often temper the heat but they in turn can create unpleasant **sandstorms** which, when combined with the high humidity, make a stay in the region almost unbearable. You can feel the energy being sapped from your body even when undertaking the simplest of tasks, and shady *qat* sessions or an air-conditioned vehicle are the best ways to survive the afternoons. Summer night temperatures of above 25°C can also make sleeping outside an air-conditioned room extremely difficult. Winter is altogether more attractive, with warm day and night temperatures – a welcome relief from the cold of the mountains.

The Foothills
(e.g. Hajjah, Khamis Bani Sa'd)

These slopes reach as far as the highlands and run parallel to the coast but are deeply split by the gorges and ravines created by the tremendous rain run-offs. Rainfall is greatest in these areas as the summer monsoon blows moist air onto the west facing slopes, causing tremendous **downpours.** The effect of this is to wash away badly made bridges, cause landslides and erode dirt tracks.

The lower areas can be classified as **subtropical** with a lot of rain, but the high temperatures quickly dry things out. The higher terracing has a more moderate climate with warm days and cool nights.

The Central Highlands
(e.g. Sana'a, Amran)

Areas of high rainfall

The mountains form a **watershed** that diverts the waters from the seasonal rains down to the foothills or into the desert. The force of the rain quickly erodes the soft layers of sandstone and limestone, sending down rivers of rich alluvial deposits that create fertile farmland where the water seeps into the ground.

The effect of **high altitude and strong sunshine** causes a difference in daytime temperatures as great as 20°C, which is exaggerated by wind chill factors. The maximum figures during the day are about the same as the corresponding minimum temperatures in the Tihama between 25° and 30°C. Summer nights are pleasant but wet, owing to the heavy rains which usually fall in the afternoon. Winter nights can be cold, reaching freezing point, with the occasional **frost**.

The Eastern Desert
(e.g. Marib, Wadi Hadramaut)

The 'Empty Quarter'

Once across the highlands the land slopes down eastwards into the Rub al-Khali, with temperatures similar to the coast, but without the oppressive humidity. This great Arabian desert is the result of the sinking of the central part of the Arabian plate. Here there is little rainfall, as most of the rain clouds have already discharged their load and the little that flows down the eastern slopes of the mountains soon seeps into the sandy ground. To the east and north there is hardly any rainfall at all in the Rub al-Khali proper, where the conditions are very hot and dry. However, Marib and Wadi Hadramaut can sometimes get torrential rain, causing heavy flood damage.

In winter it is cold at night with strong winds, but fine and clear during the day. Summers are characterised by pleasant nights, when sleeping out is ideal, but days are very hot and care should be taken.

FLORA AND FAUNA

Just as the landscape of the Yemen is determined by the climate and altitude of each area, and such human factors as irrigation and land use, so too are the flora and fauna which live here.

THE RED SEA

The Red Sea has some of the most prolific coral reefs in the world. There are over 50 genera and more than 170 species of coral to be found along its 1932km length. No permanent rivers flow into it which means a shortage of fresh water and minerals. For this reason all life would cease to exist here if it was not for the tiny entrance at the Bab al-Mandab which allows huge amounts of plankton and life-giving minerals to be flushed in from the Indian Ocean. This nutrient-rich soup drifts up past the Yemen coast reducing visibility for snorkellers and divers.

In rough weather the visibility is rather poor, but in calm conditions, the snorkelling can be superb. Regular sights are reef-dwellers like angel, damsel clown and parrot fish as well as wrasse. These are preyed upon by jacks, snappers and barracuda. You would be extremely lucky to see any type of reef shark and would need to go further and deeper to find hammerhead sharks. There are also turtles and manta rays, but they are difficult to find.

Plants

Over 2,000 different species of plant have been recorded in the Yemen, covering a vast range of habitats.

Red Sea coast

In the **northern Tihama,** there are large banks of **mangrove swamps** (*Avicennia marina*) lying just offshore that provide protection for a vast range of sea and bird life. If you travel to al-Luhayyah the route to the sea is obscured by thick mangroves. The Tihama is an arid area that nevertheless manages to support a few hardy plants such as acacia trees (*Acacia ehrenbergiana*), wild doum palms (*Hyphaene thebaica*) and broom brush shrubs (*Leptadenia pyrotechnica*)

Moving inland up the **wadi beds** you find dense areas of bananas and papaya which are well-fed by water draining from the mountains. Trees growing here tend to be the *Acacia tortilis* and the umbrella-shaped *Delonix elata*. You will also start to see the large green bush *Ziziphus spina-christi*, known locally as the *ilb* tree, which has spread throughout the country. You will often notice

Trees for nests

it because of the weaver bird nests dangling from its branches.

One plant in particular which grows all over the country – and in many other desert regions – is *Calotropis procera*, known here as *as-Shir*, which belongs to the Asclepiad family. In addition to round, light green leaves and maroon and white flowers, it has large green pods packed with seeds and silky hairs, from which the Bedouin make a type of fine string. It is usually about 2m high but can grow taller, and is found in wadi beds.

Probably the most amazing tree to see close up is the much-maligned bottle tree (*Adenium obesum*) which grows into weird stumpy shapes around basalt outcrops on steep slopes. It is only fitting that one of the world's ugliest trees should have some of the most stunningly beautiful pink flowers. Some of the large trees you will see with broad green leaves are wild fig *(Ficus)*.

Trees and trade

Across on the eastern side on the *jol* **plateau** between Wadi Hadramaut and the sea, are some isolated areas of frankincense *(Boswellia sacra)* and myrrh *(Commiphora erythraea)*.

Higher in the **mountains** are juniper bushes *(Juniperus procera)* in reasonable quantities, particularly in unspoilt areas such as Jebel Sawraq between Ta'iz and Qatabah. Coffee and *qat* are terrace-cultivated with borders of acacia, olive *(Olea chrysophylla)* and tree aloe *(Aloe sabaea)*. There are no wild cactuses in Arabia, but the imported prickly pear *(Opuntia)* is widespread.

These are quite different from the many types of prickly euphorbias, particularly the candelabra euphorbia *(Euphorbia ammak)*. These 'cactus-like' euphorbias grow at all altitudes and appear in eight different varieties. Larger ones grow all over the higher slopes but on the high barren plateaus it is the smaller hardier *Euphorbia fruticosa Forssk* (named by Peter Forsskal on Niebuhr's 1776 expedition) that flourishes. All the stony hillsides around Huth seem covered in these small prickly clumps.

Growing in the high fertile basins of the central mountain range are many types of fruit trees including apricot, pear, peach, pomegranate and quince, as well as grape vines. Some of the most pleasant to see on the slopes in early spring flower are almond and walnut.

Dwindling forests

The only remaining area of substantial **forest** is Jebel Bura above as-Sukhnah in the central Tihama. These juniper trees and the variety of wildlife that lives in and around them are under constant threat from pollution and human access.

Animals

Driving around the main roads you might think that little wildlife has survived to the present day. In fact there is still a wide variety of animal life here, including leopard, but you would be lucky on a short visit to see more than the odd lizard.

The abundance of guns over the last hundred years has driven the surviving animals into remote regions far from human habitation, and it is into these places that you must go, even to stand a chance of seeing something.

Are there any leopards?

Leopards have been reported in isolated mountain areas south of Ta'iz, and the Jebel ash-Sharafayn region in the northern Tihama. This may seem incredible, but there have been studies of leopards living in Oman and Israel, and it is quite feasible that there are limited numbers here

Animals in remote regions

living on small reptiles and rodents. There are also **striped hyenas** in several areas, and you occasionally see a young one brought into a mountain *suq*. The tufted-eared **caracal,** a small predator of the cat family also inhabits this region.

Troops of **hamadryas baboons** live in mountain caves and can be heard shrieking in the Jebel Bura area. They can also be spotted in the Mahweet, Manakha and Hajjarain areas but well away from the towns, and you will probably only see them if you are trekking.

The nocturnal **ratel** or honey badger, like many other animals, is common both in the Yemen and in East Africa, which shows that the two sides of the Red Sea were joined not too long ago. Many different species of **gazelle** inhabited this region at one time but hunting has left such small numbers that they are virtually impossible to find. There are probably still some Arabian gazelle in the Tihama, living on acacia bushes, and the exotic Queen of Sheba's gazelle *(Gazella bilkis)* still just hangs on in quiet mountain areas. The ibex, whose horns you will see decorating houses from Sadah to Seihut, has probably gone for good from the desert fringes.

Moving down the scale there are several types of **Arabian fox** in the mountains. If you do see one it will probably be the adaptable Ruppell's sand fox with large ears and a small body. I once spotted one near Kohlan *en route* to Hajjah after dark. **Mongoose, hyrax, hedgehog** and **gerbil** are widespread but the largest thing you are likely to catch a glimpse of is a speedy **hare.** Porcupines have been seen in quiet areas of Lahej and Wadi Dhahr.

Snakes, scorpions, rats and mice can sometimes be seen if you disturb rocks in quiet places, but lizards and worm-lizards will probably be the limit of your wildlife spotting.

Billions of bugs

A tremendous variety of **insects** inhabit all parts of the country – as you may well find out. The best places to see the weird preying mantis or the huge moths and crickets are petrol stations! Operating throughout the night with powerful neon lights, they attract a wonderful collection of bugs. Most of them hang around the walls and ceilings in the daytime and are easy to find, especially in the hot and humid coastal regions.

Birds

The range of altitudes and the country's unique geographical location means that the birdlife of the Yemen is more varied than in most Arab countries. The Red Sea is also a traditional passageway for migrating birds, so that the resident population is supplemented by a great diversity of migrants throughout the year.

A whole book could be written just on this subject, but I will identify some of the more common birds that you are likely to see.

There are 13 endemic species and almost 30 Afro-tropical visitors that attract bird watchers from around the world. The best place to see the native birds is in the western highlands, around Manakha.

Over 350 species have been recorded in one year, from the Arabian red-legged partridge to the spotted thick-knee.

Black kites are everywhere

In towns and villages you will see acrobatic **black kites,** the commonest of the raptors. There are over 30 of these, including five types of vulture (Egyptian, griffon, black, Ruppell's and lappet-faced) and ten species of eagle.

Travelling around you should be able to spot **stonechat** and **yellow-vented bulbul.** The **South Arabian wheatear** is a distinctive small black bird with white chest and cap, not to be confused with the other eleven types of wheatear.

In the **foothills** you will find palm dove, alpine swift, blackstart and the strange hammerkop; in the **Tihama** flocks of cattle egret, the African collared dove, little swift and bustard in northern Yemen. On the **coast** (particu-

Coastal varieties

larly around Aden) you can find greater flamingo, white pelican, glossy ibis, redshank, greenshank and various plovers. Common **waders** are the little stint and the black-winged stilt. Of the many **gulls** gathered in flocks on the beach, you are most likely to see the sooty, herring and lesser black-backed gulls. Of the twelve **terns** the most common is the lesser crested. **Wildfowl** numbers are headed by teal and pintail.

Regular **migrants** are the shoveller (with a large spatulate bill), oyster-catcher, avocet (with an upturned bill) and various swallows. Impressive **residents** include the grey hornbill (found in wooded areas), the curious hoopoe (poking around fields for insects) and the spectacular Abyssinian roller (on coastal stretches, especially the eastern Tihama). You will see wagtails (four types: yellow, grey, white and citrine) and warblers (no less than 19 varieties) some of whose nests droop from trees in almost every wadi bed. Although they are there, you are unlikely to see owls, nightjars or the blue flash of the grey-headed kingfisher (I have only ever seen one, near al-Jumah).

Brilliant sunbirds

My favourites to look out for are the four types of swooping bee-eater (the two most common are the blue-cheeked in the Tihama and little green further inland), and the nervous, diminutive flitting sunbird (with a slender curved bill, males with brilliant metallic plumage): the Palestine from 250 to 2,800m; the shining from 100 to 2,200m and the Nile Valley up to 2,500m.

Harvest time above Manakha.

ECONOMY

A turn for the better?

While it is not exactly stable, there are several elements of the Yemeni economy that are set to expand despite the recent upheavals in politics and priorities. The reliance on **agriculture** has kept the majority of Yemenis reasonably isolated from the dramatic swings of international trade, but equally this has not allowed them much opportunity to progress like their Arab neighbours. All this could change with the exploitation of oil and gas in the next few years and the associated businesses that will develop with it.

Recent problems

Most analysts agree that the Yemen came off badly in the **Gulf War**, second only to Iraq, with the loss of huge amounts of revenue from Yemeni workers in the Gulf and Saudi. Not only did these remittances dry up, but there was the added cost of receiving some one million workers back into the Yemen when they were expelled from their adopted workplaces. Other states in a similar position were Jordan, Egypt and Turkey, but they all benefited from large amounts of international aid from the Western allies. Yemen's stance of apparent neutrality excluded them from such financial support.

Long-term funding from Kuwait and the Gulf was immediately cancelled for large scale projects, and the halting of subsidised oil from Iraq, meant that the Yemen had to use its own oil production domestically at the expense of export earnings. Within six months of unification the economy was in tatters owing to a situation over which the new country had very little control.

One of the
world's poorest
countries

Before unification, both countries relied heavily on remittances from abroad and foreign aid, and without these there is now a huge **trade deficit** of almost US$1 billion. This is created by importing US$1,5 billion worth of goods, yet exporting products totalling only US$700 million. Per capita GNP works out at just US$540.

The main **imports** are sugar products, vehicles, foodstuffs, petroleum products, wood, metal and machinery, with Saudi Arabia being the chief supplier. The main **exports** are oil and refined petroleum products, with a small amount of coffee, cotton, biscuits, skins, potatoes, fruit and fish.

The future looks better for what used to be two of the world's poorest countries, and unification could prove that the whole is greater than the sum of the parts. In the long term, the development of the oil and gas industry is certain to boost the economy, but the immediate problem is domestic stability and economic survival.

Oil

A bright oil-lit
future

By far the most important sector of the economy, accounting for almost 90 percent of total exports, is oil. Still in its infancy, production is less than impressive when compared to other producers in the region but continuous improvements will increase both flow and reserve figures. Although drilling started independently, oil was discovered in both the YAR (a Yemen Hunt and Exxon joint venture at Marib) and PDRY (Soviet Technoexport at Shabwa) in 1984, with production starting in both places in 1987. The oil is light and low in sulphur. In the north it is pumped to the terminal at Ras Issa near as-Salif and in the south close to Bir Ali.

Unification saw a rush of interest from international oil companies, as various consortia jostled to obtain licences to explore other regions, including offshore. The country was sectioned into 25 blocks varying in size from just 1,300 sq. km close to known fields and with reasonably easy access, up to a massive 47,000sq km in the inhospitable Rub al-Khali desert. Twenty-two blocks are in what was the PDRY, the most intriguing being the Eyad concession which brought heavy finance from the Saudi Bin Mahfouz family, who can trace their roots back to the Hadramaut. Many of the world's leading oil companies are represented, and hopes are high for major oil production that will benefit both themselves and the new republic.

Gas

Into the next century

The immediate saviour of the Yemen's economy might well be the limited reserves of oil, but it will probably be the huge amounts of gas that will see them through the next century. It is estimated that the value of gas could well be double that of oil. The country's gas finds are possibly the second largest in the Arabian peninsula (after those in Qatar).

There is still much discussion between the government and the oil companies as to exactly what is needed to exploit the discoveries. **Gas processing plants** are being constructed in the northern fields which will go some way toward serving domestic needs, thus reducing the expensive imports of liquefied petroleum gas (LPG). It is also hoped to convert existing power stations and cement factories to run off dry gas, via a national gas grid which is to be constructed.

Minerals

Ancient and modern mining

Even though the region was known to be rich in valuable minerals for many years, very little was done to exploit them until unification. Now there are a host of mining companies, running parallel with the oil industry.

For many years **salt** was the only large-scale mining industry, which was extracted around as-Salif, with a smaller amount of **marble** also being mined. Now there are plans to extract commercial quantities of **gold, silver, zinc** and **lead** at various sites around the country, as well as **copper, nickel** and **titanium** in the north and **gypsum** in the south.

Concessions currently being worked by international companies include the search for gold around Sadah, al-Bayda, Shahara, North Ma'bar, East Dhamar and in Wadi Medden (halfway between Aden and Mukalla). Lead, silver and zinc are being sought in the Shabwa region.

Agriculture

Mainstay of the country

With the majority of the population (possibly as high as two-thirds) engaged in some form of agriculture, even if only at subsistence level, any changes in this sector would have the greatest effect. North Yemen has always been a fertile area, self-sufficient in food, and so could remain relatively independent. Throughout its history, agricultural products have shaped the society, but changes have been rapid in the last two decades.

The southern areas are different, more arid and less developed, and less than 1 per cent of the land is thought to be useful for agriculture (mainly cotton and dates growing in wadi beds).

The drift of male labour from the traditional terraced fields of the highlands and the irrigated lands of the coastal areas to the oil industry throughout Arabia, caused a severe reduction in **production.** Throughout the 1970s agriculture was left to the women, who grew just enough for their families, allowing large areas of once rich land to fall into disrepair. This was particularly true in the highlands where the intricate system of terracing requires constant maintenance to stop soil being washed down the steep mountainsides.

Women farm the land

The result was that the YAR went from being an exporter to an importer of food in a short space of time, and now much repair work is needed just to return to the same level of production. More importantly there needs to be large-scale investment in modern equipment and water supplies, but it is oil and gas that attracts the new money and there is still a problem with rural depopulation. Across the country there are projects aimed at improving agricultural potential, but they will take some time to achieve.

The Tihama Development Association (TDA) is increasing the number of wells in wadis to encourage the growing of **cereal crops, cotton** and **dates,** in an area that is otherwise only suited to livestock grazing on sparse vegetation. In the highland regions there are moves to encourage farmers to replace *qat* with **coffee, millet** and **wheat,** but there are many reasons why this is difficult to achieve (see Qat), and mechanisation is almost impossible. The inner slopes towards the Rub al-Khali have good potential and the building of the new Marib dam should show what is possible in inhospitable climates.

Qat or coffee?

Animal husbandry is an important aspect of the local economy and you will certainly see poultry farms during your visit.

Fishing

This is another potentially major industry that has been sadly neglected, but one which the PDRY at least managed to develop more than the YAR. The seas off the Yemeni coast are some of the richest fishing grounds in the world according to estimates by the World Bank, which is keen to improve facilities. New developments include storage and processing plants at Hodeidah, Mokha, Mukalla, al-Khawbah (near al-Luhayyah) and Nishtun (near al-Ghaydah).

Huge potential

The fishing industry has always been more important along the extensive south coast, which has very little else to offer in the way of employment and where it accounts for about two-thirds of the total annual catch of 70,000 tons.

Industry

A slow but
steady increase

Industrial output has never been a great contributor to the economy, and even now amounts only to about 20 per cent of GNP. The manufacture of oil products from imported crude at the refinery in Little Aden dominated the PDRY's economy, although this was mainly due to a lack of any other sizeable industries. The lack of growth is due to many factors, not least the manpower shortage which resulted when so many workers sought employment abroad. Cheap foreign labour and the training of women was originally seen as a way to expand, but now the return of many workers from the Gulf in 1990 should solve that problem.

The largest factory is a Chinese-built **textile mill** in Sana'a, but the current move is away from such traditional crafts towards more modern industries with export potential. **Cement** production is the most important, but at present it cannot even cope with domestic requirements. Factories which opened at Bajil in 1973, Amran in 1983 and al-Burh (near Ta'iz) in 1993 are expanding to raise total annual production from 1.2 to about 3 million tonnes. Exports could be possible after the completion of a new plant at Abyan aimed at producing 500,000 tonnes per year.

Salt, soap and **mineral water** production has been handled on a national scale for many years, and Hodeidah seems to be ideally placed for small units producing cigarettes and soft drinks. New foreign investment laws have given a boost to the creation of modern production lines, with South Korean involvement in a steel pipe factory at Hodeidah and a UK financed car battery plant. A lead smelter and battery recovery plant could be sited alongside.

Aden

Revitalising a
major world
port

Even though the infrastructure of the old YAR is better than that of the south, the greatest hope for the country is for Aden to regain its position as an important trade centre. By creating a **free zone** with tax and customs exemptions, it is hoped to attract international companies looking to export into the Gulf and the Far East. It was designated the new economic capital, with an excellent harbour in a strategic position and a well-trained workforce, but suffered badly as the stronghold of the southern troops in the 1994 conflict.

Studies are being undertaken to establish what modern facilities will best serve future industries, but much work needs to be done to attract investors in the first place. International traders seem unsure of Aden's claim that it is much safer for them to base themselves there,

Aden harbour.

rather than in the more sensitive Gulf ports such as Dubai. Competition is fierce, and nearby Djibouti, already with better facilities, will fight to avoid losing trade to a revitalised Aden.

Tourism

With amazing natural beauty, a unique culture and an extensive history, the Yemen should be the perfect tourist destination. Nobody is in any doubt that there is tremendous potential for the tourist industry, but equally nobody is quite sure how this potential is to be realised or what disastrous effects events like the Gulf War and internal fighting will bring.

It will need many years of sustained promotion to make the West fully aware of what the Yemen has to offer and even where it is. Government policy is to encourage the private sector rather than use its own hard currency to promote tourism, yet in terms of economic development, the industry ranks only behind oil, gas and minerals. Despite the rhetoric, the post-unification Tourism Ministry has been amalgamated with the Culture Ministry and there is not a single tourist office. What little overseas promotion there is, comes from Yemenia and the larger tour agencies, such as YATA and Universal.

Controlled expansion
Any expansion of the 50,000 visitors per year is currently severely hampered by the chronic shortage of **accommodation** at all levels outside Sana'a, particularly in the south, where camping is often the only solution. The international hotels are sometimes full of business clients, but they too wish to increase the percentage of tourists, even at discounted rates. There is no one country on which the Yemen can base it's tourist industry, but a good model to aim at would be a cross between a refined, non mass tourist Egypt and a more adventurous Dubai.

It will be some time before the Yemen is truly famous world-wide as a holiday destination, if it ever is. By then the country may have changed so much, that today's pioneer tourists could well be observing something unique and pristine.

POLITICS

Until unification on 22 May 1990, the YAR and the PDRY had distinctly differing political views, apart from the fact that both saw unification of the country as their eventual **A divided** aim. Each country interfered with each other's policies to **country** the point of assassinations and border clashes. It is worth looking briefly at the situation in each former republic between independence and unification (see also Brief History).

Yemen Arab Republic

The modern politics of the YAR (or North Yemen) surfaced in the 1940s with the **Free Yemenis** movement based in British-controlled Aden, as opposition grew to the isolationist policies and despotic regime of Imam Yahya. After his assassination by the group in 1948, any hope of change was crushed by his son Ahmed, who continued in the same vein, supported by the powerful Zaidi tribes in the north. He did make some moves towards modernisation however, by accepting British, French and American technical aid and later Soviet proposals. However, he angered the British by claiming Aden and all the protectorates, which led to frontier incidents in the 1950s.

1,000 years of   He died in September 1962 after several attempts on
Imamic rule   his life and was succeeded by his son Badr, who at first
ends   seemed intent on making changes, but then showed the same inaction as his father and grandfather. Within a week, Imam Badr's chief bodyguard, Colonel Abdullah Sallal, and Lieutenant Ali Abdulmogni signalled a **revolution** to oust the ruler. The first shots are said to have been fired by the tank that is now on a plinth in Tahrir Square. But Badr escaped to the same tribes that had supported his father, and with Saudi help conducted a bloody civil war that lasted seven years. The new YAR regime, with Abdullah Sallal as its first president, had Egyptian backing through the mid 1960s, but resources were sorely stretched by the Arab-Israeli Six-Day War of 1967.

This was a time of great upheaval in the Middle East and it became clear that both sides had reached a virtual stalemate. The British withdrawal from Aden was the excuse the Egyptians used to leave the conflict, and at this point the royalists saw their opportunity. They laid **Sana'a 70 day** siege to Sana'a for 70 days, from 1 December 1967 to 8 **siege** February 1968. The city showed great courage in resisting the siege and soon Soviet arms came to replace the Egyptian forces. Sallal was in the meantime deposed while in Iraq, and replaced by Abdul Rahman al-Iriani in the new position of Chairman of the Republican Council and Hassan al-Amri as Prime Minister. This redefined the 1962 revolution, and republican success was assured when Imam Badr was deposed as royalist leader and Qasem Munassar with his Beni Hushaish tribe switched sides (see Sana'a-Marib). Saudi Arabia's confidence was broken and it withdrew its support after royalist representation was guaranteed on the new Republican Council at the Jeddah Peace Treaty in 1970. Most royalist leaders (except the Imam and members of the royal family, who were exiled to England) returned to Sana'a and joined the government.

Northern civil war ends

Stability and reconstruction were the first priorities. The country was in tatters, with the people physically and mentally drained after almost eight years fighting. In the early 1970s, the fledgling PDRY government had its own ideas, and dealings between the two swung wildly from talks on unity to border wars. On 13 June 1974 a **bloodless coup** ousted al-Iriani and set up a seven man military junta under Colonel Ibrahim al-Hamdi. Links were forged with the USA via Saudi Arabia, which agreed to finance a huge development project and re-equip the army. This did not sit well with al-Hamdi's reunification proposals, as the Saudis feared Soviet influence from the south. He was assassinated in October 1977 and replaced by Lt Col Ahmed ibn Hussein al-Ghashmi.

Continued unrest

Within two weeks there was an attempt to murder him as well. He tried to suppress internal unrest by doubling army pay and giving all soldiers free *qat* every day! At the end of June 1978, however, the unpopular al-Ghashmi was blown up by a suitcase bomb, apparently brought by a South Yemen envoy. This attack led to further **border fighting.** The full truth of the events will probably never be known, but whatever the circumstances, it gave Lt Col Ali Abdullah Saleh the chance to become fifth President and Commander-in-Chief of the army on 17 July 1978.

Since then he has survived several assassination and coup attempts, and almost suffered defeat at the hands of the South Yemenis in 1979. Strong leadership was the only way to survive the political climate of the YAR during the 1980s and all credit should be given to the President for maintaining a reasonably stable government. He has been criticised on many points, but he modernised the YAR dramatically in his twelve year rule, and was instrumental in finally bringing about the unification of the Yemen.

Towards unification

People's Democratic Republic of Yemen

The fortunes of Aden have always dictated the politics of the southern interior, a strongly tribal and independent

The British protect Aden

region. Until 1937 Aden was governed from Bombay but it then became a British **crown colony** surrounded by the **Aden Protectorate.** This 'buffer' zone was largely based on the Ingrams Peace Treaty which required the agreements and signatures of over 1,200 sultans, sheikhs, amirs and tribal chiefs – a triumph of diplomacy. The Western Aden Protectorate consisted of 20 major sultanates and sheikhdoms stretching along the North Yemen border to Musaymir, Beyhan, Lawdar and Ahwar. The larger and more desolate Eastern Aden Protectorate consisted of what are today the provinces of Shabwa, Hadramaut and al-Mahra .

Indian independence in 1947 reduced Britain's need for Aden as a supply station and greater autonomy was granted to the Protectorate. The **Federation of South Arabia** emerged in 1959 to give the region a new structure and identity. Much of the northern revolution of 1962 was organised from Aden which then directed its energies towards setting up its own independent state.

Rushed withdrawal

In 1964 Britain agreed to grant the Federation independence by 1968, but events overtook them when the two leading liberation organisations, the communist National Liberation Front (NLF) and the Egyptian backed Front for the Liberation of Occupied South Yemen (FLOSY) began a war against continued British presence. A hurried withdrawal followed and the last British troops left Aden at midnight on 29/30 November 1967. For more details see the displays at the Military Museum in Aden.

Internal clashes marred the administration of the first president Qahtan al-Shaabi, which was supported by the NLF. Soviet backing for his regime involved the shipment of huge military supplies and the ousting of FLOSY opposition leaders mainly to Saudi Arabia and the YAR. A power struggle in June 1969 saw Salem Rubayi Ali become Chairman of a new five-man Presidential

Civil war gives way to Communism

Committee. Every business was nationalised except the BP oil refinery in Little Aden. The Soviet Union wanted access to the strategic Bab al-Mandab straits, Aden harbour and the island of Socotra and the PDRY obliged, thus aligning itself clearly with Eastern bloc countries. It became the only communist Arab state and was thus isolated within the increasingly pro-Western Arab world which preferred Islamic law to Marxist ideals.

During the 1970s there was regular talk of unification with the YAR, only interrupted by border disputes and all-out war amid claims of interference and sabotage in each others' internal affairs.

The implications of the PDRY's involvement in the assassination of YAR President al-Ghashmi in 1978 led to the resignation (and ultimate execution) of Rubayi Ali.

Prime Minister Ali Nasser Mohammed became Head of State but was soon overpowered by Abdul Fattah Ismail when the parties reorganised themselves into the Yemen Socialist Party (YSP). This started a period of even closer alignment with the USSR and China, but more internal struggles installed Ali Nasser Mohammed as President and exiled Abdul Fattah Ismail to Moscow. A gradual movement towards Arab unity was plunged into chaos with the return of Ismail in late 1985.

Continued internal fighting

Ismail and other YSP leaders were shot during political manoeuvrings, leading to **internal fighting** amongst different parties, tribes and army factions and culminating in the fierce civil war between 13 and 24 January 1986. Aden suffered greatly and it is thought that up to 10,000 people were killed, far more than official estimates. Ali Nasser Mohammed ultimately lost control and was exiled to the YAR with 20,000 of his supporters.

Collapse of communism paves way for unification

Most of the leaders involved in the struggle now concede that the fighting was mainly for tribal control and that pro- and anti-Marxism slogans were just a flimsy cover for the real issues. Haidar Abu Bakr al-Attas, originally from Hureida in the Hadramaut, returned from Moscow to become the new Head of State.

The demise of the Soviet Union led many countries to reassess their situations. For East Germany the answer was to reunite with West Germany. Unable to fund communism themselves, South Yemen decided to merge with the North.

The Republic of Yemen

Despite the rhetoric, the joining of the two halves of the Yemen had always seemed impossible. The YAR was pro-Western and a good buffer for the powerful Saudi Arabia from the PDRY's communist influence. The PDRY was an ally of the USSR and virtually isolated in world politics. Border clashes and wars did not facilitate unity, nor did the internal unrest that was generated by neighbours reluctant to see democracy on their doorsteps.

However there were several attractions. The Yemenis themselves had always considered that it was just a matter of time before they became a single country, and the problems of new oil discoveries along the border area could easily be solved if there was no border at all.

Seizing the day

Events moved quickly at the close of the 1980s. Exactly 22 years after the British left Aden, Ali Abdullah Saleh of the YAR and Ali Salem al-Beedh of the PDRY agreed to **unification** within one year if agreed in a referendum. Moves towards this were undermined by continuing tribal unrest in the north, and rather than risk further trouble running up to the referendum they simply brought the vote forward. Immediately after the referendum the Republic of Yemen was speedily declared on 22 May 1990.

Faltering steps

Ali Abdullah Saleh was promoted to General and appointed first president of the new republic, with Ali Salem al-Beedh as Vice President. A five member Presidential Council was to oversee work for 2 1/2 years until the first elections in November 1992. The transitional 301 seat parliament consisted of the 159 members of the YAR assembly, 111 from the PDRY's Supreme People's Council and 31 new members chosen by the president. Haider Abu Bakr al-Attas became the new Prime Minister with a 33-minister government drawn from the north and south.

Minaret in Old City, Sana'a.

The Gulf Crisis

Within months of setting out upon this new course, the fledgling government was hurled into political turmoil by events over which they had little or no control. Saddam Hussein's invasion of Kuwait polarised the Arab world into those that favoured a Western-backed military response and those that wanted a diplomatic solution. Being in the front line Kuwait and Saudi Arabia favoured the military option, but for right or wrong Yemen chose the latter. As a poor Arab country there were many Yemenis who were persuaded by Saddam's demands for a fair distribution of the vast Arab wealth, others, especially in the north, backed his position on behalf of the Palestinians.

In normal circumstances this stand might not have caused much of a problem, but it just happened to be the turn of the Yemen (which replaced the YAR in the United Nations) to sit on the UN Security Council as one of the two rotating members. The country therefore briefly became one of the seven most important decision makers in the world and they chose not to agree to sanction an allied response against Iraq.

Yemen on UN Security Council

This had the effect of immediately isolating the Yemen, both within the Arab world and internationally. Aid, funds and personnel were withdrawn and as if this were not bad enough, almost a million Yemeni workers in Saudi Arabia and other Gulf countries were expelled and somehow had to be reassimilated into the population. Overseas revenues, on which many people relied, just dried up and there was a great deal of anti-Western feeling.

Political Future

An uneasy alliance

It is now a priority for the Yemen to rehabilitate itself with the major nations that it alienated during the Gulf War. Internal unrest is still a big problem; the Muslim Brotherhood demanded less contact with the still communistically inclined south and would like *Sharia* law introduced. For their part, the southerners feared an end to the liberal lifestyle developed first under the British and then the Soviet-backed PDRY.

Politically, unification continues to be problematic, with renewed tension between north and south. The General People's Congress (GPC) and the Yemen Socialist Party (YSP) tried to come to terms with the emergence of a strong third force, the **Reform Party,** which is a coalition of Islamic fundamentalist groups including the strong leader Sheikh Abdullah.

New political freedom and a free Press

Some states are also doing their best to undermine the country's unity for several reasons: the Yemen now has the largest population on the peninsula; it controls the entrance to the Red Sea; it is economically tied to Egypt, Jordan and Iraq in the Arab Co-operation Council (ACC); and it is a democracy that could seriously affect the non-democratic power of the other rulers in the area.

The Supreme Elections Committee (SEC) has divided the country into 301 constituencies, each to elect a member to the parliament. This has been done by dividing the total population to give each seat a representation of 47,000 people $\pm$5 per cent. The distribution of seats is as follows, which gives some indication of the heavily populated areas:

GOVERNORATE	SEATS	GOVERNORATE	SEATS
Ta'iz	43	Aden	11
Ibb	38	Al-Bayda	10
Sana'a	36	Sadah	8
Hodeidah	34	Abyan	8
Hajjah	23	Mahweet	8
Dhamar	21	Shabwa	7
Sana'a City	18	Marib	3
Hadramaut	17	Al-Mahra	2
Lahej	12	Al-Jawf	2

First ever free elections in Arabia

The effects of the first general election on 27 April 1993 are still being digested, with every month bringing changes to the parliamentary system and the law itself. The first Speaker of the Parliament to be elected by the MPs was Sheikh Abdullah. The first 5 man Presidential Council consisted of the President and two members each of the GPC and YSP, but this changed after the 1994 conflicts. The first Prime Minister to be chosen by the Presidential Council was Mr Haidar Abu Bakr al-Attas.

A **free press** and the proliferation of **political parties** are questioning government actions, but it is uncertain how much this affects the average village worker just about surviving economically. The GPC and Ali Abdullah Saleh, accused by Ali Salem al-Beedh of trying to take total control of the country, in turn accused YPC leaders of breaking up the union. This led to an outbreak of war between the two unintegrated armies, effectively for control of the south. After spectacular tank battles around Amran and Dhamar in April 1994, and firing at each others main towns, the battle settled into a northern offensive for the main towns of Aden, Zinjibar and Mukalla. Aided by other Arab countries eager to punish the Sana'a government for their Gulf War stand, the 'rebel' southern leaders declared themselves independent of Sana'a by announcing that the south was now the Democratic Republic of Yemen. Aden suffered badly as northern troops laid siege to the final southern stronghold. By July 1994 the secessionist leaders, including Ali Salem al-Beedh, had fled to neighbouring countries, leaving Aden bombed, burned and looted.

1994 internal conflict

Birth pangs of democracy

Long term stability and prosperity seems possible through oil and gas, but it is the immediate problems of raising living standards and satisfying religious demands that are the key to the Yemen's survival.

FLAGS

From 1990 the flag of the Republic of Yemen is made up of three horizontal bands, of (from the bottom) black, white and red. The black represents the period of darkness and reactionary rule; the white symbolises the purity of the revolution; and the red is the revolution itself.

Many Arab countries use these three colours as the basis for their flags, as indeed did the former YAR A green star was placed in the centre, which indicated the fertility and richness of North Yemen. The old PDRY flag also had the three-band background, with a blue triangle entering from the left. A red star inside the blue section showed the country's communist leanings.

Many of the Aden protectorates had their own flags, some of which are impressive and colourful designs (some are on display in Seiyun Museum). Before the northern revolution, the flag of the ruling Imams was the white sword of Ali and five white stars on a scarlet background.

POPULATION

Estimates for the total population of the Yemen have always been unreliable. Through the years, highly inaccurate figures have indicated that there are roughly five times as many people in the north as in the south. Censuses in the YAR in 1986 and the PDRY in 1988 gave a total of 11 million.

Largest population in Arabia

However, for the first time in both countries' histories the government has had to establish a precise total in order to draw up constituency boundaries for the elections. Towards the end of 1992 the population of the Republic of Yemen was put at 14.2 million, including the returnees from the Gulf War. This figure gives an average density of 21 inhabitants per square kilometre, but there is a difference between the sparsely inhabited south (7 per square kilometre) and the more crowded north (48 per square kilometre).

Urban population figures are difficult to establish but governorate (not just the city) estimates are:

Sana'a	1,800,000
Ta'iz	1,700,000
Ibb	1,300,000
Hodeidah	1,100,000
Aden	500,000

Over recent years the population drift towards the cities has been significant, boosted by the returnees. But it is estimated that about 75 per cent of the population still do not live in towns and continue to earn a living in the countryside.

Infant mortality, at 130 per 1,000 live births, leads to an 'under-5' death rate of 185 per 1,000. Life expectancy from birth is 48 years and rising, but this is still amongst the lowest in the world. With a growth rate over 3 per cent, the population is very young, with over half the population under the age of 14.

Yemeni tradition of working abroad

A major factor in the country's demographic make-up has always been the numbers of men **travelling to work** in other countries. In areas with poor-quality farming and internal unrest such as Wadi Hadramaut, the men have a tradition of overseas work (to Singapore, Malaysia and Indonesia) stretching back centuries. The oldest Muslim communities in the UK are the Yemenis who settled in ports like Cardiff, London and South Shields, having worked on British ships leaving Aden in the last century. Known to be good workers in heavy industries, groups also grew up in Sheffield and Birmingham. There are similar Yemeni enclaves in the USA, in Detroit, Dearborn, Buffalo, Brooklyn and San Francisco.

More recently the Gulf States and Saudi Arabia have relied heavily on this cheap labour to develop their oil

Over half the population is under 14 years old.

Gulf War returnees

based economies. Such emigration was facilitated by easy overland travel and the waiving of official work permits.

This method of earning relatively large amounts of money to be remitted back to families in towns and villages in the Yemen has been an important source of income that has kept the local economy afloat, even though the government saw very little in the way of taxes. All this was suddenly brought to a halt by the invasion of Kuwait by Saddam Hussein in 1990 (see Economy and Politics).

Most of the **returnees** were assimilated back into Yemeni society, but those without relatives or sufficient money are still surviving in basic camp conditions in the Tihama north of Hodeidah. In addition to this there are thought to be over 100,000 Somali refugees in and around Aden fleeing the civil war there, as well as many thousands of Ethiopians waiting for an opportunity to return to their country.

Horn of Africa refugees

Ethnic Groups

Ethnically, there are three different types of people who form the base of the Yemeni population: coastal, highland and bedouin.

The **coastal** people are dark skinned and share many physical characteristics with the Africans just across the Red Sea. Their lifestyle and straw hut housing are quite different from anything to be seen in the mountain regions (see The Tihama).

The physical appearance of the *qabiili* **highland dwellers** is quite different. These slight people have more Arab than African features and live in tall multi-storeyed houses built of stone or mud (see Society).

The **Bedouins** who roam the edge of the Rub al-Khali

Bedouin lifestyle in search of pastures and water for their animals are different again. Many still follow a nomadic existence and live in their black goat-hair tents, but nowadays they move around less romantically in Toyota trucks. Their food tends to be goat, dried fish and camel meat.

The Yemen is the only remaining place on the peninsula where Bedouins still follow a traditional lifestyle; in most other countries they have been 'modernised'. The northern Bedouin tribes are more violent, owing to their smuggling activities, which have always been profitable and were least affected by the Gulf War.

These general distinctions tend to overlap, and the rapid increase in mobility over the last 20 years has helped to dilute and diffuse the groups. Urban growth has further helped to integrate them. There are still pure forms of all three, however, in remote areas.

The vast majority of Yemenis are proud, independent people with a keen sense of humour. Tribal traditions ensure the well-being of all, regardless of international (and even national) politics.

LANGUAGE AND LITERATURE

Yemeni close to classical Arabic It is probably true to say that **Yemeni Arabic**, which is the language used by locals in all informal situations at work and at home, is closer to classical Arabic than most other dialects. However there is another form of Arabic that is mixed with the colloquial, depending on the formality or complexity of the subject. This is known as **Modern Standard Arabic** (MSA), a universal form of the language learned in schools all over the Arab world. It developed from Koranic and classical Arabic through the need for Arabs from different countries to communicate with each other and is referred to by them as *fuss-ha*.

In its written form MSA is used in newspapers, books and most printed material. Orally it is heard on radio and television newscasts and formal lectures etc. It is thus through written and spoken MSA that a Yemeni can deal with say, a Syrian or an Algerian, both of whom have their own particular Arabic dialect.

There are however other influences that affect the spoken word. Through cinema, radio, television and songs, Egyptian Arabic is widely understood in many countries and for this reason it tends to be a mixture of MSA and Egyptian that is taught as 'Arabic' or appears in phrase books. To know 'Arabic' the visitor must be prepared to learn both MSA and the Yemeni dialect.

Pre-Islamic Languages

Southern Arabian scripts date from approximately 1000 BC to 628 AD, when Islam (and classical Arabic) was adopted in the region. Prior to 500 BC these languages were written in boustrophedon script – alternate lines are read to the right, then to the left. (Boustrophedon is a word from Greek meaning 'as an ox turns in ploughing'!)

The languages of the major kingdoms after this time were standardised to be read from right to left. Sabaean, Hadrami, Qatabanian, Minaean and Himyari were different dialects belonging to the epigraphic South Semitic language group.

Ancient dialects still spoken

This group also includes Arabic and modern southern Arabian dialects such as Socotri, Mahri and Shuhuri, which are all still in use today. The closest languages to the ancient epigraphic southern Arabian ones are Arabic and Ge'z. Ge'z is the language of the old Axumite Kingdom, but has survived in Ethiopian liturgical use.

The only example which exists of the literature of this time is a long poem carved onto a rock face in al-Bayda Province (between Timna and Rada'a).

Literature

Before unification, great emphasis was always placed on the ancient empires that held sway over large areas of what today we would call the Yemen. There was a revival of links with the past to emphasise the energy of unity. Inspiration came from many sources including poetry, music and literature.

The **ancient kingdoms** have left us with only a relatively few examples of their writings (also from right to left like Arabic) drawn on animal hides or carved into rocks. The seventh-century historian Ibn Sharyah tells us something of the Himyar period but was himself writing at a distance of 400 years. The **arrival of Islam** ushered in a period of intense writing and study.

The **centres of learning** which were established in Zabid, Tarim and Sana'a were concerned not just with Islam but also the study of history, grammar, mathematics, law and poetry. Many of the scholarly tomes are as relevant and important now as they were then.

Yemeni chronicler gives us window into the past

The respected chronicler **al-Hassan Ahmed al-Hamdani** lived during the tenth century and left us with a unique insight into the life of the period with his volumes of work known as *al-Iklil*. It is through his eyes that we can visualise such famous, but now totally lost, sites such as the Ghumdam Palace in his home town of Sana'a. He travelled extensively around the country, even to such remote regions as Shabwa and Wadi Do'an. His accounts are so reliable that Freya Stark used his book *Jazirat al-Arab* when touring southern Arabia in the 1930s and recommended everybody else to do the same. He died in Sana'a around 945.

Poetry is a particularly popular form of literature in the Yemen, pre-dating Islam. The works of outstanding poets have been celebrated by the tribesmen who were introduced to the texts by storytellers and singers. One of the most famous was Imru al-Qais who died in the middle of the sixth century and was later honoured by having some of his texts decorate the Kaaba in Mecca. Every period of change has had its own poet, who encapsulated the mood and feeling of the public at the time and became inextricably associated with that movement.

Golden age of the arts

Particularly glorious periods in Yemeni poetry were during the Sulayhid, Rasulid and Tahirid rule. Following the Ottoman occupation a type of poetry known as *Humayni* was developed, with the words spoken in local tongue to Sanani music; it is still popular today. One of the best exponents of this form was al-Hussein ibn Ali, the great grandson of Imam Qasim the Great, who lived at the close of the seventeenth century. Surprisingly for a member of the ruling family, he was one of the first to criticise the Imamate and its social weaknesses.

A Nationalist movement

A poet of this century who must be mentioned is **Mohammed Mahmood az-Zubeiry,** who is known as the Father of the Revolution. Born in 1909 he came to represent the liberation movement through works like 'A Shout at the Sleepers', written in 1945. Through periods of nationalist awakening, protest, resistance and finally revolution, he encapsulated current reality with dreams for the future. He was one of the original Free Yemenis and became a figurehead as first leader of the Party of God. He was murdered in 1964 but is remembered as a great revolutionary and has one of the main thoroughfares in Sana'a named after him.

In the south, poetry was used to stimulate anti-British feelings by such writers as Abduh Othman whose poem 'First Shot' recalls the uprising in the Radfan Mountains when the independence movement was started on 14 October 1963.

Arab poets are honoured much more than their Western counterparts, and poetry is as popular now as it ever has been. Contemporary poets regularly give recitals and publish works and are often feted with honours. In the Hadramaut they have a particularly high standing, with paintings of their faces displayed in public places.

Translations of Arabic poetry into any other language are only second hand versions, and if possible the works should be read in the original.

Priceless heritage

Academically it is the **religious manuscripts** that are generally considered to be the most important and new finds are being made almost every year as houses and buildings are altered for the first time in centuries. In the early 1970's 40,000 fragments of 1,000 Koran manuscripts were found when workmen were repairing the western wall of the Great Mosque in Sana'a (see Sana'a). This has now become one of the great centres for religious learning and interpretation of law. The al-Kaf library in Tarim is another centre but there are countless private places holding priceless manuscripts, the preservation of which causes much concern.

ISLAM

Islam spreads quickly to South Arabia

Religion and history are so interwoven that it is often difficult to separate the two. The earlier days of Christianity and Judaism are dealt with in other sections (see Brief History and Sana'a), and specific milestones such as the Zaidis and Rasulids are in the relevant travel sections. The most abiding religious influence in Yemen has been Islam.

ISLAMIC CALENDAR

As a traveller you are unlikely to be troubled by the Islamic calendar as most arrangements are made using the Western Gregorian calendar. However you will sometimes see references that are worth explaining. The Islamic calendar started on 16 July 622 and follows the twelve lunar months of 29 or 30 days, totalling 354 1/2 days per year. The difference of eleven days per year between this and the solar calendar on which the West works, means that important dates such as Ramadan and Haj come gradually earlier every year, until they complete a full cycle every 32 1/2 years. The year 2000 will coincide with the Islamic 1420 AH (After *Hegira*) All religious holidays refer to the Islamic year which can never be equated exactly to the Gregorian calendar (see Opening Hours and Public Holidays).

Early converts and the construction of mosques

One of the first Muslims in the country was Badhan, the Persian Governor of Sana'a, and with him were converted the whole Hamdan Federation. Yemenis are proud to say that they adopted the faith in the sixth year after the *Hegira* (the *Hegira* was the Prophet Mohammed's move from Mecca to Medina on 16 July 622). On the Prophet's own instructions the Great Mosque at Sana'a was built in the Governor's gardens at the Ghumdan Palace. The Prophet Mohammed also received delegations of sheikhs wanting to know more about the faith, one of whom was Sheikh Abu Musa who converted his Asha'ir tribe and built the famous mosque at Zabid. One of the earliest Islamic writers, Muad bin Jabal was sent by Mohammed to the then important town of al-Janad to build a mosque.

Sunni and Shi'a

The main division in Islam comes from the choice of **caliph,** the Prophet's successor. The orthodox Sunnis believe that he should be a suitable member of the Prophet Mohammed's Quraish tribe, as were the initial caliphs (Abu Bakr, Omar and Osman). The Shi'a have always held that this position should only be filled by a descendant of the Prophet, initially through his son-in-law Ali, who was also his cousin by Abu Taleb. Hence Ali was not only the fourth caliph for the Sunnis, but also the first Imam for the Shi'a. He is thought to have visited Sana'a and stayed in a house near the *suq*, where the Ali mosque now stands. *Shi'a* (or more correctly *Shi'at Ali*) means 'the party of Ali' and accounts for about 10 per cent of all Muslims.

Caliphs and Imams

Ali was murdered in 661, after which his sons Hassan and Hussein carried on the struggle against the Umayyid rulers (a branch of the Quraish tribe) in Damascus, who had usurped the title. It was shortly after the death of Hassan and Hussein (regarded as the second and third Imams), that a split occurred in the ranks of the Shi'a, when Zaid, a son of the fourth Imam (Ali Zain al-Abidin) formed his own sect, the **Zaidis.**

The start of the Zaidi imams

Unlike the other Shi'a branches, the Zaidis do not automatically inherit the imamate, but are subject to a sort of democratic election amongst the many descendants of Ali, all of whom have valid claims. Their Imams are not considered supernatural and in fact must show common sense, strength and knowledge, which by nature implies that they may make mistakes or even commit sins. They came to the Yemen in 898 when al-Hadi Yahya came to Sadah to mediate and set up his own Imamate line which lasted until 1962 (see Sadah). To the Shi'a, incidentally, the word Imam, has three meanings: leader of prayers in a mosque; religious sect leader; and unchallengable community leader. They need not necessarily be the same person.

The other sects of Shi'a consider their Imams to be supernatural beings and believe that the later ones 'disappeared' and will return as the *Mahdi* some time in the future. One such branch are the **Ismailis** (whose spiritual leader is the Aga Khan), which subsequently split into yet more sects. The main interest for us centres around the Fatimids of Egypt, who backed Ali as-Sulayhi and Queen Arwa (see Ibb) and left the Taiyibi Ismailis around Manakha as their legacy.

The main group of Shi'a are in Iran and are led by religious scholars **(ayatollahs and mullahs)** who interpret the teachings of the first eleven imams and generally keep things ticking over until the *Mahdi* is revealed. The

*Minarets
in Sana'a*

Zaidis are unique in their beliefs and are found only in the Yemen.

**Yemen accepts
Sunni doctrines**

The Sunni sect is much easier to follow, mainly because the law comes only from the Holy Koran and the *Sunna*, the Prophet's own words and actions. Of the four main branches of Sunni Islam, we are interested in the Shafi'i, named after Mohammed bin Idris as-Shafi'i born in Ghaza in 767. He travelled widely and taught conservative values, which found favour in the Yemen.

The movement really advanced with the introduction of the *madrasa* – religious schools – which were set up in Ta'iz, al-Janad, Ibb, Jibla, Aden and Zabid from the eleventh century onwards . The importance of Zabid as a centre of religious learning established the Shafi'i sect permanently in the Yemen (see The Tihama). Unlike the Zaidis, who are found only in the Yemen, Shafi'i believers are to be found in Egypt, Malaysia and Indonesia.

In many ways the Zaidi sect is more akin to the Sunni Shafi'i than to any other Shi'a sect. Great value is placed by both on educational and scholarly work, neither is particularly extreme. Religious schools in Sana'a and Zabid have created famous libraries of study for both sects. The ritual movements during praying are strictly laid down, and it is possible for experts to differentiate between Shafi'i and Zaidi by the gestures of the arms.

Islamic Law

Islam as a code for life Islamic law is a combination of Sharia law and Koranic law. Koranic law, as the name suggests, was dictated by Allah to the Prophet Mohammed through the angel Gabriel and is contained within the Holy Koran. One of the main controversies amongst experts in Islamic law is not what is in the Koran, but what is left out. This incredibly complex subject is still being discussed, interpreted and applied in a variety of ways. As far as the Yemen is concerned, legislation is based on *Sharia* law, the law practised and observed by the Prophet Mohammed during his lifetime and supplemented by pre-lslamic tribal law known as *'urf.*

THE YEMENI LEGACY

Many of the Yemenis employed as soldiers in the *Jihad* during the first century of Islam never returned to their homeland. Some of their descendants went on other campaigns as fighters, builders and administrators. Yemeni names and music spread throughout the Middle East, and there are families in every Arab country which can trace their names back to the Yemen. The Saudi oil minister in the 1970s, Sheikh Yamani, is an example of how powerful some of these families have become. In southern Spain, Yemen placenames like Hamdan and Khawlan date from the time of Moorish conquest.

Five Pillars of Islam

Duties and commitments A good Muslim, of whatever sect, should follow the five pillars of Islam, but obviously there are degrees of commitment and it is up to each person to decide how close to the 'ideal' he or she wishes to live. These basic beliefs are common to both Shi'a and Sunni.

1. **The Creed** *(Shahada).* This is the Muslim declaration: *Ash-adu an la ilaha ill Allah, Mohammedun rasul Allah –* 'There is no God but God, and Mohammed is the Prophet of God'.

The call to prayer

2. **Daily Prayers** *(Salat)*. If you are staying in the old city in Sana'a you will certainly know when it is time for al-Fajr, the early morning call to prayer, when the first traces of dawn can be seen. The call by the *muezzin* always begins with *Allah akhbar* – 'Allah is most great'. After doing their ablutions people can pray in a mosque, at home or in the fields. The act of bowing, kneeling and prostrating in the direction of Mecca in a series of cycles indicates gradual submission to Allah. A full morning's work can be done until the midday prayer, ad-Zuhr, when the sun is at its zenith. Afternoon prayer, ad-Asr is performed when the sun is at 45°. Al-Maghrib is the sunset prayer, closely followed by al-Isha, the fifth and final prayer when all daylight has gone. The most devout Muslims are physically marked on their foreheads by their repeated prostrations.

3. **Charity** *(Zakat)*. The giving of money and hospitality to the poor is an essential part of Islam. One way in which this is done is for people to calculate their wealth at the end of the year by working out what value they have in savings, jewellery and other luxuries. One-fortieth of this amount is then allocated to be given to those less fortunate. This money could go to a neighbour or friend in financial difficulty to provide basic facilities or it could be handled by the religious *waqf* foundations. Monies are traditionally handed over just before the expenses of the 'Little Id' feast. When asked about the beggars and homeless people on the streets, a Yemeni will say that Allah created poor people so that richer ones had someone to give money to.

Abstinence for 30 days

4. **Ramadan Fast** *(Sawm)*. The ninth month of the Islamic year is the month of fasting. This idea of self-denial can be traced back to Mohammed's contact with Jews and Christians, who both have similar tests of faith. In Ramadan, a combination of Lent and Yom Kippur, it is forbidden to eat, drink or smoke during the hours of daylight. In a strict Muslim country like the Yemen, where the majority of people observe Ramadan, everything comes to a virtual stop during the day. Restaurants are closed and the streets are empty until sunset, when the place comes alive until the early hours.

This would probably be the least favourable time to visit, as making arrangements becomes impossible rather than just difficult. But the nights are very festive periods. If you are in the Yemen during Ramadan, you should make allowances, as for anyone to complete the feast is a tough and admirable proposition. If you find people short tempered and frustrated, it could be because it is also expected that people give up sex for the month. Certain people are allowed to forego the fast; the old, the young, the ill and weak, pregnant women, soldiers on duty and those on extended journeys. The celebration of its completion is the festival of Id al-Fitr (referred to as 'Little Id'), which lasts about three days and is a time when gifts are given as a reward for making it through Ramadan.

Perform *Haj* at least once in a lifetime

5. **Pilgrimage** *(Haj)*. The pilgrimage to Mecca during the final month of the year is interestingly the only pillar that is not actually required. If one lives ones life as a good Muslim and follows the other four pillars, one will make it to heaven. *Haj* should only be performed by those who can afford to do so. Having said that, most committed Muslims manage to find the money, especially today, when it only requires a few weeks to complete as opposed to the months or years in older times. Since the Yemen is close to Mecca, and no air or sea travel is needed, most Yemenis who want to make the *Haj* can usually do so.

There are certain tasks to be performed during *Haj*: to walk seven times around the Kaaba; to drink water from the sacred spring Zamzam; to throw stones at the devil; and to sacrifice a horned or domestic animal. Some of these rituals were inherited from earlier pagan times in Mecca, but were 'cleansed' by Mohammed to signify forgiving of all sins. The end of *Haj* is celebrated by the *Id al-Kabir* (Great Id) which always starts on the tenth day of the month of Dhu al-Haj.

Mosques

Visiting mosques is usually difficult for tourists, as in general it is not possible to enter them, and only minimal views can be obtained from outside. However there are some that do have a loose tradition of allowing non believers inside, including al-Janad mosque and Queen Arwa mosque in Jibla. From the outside you can often observe old men reading and reciting the Koran, which is laid on a low crossed lectern. This *koursi* is used for ease of reading and to preserve the purity of the sacred book.

Tourists sometimes allowed into mosques

Two mosques which are being refurbished are al-Ashrafiya in Ta'iz and al-Airdrus in Aden, both of which can normally be entered. Occasionally there are surprises and you find you can enter, say, the great al-Asha'ria mosque in Zabid. Shoes must be removed, legs and arms must be covered and women should cover their heads. It is normal to tip a helpful guardian or imam.

The al-Asha'ria, al-Janad and Sana'a great mosque are fine examples of the earliest types, a central courtyard, later surrounded by colonnaded galleries. There are many types of layout and styles of minarets. The University Museum in Sana'a has a corridor full of different examples in photographs from around the country.

Some of the most impressive are those from the Ottoman period, with large central domes (called *qubba*), such as the al-Bakaliyah and Qubbat Tulhah in the old city.

In Yemen, the main mosque is called *jama masjid*, Friday mosque. All are open to both Sunni and Shi'a followers and are built with the northern wall facing Mecca. The *mihrab* is the niche in this wall that indicates the direction of prayer towards Mecca and in the larger ones you will sometimes find an ornately carved *minbar*, a sort of pulpit, where the imam can preach to the masses. Some mosques have segregated areas for women, who would otherwise pray at home. Old men are often seen clutching strings of beads; theoretically each bead represents one of the 99 attributes of Allah.

Praying towards Mecca

Death is not an embarrassment here, and burials are conducted in a more open way, generally within 24 hours. Only men take part in the funeral procession, carrying the coffin to the graveyard, where the person is buried in a simple shroud. Traditionally people are laid to rest sideways to Mecca, so that their head can be turned to face the Kaaba for eternity.

Most rural mosques have a **graveyard** nearby, which might be easier to visit. The huge cemetery at Sadah is full of fine carved headstones with the larger domed tombs of important Zaidi leaders, and it should be possible to look around. But sometimes visitors are ordered out, and the taking of photographs is frowned upon. The same applies at the large graveyard beside the main road in Dhamar. On the other hand, there are sites that present no problem, such as the area of graves and tombs at Einat in Wadi Hadramaut. My advice would be to enter a graveyard, unless expressly forbidden to do so, have a good look round, but be careful where you stand. Respect the dead and know that if you carry a camera you risk being asked to leave.

SOCIETY AND CULTURE

One of the most striking features of the Yemen is just how traditional culture still affects every person in daily life. The contrasts and interactions between new and old are fascinating and shape the country as we see it. Expensive limousines pull up beside 1,000-year-old mosques; international businessmen chew *qat* while sitting around on the floor; and Mig fighter aircraft scatter the sheep on the mountains around Sana'a. Many things are modern in what is a very old society.

A mixture of old and new societies

Greetings

Before going too far, you should get used to the everyday greetings of Yemeni society. Friends and relatives will warmly embrace each other and kiss both cheeks, while enquiring *'Keyf halak'* – 'How are you?' In more formal situations you might see them take the other person's hand and kiss it, as when greeting a religious leader. Men and women would rarely interact like this, when a polite verbal welcome would be more correct.

Meetings and greetings

The main phrase that you need to know is *'As-Salaam alaykum'* – 'Peace be upon you' – which can be used at almost every opportunity. It would be said by you as an individual, upon entering a group of people (indicating that you have some knowledge of Arabic), or as a welcome by a younger person to an elder, to which the reply should be *'Waalaykum as-Salaam'*. With someone that you already know, you can use the less religious *'Sabah alKheir'*–'Good morning', or *'Mesa'al-Kheir'*–'Good evening'. There are set responses to all these formal greetings, which go on for several minutes without any information actually being exchanged.

As a foreigner, you will be accorded a certain respect, and most greetings will be in the form of a firm handshake. However some men will never shake a woman's hand by tradition, so please do not take this as a snub. A final handshake concludes the meeting, when both parties would say *'Ma salama'* (More useful words and phrases are given at the back of the book.).

Social Classes

The level of tribal society into which a person is born greatly affects their standing within that group and the opportunities afforded throughout their lifetime. As with all traditions, this is changing, and some of the barriers are being broken down. However, Yemenis are extremely proud of their ancestry and are keen to perpetuate this link with the past, gladly telling you about the history of the Yemeni tribes and how it goes back to Noah's eldest son Shem (who is said to have founded Sana'a). Qahtan (Joktan in the Bible), the great great grandson of Shem, is regarded as the founder of the Yemeni tribes and all Yemenis consider themselves as the original Arabs. Islam preaches social equality, but there is a strict hierarchy, with the *sada* (plural of *sayyid*) at the top. Bedouin and urban tribal structure are different, but the following is a good overview.

Ancient religions and social order filters through

The *sayyid* class are a ruling religious group which traces its family lines back to the Prophet Mohammed. Most of the famous local leaders (as opposed to invaders) assumed power by being *sada*. The imams were *sada* who belonged to the Zaidi sect of Islam.

Other respected classes are mosque-based workers such as the educated *qadis*, jurists who specialise in

Respected religious leaders

religious interpretation and law, and ***ulemas***, religious scholars. *Qadis* are recognised by their *thuma*, a special kind of *jambia* that has a smaller, slender curve and is worn on the right-hand side, not in front. Both *sayyid* and *qadi* are sometimes immaculately dressed in a full length blue or white *zanna* (also known as a *thobe*) topped by the *imamah*, a silver- and gold-threaded cap, wrapped in white cloth.

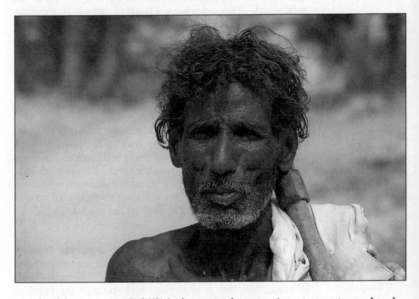

A local farmer near Qabr Hud, Wadi Hadramaut

Tribesmen and territory are the foundations of Yemeni society

Qabiili is the general name given to most people who do not fall into the other, more specific classes. It simply refers to someone belonging to a recognised tribe, whose own roots and territory are well known. This main stock comprises hard-working villagers, proud of their independence and ready to defend it at all costs. In other countries, to be called a tribesman would be to imply a lowly uneducated status, but here it indicates an individual's position in the cornerstone of Yemeni society. Most of the men that you see carrying Kalashnikovs are prosperous highland *qabiili*. The senior sheikh is the head of the village. He arbitrates between *qabiili*, and would traditionally accept the *jambia* of both men in a dispute, implying that neither would take the law into his own hands.

Below these is a class of people who practise **despised trades,** work considered unclean or religiously unacceptable, but essential within a large society. They would include butchers, barbers, tanners, cobblers and dyers. Blacksmiths are also considered lowly as they are in collusion with the evil spirits of fire!

The dark-skinned *abid* are slaves and their descendants, who were imported (usually from across the Red Sea) to serve the higher classes. Slavery continued until quite recently, mainly because the slaves themselves were happy to escape the problems of their homelands and enter into family service, where they were generally well treated. In North Yemen all slaves were officially manumitted just before the 1962 revolution. For hundreds of years in the Hadramaut it was usual to pair a slave with a family member of the same age and sex. They grew up together as friends, with the slave set for a lifetime's service to their companion.

Slavery into the 20th century

The lowest level in society are the *khadim* (plural is *akhdam*) meaning 'those who serve', corresponding to the *harijans* or untouchables in India. These lowly people do the most menial tasks such as rubbish disposal, street sweeping and cleaning. In the villages, market day is their only opportunity of making extra money by attending to the needs of the visiting traders. Another lowly class are the *dawshan* storytellers who still wander the countryside, and are always the centre of attraction wherever they recite.

This class system is still maintained in many highland village communities; choices of job and marriage partner are determined by class, and are overseen by the family and tribal elders. However, the more rigid divisions are eroding and a new 'middle class' is emerging in the modern cities, although it is still likely to be some time before a *sayyid* serves you in a restaurant.

Family Life

In view of the fact that almost 80 per cent of the population still live in country villages, it is understandable that family and tribal matters are the most important considerations in people's lives. In the main towns and cities a more western approach is taken, with family life revolving around the nuclear family, but this is certainly more the exception than the rule.

One of the main reasons for the large tower houses one sees is to accommodate the **extended family,** which will often include three or four generations. With so many people, privacy is impossible and all members of the family share in the joys and problems of each individual. The head of the family has absolute authority and his wife controls the female members. Respect for elders is paramount and is taught at an early age. There are usually enough children in a household to make a football team – and also a team to play against! Young girls are quick to assume the role of potential parent by looking after the

Respect for elders in the Yemeni family

youngest members. Women continually discuss suitable partners for those who are still single, especially during the female-only afternoon get-togethers *(tafrita)*.

The cost of celebrations such as **weddings,** as well as expenses like medical treatment for example, would be too great for one person to bear. In such cases the whole family contributes, with help from friends and neighbours.

New brides go to live with their husbands' families, which causes some concern and anguish for many young women, especially if the husband lives far from her own family. Most men have only one wife but very occasionally one might marry twice, the wives would hopefully become friends and share each other's life. Children would be brought up by both women (as well as all the sisters and aunts in the household).

Polygamy is unusual

WEDDINGS

A wedding is one of the highlights of Yemeni life, and requires a great deal of money and preparation. The women in the family are eager to matchmake between suitable couples and if successful a 'bride price' will be agreed between the heads of the two families. This is paid in the form of dresses, jewellery and especially gold, which is kept by the bride as her own personal wealth in case of divorce or some other catastrophe. Most weddings last formally for three days but carry on informally for much longer. The marriage contract is signed in the bride's family house, usually on a Wednesday when money is given to cover the costs of the forthcoming celebrations.

As a tourist the most you are likely to see of any wedding is the Thursday evening music and dancing, or the Friday festivities (see Environs of Sana'a). On Friday afternoon the men gather for a quality *qat* session in the groom's household – an expensive affair if there are many guests. In the evening the bride is accompanied by her relatives to the house of her new husband, where she will now live. Men and women celebrate in different houses, the women often continuing well into the following week to make up for all the hard work they have performed during the three days.

Education

Poor start for the school system

The level of education in the North before 1962 was pitifully low. There was one boarding school for the religious system aristocracy in Sana'a and simple Koranic schools meeting in mosques or in the open. The only school book was the Koran and the attendance rate was less than 10 per cent. The position in the South was slightly better, as the British tried to promote education.

After the revolution the YAR embarked on a series of rapid improvements which involved building one school every day. They developed a three-tier school system: six years' elementary; three years' preparatory (both

Illiteracy still
too high

compulsory and free); and three years' secondary school. Even in the 1980s, however, the figures were still worrying: adult illiteracy was 86 per cent (97 per cent for women) in the north, and 59 per cent (75 per cent for women) in the south. With over half the current population under 14 years of age, a proper and compulsory schooling system must be organised to take full advantage of the country's economic potential. The number of Yemeni teachers is rapidly increasing and they will slowly replace those from other Arab countries such as Egypt and Jordan. Women's education is of special concern as many are removed from mixed classes by male relatives at an early age. Education is one of the government's most urgent and pressing priorities.

Clothing

Traditional
clothing
replaced by
new imports

The opening up of the country during the 1960s, coupled with remittances from migrant workers, allowed people to buy a vast range of imported clothing. Until then, indigo-dyed clothing and locally woven products from the Tihama were the main choice, with some imports coming through the ports, particularly Indian cloth via Aden. The local industry has rapidly collapsed, to the point where it is almost impossible to find Yemeni produced goods. There are cotton factories still producing in Zabid and Sana'a, where artificial dyes are used, but the low prices of imported clothing from the East has swamped the market.

There are two traditional types of men's clothing. The *futah* is a colourful wrap-around skirt worn mostly in the warmer parts of the country, with a distinctive colour and shape according to region. At altitude a full or three-quarter length *zanna* (or *thobe*) is worn for warmth always with a western style jacket. In both cases, the traditional *jambia* dagger is worn inside a sheath attached to a belt. Imported *mashadda* head cloths are produced in many colours with red and white and the Palestinian black and white being the most popular. In the Tihama the expensive woven fez-like hats called *kufiyah* are popular.

Women choose
how to cover up

Women have a much wider choice of clothing. The three-piece *sharshaf* (a recent fashion borrowed from Egypt) and the one piece black *shadar* cover women completely from head to toe, but they are not particularly interesting. Black and dark colours predominate in Sana'a, but there are some variations, with brightly coloured veils popular amongst the younger women. A *sitara* is a more colourful covering, and is worn over a veil and dress. They are locally produced in Sana'a or made in India, specifically for Yemeni women.

Veiled highland village women.

Highland clothing is practical but modest

In mountain areas, many women and most young girls wear a pair of loose trousers called a *sirwal*, topped by a couple of layers of dresses in a variety of colours and materials. Some of these trousers have padded lower sections as protection against thorns and prickly bushes in the countryside. Again a veil would be added for further protection. There are many more individual pieces of clothing that can be worn in various combinations, depending on personal choice, season, fashion and availability.

In the mountain villages you will notice some children wearing the *gargoush*, a colourful hood. This is traditionally worn by all babies and by girls until married.

Music and Dance

Yemenis enjoy their music

Somewhere on your travels you will have the chance to hear live music – not in the sense of a concert, but more likely a simple get-together of two or three men playing instruments and dancing, or a wedding if you're lucky. Each region has its own speciality.

The most striking instrument is the *al-oud* (from which the word 'lute' is derived), a stringed instrument like a pregnant guitar which, when played well, is a delight to listen to. It is also referred to as the *kabanj* and the accompaniment would normally be with two small drums. The *mizmar* is a sort of small double-barrelled

Yemeni oboe whose rhythm is tapped out on a longer drum.

During wedding celebrations, there are evening music sets for all the guests. The size of the orchestra depends on the cost, but it could easily include some violins, *al-oud*, a tambourine, several drums and nowadays perhaps an electronic keyboard. Singers take it in turn to yell into the microphone and a troupe of dancers, all male of course, perform well-known movements. The drumming rhythms of the Hadramaut and Tihama regions are particularly hypnotic, beautifully offset by the deep droning and shrill yells of the dancers and singers.

The haunting rhythms of South Arabia

The final wedding day festivities as seen overlooking Wadi Dhahr on a Friday consist of groups of men dancing the bara, the Sana'a war dance, either in circles or lines of men. The music is provided by two drums hit with sticks.

Other dances that you may come across are the **raqs**, which vary from place to place. Only in the Tihama and nowadays in Aden would it be usual for men and women to dance together.

The influence of Yemeni music through Moorish conquests

Yemeni music may seem familiar, as its basic roots have been carried to many countries by Yemeni soldiers through the spread of Islam. If possible, try to hear some of the old Yemeni Bedouin songs or instrumentals that have scarcely changed for centuries, without other Middle Eastern (usually Egyptian) influence. The structure and intervals of the pieces are similar to pure Magrebi and Andalusian music, and differ greatly from other Arab music.

TRIBES

The main unit of social order is still the tribe. Individuals are born into a tribe, pledge their loyalty to it and receive protection from it. Each tribe controls a particular area of land, individual sections of which can only be bought or sold by another member of the same tribe. The borders between tribes have always been contentious issues, and most feuds stem from border clashes of one form or another.

Yemenis - true Arabs

Tribal independence is important, but when the country is faced by an invading force such as the Ottoman Turks, intertribal disputes are suspended. National identity is strong, coming from the belief that all southern Arabian tribes are descended from Noah's son Shem, through Qahtan. These Qahtanid tribes consider themselves to be the original Arabs, as opposed to the 'Arabized Arabs' from the north of the peninsula (the Adnanids) who claim descent from the much later Adnan, son of Ishmael, son of Abraham.

Such ancient lineages may seem irrelevant today but it was important during the 1962 revolution, as it united the tribes against the ruling Zaidi imams whose history went back to the northern Adnanids. The fortunes of individual tribes have risen and fallen through the centuries, but the fact that they still exist today testifies to their strength and adaptability. Allegiances are made and broken, invaders conquer and are defeated, but through it all the tribes maintain social order and discipline.

The rich heritage of tribal society

A member of a tribe is known as a *qabiili* (see Society and Culture), and is a fierce defender of his tribe's **honour**, which is determined and defined by many factors: the tribal land (many places are named after the local tribe); the leader or *sheikh*; their common lineage (Beni Husheish, for example, a tribe near Sana'a, means 'sons of Husheish'); the weekly market (e.g. the Zaraniq tribe market is at Beit al-Faqih); and such things as clothing and architecture.

The *sheikh* (elder) is the leader of the tribe who arbitrates and gives judgements between disputing *qabiili*. The *sheikh* represents the tribe on all political matters, and has a group of respected family heads as *agil* to mediate within the tribe. If a member kills someone from another tribe, he will be protected from their revenge and an amount of **diyah** or 'blood money' will be negotiated.

For greater strength, **federations** are formed amongst similar tribes, for example the Bakil Federation consists of many central and northern tribes. The Bakil also belong to the Hamdan Federation with the powerful Hashid. Such federations were another important factor in the eventual success of the 1962 revolution, as the Shafi'i tribes in the south and west formed a large anti-Zaidi movement.

You will observe tribal life in the north of the country essentially unchanged for hundreds of years. This mountainous area has been easier to defend against invaders and has ensured greater independence for the *qabiili*. You may find them slightly insular and aloof, in contrast to the more open and friendly lowland people.

Tribes are less influential in the south and west

The tribes of the Tihama have been ruled by foreigners for longer periods, and their traditions are not so strong. Further south around Ta'iz the tribes are weaker, following centuries of outside control (the Rasulids had their capital here) and the destruction of tribal society.

In the former PDRY, there was an unsuccessful government attempt to break the tribes into groups loyal only to the state. This differed greatly from the earlier British practice of respecting tribal power and using it to their own advantage. It is now generally agreed that the 1986 civil war was in essence a tribal conflict acted out under a veneer of Communism.

The position of the tribes today is very confusing. Around Sana'a and in the north they still hold great power, which reaches government level. It has often been said that whoever controls Sana'a and the Bakil and Hashid tribes, controls the Yemen. Many tribes are forming their own political parties now that multi-party elections are the new key to control. One of the interesting aspects of the fledgling democracy will be how the tribes adapt to the central government.

Previous YAR governments have always had problems with certain tribes, who enjoy virtual autonomy. The success of the new republic depends almost entirely on the co-operation of a handful of tribes and their powerful, charismatic *sheikhs*, who also know their value to external powers wishing to destabilise the democratic government of a unified Yemen.

The **Bedouin** tribes do not adhere to all the normal parameters of tribal life, but are feared as fierce marauders and fighters who do not respect borders or the agricultural life of the settled tribes.

Manipulating tribal power is the key to stable government

WOMEN

One aspect of Yemeni society, which strikes the western visitor perhaps more than any other, is the differences between Yemeni women and their Western counterparts. Whereas the men can be seen taking part in every aspect of social activity, women seem to be almost invisible around the streets and soon disappear behind their household barricades. What is it really like to live as a woman in what would seem to be a totally male dominated society?

From a Western perspective, **women's rights** in the Yemen still seem to have a long way to go, but this view is not necessarily correct. Yemeni women have the vote and, as most men will testify, they already rule the household. It is the outward appearance of repression and individuality that reinforces the male/female disparity. What you are actually seeing is a society committed totally to a religion that specifies the roles that men and women will play. In the West, we do not have such strict spiritual guidelines that separate the sexes, so the discussion should be as much about tribal and religious tradition as about sexual equality.

Women rule the households and family life

Strict Islam requires **modest dress** which is here carried to the extreme, as the majority of women cover themselves completely in a variety of dresses, cloths, shawls and veils. The veil discourages unwanted male attention and allows women to wander around freely without such pressures. **Veiling** tends to be an urban custom, and it is not even an Islamic invention but an adaptation from an earlier Byzantine practice. Do not make the mistake of thinking that because you cannot put a character or face to the person, that they are somehow living in a parallel world, unrelated to ours.

Educational and employment opportunities for women are rapidly gaining ground, yet many intelligent and qualified women still prefer to remain veiled. After a few weeks I tend not to notice women moving about and it comes as something of a surprise to suddenly hear a veiled woman say 'Hello' in a place like Sadah or Manakha. Admittedly, it always happens when there are no Yemeni men around to hear them!

Different attitudes around the country

The role of women in Yemeni society varies according to area. In the Tihama, where Zaidi doctrines are less popular, they tend to have more freedom. They are regularly seen selling produce in the *suqs* and you can sometimes see them openly smoking and chewing *qat*. These are also the only women I know who sometimes carry handguns instead of handbags.

Around Ta'iz you will see the women from Jebel Sabr without veils generally dressed more colourfully than anywhere else, and this differs greatly from the Zaidi strongholds in the northern mountains where women are expected to maintain a very low profile outside the house, or the Hadramaut, where they are completely covered. Conversely it is these strong and forceful women who play such an important part in the traditional tribal system. In an urban setting the contrast between public and private lifestyles is dramatic, typified by the high walls surrounding the houses, behind which the women are protected. This woman's enclave is thus called *hareem* (meaning 'a sacred, private place') known in a slightly different context in the West as a harem.

Large families and heavy workload

On average, women give birth to eight children. **Rural life** for women would tend to be totally dominated by the family and its requirements, as it has been for centuries. A young girl will help her mother with household tasks and agricultural work, while the son will go to school, thus continuing the imbalance in education. Almost 80 per cent of the population live in the countryside in small isolated communities, which requires the women to gather firewood, fetch water and ensure that enough food is brought in from the fields. Religious, tribal, climatic, educational and economic considerations all contribute to the way women look and behave in the modern Yemen.

COSMETICS

The use of henna to mark designs on hands and feet is widespread around the country. Powdered henna leaves are mixed with water, with sometimes a little oil added to make a long-lasting dye. The red solution often dries as a dark brown colour on the skin, but when placed on the hair (and the beards of the older men) it turns an orange-red, symbolising the celebration of life.

A natural form of sun block is achieved by painting the face with a mixture of crushed leaves, particularly in the northern highlands and the Hadramaut. This ghostly, ashen-faced appearance also makes women look unattractive, thus avoiding unwanted male attention. Particularly in the Tihama, women paint their nails with *khidab* (a manganese compound) in order to emphasise the glow of the skin.

Old men (and very young children) also join women in decorating their eyes with *kohl*. This is said to act as a protection against ophthalmia – and to ward off the 'evil eye'.

Personal choice is also an increasingly important factor. Following the revolutions, village women have had a greater opportunity to change their outlook and expectations if they wish. Roads now provide access to even the remotest settlements, creating greater mobility but also more exposure to outsiders and thus more veiling.

Viewing the rest of the world

Television has opened up a whole new vista of lifestyles and attitudes, and education offers exciting futures. The movement of women (albeit as wives of male workers) to other cities and even other countries, broadens their knowledge and experience. Even those women who stayed behind when their husbands went to work abroad, had to become more independent to farm and survive for themselves.

A warm reception for visiting women

Women travellers are eagerly accepted by Yemeni women, and are thus in a unique position to observe the lifestyle of both sexes, something impossible for a foreign man. Whereas a male visitor will be invited to chew *qat*, females might be asked to join the women in the afternoon for their *tafrita* get-togethers. *Qat* and tobacco will be handed around, and some very personal questions asked. Local women are just as inquisitive about you as you are about them, so accept any invitation that gives you a better insight into the 'hidden' world of Yemeni women.

JEWISH YEMENIS

Importance of Jewish traders

Some of the success of the Yemen as a trading centre throughout history has been due to the merchants, ministers and soldiers who followed the Jewish faith. At various times a sizeable proportion of the population were Jews who interacted with other Jewish and Muslim merchants in distant trading centres such as Egypt, Persia and India.

Biblical evidence

The precise origins of Jewish settlements in the Yemen are unknown. The Bible tells us that during the time of Solomon, Israeli tribes settled in Arabia and that the King sent Jewish soldiers to protect the returning Queen of Sheba. And Strabo tells us that in 24 BC 500 Jewish soldiers were sent by King Herod to help defend southern Arabia from the Roman troops of Aelius Gallus.

In the fourth century AD, the ruling Himyar tribe appears to have converted to Judaism, partly as a policy of remaining independent of Rome. Trade flourished for two centuries and close contacts were recorded between the Jews of Himyar and towns in upper Galilee. Tension finally erupted between the two major religions when southern Arabian Christians were massacred by the last Himyar ruler Yusuf Dhu Nuwas (Ash'ar Yath'ar). The Axumite Empire quickly responded by defeating the Jews in 570, possibly the same year in which the Prophet Mohammed was born.

Throughout the establishment of Islam, Jews from the Yemen continued to trade and set up small communities from Babylon to Spain. Likewise, some Jews from other countries set up communities in the Yemen. The **regulation of Jewish practices** in southern Arabia, the stronghold of Islam, reached a peak under Caliph Umar, who introduced the 28 Umar Conditions. Amongst these were bans on praying aloud, building new synagogues and living in houses higher than those of Muslims. Jews were not allowed to ride horses, only unsaddled donkeys. The strictness with which these conditions were imposed varied with the prosperity of the country, but generally the Jews led a relatively independent life alongside their Muslim neighbours.

Impositions on Jews

The lengthy battles against the invading **Turks** in the seventeenth century caused severe famine and plague in the rural areas, driving most Jews to Sana'a. In 1676 the Imam al-Mahdi forced many Jews to become Muslims by decreeing the Yemen to be 'consecrated ground', stating that is was impossible for the two religions to co-exist. The appearance of a false Messiah, one Shabbatai Zvi from Smyrna, caused the Jews to rebel openly against the Imam, who responded by expelling them from the city.

The Jews mistakenly follow a 'false Messiah'

By 1679 all Jews from Sana'a had been banished to the hellish environment of Mawza, 25km inland from Mokha. However, it soon became obvious that daily life in the capital could not continue without their expertise in the production of tools, utensils and jewellery. They were therefore allowed back, but their houses had been taken over by Muslims and so they were given an area outside the old city walls. Thus began a tradition of a Jewish section in Bir al-Azab, known as al-Qa.

Much of the **coffee trade** in Mokha was run by the Jews, and with the decline of the port, many settled in Aden to participate in the boom years there. Under British rule, Jews and Muslims enjoyed the same rights, and some Jews prospered enough to set up trading **International** branches in Bombay and Calcutta. Meanwhile in the **Jewish trade** northern highlands, wealthy Jewish artisans based in Ta'iz and Manakha who imported goods from India and the Far East suffered when Imam Yahya took control in 1904 and immediately reimposed the strict Umar Conditions. He also added some of his own, the most bizarre being a ban on Jews raising their voices or accidentally touching a passing Muslim. A refinement to the unsaddled donkey law meant that they could now only ride side-saddle – without a saddle! The latrine law of 1846 was also reintroduced entrusting the cleaning of all public toilets to Jews.

Such harsh treatment helped to disperse the Jews around the country, where they formed as many as 1,000 settlements in towns and villages, totalling 100,000 people. As artisans and traders, the system of weekly markets were important outlets for their products and also opportunities to meet friends and relatives, obtain news and exchange letters.

Almost all the The final chapter in the story comes with the estab-
Jews leave for lishment of the **State of Israel** in 1947. The Arab-Jewish
Israel ... war of 1948 led to a mass exodus of Yemeni Jews to Israel. This massive airlift from Aden, known as Operation Magic Carpet, meant that many Jews had to walk for weeks from their homes in the north. However, it was the settlements in the south and centre that were most affected by anti-Jewish feelings, and all the Jews of Habban and Aden left. Such a mass exodus meant the overnight loss of many traditional trades.

Jewish Yemenis in Israel still refer to the Yemen as their homeland and even continue to chew *qat*, despite the fact that the trees in Israel produce a rough, poor quality leaf.

... but there are The result of this exodus is that the visitor today is
still a few left unlikely to see any Yemeni Jews, with their side locks of curly hair. There are small communities in Raydah and Sadah, where you might see them around the southern gate. Very occasionally you can see them selling silverware as itinerant traders at the Bab al-Yemen in Sana'a. But the numbers are small, which indicates that their future in the Yemen must be uncertain.

Selecting Qat *shoots.*

QAT

If there is any one aspect of everyday life in Yemen that is totally unique it has to be the obsessive chewing of the plant *Catha edulis*, better known as *al-Qat*. *Qat* is big business for all involved: growers, owners, transporters, traders and even the people who produce the red plastic wrappings. Some visitors show concern at the glazed look of their driver as he twists the vehicle around tight mountain bends, but it is far better to have him 'awake' on *qat* than asleep at the wheel.

Qat as a daily local industry

The plant grows best at altitudes between 1,500m and 2,500m and thrives in areas receiving annually 500–1,000mm of rain. Cultivated bushes are usually between 2 and 5m in height, but there are shorter varieties, which need regular pruning in order to stop them growing up to 10m. Travelling around the highlands you will see small fields of *qat* on the plateaus and neat rows evenly spaced along the terracing higher up. The leaves are a shiny dark green in appearance which give it the name 'the emerald leaf'.

Qat is also grown and chewed in Somalia, Kenya and Ethiopia and it is probably from the latter that the plant was introduced into the Yemen some 700 years ago. It also occurs naturally in Central Asia and East, Central and South Africa, and has been successfully introduced into Israel for consumption by Jews of Yemeni origin. It was mentioned and named by the botanist Peter Forsskal on Carsten Niebuhr's expedition in 1763, who latinised *Qat* into *Catha* and added *edulis* because it was 'eaten'.

The easiest crop to grow

Cultivation is easy and can begin within two to four years of planting. Small shoots are taken from the base of existing plants and laid just below the surface, which produce new shoots after being watered for a few weeks. Only the most tender parts of the plants are cut for chewing, a continuous process which can last for up to 50 years providing the plants are well watered. For transport, large amounts of *qat* are wrapped in leaves of other plants to keep them fresh. Driving around the wadis you can often see van loads of banana stalks being taken up to the *qat* fields, as these leaves are good for the wholesale wrapping of *qat*.

Qat must be fresh

The journey from field to *suq* is often done at break-neck speed so that the *qat* arrives as fresh as possible. Throughout the morning you will see powerful Toyota Land Cruiser trucks loaded with massive bundles speeding along the highways, Kalashnikov-laden minders grimly hanging on for dear life. Unlike coffee which grows in similar conditions, *qat* must be harvested and sold quickly, which makes it impossible for the lucrative business to be taken over by powerful merchants. The coffee trade is seasonal and can be well controlled by storing until prices are favourable, whereas *qat* is a year-round product and impossible to keep.

Thus the *qat* **trade** is still in the hands of the small farmers and landowners, who have three choices of how to sell it. They can take the produce to the village *suq* themselves and sell it on the street for local consumption, or if urban prices are higher, direct to the main cities. Secondly they can sell to city based traders who travel into the country to buy at advantageous prices. But more likely, they will deal with a wholesaler or a retailer, known as a *mufowadeen*, who will sell on their behalf, charging a commission of about 10 per cent.

Finding the right market

There are many different types of *qat* and it is hard for the casual bystander to understand the difference in price between a veritable bush of twigs and leaves and a small high quality spray costing ten times as much.

The *qat* sections of a *suq* are always the liveliest and noisiest places, with everyone wandering around looking for the best quality within their budget. Bundles are inspected and stiffly rejected, and bargaining ensues with great passion until both sides are happy and the satisfied customer departs clutching his *rubta* wrapped in a thin polythene sheet. There then follow discussions of where to chew, which will nearly always be in a private house. Men take it in turns to offer their houses as venues for the afternoon and those with a large *mafraj* (the room for entertaining guests, usually at the top of the house) are most popular. After the morning purchase, a large lunch is taken which offsets the loss of appetite following a *qat* session. Midday prayers will also be observed.

Hard bargaining

At a typical daily **chew,** all guests would bring their own bundles but the host will be expected to provide drinking water and a pipe for smoking. For a special occasion such as a wedding, the host will purchase and distribute *qat* amongst his guests. The participants start to gather at around 14.00 for a session that will last about four hours. This is the average time taken for a person to slowly chew his way through a *rubta*. It is romantic to imagine every *qat* chew taking place in a bright, open *mafraj* at the top of a tower house overlooking roofs and countryside. Such venues are at a real premium in the capital, and the majority of chews take place in a lower room, known as the *diwan*, normally the general family living room. In areas where there are no tower houses, men chew *qat* in a ventilated room or an open shady area beneath a tree, as in the Tihama.

Etiquette at a *qat* chew

Certain places have become popular for chewing *qat* **outdoors,** and you can quite often see groups of men enjoying a vista whilst sitting in the shade halfway up a cliff face, or under the canopy of a petrol station on the edge of an abyss. The main thing to realise is that it is not just the act of chewing that creates the atmosphere, but the fact that one is socialising in a particular group. At high-level *qat* chews, important issues are discussed and determined in a way that is difficult for the outsider to comprehend. In the Yemen, social climbers attend all the best *qat* parties and try to arrange who they sit next to.

Infusion through the lining of the mouth

For a couple of hours, the tenderest young leaves are plucked and cleaned with the fingers, and then placed in the side of the mouth. The leaves are not swallowed, but are chewed to produce a green mulch which is kept in the cheek. With skill, they can be rolled around to form a solid ball, from which the juices are slowly extracted and absorbed into the blood stream. Travelling around you will see some men who are greatly admired for the size of their cheeks, looking like off-duty glass blowers.

If any member of the group runs out of leaves he will be tossed a twig or two by his fellows. A miserly person is therefore described as 'never having thrown a bunch of *qat* at anyone'.

A drug, or not?

Tests on *qat* have shown it to contain two substances, *cathin* and *cathinone*, which have the same effect as amphetamines, i.e. raising blood pressure and body temperature, and releasing adrenaline. Chewers become excited and talkative, weary souls experience renewed energy and vigour, it stimulates and soothes. The spirit is said to spread its wings in a search for satisfaction and some mystics use *qat* to communicate closer with Allah.

Such claims can seem far-fetched in the late afternoon when one steps into a shop to see the owner slumped against the wall, looking definitely one twig short of a *rubta* – and not only looking, but also sounding, as it is almost impossible to tell what people are saying with such an obstacle to speech lodged in their mouth.

Excessive use of *qat* can inflame the prostate and cause mild shrinkage of the genitals, which could explain the loss of sexual appetite!

The dryness of the leaves causes **dehydration,** which is combated by the constant sipping of water or soft drinks. By now the heap of foliage and unsuitable leaves in the middle of the floor could well hide one side from the other. After about two hours the mood changes as the group is happy to relax and contemplate the rhythmic sounds of the smoke bubbles being sucked through the

Peace at the end of the day

water of the *mada'ah* pipe. This idyllic scene is completed with the late afternoon sun shining through the coloured windows. The call of the *muezzin* at sunset signals a slow revival amongst the chewers, when some will clear their mouths of the remaining wad and start to make their way home. Other chewers continue well into the evening.

Depression, sleeplessness, indigestion and a loss of

appetite are typical 'hangovers' suffered by irregular chewers, symptoms that are said to reduce if you chew every day. A beginner would also experience extreme soreness in the mouth, a painful back and a numb rear-end after squatting for so long.

Visitors should not expect too much of a reaction

The slight 'buzz' one gets from *qat* is only a tiny part of this fascinating ritual. It is the whole social aspect of *qat* parties that is important and you are unlikely to appreciate this by chewing a few bitter leaves in the back of a bouncing Land Cruiser. A foreigner would need to be confident enough of how he chews and behaves, while not fidgeting or getting cramp, before he could accept an invitation to a real *qat* party.

If you want to try (and everybody should, even if it is just to prove to yourself how horrible it tastes) get a local person to help you choose a reasonable *rubta* for the amount that you want to spend and find a hostelry where people are chewing. In the cities you can find these all over, usually in a first-floor room above a local eating house. With luck there should be someone who speaks English, who would be prepared to help you.

Women also chew *qat*, but not as openly as men. A man will normally buy for his wife, who will chew in her own women's group, inside one of their houses. Before the revolutions, *qat* was priced out of the reach of most people and only available in certain *qat*-growing areas. Since then it has become readily available, even more so since unification as it was only permitted in the PDRY on Thursdays and Fridays.

A habit that costs too much

There is widespread concern about the amount of money spent on this indulgence, which sometimes amounts to one-third of the household budget. Supporters argue that it is not an addictive drug, nor is it banned specifically on religious grounds. It also helps to spread money from the cities into the countryside.

Objectors point to the minor health hazards and the crippling effect it has on economic production, not to mention the reduced family budget. But while there is still a flourishing market, farmers will continue to cultivate *qat*, which gives them a good steady income at about five times the profit of any other agricultural product.

ARCHITECTURE

The **tower houses** of Sana'a, Shibam and the highlands are world famous, and rightly so, but these are just a few examples of the wealth of unique building styles employed in the Yemen. Before travelling out of Sana'a, try to visit the third floor of the National Museum which has models and details of types of houses from around the country.

Architectural details are provided in the relevant

travel sections, so Sana'a tower houses, for example, are described in the walk through the old City. But even many modern buildings use traditional methods and styles: mud brick houses in the Hadramaut, stone buildings in Manakha, or simple huts in the Tihama – all determined by climatic conditions and the available material.

Many unique traditional styles

White paint and white decorations are seen on many buildings, especially houses. It is a sacred colour, and was initially confined to mosques, but it was later used to decorate window surrounds by pilgrims returning from Mecca. Nowadays the white window borders are said to attract light, but repel flies. In many regions different symbols are used to bring good luck. The most widespread are horns of animals (particularly the *w'il* or ibex) which are attached to the corners of tall houses, where they are supposed to ward off the 'evil eye' and protect the house from bad spirits. Other symbols include representations of snakes (see Sana'a) and metal prongs in some mountain villages.

Modern pressures require quick and cheap solutions

However, **social changes** are affecting the use of traditional styles. If a modern city family wants to live separately from their relatives, they will choose a small house or flat in the suburbs. Likewise a Tihama couple may move to Hodeidah to live in a quickly constructed breezeblock building, as it is impractical to build reed huts in a rapidly expanding city. All major towns and cities are experiencing an unprecedented influx of people who have to be housed, and generally there is neither the time nor the inclination to construct fine examples of traditional Yemeni architecture. There is also the problem of temporary accommodation for the returnees expelled from Saudi Arabia and the Gulf countries, especially north of Hodeidah on the road to Jizan.

You can see the best examples of Yemeni buildings in the preserved sections of cities like Sana'a and Shibam. Next in importance are the old centres such as Sadah, Zabid and Seiyun, although as provincial capitals they are rapidly expanding and therefore losing their character. For modern buildings that still use traditional styles, you should go to small out-of-the-way places such as Thulla (near Sana'a), Hajjarain (Hadramaut) or Qureish (near Khushm, Tihama). The construction of three large cement factories (Amran, Bajil and Ta'iz) can only lead to more Western-style convenience housing, even though current production falls far short of demand.

WEEKLY MARKETS

The practice of villages and towns holding markets on particular days of the week stems from the tradition of each tribe selling its goods on its own territory each week. Thus a **rota system** of intertribal trading has evolved throughout the whole country, especially the north. It is the responsibility of the host village to ensure protection for all traders and buyers, and the market area is temporarily declared a *haram* district, which forbids any physical assaults even during times of war.

Initially, some places only existed because of the market and were often known as such – one example is Suq al-Khamis ('Thursday market') in the Tihama. In some towns and cities markets are now so busy that they have to operate daily, but in rural areas the weekly cycle persists. The following description is of ar-Rujum Monday market near Mahweet, but much of the same applies to almost every market you will see.

Description of a typical market day

The **traders** start arriving around dawn to lay out their wares for the day, some having travelled many miles from the surrounding mountains. All the town centre shops are soon open with casual traders filling the gaps and creating whole new 'streets' of goods. They are grouped into various general items: fruit and vegetables; meat; household goods; spices and grain; and, as always, the lively *qat* section.

The **livestock market** is on open ground towards the edge of the town, cattle and donkeys separated from sheep and goats. Hard bargaining often requires the entire morning for the purchase of a single animal, the whole process being overseen by a *musalih*, who ensures fair play and receives his 10 per cent commission upon completion. Half of this fee will go to the influential *Sheikh al-Suq* of the host village. Some of the traders are women, who are known to be tough in business. To one side of the animal area are the slaughter men, who have a particularly low standing within the tribe, surrounded by bloody-mouthed dogs eager for the poorest scraps. A goat or sheep is handed over, its throat is slit, the blood is drained, the skin is removed and the carcass is hoisted onto a temporary three-pole support. Joints are cut from the dangling animal and weighed for sale.

Same time, next week

By noon the impetus has gone and attention focuses on the homeward journey and a well-earned *qat* session.

Markets are great places for friends to meet and exchange news. Often you will be held up in your wanderings by old men embracing and kissing each other. The scene is lively and colourful, and forms the whole basis of trade outside the cities. Eight-year-old porters crash into your shins with speedy wheelbarrows and eighty-year-old men almost blind you with their lethal walking sticks, but to wander around a weekly market is one of those timeless experiences.

*Dar al-Hajjar
(Rock Palace).*

SECTION 2:
AROUND YEMEN

Old City, Sana'a.

SANA'A

INTRODUCTION

Sana'a is arguably the oldest inhabited city in the world, although Damascus disputes this claim, and there certainly is a wealth of history contained within its walled city.

A city in the mountains

It is more than 2,000m above sea level, so one of the first things you will probably notice is a shortness of breath and occasional dizziness, especially if you are climbing seven floors of a tower house! You would also be advised to eat your main meal at midday as the locals do. Their reason is that the afternoon *qat* session reduces hunger, but there is also the fact that many a bad night has been spent trying to digest a heavy evening meal owing to the slowing up of the digestive system at such altitudes.

A tour of the old city and *suq*, a visit to the two central museums and an initial trip to some of the surrounding countryside such as Wadi Dhahr, Thulla and Kawkaban are all worth fitting in at the beginning of your visit.

HISTORY

The Yemen has had many capitals over the centuries. This, coupled with the country's past isolationist policies means that Sana'a is not one of the more recognisable capitals in the world. This may be one reason why the city (and the country, for that matter) remains a well kept secret.

Before 1000 BC Sana'a appears to have developed as a relatively unimportant town on a secondary **incense trading route,** controlling a narrow gap in the highland plateau. The main route lay to the east on the very edge of the desert, through the Sabaean capital of Marib, which became the greatest power in the region.

The Sabaeans controlled the fabulous wealth heading north by setting up fortifications along the various connecting routes from the Tihama and Aden. The town which grew up around the cross-roads of these east-west and south-north routes was simply known as the 'fortified one' – Sana'a. Like many ancient places in southern Arabia there is a lack of hard evidence to substantiate much of the city's history, so we have to rely on colourful stories to fill in the gaps.

Beginning with a myth

One such tradition concerns the **founding of the town,** which it attributes to Shem, the eldest son of Noah, who was led by a bird to a spot below Jebel Nuqum. One of Shem's descendants was Joktan (Qahtan in Arabic) from whom all Arabs claim their descent. Two of the sons of

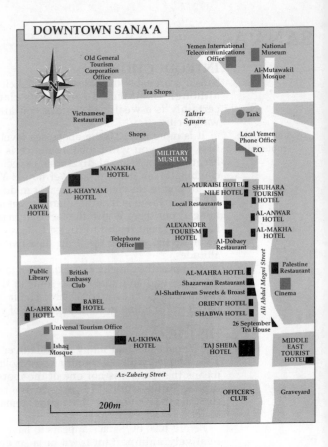

DOWNTOWN SANA'A

Yemen International Telecommunications Office

National Museum

Old General Tourism Corporation Office

Al-Mutawakil Mosque

Tea Shops

Tahrir Square

Tank

Vietnamese Restaurant

Local Yemen Phone Office

Shops

P.O.

MILITARY MUSEUM

MANAKHA HOTEL

AL-KHAYYAM HOTEL

AL-MURAISI HOTEL
NILE HOTEL

SHUHARA TOURISM HOTEL

ARWA HOTEL

Local Restaurants

AL-ANWAR HOTEL

ALEXANDER TOURISM HOTEL

AL-MAKHA HOTEL

Telephone Office

Al-Dobaey Restaurant

Public Library

British Embassy Club

AL-MAHRA HOTEL

Palestine Restaurant

Ali Abdul Mogni Street

Shazarwan Restaurant

Al-Shathrawan Sweets & Broast

Cinema

BABEL HOTEL

ORIENT HOTEL

AL-AHRAM HOTEL

SHABWA HOTEL

Universal Tourism Office

26 September Tea House

Ishaq Mosque

AL-IKHWA HOTEL

TAJ SHEBA HOTEL

MIDDLE EAST TOURIST HOTEL

Az-Zubeiry Street

200m

OFFICER'S CLUB

Graveyard

Biblical references

Joktan mentioned in Genesis are relevant to this region, one called Hazarmaveth (Hadramaut) the other Uzal (also called Azal, another old name for Sana'a).

In the early years of **Christianity,** the Kingdom of Saba grew to be a federation, and Sana'a became as important as Marib itself. Possibly because of its climate, Sana'a became the chief residence of the Sabaean kings. Several times the town came to the aid of Marib, which always seemed to be at odds with neighbouring kingdoms. The **Ghumdan Palace** is thought to have been built around the third century AD for one of these kings, possibly Sha'r Awtar. The great Arab chronicler al-Hamdani, writing some 600 years later, tells us that the palace was

The world's first skyscraper?

20 storeys tall, each wall made of different-coloured stone, with an alabaster roof through which birds could be seen flying. At each corner of the roof was a bronze lion which roared as the wind passed through it.

Throughout its history, Sana'a seems to have benefited

from its *haram* status, meaning that people had free access to markets and trade even in times of war. Once inside the walled town, all disputes and conflicts were suspended. Most of the surrounding land was taken up with providing enough food for the massive army. The established religions of Christianity and Judaism attracted followings among the traders who frequently visited the north and the whole region became a political battleground between Byzantium and Persia. Until then people worshipped a moon god and sun goddess, whose crescent and ball symbol can be found on many inscriptions all over southern Arabia.

Sana'a grows in importance

When the **Himyars** finally defeated the Sabaeans in the fourth century AD, they built a new capital at Dhafar, near Yarim. With this move the major trade routes also moved into the mountains. Details of this period are at best sketchy, but it seems that Sana'a hung on to its importance long enough to become capital again when the Abyssinians of Axum (Ethiopia) conquered the highlands from the declining Himyars. The Abyssinians had long controlled the Tihama and used the excuse of Jewish atrocities on the Christians of Najran to launch a Byzantine-backed invasion early in the sixth century.

Centre of Christianity

By 537, the Axumite leader Abraha had secured funding from the Emperor Justinian to build a great **cathedral** for Christian pilgrimage in Sana'a. To boost its credibility, a far-fetched legend grew up that the new cathedral was built on the site of Jesus's visit during his wanderings in the wilderness. The Qalis as it was known (see Old City Walk), became a religious centre to rival the pre-Islamic centre at Mecca, and was the focus of Christianity south of the Mediterranean.

Abraha's death, shortly after his ill-fated attack on Mecca in 570, gave the Himyars an opportunity to regain control. For this they enrolled the help of Persian troops who succeeded in defeating the Ethiopians, but then refused to leave and added Sana'a to the Persian Empire.

Connections with the Prophet Mohammed

The importance of Sana'a just prior to the coming of Islam is shown by the fact that Mohammed's father travelled there and his great uncle is said to be buried in the city. With such strong links with Mecca it is not surprising that within six years of the *Hegira*, Sana'a became one of the first cities to embrace the new religion, during the rule of Badhan, the Persian Governor of the city.

Initially religious tolerance was the order of the day, but confrontations led to the destruction of the Qalis as well as the Ghumdan Palace. Carved stone blocks from both buildings were then used to construct a new place of worship, the Great Mosque. One of the envoys from Mecca is said to have been the Prophet's son-in-law Ali

117

A much fought-over trading centre

bin Abu Taleb, who stayed in a house near the *suq*. A small mosque which bears his name now stands on the site.

When Ali assumed the Caliphate in 656 (35 AH), a **civil war** broke out between rival factions, with Sana'a supporting Ali. However, the city fell to the Umayyids of Damascus who controlled it through appointed governors. Later the Abbasids of Baghdad took control and the city prospered particularly under Mohammed bin al-Barmaki, who provided the water supply and constructed a mint. In the middle of the ninth century, a local tribe from Shibam-Kawkaban under Yufir bin Abderahman al-Hiwali captured Sana'a and, although they remained loyal to Baghdad, they established Yufirid rule for almost 200 years. This period also saw the rise of the northern Zaidi imams (see Sadah), who continually tried to seize power.

It became clear that whoever controlled Sana'a and the surrounding tribes, controlled the Yemen. Confusion and anarchy reigned until the establishment of the Fatimid dynasty under Ali bin Mohammed as-Sulayhi, who took Sana'a in 1047. The Fatimids of Egypt provided the power for the Sulayhis to subdue the Tihama and Sadah regions. A short-lived empire flourished until the death of Queen Arwa at her new capital Jibla, while local sultans controlled Sana'a.

Sana'a - a city in constant conflict

With the **Zaidis** establishing themselves in the north and tribal unrest throughout the land, another Egyptian force invaded. Saladin's brother Turanshah took Sana'a in 1173 but soon lost it to Sultan Hamdan. However Ayyubid control was regained when another of Saladin's brothers, Tughtakin established his capital in the city in 1189. As power slowly shifted southwards towards Ta'iz, Sana'a found itself continually in the midst of an Ayyubid-Zaidi conflict, which remained unresolved until the Rasulids emerged from the Ayyubid embers in 1228. A golden age of peace and trade placed Ta'iz above Sana'a, which declined to a lowly fiefdom. Eventually the Zaidi imams claimed Sana'a and ruled for over 200 unremarkable years, although few details emerged from this period.

Much of Sanani and Yemeni history was later determined by the expansion and protection plans of **Egyptian rulers** wanting to control the southern Red Sea coastline and supply routes. By the early sixteenth century the Mameluke Sultans in Cairo had taken Sana'a by expelling the Zaidis, who fought a rearguard action from Thulla. Within two years, Egypt itself had fallen to the Ottoman Turks from Constantinople, which gave the Zaidis the opportunity to return to Sana'a in 1517. Conditions in the city were appalling and a plague in 1527 is thought to have claimed over 10,000 lives.

The first period of Turkish occupation

Ottoman expansion naturally included southern Arabia, and Sana'a fell to them in 1547. The citadel became the residence of the Turkish Governor, but was recaptured by the Zaidis 20 years later. A strengthened Turkish force under Sinan Pasha retook the city and some stability returned until the arrival of a great Yemeni folk hero, al-Qasim ibn Mohammed – known as **Qasim the Great,** who plotted the downfall of the Turks in Yemen.

A thousand years of Islam was celebrated by the rise of this new Zaidi imam, who rallied the tribes of the north and fought glorious battles against the Turks from his mountain stronghold of Shahara. The long campaign was continued after his death in 1620 by his son Imam Mu'ayyid, who besieged Sana'a for three years. By 1635 all the Turks had been expelled, even from the Tihama, and Sana'a slipped into a peaceful existence. By the seventeenth century all the trade was concentrated on Mokha and the Tihama, while the imams ruled serenely from Sana'a, content to achieve isolation and peace.

A century and a half of inactivity led to instability and insurrection. The Turks had always wanted to re-establish themselves and took the opportunity to occupy the Tihama. In 1849 the weakened imam was forced into a one-sided agreement which allowed Turkish soldiers to be stationed in Sana'a. Half the country's revenue went annually to Constantinople. The locals rose up against such conditions and slaughtered almost 1,000 troops. Not surprisingly the Turkish reprisal was fierce and bloody: petty leaders fought amongst themselves; the city was looted, plundered and racked by poverty and disease.

Turks finally expelled

Ironically it was the Turks who were invited by the elders of Sana'a to restore peace amongst the warring tribal factions. But 20 years of Turkish plunder and oppression was enough to unite the tribes under Imam al-Mansur Hamid ad-Din, who led a war of independence. The beleaguered city was besieged several times as invader and defender both gained the advantage. Imam al-Mansur died in 1904 and was replaced by his son Yahya, who continued the aggression at the expense of Sana'a. In 1911 an agreement was reached whereby the Turks only controlled the Tihama, but by then Turkish power was diminishing and had totally disappeared by the end of the First World War.

The rule of the Imams

Imam Yahya ruled from Sana'a, adopting isolationist and independent policies for over 30 years until his assassination in 1948. The old city was looted as a reprisal by tribal forces supporting his son and successor, Imam Ahmed, who then established his new capital in Ta'iz.

Capital of the new republic

During the civil war following the revolution, Sana'a suffered a 70 day siege when the royalists unsuccessfully tried to regain the city in 1967-8. With the proclamation of the YAR, Sana'a became the capital again, its importance reinforced when it became capital of the unified Yemen in 1990. There has been a rapid expansion of the city over the last 30 years as Sana'a tries to catch up with the twentieth century, but international concern over its unique heritage has placed the old city under the protection of United Nations agencies to minimise the damage done to it in the process. During the May 1994 conflict, the city received several scud missile direct hits from southern forces, but none in the Old City.

Garden and houses in the Old City, Sana'a.

MUSEUMS

National Museum

Not to be missed

Before touring the country it is a good idea to visit the National Museum, situated 100m north of Tahrir Square, just past al-Mutawakil Mosque. The tall circular tower beside the road was one of the secure places were prisoners were held during the rule of the imams. At one time, Imam Yahya even had three of his own sons locked up – one here, and two in the citadel!

The museum is open 8.30–13.00 and 15.00–17.00

Saturday–Wednesday and 8.30–12.00 Thursday; it is closed Friday. Entry is 10 YR and cameras and bags are not allowed. The building is called Dar as-Sa'ada ('House of Good Fortune'); it dates from the 1930s, and was one of the later imamic palaces.

First impressions   On the **ground floor,** immediately upon entering the building, you are faced by the giant bronze statues of the Himyar Kings Damar Alay Yuhabirr and his son and successor Tharan. Sections of these impressive 2.4m high figures were found in 1931 at Nakhlat al-Hamra, the Himyar palace site east of Ma'bar, halfway between Sana'a and Dhamar. In 1977 the pieces were taken to Mainz in Germany, where restoration work was carried out, and they were returned five years later as complete figures.

Their unusual Roman appearance is explained by the fact that they were indeed made by a Roman called Phokas, working under the supervision of a southern Arabian master. The name of Phokas is inscribed in Greek (which was normal for the eastern part of the Roman Empire) on the left knee of the younger king, with a carving of a goat behind the knee. Reading from right to left in southern Arabian script across the chests of both figures, other inscriptions tell us who they represent and they have been dated to between 270 and 310 AD.

Important Yemeni information   Information on the ground floor is in German and Arabic, but in English and Arabic on the **first floor.** Here are details of the pre-Islamic history of Marib, Sirwah and Dhafar, as well as a model of the temple of as-Sawda in Wadi al-Jawf. Interesting maps show Neolithic, Palaeolithic and Bronze Age sites. Discovered at the Bilqis Temple at Marib in 1952, the famous eighth century BC bronze statue of the Sabaean prince Ma'adi Karib takes pride of place. His *thuma* (a special type of jambia reserved for holy men) can be seen tucked into his belt. There are also examples of the precious trading commodities before burning: frankincense is similar to rounded globules of alabaster; myrrh looks like shattered bits of toffee; and incense is like dark crystallised Kendal mint cake!

The **second floor** is dedicated to Islam in Yemen, with examples of script and carvings. There is a large display of armour through the ages, coins and manuscripts. If you intend to visit Rada'a there are details of the restoration of the al-Ameriya Mosque, which was begun in 1984.

Lifestyles from around the country   The **third floor** has life-size displays of craft work and industry. Agricultural methods, fishing techniques, weaving, jewellery and pottery-making are shown in relation to the area in which they appear. There are also models of the different types of houses seen around the country.

Military Museum

This is well worth a visit, even if just for the curiosity of what is considered to be military. The museum is fronted by two huge howitzers and a torpedo, where Gamal Abdul Nasser Street enters Tahrir Square. Entry is 10YR and you have to pay 10YR to use your camera. It is open 9.00–12.00 and 16.00–20.00 every day except Friday and the last Thursday of the month.

The build up and execution of the revolution

Various halls tell the story of military activity through the centuries leading up to the revolution, with displays of guns, shells, uniforms and medals, including a peculiar Skoda camel-mounted cannon – imagine the recoil! There are gruesome photographs of executions during various uprisings against the Imam and examples of instruments of torture.

Amongst all these are some **non-military objects** like ancient inscribed blocks, tombstones, horse-drawn carriages and a Ford Super Deluxe car. There is even a set of rusty wheels from the ill-fated Turkish railway at Hodeidah, with pictures of the wrecked train also. Just when you think it is all over, the exit is through the back garden which contains two bullet-ridden cadillacs belonging to the Imam – note the nine thicknesses of glass in the windows! There is also a complete Mig 17 which played a part in the 70-day siege of 1967.

Old University Museum

On the edge of al-Qa, the old Jewish quarter, is the old university complex. The archaeology department has a small museum open to the public daily 8.00–13.00 except Friday. Entry is free but no cameras are allowed. To find the right building, ask any of the students for the 'mummy' – this refers to the collection of mummified figures.

The entrance passage is a line of pictures of almost every possible type of minaret to be found in the country. Not many tourists come here and you might have to get the key for the mummy room from Dr Abdul Ghalib himself.

Mummification as an ancient art

The **mummies** are in a good state of preservation, and are displayed with funerary items such as necklaces, leather shoes and wrappings which compare well with their ancient Egyptian counterparts. The bodies are modestly displayed with only the heads, hands and feet showing. They were found at a variety of sites around Sana'a including Mahweet, Shibam al-Gharas (on the way to Marib) and Thulla. There are also some coins and alabaster heads.

Links with religion and the past crop up all over the place, such as in the motto of the university. When the

Prophet Mohammed received Abu Musa bin Ash'ari of Zabid, he is reported to have responded to the profound understanding of the Yemeni visitor by saying, "Faith is of the Yemen and wisdom is Yemeni".

OLD CITY WALK

This 2–3-hour walk, from Tahrir Square to Bab al-Yemen, is not intended to be a definitive tour of the Old City, but it should establish the main points of interest. It should also give you the orientation to delve around on your own, in what is a truly unique area of world architecture, containing 14,000 amazing **tower houses.** The walls of Sana'a used to contain as much to the west of present day Tahrir Square as it did to the east, but it is the tower houses of the eastern section that are the real gems today. As a general guide for orientation, the *saila* (dry riverbed) runs south-north. To go east, head for Jebel Nuqum, the mountain that towers above the city and is distinguished by the flat Turkish fortifications on the summit (out of bounds – military!).

From the tank on the plinth in Tahrir Square, cross Ali Abdul Mogni Street and head east down the pedestrianised **Bab as-Sabah Street.** This gives a good idea of what to expect in the old suq with many shops and traders selling *qat*, food and meat all spilling out into the street. At the end is the *saila*, which concentrates the seasonal floodwaters between the newer and older

A city unique in the world

Street traders and everyday life

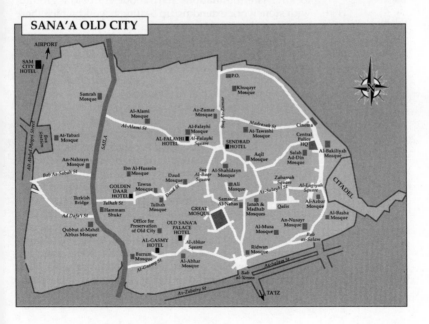

SANA'A OLD CITY

sections of town. On the left is the small an-Nahrayn Mosque just poking above the shops.

Turn right and cross the *saila* by the old Turkish stone bridge. Looking south from the bridge there is a fine view of the **Qubbat al-Mahdi Abbas Mosque** to the right.

Turkish baths, before the Turks

Closer on the left is the **Hamman Shukr** bath-house. This is one of the three baths that can be dated to before the Ottoman occupation and hence should not be referred to as Turkish baths. Men and women use the *hammams* on alternate days, but it's never too far to the next one. A sweat and scrub down is great value and an invigorating experience.

Continue eastwards along Tulhah Street until you see **Miqshamat al-Kheraz Garden** on the left. One of the features of the old city is the number of walled gardens *miqshamas* – often hidden away from sight in sunken areas. This is due to the earth being taken to build the nearby houses. These gardens are owned by the religious *waqf* foundations, and all produce is sold to the locals or in the *suq*, with the proceeds going to the mosques. The palm trees and greenery add much-needed colour to the dusty surroundings.

Hidden gardens

By studying the houses across the garden, you get a good idea of their **construction** and **use.** The primary building materials are clay derivatives and stone, decorated by gypsum plaster (plaster of Paris) and water-proofed by lime whitewash – all materials which occur locally. The foundations start about 1m below ground, with stonework extending up 3–10m, beyond which there is exposed brickwork.

Solid staircases built on solid foundations

These houses – up to nine storeys – derive their main strength from the massive **central stone staircase** as well as the crosswalls on each level. For stability the thickness of the walls decreases as they rise, but amazingly it seldom exceeds 70cm at ground level. Rubble is used as a core between the smooth external and the rougher internal facing stones.

Traditionally the **ground floor** accommodates the animals and the **first floor** is used for storing grain, fruit and vegetables. Upper floors are made of tree trunk beams with the gaps filled with bundles of sticks. This is then covered with earth and smoothed off with stone slabs or plaster. A band of decorative brickwork separates the stone and brick levels, usually in a zigzag design.

The first **living level** contains the family rooms, and above this is the *diwan*, a large parlour for special family occasions such as weddings and births. Next come the kitchen, the women's room and more living rooms. Each higher floor has a bathroom with a long drop toilet down to ground level.

The **roof terrace** often has a protruding *mashrabiya* (from *sharab*, 'to drink'), which keeps water cool and fresh by evaporating surface water from earthenware jars. A similar projecting window box, called a *shubbak*, allows the women of the house to observe who is at the front door without themselves being seen. Sometimes a long cord can open the front door latch from many storeys up.

The *mafraj* is the pinnacle of Yemeni building and decoration

Finally there is the ***mafraj***, the most decorated room in the house, perched on top. Here guests are welcomed, *qat* is chewed and *mada'ah* pipes are smoked, all in the relaxed atmosphere of fresh air circulating through the open windows. The naturally air-cooled room is kept at temperatures much more tolerable than outside. The word *mafraj* has it's roots in *faraja*, meaning 'to dispel grief or anxiety', also *tafarraja* – 'to look upon something'.

Window shapes play a large part in the decoration of a house, both inside and out. The main shuttered windows are fairly low, allowing people to sit and look out. Above these are the fanlights which enhance the exterior design and give the interior warmth. These arched, semi-circular and round windows used to be filled with thin alabaster sheets, which were quarried locally. It was very difficult to cut such large sheets for these *qamariyah* windows, so a unique design was created made of small segments held together with plaster. Over the last 200 years these stucco *takhreem* windows have tended to use coloured Venetian glass, but now it's all coloured plastic.

The house that separates the garden from the Bustan Dalal Orchard further along is **Dar al-Dhahabi,** one of the few remaining examples of a Turkish style villa. It is unusual in having the *mafraj* on the ground floor, opening onto a courtyard. A unique feature is the central well-ramp which runs from the back of the house to the front. It used to fill a small *sabil* (public drinking supply) on the street and also watered the now abandoned orchard. The house and orchard are among the conservation projects of the General Organisation for the Protection of the Historic Cities of the Yemen GOPHCY), which is funded by UNDP and UNESCO. It is intended to use Dar al-Dhahabi as a women's vocational training centre and kindergarten, with Bustan Dalal as a playground and rose garden – in the past, Sana'a was famous for its roses.

Protecting old buildings is a priority

The next building on the left is the Golden Daar Hotel and further left down the same street can be seen the minaret of the Ibn al-Hussein Mosque. Continuing along Tulhah Street, straight ahead is the small **al-Tawus Mosque** on the left. Little of it can be seen from the street, and it is in a poor state of preservation. It is one of the oldest mosques in the Yemen, dating from about 725 AD and has a *sabil* built into the wall, with a small house built over the ablution block. Around the bend is **Qubbat Tulhah Mosque** to the right, whose minaret has unusual proportions. The stonework base is too high for such a squat tower but it does have some beautiful decoration. It dates from around 1620 AD, and the large Ottoman style dome with corner turrets has some fine designs.

Ahead and left, down a narrow alley called Daud Street, past the Taj Talha Hotel, is the minaret of the Daud Mosque. Opposite the hotel are two houses on the left. Look carefully at the tops of the stonework bases, about 10m off the ground, and you can see small metal snakes attached to the corners of the houses. These are good luck symbols protecting the building from evil, an idea possibly taken from an old legend that no snake could enter the city gates and survive.

Snakes bring good luck

The alley leads into the small square **Suq al-Baqr,** the geographical centre of the old city, where there is another pre-Turkish bath, Hammam Mahmud, just to the north. Turn right at Attaefie Drug Store and note the unusual house immediately on the right. This is completely built in stone with the intricate use of light and dark blocks, and is held together by a thin mortar. Compare this with the house next door, which is built on much more traditional lines using stone only for the lower floors. Note the exposed wooden beams, sometimes of apricot wood, which is used for its hardness and durability. You will usually not recognise these beams, as they are normally whitewashed for protection against the weather.

The circular fanlights made of brick above the shuttered windows indicate older houses. As I have said, these were originally fitted with thin alabaster sheeting. They are usually single rondels but here they are in a double circle form. Continue to the collapsed house, which shows the extensive use of wood in the exposed structure. Turn left, then first right and first left around some small shops and enter the Suq al-Najjarin ('wooden articles').

The *suq* has changed much over the centuries … in some ways

Suq al-Milh ('salt market') is the name given to the general *suq* area, but within this there used to be 40 smaller *suqs*, each dealing in specific items. Some of these have now changed commodities or disappeared completely. Pass through the arch and look up at the wooden beam and stick construction of the arch roof, as used in house ceilings. You are now facing the northern wall of the **Great** or **Friday Mosque** (al-Jama al-Kabir).

From here we will turn left into the *suq* proper, but it is worth wandering around the outside of the mosque, which is built in the Kufic style of four roofed galleries around a central courtyard. Halfway along the northern wall you can see the indentation of the central *mihrab* and several doorways now blocked off. Look carefully at the two carved stones on either side of the farthest blocked doorway. They depict a pair of doves and are probably taken from the Qalis (see below). If you walk down the eastern wall you can usually catch a glimpse through the doorways before being ushered on.

The first mosque in the Yemen

This mosque was built according to instructions from the Prophet Mohammed himself and thus claims to be the oldest in the Yemen, but very little of the original building remains. For its construction pre-cut blocks were taken from nearby buildings such as the Ghumdan Palace (the mosque is said to have been built in the garden of the palace), the Axumite cathedral, the Qalis, and even Sabaean temples. Many of the columns, capitals and bases supporting the flat roof are of pre-Islamic origin.

It was extensively enlarged around 710 and again after flooding in 878. Much building was carried out in the tenth century and beautiful ceilings were added by Queen Arwa in the eleventh (see Ibb). The two uniden-tical and asymmetrical minarets were extensively rebuilt in the thirteenth century, when the ablution area was added. The library was not built until 1936, by Imam Yahya. A great discovery was made in the early 1970's when a vast collection of ancient manuscripts was found in a suspended ceiling during repairs. Some date from the first century of Islam and now constitute an important source of early Yemeni Koranic calligraphy, including some unique illuminated frontispiece volumes. Scripted at a time of early Koranic experimentation, holy writings should never be destroyed and so they were 'buried' in the mosque.

Old manuscripts discovered

The mosque is unique in possessing a central *kaaba* (the only other is at Mecca). You can sometimes see a corner of its black and white striped blocks through an open doorway. From the south-eastern corner you can get the best, but still not very good, view of the minarets. Before you return to the north-eastern corner, there is a small hill on the right, now hidden by modern buildings, which is possibly the site of the Ghumdan Palace.

Into the *suq* proper

Continuing eastwards the pathway narrows past pottery and *jambia* belt traders, to enter the wider **Suq al-Inab.** On the left-hand corner is one of the places being restored – the Samsarat al-Mansuriyah, an eighteenth century caravanserai or *khan*. Each of the 40 *suqs* used to have its own *samsarat* to act as warehouse for the goods and to provide shelter and accommodation for the overland traders. Less than half of these now remain, although some are still being used, and one of the prior-ities of the restoration process is to rebuild these great buildings. This particular project has been financed by Germany and the building is the new National Arts and Handicraft Centre.

THE *SUQ* TRADE

Each trade has its own association which controls bulk supplies and in effect guarantees competitive equality. The associations elect one member to the Chamber of Commerce, a body which regulates foreign merchandise and levies taxes. They elect the **Sheikh al-Layl** – literally 'headman of the night' – a highly prestigious position. It is his responsibility to ensure that all goods are safe throughout the night, when many traders leave their goods piled up, protected only by sheets. He must therefore be trustworthy and financially secure in order to make good any losses of goods under his protection. His night watchmen also work as porters through the day, transporting goods from the *samsarat* to the shop. Only free tribesmen capable of supplying a guarantor can become such porters and guards.

Narrow street crammed with goods

The route now enters the Suq al-Henna, specialising in henna (see Women) and tobacco. On the left are the narrow alleys of the Suq al-Tawra, which sells general goods. 80m past the al-Mansuriyah turn slightly left (turning right would bring you quickly to the Bab al-Yemen) and follow the main path east into the shoe *Suq*. On the right are the twin mosques of Janah and Madhab, sharing one minaret. This tower is unusual in not having a balcony for the muezzin, who had to yell through a set of windows instead. On the left is the chaos of the Suq al-Hubz, now referred to simply as the Suq al-Milh. This is the Old City's equivalent of fast food, where fish, eggs, bread, kebabs and fruit drinks are served for immediate consumption – all at great value.

Carry on up as-Sulayhi Street and turn right down a side alley just before the slight kink in the road. After 50m enter a small square which used to be at the centre of the old Persian Quarter. Looking back into the square, you will notice the animal horns adorning the tops of the houses, another good luck symbol. You are now standing at the south-western corner of what used to be the site of **Site of the old cathedral** the old Axumite cathedral, the **Qalis**. This square is the remnant of the open area fronting the main door of the Qalis. The cathedral was apparently made from precious woods, gold, silver and marble, and is thought to have followed the outline of the present-day houses on the left. Turn left and walk east along the southern edge of where this magnificent cathedral once stood.

Following the Axumite conquest of southern Arabia in the sixth century, Sana'a became the capital and its new cathedral was a place of pilgrimage for Arab Christians. The block measures roughly 80m x 25m, with a circular walled pit at the eastern end, the site of the crypt. This was covered by a large dome that contained a pulpit of ebony and ivory, with gold and silver crosses, illuminat-

'The Major.'

Local woman in Wadi Hadramaut.

Camel-trader tribesman near Bayhan.

Women at gate, Thulla.

Southern native, near Lahej.

ed by a huge sheet of thin alabaster set in the wall. Walk around the walled pit and look in at the sunken swamp.

From the pit, return north to as-Sulayhi Street and turn right. After 50m you can just make out another snake design on the corner of the first turning left, this one carved on a single block about 5m off the ground. Continue into al-Lagiyah Square. Ahead is the **Qasr as-Silah** citadel, the oldest part of the city. The only excavations allowed in Sana'a have been here at Beit al-Ambasah and it is understood that this was the site of a Sabaean fortress. The history of the site might date back to the Queen of Sheba, as it controls the narrowest point of the plain where two main trading routes crossed.

The Citadel is still well protected

The word Sana'a means 'the fortified one', and the name could date from this time. Over the centuries successive occupiers of this strategic site have built and reinforced the buildings. The last were the Turks, who constructed massive defences less than 100 years ago. It is still in the hands of the military today – and thus out of bounds – so be careful where you point your camera or the guards will soon be over. However, it is hoped that the area will be handed over to GOPHCY, and that a serious study of the hidden layers will be made and the whole site become a museum.

Sights of old Constantinople

Turn left and walk up the busy al-Lagiyah Street towards the impressive **al-Bakiliyah Mosque** across the road. This fine building was erected by the Ottoman Governor Hassan Pasha in 1597. It was named after the Governor's friend, who died here and was eventually buried in the corner of the mosque. It is beautifully built in the metropolitan style of Constantinople, but much smaller. It was restored during the second Turkish occupation as part of the general improvements of all buildings between the citadel and Bab Shu'ab, making this the fashionable quarter with shops, cafes and tree-lined avenues. Unlike the mosques in the crowded streets, you can stand back and admire this one from a distance and compare it with its picture on the 10 YR notes.

Returning back into the maze of alleys

Twenty metres beyond the al-Bakiliyah Mosque, turn first left after the Central Police Headquarters down a lane with a Pepsi sign on the corner, then bear left after 80m. Follow the winding alleyways until you pass under an old archway. Swing left and after 25m look back to get a good view of the tilting minaret of the Salah ad-Din Mosque. Built of baked brick, decorated with gypsum and standing on a square base, this is a typical example of a unique Sanani minaret.

Follow the main street for about two minutes back towards the *suq*.

At the T junction, the minaret of Janah and Madhab

Minaret to topple over

can again be seen to the left beyond the fast food, but turn right and follow the curved wall towards the **AqiI Mosque,** whose minaret tilts precariously over the Suq al-Aqil area. This mosque was ruined as early as the sixteenth century, but rebuilt in ancient form by the son of Imam Sharaf ad-Din in 1540. The minaret was added by Amir Iskander al-Kurdi in 1560, but now needs some urgent work to its foundations. Turn right into a fabric *suq* where every type and style of women's veil can be found.

Some gates have disappeared

Follow the paved road until you reach Suq az-Zumar Street. We will turn left here, but it is worth going a few metres to the right first to look down this wide street full of general traders, which stretches all the way to Bab Shu'ab (now dismantled). The change in Sana'a has been incredible when you think that until 1962 all the Old City gates were still in place and closed every night at 20.00 to protect the town.

Just on the right is the Sendbad Hotel in a fine old tower house known as **Beit Abu Taleb.** The courtyard is a good place to take refreshments and with luck the staff may even take you up to the *mafraj*. Turn left and head towards **al-Shahidayn Mosque** along a newly paved street. Note the new black and white stone building with shops to the right. Keep the mosque to your left, and notice the small shops making and selling *makhbezah*, the mushroom-shaped utensils used for placing flat dough onto the inner wall of hot *tannur* ovens. This is the Suq Harat al-Madar.

The story of the mosque is intriguing. Al-Shahidayn means 'the two martyrs', and relates to an incident around 660, in the very early years of Islam. The incoming Umayyid Governor murdered the two infant sons of the Alid Governor in a small nearby prayer hall called the Musallat al-Mansi. The mosque is thought to have been built on the site of a *hammam* which was used to store the bodies. A tomb inside the entrance to the mosque garden is said to be that of the murderer himself. Many pre-Islamic stones and columns were used in the mosque's construction and still remain, despite extensive rebuiding at the turn of the century. The minaret is a late addition dating to approximately 1885, with the same patterned brick as many earlier ones. The brick minarets resemble those of ancient Persia and Central Asia.

Animal sanctuary

Heading uphill away from the mosque, turn first left and then immediately bear right at the *sabil*, up a steep rough path into an open area. What you are now entering is a curiosity of Sana'a. The **Suq al-Bahim,** also known as Suq al-Arj, is where old, sick and deformed donkeys are cared for at the expense of the local traders. Go diago-

Mosques of the Old City.

nally right towards the sound of metal beating and enter the extremely narrow alleys of the blacksmiths' quarter.

Beating metalwork

This trade has been practised for over 1,000 years in much the same way as you see it now, in small cramped workshops with hardly room to swing a hammer, sparks flying everywhere, amid a deafening noise. The workmen help each other with the heavy tasks of beating hot metal into fittings for windows and doors, agricultural tools and *jambia* blades. Conditions are tough, with local demand suffering from cheap modern imports, and help is needed if this trade is to continue into the next century.

An Aladdin's cave

Pass straight ahead and you will drop into the **Suq al-Haddadin** ('iron articles'), an Aladdin's cave of shining metalwork, which was destroyed by fire in November 1992. The shops which escaped are almost hidden behind piles of pots, pans and glistening cooking utensils, decorated by intricate sieves and draped with lengths of chain. Exit at the opposite corner into the main street. The small minaret to the left belongs to the Ali Mosque, which dates from the twelfth century and is in need of restoration. This is the mosque said to stand on the site of a house visited by the Prophet's son-in-law Ali bin Abu Taleb (see Sana'a History).

Behind are the *suqs* specialising in *mada'ah* (water pipes), ropes and leather. Turn right and 50m ahead is the Samsarat al-Mansuriyah on the right hand side. This area is generally known as Suq al-Halaqah, famous for tin and iron articles. However, if you turn left under an over-hanging watchtower decorated with wooden horns you will enter the Suq al-Bazz, a street full of money changers.

The imposing looking building to the left is the ruined **Samsarat Mohammed bin al-Hassan bin al-Qasim,** which dates from the seventeenth century. Named after a renowned Amir, this vast building was used as a deposit for cash. It was known as the Dar al-Mal ('House of Money') at a time when there was no other form of banking system in the country. Despite its heavy fortifications – including eight domed watchtowers – it was attacked and looted in 1948 by tribesmen paid by Imam Ahmed, as a reprisal for the assassination of his father, Imam Yahya. The building is now in a dangerous state and the roof has collapsed, but the long term plan is to re-establish it as the only bank inside the Old City, possibly with Swiss backing.

A building full of money

At the end of this street is the compact Suq al-Zabid, which specialises in raisins and seeds. Carry straight ahead into the Suq al-Hulba wal-Milh and you will be assaulted by the aroma of spices and cereals stacked to the roof. Turn left at the end and then first right. Almost opposite is the low gateway to the **Samsarat al-Mizan,** the 'caravanserai of the scales' – which can be seen from the street. All goods came here for weighing to determine the customs duty, and were then taken to the respective *suqs* and *semasir* (plural of *samsarat).* Today the scales are still used to weigh sacks of coffee beans and, if you ask the headman nicely, the occasional tourist. Above the amazingly uneven floor are the old living quarters.

Weighing it all up

Leaving the scales, turn left past the *qat* sellers and then first left into the Suq al-Saman. This becomes the Suq al-Mukhlas and contains many gold and silver shops. Set back in a corner to the left are more huge scales. Turn left at the end, past menswear and enter a small square with rows of *jambia* makers and sellers. We will be passing up this line of traders, but it is worth quickly turning right as if going back down to the Aqil Mosque. Twenty metres on the right are the large wooden gates and entrance to the **Samsarat al-Jumruk,** recently restored, where merchants still deal in huge sackfuls of dried fruit. It is sometimes possible to climb the steps behind the metal gates to get an elevated view of the *samsarat* and also to see some of the small stores, which were previously used as temporary accommodation. Return to the *jambia* sellers, pass them and turn left into the Suq al-Qishr ('coffee husks').

Gold, silver and jambias

The route now leads through the heart of the *suq* all the way to the Bab al-Yemen. Pass the spice dealers and continue to the end of the Suq al-Habb. Turn right and then first left, crossing an earlier route. Just on the right is the newly restored **Samsarat al-Nahas,** now the National Centre for the Development of Handicrafts. This is a good place for local souvenirs; almost all the products are made by local artisans with natural materials. It is open from 9.00–12.00 and 15.00–18.00 Saturday–Wednesday, 9.00–12.00 Thursday, but closed on Friday.

Outlet for artists

If you climb up to the third floor, Gallery No. 1 has a small studio selling paintings by local artists as well as the excellent prints of Fuad al-Futaih. The staff may let you have the key to go onto the roof for a superb *muezzin's* view over the *suqs*. The ancient core of the *suq* can be seen bounded by the four old mosques of Ali (with the stubby minaret), al-Shahidayn, Aqil and the double Janah and Madhab just below you.

Chaos at the main gate

Back in the main alley, turn right and pass the money changers and general traders. Just before you reach the **Bab al-Yemen** turn right at a small square and slightly double back up a slope to see an old camel driven sesame mill low down in a basement on the left. Upon entering the square in front of the Bab, have a quick look at the minaretless Ridwan Mosque on the left corner. This busy square is usually packed with merchants selling all types of useful objects.

By now you could probably do with a drink and there are several small *chai* shops inside the Bab, or you can go through the gateway and climb some rickety steps on the right to a narrow balcony and have *chai* while watching the chaos below. From here, little minibuses run down az-Zubeiry Street, passing along the restored sections of city wall to the *saila*.

Returning by another route

However if you want to walk back to Ali Abdul Mogni Street by a different route, but still inside the Old City, head down the street with the Dar Saam Tourist sign on the wall. This leads to al-Abhar Square, which contains the Old Sana'a Palace Hotel, with a central plaque commemorating the restoration work. Continue west past al-Abhar Mosque on the left and down al-Gasmy Street to the Al-Gasmy Palace Hotel and Restaurant. Continue past the Miqshamat al-Gasmy Garden on the right to overlook the *saila* at the end. From here you can reach az-Zubeiry Street by going up the *saila*, or walk back down to the white-domed Qubbat al-Mahdi Abbas Mosque. The small arched shops in front are the old lapidary shops. Turn left up ad-Dafai Street, passing the office of the Sultan's Palace Hotel and many more gold and silver shops. The road enters Tahrir Square 20m from where you started.

ENVIRONS OF SANA'A

Plenty of choice for short trips

Within an hour's drive of the capital there are medieval villages and superb natural sights. Beit Baws, Hadda, ar-Rawdah, Wadi Dhahr, Thulla, Shibam-Kawkaban, al-Huqqa, Jihanah, Jebel Marmar and even the highest peak Jebel Nabi Shu'ayb, are all within easy reach of Sana'a, making ideal half- and one-day trips. Many of these will be incorporated in group tour itineraries to other destinations. Jebel Marmar is described on the way to Marib, and Jebel Nabi Shu'ayb on the way to Manakha.

SANA'A ENVIRONS

Beit Baws

This small village is not on the way to anywhere and needs to be visited separately. Hidden from the Sana'a plain by a small range of hills, it is a fascinating mountain village, too often overlooked by tourists. It lies about 7km to the south-west of the city, beyond the new suburb of Hadda, and can be reached by two routes. Head up Hadda Road beyond the Ring Road and turn left just past the Bella Venezia restaurant towards Hadda New Town (*Hadda Medina*). Pass through the modern housing and the track will meet up with the other route – a continuation of the Old Airport Road. The main red dirt road swings back south to strike the Ta'iz road, but you must turn right for the old village of Beit Baws seen on top of a rocky outcrop.

Abandoned through lack of water

The new village has grown up around the base of the outcrop, but it is the old deserted higher village that is of most interest. Climb up through the houses (probably accompanied by a hundred yelling children) onto an expanse of cactus-covered rocks. At the base of the outcrop, inspect the smooth rocks for old pre-Islamic inscriptions. The small houses balance precariously on the clifftop and seem impossible to reach, but you can get to them through a gateway around the back, overlooking a large wild fig tree and cistern.

A few people still live here, but most have moved to the newer houses below, which are served by a better water supply. Old Himyar inscribed blocks have been reused in the construction of some of the houses, and with care it is possible to clamber around the recently abandoned properties just to see how cramped living conditions really are. There are good views over the southern end of the Sana'a Plain towards Wa'lan, and across a small valley to the earlier dwellings cut into rock overhangs, which used to house the Jewish population until the late 1940s.

Hadda

Instead of going straight back to the city, return to the Hadda Road and continue into the foothills of Hadda Mountain beyond the Hadda Hotel. The road winds gently uphill to Hadda village, and becomes a pleasant walking track through small orchards of apricot, walnut and almond trees. There are many ruined buildings including an old Turkish watermill and a mosque to poke around. The area is at its best at the beginning of the year when the almond trees are in full blossom. Climbing through the small village of al-Ain and upwards above the tree line, you arrive at a series of mines and quarries which look as though they should be out of bounds – and probably are. Similar mining activity can be seen behind the Hadda Hotel and the Bella Venezia, and I have been marched away from it at gun point! From al-Ain it is possible to walk along the edge of the hillside through as-Senna and Beit Zabatan to Beit Baws in about an hour.

Suburban walking

Ar-Rawdah

The name of this village means 'garden meadow' and it used to be a peaceful resort for many of the imams. Nowadays it lies just to the east of the international airport, and is often 'buzzed' by low flying military jets. The **Rawdah Palace Hotel** is one of many finely decorated houses, formerly a five-storey palace in quiet gardens with a swimming pool. Even if you are just passing, try to get up onto the roof for a great view over the town and surrounding countryside, which is famous for its sweet grapes.

Down the road from the Palace is the mosque of Ahmed ibn al-Qasim, Imam of the Yemen for five years from 1676, and grandson of the famous Qasim the Great who defeated the Turks earlier the same century. From the roof of the Palace you can see the central square courtyard of the mosque, surrounded by four galleries. The best day to visit Ar-Rawdah is Sunday, when the weekly market turns this otherwise sleepy suburb into a bustling mass of buying and selling.

Best weekly market near Sana'a

Wadi Dhahr–Thulla–Shibam–Kawkaban

Six kilometres north-west of the Ring Road, past the Kuwait Hospital, is the suburb of Shamlan, where they produce bottled mineral water. The main road goes left to Shibam and Thulla, but if you go straight ahead you will quickly reach the look out positions over **Wadi Dhahr.** As a first impression on your first day in the Yemen, this is an incredible sight; seeing it at the end of a tour, you will be a bit blasé. From the clifftops you can look across to the world famous Dar al-Hajar ('Rock Palace').

Friday is a good day to join the locals

If you can arrange to visit this point between about 10.00 and 12.00 on a Friday, you will not be disappointed. Over the last few years a tradition has developed for **wedding groups** to assemble here as part of the final celebrations. Fleets of beribboned cars carry all the male guests to a stretch of rough ground, where there is impromptu singing and dancing to a simple three- or four-piece band. Old men show off their agility and encourage the younger ones to get up, with group dancing in circles and lines, glistening *jambias* waving around their heads.

Every now and then there will be a deafening crack of a rifle or machine gun as it is fired against the rock face across a small ravine. The groom – resplendent in beautiful clothes with a ceremonial sword or the family Kalashnikov – is surrounded by relatives and well-wishers. Often he will have fresh sprigs of basil tucked into his headwear. Different groups try to outdo each other with noise and movement, and it is difficult to tell which people belong to which party.

These are the weddings of the wealthy Sanani families, who are proud to show off their position. Expensive 4x4s and luxury Mercedes and BMWs bounce along the tracks, horns blasting, in a continuous stream of vehicles in and out of the site. In such a festive atmosphere the participants are usually more than happy to pose for photographs in their Friday best.

A line of *nubas*, fortified towers overlooking the wadi, indicate that this narrow fertile basin has been protected for thousands of years. You can take a vehicle down the road into the wadi, or clamber down the gully just to the right, emerging in the fields at the bottom. A dirt track runs the length of the wadi up the *saila* and it is possible to wind around to the head of the valley through dense plantations lying below splendid vertical walls of eroded rocks, to emerge at the village of Beit Na'am on the road to Shibam. **Dar al-Hajar** itself suddenly looms up against the mountain backdrop, and moving closer you can see the palace stark against the blue sky. This is definitely worth a few photographs from different positions and settings.

The most famous building in the country

The palace itself only dates back to the 1930s, and was built for Imam Yahya, but it is clear that a settlement of some sort has been on the site for many centuries as a roughly cut well reaches down to secure a water supply.

Entry to the house and grounds is at the discretion of the guardian, who tends not to be around on Fridays or at lunch times. For years the palace has been on the verge of becoming some form of hotel or museum, but until then a small tip should get you in to see the well, storerooms, passageways, beautifully decorated rooms and stunning view from the roof – but do not go too close to the unprotected edge.

Behind the palace is a school; beyond that the village of **Qaryat al-Qabil**. The houses huddle around the base of steep cliffs containing old cave dwellings, topped by a ruined fortress. Enter the village, leave it through the cemetery and cross the fields to a small rock outcrop. Behind some metal gates are dozens of rock carvings on a smooth rockface, some of them possibly dating back to 4000 BC. Many are difficult to distinguish, as they are badly worn and overlap each other, but the larger figures of mountain goats can be seen. The chiselled outline of a man is modern graffiti. Return to Qaryat al-Qabil, from where a tarmac road leads 3km out of the wadi onto the road to Sadah. The hills around this area are good for easy walking, as you can never go too far astray, they are all within an hour of Sana'a.

Rock carvings testify to ancient habitation

Back above Wadi Dhahr at the Shamlan turning, take the main road west towards Shibam-Kawkaban through the village of Dhola'a, which contains the house of the unpopular former YAR president Ahmed ibn Hussein al-Ghashmi, who was assassinated in June 1978 by a suitcase bomb delivered by a PDRY envoy. Seven kilometres after climbing out of the Sana'a Plain, you come to Beit Na'am, a village with a crowded Wednesday market, from where it is possible to do some rough walking back down to Wadi Dhahr. Just beyond is a good view of al-Qurza hill village, built into a volcanic cone about 1km away on the right behind a petrol station, with Jebel Tin (and its telecommunications mast) in the far distance. The road to Sadah runs at the foot of Jebel Tin, and a very rough 4x4 track reaches it from here.

Crossing a lava-strewn rockscape

The massif rising up to the left on the horizon includes Jebel Nabi Shu'ayb. The small village of Hajar Saeed lies in a fertile shallow wadi further along on the left. Just before the road to Thulla splits away, there is a fine example of a single storey travellers' rest house on the right built around old stone pillars and arches. These rest houses were built at convenient sites between the main towns, and travellers of old could find shelter and safety there.

Thulla

Thirty-two kilometres from Shamlan and just before Shibam, a signpost indicates the road towards Thulla, which crosses a flat plain and rises up to the village. Get out just beyond a metal archway – when you can see the old walls to the left – and walk up to the southern gateway. This ancient town, where one of the mummies at Sana'a University Museum was found, is the most perfect example of the use of local stone and rock. Throughout the day, sunlight changes the mood of the town from stark brightness to mellow shades. Narrow alleys slither between the tall buildings, slowly rising towards the cliff face. There are pre-Islamic inscriptions and carvings.

The most aesthetic village

The **fortifications** above the town, initially dating from the Himyar period and later extended from the sixteenth century, contain watchtowers, a mosque, food silos and plenty of water cisterns. This served as a final refuge during times of attack and shows the same sort of symbiotic relationship as Shibam-Kawkaban. The Egyptian Mamelukes forced Imam Sharaf ad-Din and his troops into the fortress in 1517, as did the Ottoman Turks to Imam Mutahar 50 years later, but neither managed to conquer the town despite having far superior troops and weaponry. It is only a 15-minute climb up to the fortress but for the last few years it has been placed out of bounds by the military.

The southern gate has a twisting approach (similar to the Najran Gate at Sadah), making it easier to defend, and small watchtowers along the walls can be climbed for better views. The main attraction is the white dome of the al-Qubba Mosque which can be seen from a great distance. To the left of the gate is a large water tank, beyond which is a religious school *madrasa* built into the walls. It is possible to walk around the streets in relative safety, but some Westerners have had stones thrown at them from rooftops by children.

Thulla was the country residence of another former YAR president. The revered Colonel Ibrahim al-Hamdi led a seven man military junta which seized power in a bloodless coup on 13 June 1974, but he was assassinated in Sana'a in October 1977.

A popular destination for visitors

The **main square** in the centre of Thulla is cashing in on its proximity to Sana'a and the number of tourists who therefore include a visit to the town in their itinerary. Shops are becoming souvenir outlets, something which would have been unheard of even in 1990. The pleasant *fonduq* lies off the square and is the former residence of the imam. Tea and coffee can usually be bought upstairs in the *mafraj*, and overnight accommodation is also available. The walk to Amran initially follows the contours around the mountain until it drops into the al-Ma'mar plain, and takes about four hours.

A 4x4 track leads north from behind the town and

A westerly track climbs onto the plateau. This tremendous route follows the ridge that lies south of the Amran–Hajjah road, with various tracks dropping into the valley around the cement factory. However it is possible to continue climbing for an epic journey to Beit Adhaqah, below Jebel Maswar, and on to Hajjah in about nine hours of tough but rewarding driving.

Friendly locals in the northern highlands.

Shibam

Ancient beginnings Retrace your route for 9km and turn right towards at-Tawila. Shibam can be seen lying at the foot of an impressive escarpment, topped by its twin Kawkaban, which suffered badly during the civil war. Shibam is an old town with a Friday market. Exactly how old it is, nobody knows for certain. The inscribed blocks which have been reused in the gateway, mosque and houses come from the Na'it area. Easily defended, Shibam-Kawkaban has always taken the opportunity of asserting its independence when the greater powers of Saba or Himyar were in decline. However, it was during the spread of Islam that their greatest leader Yufir bin Abderahman al-Hiwali laid siege to Sana'a, captured it in 847, and declared Shibam the new capital. Yufirid rule was always uneasy, as the rulers had to contend with the initial rise to power of the strong Zaidi imams from Sadah, but they did hold out for almost two centuries.

139

It was during this time that the Great Mosque was built, as well as the strong defences around Kawkaban. The small *suq* shops have ancient circular pillars supporting the roof, similar to those at Amran. There is little to see in Shibam itself after a quick walk around, which most people include with their walk up or down from Kawkaban. A few shops below the gate sell souvenirs, with a small *fonduq* out on the local road towards at-Tawila for meals, drinks and basic accommodation.

Kawkaban

Spectacular by road
The rough and steep 4x4 track up behind Kawkaban has been improved and asphalted as part of the contract for the new German road to Mahweet. The climb gives superb views over the protected Wadi Na'im, which produces good-quality *qat*. Towards the top of the track at the steepest and windiest part, notice the strange interlocking hexagonal intrusions of basalt columns, where volcanic activity has punctured through the overlying sandstone.

The approach to Kawkaban is spectacular, as it occupies a narrow peninsula of clifftop which juts out above the plain. A twisting entrance passes through an
A mountain-top ghost town
impressive gateway, which until recently was closed at night. Much of the town is still ruined, as it suffered badly during the late 1960s, when it was a royalist stronghold. There are several mosques, water cisterns, grain silos and large houses, two of which have been converted into *fonduqs*, in the middle of the town. The older Kawkaban Hotel offers meals and drinks, and is a good overnight base for walks in the area.

At the far end of town are spectacular views down to Shibam and across to Thulla – an ideal place for a relaxing and memorable picnic, but some women travellers have felt threatened by stone-wielding boys on this exposed promontory! There is a strong Shi'a presence in the town, which can cause problems for Western visitors, especially women. Keep covered up and I advise women not to wander alone around town or walk to Shibam unaccompanied.

Spectacular by foot
Walking up or down the direct footpath between the two towns is a spectacular mini-trek and is worth attempting, even for the laziest visitor. The height difference is 350m and the walk takes about 45 minutes down, one hour up, all of it on large blocks formed into steps. Make sure you keep to the footpath and do not follow the vehicle track which you will meet halfway. From Kawkaban the walk starts immediately outside the gates, by turning right down the huge cleft in the mountain.

Hotels

Both 'hotels' offer *fonduq*-style rooms with mattresses in a friendly family atmosphere.

Kawkaban Hotel: Eight rooms. They offer bed, breakfast and evening meal, as there is nowhere else to eat. Good value, and ideal if you are planning to walk along the plateau.

Hotel Jebel Kawkaban: The newer establishment, next door to the above.

Walks from Kawkaban

Trekking along the wild plateau

A very quiet night can be spent in Kawkaban before attempting the full-day walk to at-Tawila across the plateau, but be fully prepared (see Trekking). However an exciting half-day walk can be made from here around the back to Hababah and thence to Thulla or Shibam. The route is initially the same, heading across the plateau directly away from the town. Essentially Kawkaban is at the end of a very long, narrow plateau with vertical 350m sides. Always keep to the 4x4 track which splits off from the road back down to Shibam. This track will continually split and rejoin, and it really makes no difference which you follow as they all ultimately head west along the plateau. Never take a track which starts to drop down off the edge. After 45 minutes you will start to see views from the north-eastern edge down to Hababah and Thulla.

Any of the tracks down to the right from here will get you to Hababah, which should take two or three hours from Kawkaban. Thulla or Shibam will be one hour's level walk from Hababah.

If you are continuing to at-Tawila, walk on until you come upon a large travellers' rest hut, about two hours from Kawkaban. From here you need to head to the small village of Na'dah which has a new school with a distinctive white roof. A large canyon cuts in from the left sending you around to the right. The next objective is the single tower of the village outcrop on the edge of the plateau due west. If you want to take the 4x4 track off the plateau, follow it to where it drops down to the left of Husn Bokur.

On the edge of a precipice

If you want to see **Husn Bokur** go further right through Bokur village itself. If you do not employ a local boy as a guide, they will say that the Husn is *memnur* 'forbidden' – but keep heading towards it. The path drops 100m to cross over a col onto this amazing outcrop of houses built into the eroded overhangs. About 50m before the Husn gate, note the path you need: left will go down to meet the 4x4 track to Safei and is the more direct route; right will go to Aled but is longer. So also is the path through Beit Ma'ain, with both routes eventually getting to Safei, on the far side of Husn.

The policeman/guard of the Husn gate will probably also say that a visit is *memnur*, but this ban can usually be overcome by a small donation to the 'Police Benevolent Fund'. A visit is well worth the effort, as there are grain silos, cisterns and steps cut into the wrinkled rockface, topped by a very dangerous watchtower. These views are stunning around midday, and they help you to plan out the next bit of the route to Safei, but in the afternoon mists could start rising up from the Tihama.

Taking the unmarked route down the south side of Husn can be a bit of a gamble, but quite often you will find that there are some unseen locals keeping an eye on you from above, who will shout instructions if you go the wrong way! Once on the 4x4 track, go left around Safei; the track is almost flat until Dera, where you also pass to the left. Keep to the 4x4 track until you reach a small cut, and turn left at the T junction. There are now magnificent views over to the right all the way to at-Tawila, which you approach from above and behind. Drop down through the town onto the new Mahweet road. This is a full day's hard walking, taking about eight hours. You can stay overnight at the two basic *fonduqs* in at-Tawila or get back to Sana'a via Shibam in about two hours.

**A long day ...
but it's worth it**

Al-Huqqa and Haz

**A seldom-
visited site**

Al-Huqqa is the site of a famous ancient temple about 20km north of Sana'a, just beyond the village of Beit al-Hauri. The temple dated from about the third century AD and was probably destroyed in the eruption which caused the great lava flow nearby, known as the Harra of Arhab. An excavation of the site in 1928 by Rathjens and von Wissman uncovered some fine carvings and columns, all of which are now held in Sana'a Museum. Little remains to be seen at the site, and it is generally missed by most visitors.

Haz is an old village about 30km north-west of Sana'a, on the road to Thulla. It lies about 3km down a track to the right. It is an area rich in pre-Islamic history, with many cisterns and old foundations. An old citadel lies inside the town and almost every house has some form of inscribed block in its construction. The town had a distinctive Jewish Quarter before the exodus in the late 1940s.

**Other walking
options**

This is a marvellous area for walking, as it is possible to link Thulla, Haz, al-Huqqa, Beit Na'am and Wadi Dhahr. First make sure from locals or tourist agencies that the area is safe, however, as there have been hold-ups of tourists during anti-government demonstrations by locals.

Jihanah

This is a very worthwhile excursion, which is usually omitted by visitors. The route covers the first section of what used to be the track to Marib before the building of the more northerly asphalt road to Marib. From Bab al-Yemen take the road south towards Ta'iz for 9km, turn left at the village of Dharsan and climb up through flat scrubland. After another ten minutes there is a Y-junction, where you need to turn left (taking the right fork would bring you to Beit al-Ahmar where President Ali Abdullah Saleh was born in 1942). The rolling rockscape sometimes allows the smallscale growing of *qat* and grapes, which are watered from nearby wells.

Home town of the President

The first main village off to the left is **Esnaf,** a stone-built place similar to Thulla, but completely unspoilt by tourists, and full of friendly, busy people. Narrow lanes climb between the houses up and around the slopes, complicated by a maze of water pipes. The open country-side around the back shows traditional agriculture unchanged for millennia. The difference between Esnaf and Jihanah, only 4km further on, is incredible: not a gun is to be seen in the former, but the latter is bristling with almost every type of portable firearm.

Outlets for the arms dealers

When you see Jihanah off to the left, turn onto a track just before the petrol station and bounce up to the *suq*. This small stone town, set in a low basin of hills, does not have the usual range of shops; every other establishment has a display of automatic weapons, handguns, machine guns and even hand grenades. The owners will proudly run through the countries of origin of the equipment, but there is always an air of tension hanging around this mini Peshawar. The town has a new Jama al-Kabir Mosque, with the older, smaller Jama as-Sanani next door. Just beyond Jihanah, tarmac gives way to a rough but spectacular 90km track that leads through totally unsafe tribal country to Sirwah, and eventually Marib. This route is off-limits to tourists.

Sana'a Hotels

The star rating is my own.

***** **Taj Sheba,** Ali Abdul Mogni St, PO Box 773. Tel: 272372; Fax: 274129.
200 rooms. The best hotel in the Yemen, with top international standards of both food and service. Restaurants and coffee shop, health club and swimming pool. Ideally situated in the centre, near Tahrir Square.
***** **Sheraton,** Dahr Himjar, PO Box 2467. Tel: 237500-3; Fax: 251521.
300 rooms. International chain hotel with all facilities. Restaurants, coffee shop, fitness centre and pool. On the

Ring Road about 3 km from Tahrir Square.

**** Hadda, Hadda St, PO Box 999. Tel: 215215/4; Fax: 263094.

136 rooms. Also known as the Ramada Hadda (but now not part of the international Ramada group), good hotel with the usual facilities including health club and pool. About 5 km from centre.

*** Dar Al-Hamd, Al Hay al-Izaya, PO Box 2187. Tel: 203055/4.

35 rooms. Former palace of the Imam converted into a hotel. Traditional style, north of al-Qa, 15 minutes walk from Tahrir Square. Interesting.

*** Sam City, Al-Qiyadah St, PO Box 10127. Tel: 270752, 76255; Fax: 275168.

80 rooms. Reopened after extensive modernisation. Roof restaurant. Ten minutes walk along Ali Abdul Mogni Street from Tahrir Square. Good value.

*** Rawdah Palace, Ar-Rawdah village, close to airport. Tel: 340226/7.

34 rooms. Another former Imam's palace set in well laid-out pleasant gardens. Not much to do in the village, about 10km from Tahrir Square.

** Bir Al-Azap

38 rooms. To the west of Tahrir Square. The recently converted former US Embassy. A traditional house, similar to the Dar Al-Hamd Hotel, except that it is mainly used by tour groups and must be booked through the Universal agency.

** Al-Ikhwa, Seif St, PO Box 344. Tel: 74127, 74026.

40 rooms. Slightly overpriced older hotel, but with a central position behind the Taj Sheba, and good food in the restaurant on the fourth floor.

** Middle East Tourist, Az-Zubeiry St, PO Box 99. Tel: 272654.

24 rooms. Clean and friendly place between the Taj Sheba and the *saila*, but on a noisy main road. The management also run the **Kuwait Tourist** (Tel: 275722), with 24 rooms, on the outskirts of town near the Kuwait Hospital.

* Alexander Tourism, Tel: 272934, 272942.

32 rooms. Two streets behind the Al-Makha Hotel. A good enough place in a central position.

* Babel, No 5 St (Near Al-Ikhwa hotel). Tel: 272267.

20 rooms. A good, clean local hotel.

* Al-Ahram. Tel: 270861, 76332.

17 rooms. Behind the Al-Ikhwa, near Universal Tourism office. A good value practical hotel, busy with local guests.

One of the best developments since unification is the conversion of several tower houses in the Old City to comfortable traditional-style hotels. Classification is pointless as they are all clean and good value, in totally unique situations. Most rooms have mattresses on the floor, and shared bathrooms.

Sendbad, Az-Zumar St. Tel: 222677.
10 rooms. Near the *suq*. Beautiful seven storey house with sauna and courtyard. Check out the *mafraj* on the sixth floor. Great view from roof. Great place.
Old Sana'a Palace. Tel: 76990.
60 rooms. Near the al-Abhar mosque, very central. A large rambling place with good *mafraj* on top. Reasonable food in the ground-floor restaurant.
Golden Daar, Tulhah St. Tel and Fax: 222949.
22 rooms. Between the *saila* and the *suq*. *Mafraj* and restaurant on top, great views.
Al-Gasmy Palace, Al-Gasmy St. Tel: 273816; Fax: 271997.
22 rooms. Also between the *saila* and the *suq*. Tends to be booked up, as it is popular with tour groups. Courtyard restaurant.
Taj Talha, Daud St. Tel: 237674; Fax: 223921.
30 rooms. Between Golden Daar Hotel and central *suq*. Beautifully preserved old house.
Dar Al-Diyafa. Tel: 222997, 77785; Fax: 241805.
16 rooms. Near al-Falayhi Square, north-west of the *suq*. Great view from the restaurant on the fifth floor. Difficult to find, but worth the struggle.
Sultan's Palace. Tel: 273766, 73702.
A new conversion to the west of the *saila*, only five minutes walk from Tahrir Square.

Many good hotels are springing up all the time around the full length of the Ring Road. These offer value for money for the visitor prepared to be based 2-3 km out of the centre.

There are many local one star hotels in Ali Abdul Mogni Street between the Taj Sheba and Tahrir Square. Most cater for local visitors, with tourists expected to pay a premium rate for a central location but poor facilities. They include the **Al-Nasser (Egypt Hotel), Al-Muraisi, Nile, Al-Anwar, Al-Makha, Al-Mahra, Orient, Shuhara and Shabwa.** All are basic and for years were the only budget hotels for travellers. Today, they are not good value, considering what is available in the Old City.

The same can be said for the Bab al-Yemen area, which also has some poor-value hotels for the seasoned traveller, including the **Himyarland, Aden Tourism and Al-Salam Tourism.** If you stay here without sleeping bag, you might have to nip across to the *suq* and buy a sheet or two.

At the western end of Tahrir Square, about 200m up Gamal Abdul Nasser Street there are three small hotels worth considering, with many local restaurants nearby. The **Manakah Hotel Tourist** (Tel: 74079) is the former Sana'a Hotel, refurbished, with 25 rooms and very clean. The **Arwa** (Tel: 73838, 275103) has 30 clean rooms and is usually busy. The **Al-Khayyam** (Tel: 71795, 74045) has 17 rooms, but is a bit threadbare.

Restaurants and Eateries

A wide range of standard, cost and choice exists in the capital. There has been a growth in specialist restaurants to cater for the expatriate community, particularly on the outskirts of the city near the housing complexes.

All the top hotels have international-standard food in their restaurants, particularly worth mentioning is the **Golden Peacock** at the Taj Sheba, which also has theme evenings with food from around the world. Being Indian run, the food at the Taj is usually excellent.

Yemeni

Local restaurants can be found all around the city; many do not even bother having a name. The following are particularly good:

Al-Halwani, Az-Zubeiry St.
50m beyond the end of Hadda Road. Good Yemeni food at cheap self-service prices. Crowded at lunch times. More traditional small restaurant upstairs.

Al Dhiyafah Al Arabiyah, Ali Abdul Mogni St.
Between Tahrir Square and the Sam City Hotel. A good, small self-service place with a pleasant atmosphere. Open area at rear.

Palestine and **Shazarwan,** Ali Abdul Mogni St.
Two restaurants on opposite sides of the road between the Taj Sheba and Tahrir Square. Good-quality local fried chicken and kebab places. Beside the Shazarwan is the similar **Al-Shathrawan** broast (grilled) chicken and chips, sticky desserts and pastries.

Al-Afrah, Az-Zubeiry St.
Good local chicken place near the Middle East Tourist Hotel.

Arabian Nights
A large, reasonable chicken restaurant, 2km from Tahrir Square, near the corner of Al-Sabain Youm (Old Airport Road) and Abulhabai Street.

Al-Musbahi, corner of Hadda Rd and Ring Rd.
2km before the Hadda Hotel. Great value and quality.

Hadda Touristic
2km beyond Hadda Hotel on the right-hand side. A very local place with good prices on the slopes of Hadda.

Sunflowers
A large place in the middle of al-Qa Gardens. Open all day.

Non-Yemeni

Specialist places are opening all the time; some worth mentioning are:

Al-Bustan
Five minutes walk from where Hadda Road meets Az-Zubeiry Street. A large Lebanese restaurant in sectioned gardens, popular with wedding parties at weekends.

Abu Nawas
A reasonably up-market Palestinian restaurant in its own pleasant grounds. Near the Al-Bustan and Al-Halwani restaurants.

Chinese, Hadda Rd.
5km from Tahrir Square, almost opposite the Hadda Hotel. Small, but with good Chinese and Oriental food.

Concord Patiserie, Hadda Rd.
1km from Az-Zubeiry St on the left-hand side. A quality cake and pastry place.

Vietnamese
On the western corner of Tahrir Square, near to the old General Tourism Corporation office. Very popular with good food, but lunchtimes only. Get there early.

Bella Venezia, Hadda Rd.
lkm before the Hadda Hotel on the right-hand side. Inconsistently good Italian style food at reasonable prices. Highly recommended by expatriate workers, but sometimes closed.

Sana'a Tourism, St. 36.
Near Yemen International Communications, opposite the Chinese Embassy. Ethiopian food at good prices. Spicy *zigny* chicken is a speciality.

The Mahweet region.

NORTH OF SANA'A

SANA'A–AMRAN

Only one main road heads north, but there are two ways of leaving Sana'a to reach it. The more interesting route passes Dar al-Hajar (see Wadi Dhahr). The more direct route is as follows.

The main road north swings off Airport Road onto Manamah Street, just before the modern glass-fronted Yemenia head office (4km from Tahrir Square). The National Stadium can be seen to the right after 8km and beyond are the suburbs of housing and light industry that are constantly extending along the main roads. After **Passing close-by** 15km a signpost points left to Arrowd along the tarmac **Dar al-Hajar** the road to Dar al-Hajar. The palace itself can just be seen from further up the main road. There are also the remnants of lava tunnels on the right where the road follows the lava flow.

The scenery on the **al-Ma'mar plain** alternates between *qat* fields and black lava flows, sometimes topped by exposed volcanic cones. Beyond al-Ma'mar town (23km) the road climbs a 2,600m pass amid a boulder-strewn landscape with many extinct volcanoes. A few kilometres further is Beni Maymoon hill village on the left. The white-domed mosque of Thulla stands out low down against the distant mountain backdrop. Further round the escarpment, even the buildings of Kawkaban are visible.

Amran

Fifty kilometres from Sana'a is Amran, which lies in the centre of the fertile al-Bawn Plain, and can be seen as the **Small, compact,** road drops down from the hills. Modern buildings **old walled town** sprawl around the old walled town that lies hidden within; almost everything in the vicinity is covered by a thin layer of white dust, courtesy of the nearby cement factory.

It is a bustling centre in its own right, but it is still part of Sana'a Governorate. There are calls for it to become the centre of a new governorate, a move which will improve the poor services and facilities: educational, medical and municipal services are lacking, and the water and electricity supplies are poor.

The road north passes just to the east of the old town, but to visit the town turn left along the Hajjah road. After 500m is the main cross-roads, with a good local restaurant on the left-hand corner. Diagonally opposite, notice the carving of a snake (again for good luck) on one of the wall blocks, halfway up the steps to the *qat* and tobacco joint. Turn right and pass the regular daily traders to the square at the end, before turning right again. The alley straight ahead leads to the main gate of the old town. Many of these northern traders still use old Maria Theresa dollars as everyday currency and will sometimes offer them for sale to tourists. Check their current value in rials before buying.

Old coins still used as cash

MARIA THERESA DOLLARS

Known locally as *rial fransi* these large silver coins were introduced into the Middle East by Napoleon in 1798 when he conquered Egypt. The high silver content meant that their value was universally accepted and they became the standard currency in most Red Sea countries. Until the revolution, the Maria Theresa thaler (the word 'dollar' is derived from this) was used for all money transactions, as there was no banking system whatsoever. There are stories of the imams even in this century transporting mule-loads of the heavy coins across the mountains to pay for tribal support. It became totally unsatisfactory as a standard currency because the value fluctuated wildly as the price of silver rose and fell. There was no distinction between the finances of the state and those of the imam, and financial problems arose when great hoards of coins were suddenly taken out of circulation.

The coins were minted in Austria from 1780, but they always bear the date 1780 regardless of the date of manufacture. For many years they were minted by the Bank of England, but production eventually ceased in 1960. In the mountains, the magnificent coins are still used today, with a set value in Yemeni rials. They make good souvenirs but are disappearing rapidly.

Unlike many other large towns with old walls, Amran's defences are intact and can be walked for many sections. The main **gatehouse**, which is now used as a prison, is a three storey stone building with small Turkish style wooden shutters. Be careful taking photos. Beside the gate runs a row of tiny shops built into the outside of the wall, each with a column of circular blocks supporting the roof. Some of these old *suq* shops have very ornately carved wooden doors. The best days to find them open are Friday and Saturday, when the market is busier than normal. The houses outside the wall belong to the old Jewish section. A smaller gate with wooden doors and Islamic inscriptions pierces the walls about 100m from the main gate.

Ancient blocks used for walls and supports

Passing into the main gate, you can see a huge block on the right with a Sabaean inscription (always referred to by the locals as Himyar). Several walls and houses in the old town also have inscribed blocks. The 3m high **walls** themselves are made from a random mixture of dark (volcanic) and light (limestone) blocks. These are

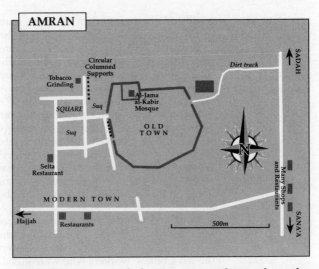

finished on the outside but are extremely rough on the town's inner wall. If you turn left inside the gate, you will quickly come to the al-Jama al-Kabir (the main mosque) with a large brick minaret. Walking directly through the old town you will reach the opposite gate in about five minutes.

The ground floor walls of the buildings tend to be of stone, with higher ones made of mud-brick faced by smooth mud and punctuated by small irregular windows with rough surrounds of white gypsum. The old town has neither the grandeur of Sana'a nor the remoteness of Sadah, but it does have a rough 'lived-in' quality sometimes lacking in the 'museum' showpieces.

The functions of the various floors of the houses are much the same as those of a Sana'a tower house, but notice how many of the ground floor doors and archways are **Rising** now only 1m or so high, due to the rising street level over **street level** the years. Family life, at least in its outward appearance, cannot have changed very much in a thousand years.

AMRAN–HAJJAH–TIHAMA

This 80km road is one of the most spectacular in the country. Heading west out of Amran with its preponderance of second-hand car dealers, you will see the busy cement factory on the left. Just when the road starts climbing at the head of the valley, look out for Beit Bady, a hilltop village to the right with three large round fortress houses. 10km further up, the farming village of Mantaqat Karen has a similar large walled circular house, **Fossils to find** which is much closer to the road and is popular with **or buy** photographers. The children here sell all types of fossilised shells found in the area, many of which are much more valuable than the few rials they charge.

From the 2,800m summit (20km), there is a very rough track branching left for 17km to Beit Adhaqah, which lies under Jebel Maswar, where the 4x4 route from Thulla arrives at the escarpment. Beyond Beit Ashmour (22km) the road descends for an amazing 27km. Stop at the initial look-out point for stunning panoramas; Kohlan can be seen halfway along the mountain range straight ahead.

The distant mountain due north is Jebel Shahara, over 50km away. In clear weather and with good binoculars it **Possible to see** is just possible to see the bridge at Shahara at the bottom **Shahara Bridge** of the 'V', just below the summit on the right. The ground is rich in fossils, with thousands of bivalves indicating an ancient sea bed.

Further down the road are equally good views to the left across Wadi Sharas, with Hajjah in the distance at the top. A single rock pinnacle, Shanif Caderie, is a shrine to the ten Chinese workers who were killed whilst building this difficult section of the road. The low Chinese railings do not offer much protection, so this is not a place for sufferers from vertigo. One kilometre further on is the right turn for the short climb up to **Husn Kohlan.** Try to be dropped 50m beyond the 'No Photo' sign, referring to photographs of veiled women collecting water from the large open cistern, and tell your driver that you will walk down and meet him at the *suq*. Walk uphill between the two *mudhir* (managers') houses, past the white mosque and down the paved steps.

An easy walk In some ways I prefer this short walk (less than 30 minutes) to the more popular Kawkaban-Shibam walk, as it passes through mountain village life at its rawest. If you are feeling fit, you can keep to the higher path about 50m past the mosque and climb up to the citadel through two fortified gates. The guardians are friendly but reserved, and might let you into the main building from the small courtyard and well.

There is a bewildering maze of paths around the lower houses, but the locals are helpful. Generally you need to head left and down to reach the tarred street. Turn left to meet your vehicle at the *suq* square (referred to rather grandly as Kohlan City). If you are there on a Monday morning, the weekly market runs the length of this street and is a seething mass of colourful bargaining – with the traffic problems that go with it. Try to get a glimpse of the unusual old al-Meshed Mosque on top of a rock outcrop about 100m north of the square.

Twists and Rejoin the mountain road and continue downwards. **turns forever** The ingenuity of Yemeni builders never ceases to amaze – **downwards** many houses are built into the sloping cracks high up on the rock face. This is a rich agricultural region where anything will grow, including wild trees and bushes such as *ilb, as-Shir* and bottle tree. The 1,800m drop ends at the bridge over Wadi Sharas, where a small pavilion at Suq al-Sharas commemorates the 1982 Chinese road project.

**The climb up
to Hajjah**

The scenery is now very lush with large trees shading banana, papaya and coffee plantations beside the wadi. The road then swings away from Wadi Sharas to climb up another 700m to Hajjah town (80km).

Hajjah

If Ibb was not already called the 'green province', then Hajjah surely would be. Throughout the day, enormous clouds build up as the air rises above the mountains from

**Storm clouds
and green fields**

the hot Tihama, and these clouds sometimes develop into violent thunderstorms. The resultant high rainfall gives as many as three harvests each year, ensuring a continuous greenery on the many terraced hillsides where coffee is still grown.

As provincial capital, the town of Hajjah enjoys good connections with Sana'a, yet overlooks the Tihama plains, amid rugged and isolated mountains. The town is slightly confusing, centred on a main roundabout but spreading over several small peaks connected by steep, winding and very similar streets.

**Strategic
importance**

It has never been a great city, and only came to prominence when it was fought over by the invading Turks (who were always strong in the Tihama) and the defending Zaidi imams (who were powerful in the mountains).

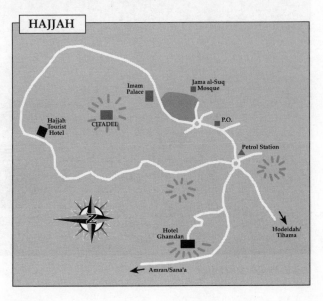

153

A grim fortress

As a Zaidi stronghold, it has **dungeons** dug beneath the citadel, which apparently contain some gruesome scrawlings on the walls, made by prisoners of the imams. These dark caves, known as Nafi Prison, were guarded by merciless soldiers who tortured and murdered the inmates. Over 800 Zaraniq tribesmen died here after declaring war on the Imam. They demanded UN recognition for a separate Zaraniq state in the Tihama, but the response from the Imam was swift and brutal.

To subdue similar uprisings and to ensure the support of the tribes for the imam, it became a frightful tradition to imprison the eldest son of every sheikh. In 1948 Imam Ahmed rallied his troops in Hajjah before ordering them to loot and destroy Sana'a as a reprisal for his father's assassination. Royal support during the civil war also cost the Hajjah region many lives and severe damage from aerial attack, with the result that there is little for the tourist to see.

Suffered heavily in civil war

The two most interesting attractions, the citadel and the Imam's Palace are closed to visitors, being in the hands of the military and government respectively. The Palace can be viewed from the road beside the *suq*; it is quite an unusual building of light stone, white cement and brown wooden shutters. The *suq* itself is small but interesting and contains a mosque, not surprisingly called al-Jama al-Suq.

4x4 driving near Hajjah.

The Ghamdan Hotel is perched on the edge of town and is a good place to stay, with great views across the wadi. If intending to walk in the Maabien region, you can plan most of your route from the panorama roof view. In the clear early morning you can also sometimes see the Shahara mountain range to the north.

Hotels
*** Ghamdan. Tel: 220420.
32 rooms. The best hotel in town. Good rooms and food, excellent views from the roof. It is just possible to see the bridge at Shahara on a clear morning.
Hajjah Tourist. Tel: 220285.
At the time of writing, this place was no longer open for business, but it might just be waiting for trade to pick up.
Restaurants
There are many good local eateries in and around the town centre, including the **Al-Andlus,** on the right when walking from the roundabout towards the Ghamdan Hotel.

Walking in the Hajjah region

Some of the best walking in the country

There are splendid walks in almost every direction, but it is sometimes considered to be an unsafe area for tourists. The range of mountains on the opposite side of Wadi Hajjah to the north contain seldom-visited villages right up to the peak of Maabien. Start by heading for the weird hat-shaped peak and follow the 4x4 track up to the right. **Maabien** lies behind the peaks that you can see from Hajjah, and if you climb into the citadel you can meet the warders of the local jail and offer cigarettes to the prisoners. This village was another royalist base in the civil war and many of the houses are no more than bombed ruins. The views west are simply staggering as the land drops 1,600m to the Tihama. Return via a more easterly route passing through remote settlements as you drop down into Wadi Hajjah, and then have to climb back up the other side to the town.

A half-day walk to Wadi Sharas

To the east, it is possible to make your way to the edge of Wadi Sharas at roughly the same height as Hajjah, and drop down to Suq al-Sharas. Take the road past the Hajjah Tourist Hotel and turn down a track towards the hilltop village of Kawkaban (another one), ask any of the locals for "Wadi Sharas". After 30 minutes the track splits, take the right fork and drop over the col to descend for about two hours along paths and an old Turkish stone road. Head for a huge tree in the wadi bed. It is then about 30 minutes walk down the wadi bed to the bridge at Suq al-Sharas. Taxis can be taken from here to Hajjah. Carry plenty of water for this five hour trek.

Trekking even higher

A longer walk (see Trekking) needing an overnight stay would be up the wadi bed itself, ending with the enormous climb of Jebel Maswar. Keeping to a lower altitude you could cross the western col behind Hajjah to enter the upper reaches of Wadi La'ah and descend to at-Tur in a couple of days. Alternatively, you could then climb up the southern range and make for at-Tawila or Mahweet. The possibilities are endless and at the present time they would be almost all trail-blazing treks, amongst bewildered locals.

Villages on the lower slopes

A shorter route into Wadi La'ah would be to drop down to the south of Hajjah via one or other of the villages of Bani an-Nihari, Nu'man and ash-Shaqhadirah. It is then possible to climb up to Mahweet in a total of two days, or to at-Tawila in three. One journey I would like to undertake would be to go down Wadi Sharas from the bridge to its junction with Wadi Mawr (20km) and to then turn right and walk up Wadi Akhraf to the foot of Shahara (about 45kms) and onto Huth (85kms). Unfortunately this area is still regarded as rather dangerous from the tribal point of view.

Hajjah–Tihama

It is 64km from Hajjah by road until you meet the main north-south Tihama road at the village of Khushm, 117km north of Hodeidah. The route descends through heavily terraced and cultivated areas which benefit from the abundant rainfall. Almost immediately you will start to see both men and women in the fields wearing typical Tihama straw hats to keep off the sun.

Suq al-Aman (16km) is a sort of large outdoor DIY centre where every building requisite is on show. Twenty kilometres further on the right-hand side is the small mountain of Jebel Hassan Sulayman, topped by a small fort. The track that heads north from here goes to al-Mahabishah, 60km away in the remote Jebel ash-Sharafayn, a possible leopard area. The scenery after crossing Wadi Mawr for the rest of the way to al-Mahabishah is well worth the rugged ride. From here Abs can be reached down Wadi Qawr.

Down to the coastal shelf

At-Tur (37km) is the main town *en route*. In fact it is a small modern village in a strange boulder-strewn landscape. The ruined Turkish fort behind the *suq* is the local police station. A kilometre out of town the track crosses Wadi La'ah which drains the huge basin stretching all the way to distant Kawkaban. Once on the Tihama coastal plain, the mountains become small hills separated by vast fields of *dhurra*, tended by locals living in straw huts. The track is fast and straight to the main road.

AMRAN–HUTH–SADAH

North of Amran the road crosses the basin through well cultivated fields and small villages with unusual circular tower houses built for easy defence.

Following the
ancient
mountain
trade route

Raydah (70km), like many of the towns up to and including Sadah, can trace its history back to pre-Islamic times when it lay on the old Himyaritic trade route from Sana'a to Mecca via Najran. Parts of the old town can be seen high up on the left on top of Raydah Hill, but today it suffers from a disease affecting many main-road settlements – uncontrolled ribbon development. Car mechanics and workshops, spare parts dealers, restaurants, doss houses and photography studios all cater to the through-traffic. The most exciting day to be in Raydah is Tuesday when the large market attracts people from as far away as Sana'a for the goods that make their way here unofficially from Saudi Arabia.

Dhi Bin

From Raydah a side road runs north-east between Jebel al-Kalbiyn and Jebel Hays 30 km to the village of Dhi Bin, famous for its thirteenth century mosque belonging to the Zaidi Imam Abdulla ibn Hamza. The village lies 2km to the north of the road and above are the large impressive ruins of **Dhafar** (not to be confused with the ruins of the same name near Yarim). Some visitors have reported local aggression from both children and adults alike, so although it is possible to hire a taxi in Raydah, it is preferable to take a Yemeni escort for safety.

There are several routes up the southern and eastern side of the mountain branching off tracks that can be used with a 4x4 vehicle. On the summit is a commanding fortress with cisterns, towers, houses and a mosque. Allow half a day for the return trip from Raydah.

On the edge of
Wadi al-Jawf

This is as close as tourists can get to the troublesome Wadi al-Jawf (see Sana'a–Marib). Hopefully in the future it will be possible to continue into it and perhaps even take the track that heads south from just beyond Dhi Bin through al-Hayfah to get back to Sana'a. Al-Hayfah is the village nearest the ruins of Riyam and Na'it, where there are two pillars similar to those at Marib and also some rock cut tombs, pictures of which are at the Sana'a University Museum. Both sites are off-limits to tourists.

Raydah–Huth

Eight kilometres beyond Raydah the road climbs a steep pass to the village of al-Ghoolah. At present the road to Sadah is open to tourists and hopefully will remain so, but the troubles in Wadi al-Jawf sometimes spill over into Armed conflict this area. I have passed along this road amid crackling machine guns with lines of troops and tanks spread across the hillsides attacking a tribal position. Many of the checkpoints you now encounter are as much tribal as they are governmental and almost every male over twelve carries some form of gun, usually an AK47 Kalashnikov.

The old stone town of **Khamir** (96km) appears on the left of the healthy modern buildings near the road. Some of the stone houses of this local administrative centre have an odd upper floor made of mud. Sunday is market day and attracts battalions of well-armed tribesmen from all over this troubled region. By tradition Khamir must give sanctuary to the Hashid tribe, whose leader Sheikh Abdullah bin Hussein al-Ahmar is the most important tribal chief in the country. His power stretches back to the part he played during the civil war and he is now involved in politics, with his own movement, the pro-Islamic Islah Party. His residence in Sana'a is the large mansion opposite the Yemenia headquarters.

Sheikh Abdullah - a charismatic leader

Before continuing north there is an opportunity of a break at a small roadside eatery to the left on the outskirts of town.

HASHID AND BAKIL TRIBES

Both these tribes are famous for their bravery and fighting abilities. Burckhardt travelled here almost two centuries ago and described the tribesmen around Huth as serving in the forces of the Imam. Many went to India by way of Shihr and served in the armies of the Indian princes, where they were preferred to any other class of soldier.

Together the tribes from the Hamdan Federation which has exerted power in the region even from the time of the Sabaean Kingdom. Conquerors have sought to gain their support but for the most part the Hashid and Bakil have been called the 'wings of the imamate', owing to their almost continuous support of the Zaidi imams. It should be noted that they have always remained allies rather than subject of the Imam. Before the civil war, the Imam was responsible for the murder of the Hashid paramount sheikh and his son while in their care. The Hashid tribes vowed never again to support the Imam and sided with the republicans.

YAR government could only operate successfully if they contained the right balance of Hashid and Bakil representatives. The President of the Republic Ali Abdullah Saleh is a member of the Hashid tribe and thus closely associated with Sheikh Abdullah of Khamir.

The rubble strewn plateau now takes on a different appearance, with thousands of small euphorbias and succulents sprouting up among the rocks. On a clear day, the plateau before al-Rayan (116km) gives a good view to the left of the Jebel Shahara range. The area is also rich in small fossilised shells and sea creatures, showing that this

Euphorbias and fossils

whole region was once under water.

At the point where you can look down onto Huth (127km) it is worth stopping to inspect the ruins of an old pre-Islamic trading town on the right. Situated on twin outcrops and split by a small ravine are the foundations of several houses, three rough upright columns and sections of the outer wall.

Ancient town clings to life

Huth lies halfway between the capital and Sadah, and is a good place to stop for lunch. Many travellers call at Hussein's to the left of the road, as witnessed by the many tour stickers it displays. Here you can get good local food in typical style. There are usually a few stalls for fruit across the road even when it is not Friday, market day.

Huth was previously an important Zaidi religious teaching centre, but it has reverted to a sleepy roadside halt. The main mosque, about 100m across the road from Hussein's, is of local design with unusual outer wall decorations and a squat minaret. The best view is across the water tank from the far south-eastern corner. The whole place has a rough 'frontier' feel about it, as though the fortress houses could easily become derelict and turn it into a ghost town.

Huth–Shahara

Turn left for Shahara

Huth is the place to load up with supplies before heading west to Shahara, one of the highlights of any trip to the Yemen. Logistics are a bit awkward as a visit will take two days and requires a 4x4 vehicle. The night can be spent camping at al-Gabei, which lies at the base of the mountain, or up at the *fonduq* in the town itself.

The rough track begins at the petrol station south of Huth. It is a mind- and body-numbing journey of about 10km that seems more like 100. The descent into Wadi Lissam ('tongue') is via the Naqil Lissam, at the foot of which are two tracks. One heads north to al-Qaflah, but the one you want swings south through a very fertile wadi where all sorts of fruits and crops are grown in an almost perfect agricultural climate. Al-Ash'shar, a ramshackle collection of houses and abandoned armoured vehicles is only 17km from Huth, but it will take you the best part of an hour to get there.

For many years there have been plans to link Huth with the town of Harad in the Tihama. If the plans ever come to fruition, the road will involve another amazing drop off the plateau for 120km.

Thirteen kilometres further on is Suq al-Ahad ('Sunday market') where weaver bird nests weigh down many branches of the large *ilb* trees. Eventually your 4x4

Base camp

will bounce it's way into the **al-Gabei** station, where all visitors are forced to abandon their vehicles, and 'hire' other (far worse) 4x4s to reach Shahara.

To walk or ride?

The locals here are so powerful that they can quite freely exploit those wishing to visit the area. If you do not pay, you do not go – or you walk. Basically you have three options: walk up, drive up, or drive to Araba and then walk up for the best bit. Do not underestimate local tribal problems.

By walking the whole way, you avoid paying the 4x4 toll but you would need to camp somewhere nearby, as it takes between four and seven exhausting hours to climb the 1,500m (roughly equivalent in height to the north face of the Eiger!). Even if you hire a 4x4, the journey takes two hours. Personally, if you have time, I think the best choice is to come from Sana'a or Sadah in the morning, hire a 4x4 to Araba (you can bargain a price far lower than the full Shahara rip-off) and walk from there. Stay overnight in the rough *fonduq* (take sleeping bag and make sure there is room for you) and walk or drive the whole way down, and you can be back in Huth for lunch.

Steep tracks and sharp bends

The route for both 4x4s and walkers is about the same from al-Gabei to Araba, roughly halfway up. In places the track is cut so steeply into the rockface that it looks impossible and highly dangerous for any vehicle to attempt it, let alone the wrecks that you will be in. On my last visit the road was being widened lower down and it might now be safer.

Araba is the third small settlement you pass, and is situated immediately below the double mountain of Shahara. From here the bridge can still not be seen, but you can clearly make out the stone path leading to it just below the summit. Beyond Araba the 4x4 track levels out for about 1km as it follows a terrace to the left and goes around the back of the mountain to approach Shahara. An easy walk is through the Bab al-Nakhlah gateway, but I prefer a more southerly route. Do not worry about getting lost if you walk. Armed with the usual walking equipment (see Trekking) and this book, you *will* get to the bridge!

Walk the last bit

If you are planning to walk, leave the small shops and houses as if you were continuing along the 4x4 road. At the end of the village, turn right up a path towards some higher houses, following a metal water pipe. This becomes a paved road that gives tremendous panoramas to the right. A hundred metres further up, you pass a house on the right and leave the road and water pipe, just past a water cistern, also on the right. Take the small mule track going left beside an old travellers' hut.

Your next objective is a round fortress tower, which you can see by looking left to a small grey hut on the same level about 200m away. The round fortress is 200m vertically above the hut, but hard to distinguish against the rock background. Follow the path along the *qat* terracing as it winds around the slope, sometimes up steps but always heading for the fortress, which has a small open stone side doorway.

Your next objective is the old stone gateway high up above your right shoulder. Soon after the fortress, when you get your first view of the bridge, turn right up a steep path (straight ahead would lead you back down to the 4x4 road). The size and quality of the path improves until you reach the gateway with its heavy wooden doors, built in an easily defendable defile. Follow the path to a cistern and a small mosque perched on the edge of the mountain.

A bridge joining two mountain top villages

From here the path heads straight up the mountainside to Shahara tel-Feesh, the village on top of the other peak and the whole reason for having a bridge in the first place. From above the houses follow any path heading left along the terraces (locals will point you in the right direction as it is pretty obvious where you are going) around the hill to the bridge. It should take between an hour and a half and two hours to get there from Araba.

The uniquely constructed **bridge** is approached from above and you will walk down to it. It dates from the early seventeenth century and was built by a famous architect, Saleh al-Yaman, using two support bridges below. If it were easier to get to, this bridge would surely be one of *the* great tourist sites of the Middle East. As it is, the locals simply consider it to be a way of getting from one village to another, which a few crazy foreigners come to look at for ten minutes.

The impact of the ancient architecture has been reduced somewhat lately with the addition of the metal water pipe which snakes down the steps and across, and which is impossible to hide in photographs. From here it is ten minutes' walk to the centre of the village and the *fonduq* behind the mosque. *En route* are numerous cisterns that have supplied water to the inhabitants during times of siege.

Royalist stronghold

Because of its virtually impregnable position, **Shahara** has always been a place of refuge for the Zaidi imams whenever they have come into conflict with invaders or rival leaders. Such tactics were successful under Imam al-Qasim ibn Mohammed (Qasim the Great) in the early seventeenth century. He masterminded the expulsion of the Turks, and the job was completed by his son Imam Mu'ayyid in 1635. From here, almost 300 years later, Imam Yahya led the battle, also against the Turks, that gave North Yemen its independence. More recently, it was a royalist stronghold during the civil war, and suffered greatly from the aerial bombings of the republican and Egyptian air forces.

Unforgettable views

There are impressive views wherever you look from Shahara. The 4x4 track rumbles down to the west, and an old cannon commands the abyss to the south beyond the graveyard and ruined shops. Behind the *fonduq* is a large cistern with a look-out position giving stunning views across to the small villages perched on equally remote mountain tops, almost close enough to touch but hours away by vehicle. The sun sinks into the Tihama leaving bands of orange and purple, as mists rise over the jagged peaks. There is something primeval about this scene, something that should not exist in this day and age. This is Nepal, Morocco and Jordan rolled into one amazing panorama. As you can imagine, a night spent up in this eagles eyrie is quiet and magical.

Getting back down . . .

For the return journey, a good price can be negotiated, possibly as low as 25 per cent of the upward cost, as the 4x4s have to go back down to al-Gabei anyway. The walk down has taken me as little as an hour and a half to Araba, followed by an hour and a quarter to al-Gabei, but this pace is very wearing on the knees.

. . . in one piece

One thing to note is that walking tourists are targets for the many stone-throwing children. Walking up does not seem to be so bad, as you might well be bringing gold, francs, cents and marks to distribute amongst the children. But walking down away from the villages can be quite dangerous with large stones and even rocks raining down. All this seems to be a way of reasserting their independence, as I have watched children (girls as well as boys) throwing stones and appearing to be encouraged by nearby adults. If it were not for the 4x4 extortion, the rock throwing and abuse, this would be the best excursion available, but unfortunately some visitors are left with a very bitter after-taste, not to mention cuts and bruises, from this dangerous tribal area.

Huth–Sadah

Heading further north to Sadah

Between Huth and al-Harf there is a short pass reaching 1,700m. Al-Harf (163km from Sana'a) is the western end of any journey through Wadi al-Jawf (see Sana'a–Marib). From al-Harf one track descends 67km south-east to al-Matamah, while another goes north-east across Wadi Madhab to reach al-Marashi after 37km. Twenty-eight kilometres due north of al-Marashi is Suq al-Inan, which is famous for its many beautiful mud houses. The houses are fortresses themselves, similar to those around Habban but built in the *zabur* style (see Sadah). Sixty-seven kilometres due east of Suq al-Inan is al-Mahjil, which lies in a stunning desert where Wadi Khabb disappears into the Rub al-Khali. Unfortunately, unless you work for one of the oil companies you are unlikely to see any of it, the whole area being out of bounds.

Spectacular mountain pinnacles

Beyond al-Harf the road heads towards the impressive jagged peaks of Jebel Mafluq before swinging west around it. This area saw some of the fiercest fighting during the civil war. The countryside opens out into sweeping barren slopes until the 1,900m pass, which is topped by the tin-hut roadside car parts and fuel centre at al-Ahmar. Here there is a Tuesday market and a high population of car mechanics.

A perfect village?

From here to Sadah is an area of small unique **mud villages,** most of whose houses are built on fine clean lines with tiny windows. The colour of the mud harmonises perfectly with the countryside. Most are surrounded by well-cultivated strips of farmland including the famous local black grapes dangling from wooden trellis-work.

One village set back from the road on the right is **Faroowah** (10km before Sadah). It is reached by a farm track that winds around the tamarisk trees found all around the Sadah region. You can stop in the field beside the village and compose some spectacular shots of the houses while wandering around. Children are already learning to sell small handicraft baskets, souvenirs and fossils, but it is nevertheless worth a half-hour stop. You should see some yellow-vented bulbuls flitting noisily around the nearby plantations.

The road then descends into Sadah, an ancient walled town that only recently has needed to spread beyond its gates.

SADAH

This Zaidi capital has a proud past and, like Marib, seems to hover nervously between provincial capital and anti-government stronghold. Around here borders are undefined and fluid, and practically anything can be purchased, regardless of its legality. The town lies on fertile ground where several wadis discharge silt before flowing north-east into Wadi Najran. As several routes meet here, Sadah has always been the main collection point for pilgrims heading north to Mecca. It used to take seven days to walk from Sana'a to Sadah and then a further 36 days for the pilgrimage to Mecca.

History

Home of the imams

Like Sana'a, Sadah lay off the old trading routes which passed along the edge of the Rub al-Khali to the east, but became important when these routes moved into the mountains during Himyar rule. Iron mining and tanning are the traditional trades of the area.

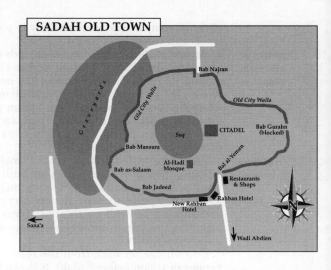

SADAH OLD TOWN

Towards the end of the ninth century, a respected arbitrator was brought in to settle prolonged disputes between rival tribes. The arrival of the Iraqi born **Yahya ibn Hussein ibn Qasim ar-Rassi** in 897 from Medina was the start of a line of rulers which lasted for over 1,000 years. Through his successful mediation he gained the respect and support of the local population to the point where he became their Imam, having fulfilled all the necessary requirements, including being a descendent of Ali (see Islam).

The founding of the Imamate

The founding of the Imamate was arguably the most important event in the Yemen, as his successors played a crucial role in determining the country's future. He took the title of al-Hadi (meaning 'trustful person') and set about filling the deep spiritual need of the people, left by earlier clashes between Jews and Christians in Najran. He brought religious order and established Sadah as the capital of the Zaidi state and centre of Zaidi teachings. Throughout their history, the imams moved their capital all over the Yemen, but Sadah was, and still is, their stronghold.

The legacy of Al-Hadi

Al-Hadi Yahya ruled as imam for ten years and is buried in the Great (al-Hadi) Mosque, which is still the centre of Zaidi learning. The inhabitants of Sadah have always been at the centre of Yemeni affairs, but after a millennium their power is fast disappearing. The revolution ousted their imam and replaced him with an unwelcome republican government. The recent unification of the YAR and PDRY has since shifted the balance of power even further south and allowed in Communist (atheist) and Western influences.

Walking around Sadah

As the provincial capital of a rugged mountainous and desert region, Sadah has many new government buildings totally out of keeping with the old walled town. With every visit there seem to be new buildings stretching down the main road, so that Sadah is now shaped like a tadpole, with the ribbon development as the tail and the old town at the head. But despite recent modernisation the **walled town** is still a real gem of unique mud architecture.

Walking along the walls

You will invariably arrive at the south gate (Bab al-Yemen), note the pre-Islamic carvings, from where you can continue into the main square, or climb up onto the solid mud walls which run continuously around the town, except for a few minor breaks. There is access onto both sides from the gate; the right (eastern) section is the quieter walk, whereas up to the left the wall passes close to the new constructions. Either way, with a bit of improvisation you can walk around to the Zaidi graveyards and the northern Najran Gate.

The walls are wide and were fully rebuilt in 1992/3. By walking along them you get a tremendous view across the rooftops of the mud houses, with great opportunities for pictures of children hanging out of open windows.

Clean lines of the mud walls

This style of *zabur* **architecture** is common to the north and east of the country but as these areas are either out of bounds or impractical to reach, Sadah offers the best examples. As good stonework is scarce, blocks are only used for foundations and can just be seen at ground level. The layers of the walls are built up in stages of about 1/2m, a process that takes at least half a dozen men. Mud clay is mixed with chopped straw and water, and made into handy-sized lumps that are stacked by the head builder who sits astride the wall. The faces of the layers are smoothed with mud by hand, and are then allowed to dry before the next layer is added.

This pleasing style has also added strength in the corners, which are raised and lean gently inwards. For protection there are usually no windows on the ground floor which tends to be used to keep animals anyway. Higher windows with wooden shutters are sometimes protected by a rough surround of gypsum, as is the roof level which is often decorated with beautiful stepped designs.

A gate to keep out invaders

The **Najran Gate** has a twisting entrance similar to that at Thulla, where invaders could be easily attacked from above, before they arrived at the gate itself. Walking away from town to the west you will come to the walled graveyards famous for the large intricately carved headstones. There are several cemeteries running along to the west, some containing the large domed tombs of distant important Zaidis. Children will often accompany you and impose their own ban on entry. It is up to you to decide whether you enter for a respectful visit or run the risk of being stoned.

Just inside the Najran Gate are narrow streets of tall houses, some with old wooden lintels with carved Koranic inscriptions. Further towards the centre is the citadel on a slight hill to the left of the central square. This is a government building and should not be photographed or entered. Slightly to the right is the main *suq* which operates throughout the week, even though Sunday is officially market day. Silver and metalwork are in good supply, offering good value, along with locally produced necklaces.

Zaidi suspicion of Westerners is likely to be felt here more than anywhere else (except Shahara of course), and the traders can be somewhat offhand. But there are still some friendly locals offering local produce, even though their friendliness might be because they run one of the new souvenir shops that have recently sprung up. If you are going to see a Jew then it is likely to be here in Sadah, where they enjoy the same rights as any Yemeni citizen: freedom of movement, ownership of land etc. (see Jewish Yemenis). Recently they have opened a Jewish community school in their village, teaching Jewish doctrines and Hebrew. Some Jewish silversmith families own the shops around the Bab al-Yemen; opening times are different and they are closed all day on Saturday.

**A small *suq*
with some Jews**

To the west of the south gate is the **Great** or **al-Hadi Mosque** with its brown and white minaret towering over the cupolas and tombs of al-Hadi Yahya, who died in 911, and eleven other imams. It is worth making your way around to the back – the side nearest the town wall – for a good view across the small graveyard to see the mosque in its entirety. The tradition is that it is built on the site where Prophet Mohammed's camel rested. The building dates from the twelfth century but was altered and enlarged in the seventeenth.

**Places around
Sadah**

As there is no northern through-route for tourists, you have to follow the same road back to Amran. It is a long way to go for just one night and many group itineraries therefore drop Sadah altogether in favour of the new opportunities in the south. If you are staying for more than one night, there are some very interesting places around which are not visited by many tourists. Umm Layla and as-Sinnara castles can be found easily, but for everything else you will probably need a local guide, as good maps of the area do not exist.

Umm Layla

The furthest north you can visit

Sixty kilometres north-west of Sadah on the road to Baqim near the Saudi border is Jebel Umm Layla ('mother of the night') a group of **mountain-top defences** controlling the pass to the north. From the road they can easily be seen, but the route up is neither easy nor obvious and it will take about 45 hard minutes to clamber straight up. The view from the top is stunning, looking across tiered and eroded outcrops to the east and up to the rugged mountains in the west.

This was an important control point back in Himyar trading times, as testified by huge slabs of rock with lines of script. The whole fortress is walled and contains large cisterns, a mosque, houses, granaries and a central citadel. Many of the buildings are in a good state, considering the military activities that have taken place this century, with impressive flights of steps and stone arches. It is a worthwhile excursion that will last about three hours in total from Sadah, but often it is off-limits to tourists.

Unknown mountain area to the west

Roughly halfway to Umm Layla is the village of **Majz**, which has a Thursday market and is the starting point for a great 4x4 adventure into the Jebel Asayah region. This wild area offers unspoilt villages and tremendous scenery, but it is frequently unsafe for outsiders and sometimes forbidden because of its proximity to the Saudi border.

If you do manage to get in, a spectacular track winds around the mountains to an-Nadir and al-Malahit, from where there is a rough track to Harad in the northern Tihama, 125km from Sadah. From al-Malahit another track leads 27km east to Haydan, which has a bustling Wednesday market, and then north-east to Saqayn. This whole area was the last enclave of Imam Badr in his fight against the republicans and is still impossible for the government to control. Saqayn has a Friday market and some fine rock inscriptions, and is only 36km from the Sadah–Sana'a road.

SADAH ENVIRONS

Umm Layla

Airstrip

→ Al-Buqe

SADAH

Outcrops with rock carvings

Rahban Village

Sana'a

As-Sinnara Castle

Al-Gufel Castle

→ Al-Buqe

N

Faroowah village near Sadah.

Suq at-Talh

A market where anything goes

If you are in Sadah on a Saturday, make sure to visit the market at Suq at-Talh, 10km up the Umm Layla road. This has a reputation for being the main centre for goods smuggled in from Saudi Arabia, everything from electrical goods to heavy armaments. Recent Saudi moves since the Gulf War have restricted this trade but it is still well worth a visit.

The north-eastern road to Najran, also near the border, is not so good or interesting and is likely to be restricted. After 30km another track splits off east to al-Buqe, a border desert town some 140km from Sadah. A weekly scheduled flight from Sana'a arrives there but unless you have special permission you are likely to be bundled straight back to Sana'a.

Rock Carvings

Pre-historic inhabitants

Still in the east but closer to Sadah, is an area of rock carvings of dubious age, many situated under weathered rock overhangs and open caves. The area is well culti-vated and has been so for many thousands of years, judging by the number of carving sites that appear on weird eroded blocks of stone rising out of the flat acacia strewn landscape. Deep cuts in the rock depict mountain goats and ibex, and are of much better quality and quantity than those in Wadi Dhahr.

As in the Tassili plateau in Algeria, these sites must have had particular significance, as figures overlap one another while other rockfaces are left bare. You would need a local guide to show you these many hidden treasures, of which little is known. From the top of any of these outcrops there are great vistas across to other eroded rocks. On the top of many are ancient water cisterns carved out of the rock and the remains of defensive walls.

Wadi Abdien

Flat, easy walking

Five kilometres to the south of Sadah is Wadi Abdien which forces its way through a narrow gorge in the mountains. This can be a good half day walk starting down the track directly opposite the Rahban Hotel outside the south gate. The village of Rahban is about halfway and it would be interesting to look around its fine clean buildings if it was not for the stone-throwing children.

Fortifications

The castle of **as-Sinnara** can be seen strategically rising out of the bare rock hillside, overlooking the gorge on the eastern side. At one time there was an ancient mud dam built across the wadi. Nowadays the wadi is an irrigated valley floor of bulging orchards and vineyards interspersed with a few small villages. The castle as seen now only dates from the 1930s but a fortress of some sort has guarded the wadi entrance for centuries. During times of trouble further south the Zaidi imams could always retreat here. It was in this castle that Imam al-Hadi Sharaf ad-Din died in 1890 while virtually the whole of the Yemen was under the second Turkish occupation.

Almost opposite as-Sinnara is the smaller al-Gufel fort that helped control the old trade through the wadi. As-Sinnara is in good condition, but unfortunately is still a military garrison. There are cisterns, towers and older fortresses on the slopes, but you will probably be turned away after struggling up the cliff.

Sadah Hotels

All hotels are on the main road from Sana'a.

*** Al-Mamoon. Tel: 2203 or 2459.

45 rooms. A new hotel about 2km from Bab al-Yemen. Good.

** Rahban. Tel: 2856 or 2848.

50 rooms, all without air-conditioning, so there can be problems with mosquitoes. Good views over the city walls at the rear. Centrally located near Bab al-Yemen. New Rahban is being built next door, and will be the best in town.

* Marab

A small reasonable hotel about 1km from Bab al-Yemen.

SANA'A–MAHWEET

Take the road out to Shibam-Kawkaban (see Environs of Sana'a)and by-pass Shibam on the new German-built road (45km from Sana'a). Just beyond the road up to Kawkaban (47km) a tough 4x4 track turns off left towards Jebel Nabi Shu'ayb and skirts around the upper reaches of Wadi Surdud, eventually joining the main Sana'a–Hodeidah road just north of Matnah.

New road brings new opportunities

The new tarred road will open up many tourist possibilities in the Mahweet area which previously required an overnight stay. The road drops into Wadi Ahjar (51km) which feeds Wadi Surdud (you will see it at Khamis Bani Sa'd *en route* to Hodeidah), with the town of al-Ahjar off the road to the right. The town lies at the foot of the Kawkaban-Tawila plateau and is surrounded by spectacular waterfalls draining the plateau in the wet season. Beyond a jumbled landscape of volcanic rocks, weathered sandstone and shallow terracing, the village of Beit Gadeena rears up on an outcrop to the left.

At-Tawila

At-Tawila (79km) is an unassuming town set in a remarkable giant rockery. Outcrops of the weathered remains of a layer of sandstone lying on a bed of Amran limestone give the town a picturesque appearance, in a rather grubby, chaotic way. Huge boulders form part of the scenery as the houses are built around, on and even in them. The small **Fonduq as-Salam** on the main road can offer food and drinks before you cross into the narrow lanes that makes up the old *suq*. It also offers accommodation in two medium-sized rooms with mattresses, and is good and clean. If it is crowded, another house, just across the road, also offers accommodation.

Jabbawockyland

The shops in the town seem tiny, but perhaps it is just the larger-than-life scenery. It is a fascinating place to look around, the atmosphere is good and there is the option of climbing the lower slopes for better views. Most of the towering peaks still have summit fortifications, but it is possible to climb up one or two. From here it is a long day's walk across the plateau to Kawkaban or Thulla (see Environs of Sana'a), or plan for two or three days to Hajjah, Beit Adhaqah or Mahweet.

At-Tawila–Mahweet

The boulder house

Back on the road it looks as though the locals have entered a 'craziest house' competition! Just to the west of the town, there are doorways in the sides of boulders where the rooms have been hacked out of the solid rock. As you cross Wadi Maswar, which runs north into Wadi La'ah, by the graceful new bridge (84km), notice the old stone arch over to the right.

Before **ar-Rujum** a 4x4 track goes left for 13km and then becomes a footpath down to Wadi Mashar, which runs into Wadi Surdud. There are splendid two- or three-day walks from here up the wadi to Shibam or Jebel Nabi Shu'ayb, down to Khamis Bani Sa'd or a tougher one up to Manakha. Ar-Rujum (103km) – pronounced quickly as 'Arjum' – is a village on the edge of a well cultivated plain. It has a lively Monday market (see Weekly Markets).

Mountain sides covered in small villages

Climbing up to Mahweet there are superb views northwards across Wadi La'ah with a spread of villages lying on the lower slopes below Hajjah. If this does not make you want to spend the day walking, nothing will. Beit Gawzah (116km) has a large number of shops, and after 121km you reach Mahweet.

Mahweet

Officially this small town should be called al-Mahweet but like al-Hodeidah, the prefix tends to be dropped in general conversation. Conditions here have always been favourable for human settlement, and there is evidence of early man having lived in caves worn out of the soft rock. The most complete and best-preserved mummy in the Sana'a University Museum was found nearby. Much of Mahweet's history is closely associated with that of Hajjah to the north, and it too can be a problem area for tourists.

The old **citadel** is perched high on a central pinnacle with the new town sprawling below. Only 4x4s can make it to the top, but it is easy to walk to the look-out point facing south. At one end of the terrace is the police station, but the old houses can be seen by entering the gateway at the opposite end. Inside is a maze of twisting alleyways, tunnels, bridges and steps. Take the steps down to the newer section of town, but once you have looked around the modern shops, and the mosques, there is little else to do.

A busy town centre

Like Sadah and Hajjah, this provincial capital is rapidly being improved and modernised and, as with the latter, the main interest for tourists is getting here. With the new road the return journey can now be done in a day from Sana'a, but an effort should be made to plan an onward journey to the south or west. If you plan to stay, the **Fonduq Nile** offers basic accommodation in six rooms, in the new part of town. There is a local restaurant just down the road.

South and West of Mahweet

The route south, down Wadi Hufash (Wadi Sara) is a bird watchers paradise, and has in the past been part of tour-group itineraries, but it now tends to be less popular as Mahweet itself becomes more accessible. A whole range

*Beit Showta
near Mahweet*

**Another route
to Hodeidah**

of vegetation is encountered as the track drops 2,000m in 25km; this would be a fine route for walking with 4x4 back-up. The road passes the small shops and restaurant of Souk al Jama (meaning 'Friday Market') and runs down through narrow rock gorges and plantations of tropical fruits another 37km to Khamis Bani Sa'd (see Manakha–Hodeidah).

The westerly route is also a vehicle track, but much more thrilling. This is superb trekking country, with 4x4 back-up if required. The track initially keeps to the ridges of Husn Ma'aman, Beit Shair and al-Urgup villages, before dropping southwards across rough open highlands into **Wadi Lahima**. After following Wadi G'da (23km) for a short way, it then climbs steeply northwards, again following Wadi Lahima, to al-Mirwah village (35km), where there is a very small *fonduq*. The next 16km offer some of the best views in the whole country: for 9km the track clings to the mountainside through Haddah and Shamsan villages, with superb views south over the double mountains of Jebel Hufash and Jebel Milhan.

**Adventures in
the foothills**

At **as-Sharaf** (45km) four intriguing mountain routes meet. South would take you through as-Safaqayn on the tough track lying between Jebel Hufash and Jebel Milhan on to the Sana'a–Hodeidah road, west of Khamis Bani Sa'd. The route west goes to Namira, but initially also heads for as-Safaqayn. From Namira the track drops into the Tihama and runs to al-Qanawis.

The shortest and most dramatic route goes north and drops down the side of Jebel Juba 14kms to at-Tur on the Hajjah–Tihama road. This descent is steep and dangerous and should not be underestimated by 4x4 drivers. The 59km drive from Mahweet through as-Sharaf to at-Tur takes about five hours, and could be walked in a hard two days by staying overnight at al-Mirwah.

EAST OF SANA'A

SANA'A–MARIB

Travelling north or east from Sana'a there is a good chance that you might have to show your passport at one of the many checkpoints, so make sure that it is always at hand. Many of the rough-looking local roadside restaurants on the way to Marib serve excellent *selta* if you happen to hit them at lunchtime.

Marib is 175 km due east of Sana'a with a theoretical choice of two routes. Tourists travel on the northern tarred road, which can also include a side trip to Baraqish. The southern route via Sirwah requires a 4x4. It passes through more spectacular scenery but is out of bounds owing to the tribal problems in the area.

From Sana'a the tarred road passes east of the airport and the suburb of Ar-Rawdah (10km). Beyond this the Sana'a Plain is known as the region of the **Beni Hushaish,** a powerful tribe which played an important part in ending the civil war. Initially royalist fighters, the tribesmen became republican supporters in 1968. Be careful taking people's photographs. This area is noted for its high-quality *qat* and grapes, especially towards the end of summer.

Shibam al-Gharas (30km) is a small village off to the right at the foot of the spectacular Jebel Marmar range. It was in the nearby caves that some of the mummies in the University Museum were found. The old white-domed **al-Hadi** Mosque nestles quietly at the base of the cliffs, with a deep well and water channel leading to the ablutions pool. Looking directly up to Jebel Marmar, there are old city ruins that contain a citadel, a mosque, houses and water cisterns dating back 1,000 years. Once controlled by the Sultans of Beni Hatim, it is one of the places of pilgrimage for members of the Ismaili Taiyibi sect which now has its headquarters in India. It is possible to climb the 700m to the top, but you should have a local guide and plenty of water and supplies, allowing a full day for the adventure. This is an area where gypsum is mined and burned in kilns.

Ismaili pilgrim site

The road climbs out of the Sana'a plain over the Naqil bin Ghaylan pass and into another basin covered in *qat* trees. From here Wadi al-Kharid strikes due north and runs into Wadi al-Jawf. Should this region ever be opened to unrestricted travel, it would be a superb 70km adventure by 4x4. Beyond Barran, lying at the foot of a spectacular sugar loaf mountain on the right, is an important checkpoint with much military hardware on show.

Into the 'Empty Quarter'

This is the start of the **Eastern Desert,** where the local tribes have greater autonomy, and control many of the ancient sites which are currently out of bounds to tourists. Most men in these wild areas saunter around with a formidable arsenal (an English word derived through Italian from the Arabic *Dar accina'ah* meaning 'House of manufacture'). It is quite normal to see men with not only *jambias* and Kalashnikovs, but pistols, cartridge belts and even brightly coloured hand grenades.

Personal protection

The road cuts through the Naqil al-Fardha pass giving breathtaking panoramas over the edge of the Rub al-Khali, the Empty Quarter. On the desert floor another checkpoint (100km) marks the start of the road north to Baraqish. The sign says 'Baraqish 30km' but it is actually 33km to this most impressive fortified town rising out of the desert wastes.

Baraqish

Ancient capital looms out of the desert

Baraqish was known as Yathul during its heyday as capital of the Minaean kingdom, and like most of the towns on the incense road its fortunes rose and fell with the trade. Lying in Wadi Fardha, the town received taxes from all the traffic passing from Marib northwards into Wadi al-Jawf and beyond. Initially the Sabaeans controlled this whole area, but slowly independent states rose to rival Marib. Baraqish proved to be a valuable outpost for the Minaeans from 500 to 100 BC, even becoming capital for a few years around 400 BC. After the demise of the trading route, it appears to have limped along for over 1,000 years, until it revived temporarily between 1200 and 1700. The foundations of these later houses are now almost level with the top of the walls, indicating that there are many layers of older buildings below.

There are more than 50 stone towers built into the elliptical fortifications resting on a small hillock rising out of the wadi bed. To the east of the town are the remains of a small dam just inside the perimeter fence. The walls are breached in several places allowing access into a bewildering mass of stones and rubble; most of what can be seen dates from the later Islamic period. The central point of interest is the excavations begun in 1990 by the Italian Institute for the Middle and Far East on the small Barran temple (temple of Nakrah) on the western edge. So far they have uncovered several pillars and beams similar to those at Marib, their depth giving an indication of how many other fascinating buildings there must be below the current ground level. Many of the objects they have found are now at Sana'a Museum awaiting classification and display.

Recent excavations

In the centre of the town there are the remains of a small mosque with a ruined dome, a stone tower and a deep, dangerously unprotected well. From the outside, the western wall provides the most interest. The highest tower is 14m, the original maximum height as the top layer of finished carvings can just be seen. Along the wall-blocks in various heights are rows of Minaean inscriptions, some in their original position, others moved to repair fallen sections. On the north-western corner there are several different types of inscription, including carved snakes.

Keeping the peace

Until 1990 it was usual to arrive at Baraqish to be met by gun-toting tribal children who demanded money for simply being there. Since the Italians started excavating, however, the troublesome tribes people have been kept away by a heavy army presence. It is an uneasy peace which allows tourists access to the site under armed escort. The whole site has a morose atmosphere as though it hides violent and disturbing secrets.

Wadi al-Jawf

A forbidden land

Baraqish is on the very edge of the safe area for tourists. The provincial capital al-Hazm is only 26km north of Baraqish, but it is in an area which is unsafe for travellers. The tribes around Wadi al-Jawf lack neither money nor arms, regularly accepting 'gifts' from both the Saudi and Yemeni governments. This undefined border region, once the domain of the wandering Bedouin, is highly prized by both governments, who try to buy the favours of the fiercely independent tribes. The Yemen wants peaceful relations with the locals in order to facilitate the search for new oil and gas fields. The Saudis are keen to ensure the security of the region, and so reduce the threat of another major conflict.

The locals are well armed, sometimes for self-protection, at other times to take advantage of the opportunities for self-enrichment offered by visiting oil company personnel who are granted permission to enter. Many brand new 4x4 vehicles have been ambushed and stolen from the oil companies. The occupants of the cars are usually released unharmed, having only to contend with the long walk back to camp, but occasionally they are held hostage by the tribes who then bargain their release with the authorities.

Within this troubled area there are several important ancient sites along the northern continuation of the trading routes from Marib. **Ma'in,** which lies just a few kilometres from al-Hazm, took over from Baraqish as the capital of the Minaeans in the fourth century BC. There are some fine sights there, including a shrine inside the old city and the Athar temple outside. Other sites are al-Lawd, Anbba, Kharbat Hamdan, Kimna, Kharbat Abi Thowr and the more famous as-Sawda and al-Beida *en route* to Najran. Unfortunately at the moment the only way to see what they are like is through photographs in

Many important sites

museums or specialist publications.

It may be possible one day to get to Wadi al-Jawf and follow the route up to al-Harf, where it meets the Sana'a–Sadah road. At the moment, however, the only way out of Baraqish is to retrace the road back to the checkpoint at the junction (100km from Sana'a) and head east to Marib. During the summer rains this area of semi-desert is home to many of the nomadic Bedouin, who feed their herds of goats on the sparse vegetation before disappearing back towards the Rub al-Khali.

Towards the Queen of Sheba

The road runs along the edge of sand dunes almost at the foot of the chain of mountains that extend eastwards into the vast emptiness. Just before reaching Marib the scenery breaks up into a series of black lava flows separated by bright yellow dunes.

MARIB

The airstrip on the left-hand side of the road at Marib was the arrival point for visitors until the completion of the road. The new town is on the opposite side, with the two major hotels on the outskirts reached by impressively under-used dual carriageways. The main road running away from the airstrip has several shops and local restaurants, although many visitors will eat at the Bilqis Hotel. Every time I come here, it reminds me of El Kharga oasis in Egypt's New Valley – a modern desert town, a few ancient sites, wide open roads and yet hardly any cars or people, all in a very inhospitable climate.

Optimism in the desert

Awwam Temple, Marib.

History

Archaeologists have identified **Neolithic** and **Bronze Age**
sites to the south and west of Marib, which indicate that
these areas were settled at a time when the climate was
not as harsh as it is at present. Like so many of the other
towns on the trade route, Marib was at the mouth of a
fertile *wadi*, on the very edge of the Rub al-Khali.
Seasonal rainfall was collected as it flowed through the
narrow gorges and diverted to the fields.

The ancient history of the entire country is closely
associated with the **Sabaean Kingdom** which controlled
the southern end of the Gold and Incense Road for 1,000
years. Sirwah became the first capital around 1200 BC.

**Collection
points for the
precious goods**

There were several different routes inland from the
east and south depending on local conditions, but it is
generally accepted that it all filtered through Shabwa and
Marib. Here it was joined by goods from Aden and Muza
(north of Mokha) and repackaged for the journey northwards (see The Gold and Incense Road).

As the trade increased so did the importance of Marib
which profited from its position further along the route
and its abundant supply of water, and it replaced Sirwah
as capital. The Kingdom of Saba also soon controlled the
sea trade, bringing luxury goods from India and East
Africa. The name Saba comes from one of the descendants of Noah (possibly of the seventh generation),
whose brothers gave their names to areas of southern
Arabia; Hadramaut, Azal (an early name for Sana'a), and
the now lost Ophir.

Little is known about the Saba Kingdom and almost
nothing of the period until the tenth century BC, when
one of the great stories of Arab tradition took place, a
story that also found its way into the Koran and the Bible
– the meeting of the **Queen of Sheba** (Biblical Saba) and
King Solomon. Of all the rulers of Saba, the Queen
(known as Bilqis to the Arabs) is by far the most famous,
and although there is as yet no mention of her in inscriptions, there are simply too many historical references,
stories and poems to dismiss her as a mythical figure.

**The Queen of
Sheba meets
King Solomon**

Even though we know very little about her, we can at
least date Solomon as ruling for a period of 40 years from
about 965 BC. From the Koran (Suras 27 and 34) we know
that Solomon first heard about the Queen of Sheba from
his magical messenger bird, the hoopoe, who extolled the
greatness of her kingdom. They exchanged many letters
and as their kingdoms and trade overlapped, she
eventually travelled to meet him.

According to the Old Testament, which only refers to
her as the Queen of the South (1st Kings 10 and 2nd
Chronicles 9) she travelled along the Gold and Incense

Road to present great gifts to King Solomon in Jerusalem.

A historic meeting

There are many tales about this meeting, greatly embellished by classical scholars and artists captivated by this historic event: she set him 'hard questions' which he cleverly answered; she was tricked into showing her hairy legs; her foot was like a donkey's hoof; he tricked her into bed, an event that led to the birth of a son called Menelik. She returned to Marib after Solomon 'gave her all that she desired' (Kings 1:10) and for the next 500 years trade prospered under the Mukarrib Kings and rulers, making the Kingdom of Saba the greatest in the region.

KING MENELIK

Menelik, the son of the Queen of Sheba and Solomon, grew up with his mother and later visited Jerusalem, where he was introduced to the Jewish faith. Solomon was impressed with his son and sent him with many followers back 'home' to Axum in Ethiopia taking with him, it is said, the Ark of the Covenant. Menelik (or Ibna Hakim, a local name meaning 'son of the wise') is said to be buried in Axum and the sacred Ark of the Covenant is thought by some to be inside the Church of St Mary of Zion at Axum.

Ethiopia and Arabia had strong links in the past and it is probable that the Saba Kingdom did in fact stretch over both sides of the Red Sea. The legends are recorded in the **Kebra Negast** ('Glory of the Kings') compiled by the monk Yetshak in the early fourteenth century, some 2,500 years after the events. The rulers of Ethiopia have always claimed descent from Menelik, and Emperor Haile Selassie was the 225th and last monarch in the Solomonic lineage.

The world's first great dam

This prosperity allowed the Sabaeans to undertake great civic projects such as the building of strong defensive walls, temples and the great **Marib Dam.** This last huge project turned the desert into a paradise of cultivated land under shady trees, famous around the known world (see below). The irrigated lands produced greater supplies of food for the increasing trade caravans, which in turn provided more taxes and revenues to build bigger and better facilities. The mysterious neighbouring Kingdom of Awsan and its port of Aden fell to the Sabaeans, but it is still uncertain exactly where the capital was. During this period a single religion worshipping the moon god 'Almaqah' was generally followed, but there is new evidence concerning a sun god.

Roman envy

Several of the minor towns along the route became independent and rose up against Marib during the fourth and third centuries BC. The **Romans** failed to take the city in an ill-fated expedition under Aelius Gallus in 24 BC (some scholars think the army might have made it to Shabwa and been defeated there).

The Sabaean monopoly of trade was eventually

**Collapse of
an empire**

broken, however, and this led to the collapse not only of the dam, but of the whole empire.

The **Himyarites** began to battle for supremacy and soon defeated Saba, moving their capital to Dhafar, in the unconquerable mountains. The **Ethiopians** (links with Menelik?) took Marib in 525 AD, but were defeated at Mecca during a period when the dam finally collapsed for the last time.

The order in the Arabian peninsula was rapidly changing, and there was no room for Marib, which sank back into obscurity until curiosity led early travellers there in the last century. With the recent oil boom it is once again rising out of the sand and the new dam will help sustain a new population. The town is slowly awakening after a 1,500 year slumber.

Sites are nearby

All the sites of interest – the dams, temples and old town – are conveniently located within 10 minutes' drive of each other, allowing ample time to look around. All are to be found by heading towards the ruins of the old town, temptingly situated on a small hill overlooking the lower Wadi Adhana.

The Old Town

The main road swings off right to run around the old town but to visit it, head directly towards it after passing the checkpoint. Even before the ruins you can see the lines of old walls, water channels and heaps on the ground that indicate the sites of old houses. Inspect these

**A dusty
ghost town**

while you take a panoramic photograph of the old town just after passing through the wire fence.

Almost everything is in ruins, but there are a few families still living in the tower houses built of mud brick and stone. Wandering around you can see how some of the blocks from nearby Sabaean buildings have been

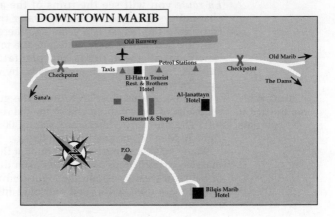

reused. It is easy to get good photographs by climbing (with care) to the tops of some of the abandoned houses. The views over the town and Wadi Adhana are superb. The whole place is like a bomb site, which is hardly surprising as it was heavily bombed as a royalist stronghold during the civil war.

Ruins and ruins

Alongside the town are the ruins of the **Suleyman Mosque** which is also well worth a look around. The wooden beam and stick roof was supported by 42 columns, all different. Though some of these have now collapsed, it is possible to see that some were made from old Sabaean pillars looted from the nearby temples.

The **Imam's former residence** is a smart ruin about 400m south of the town and can be seen to have received some direct hits during the bombardment. The door is usually locked but a local guardian nearby has the key.

Bad planning

Between this and the old town is a large unstable building in black and white blocks which was to have been the residence of the **Hakuma** (local governor). It was started in 1977, but foundation problems caused it to be abandoned. If you go around the corner to the entrance on the right there are some fine examples of reused blocks in three different-sized inscriptions.

A ruined mud town lying on a mud hill creates lots of dust in the dry season, which here is virtually all year, so be sure to have plenty of water to quench your dry throat. Even though I have always found the locals friendly, I know some visitors who have been stoned, normally for refusing to pay money to take photographs, so beware. You can take the same road back or head directly south past the Imam's house towards the dams.

The Old Dam

The remains of the old dam are 14km from the modern town of Marib, across a narrow part of Wadi Adhana. *En route* you will see the ruins of the ancient raised channel system for distributing water through feeder troughs in the fields. Ten years ago there was nothing growing here and even now despite the proximity of the new dam, all these fields and plantations growing citruses, fruits and cereals are irrigated by water pumped up from wells.

Remarkable construction at the time

The mountains close in to form the gorge, with the remnants of the southern end of the old dam over to the left. The northern sluices are about 300m over to the right, hidden behind small mud hills.

Many smaller dams had been built at the site until the massive constructions were undertaken during the peak of Sabaean wealth around the eight century BC. Rough stones were used, with sand and mud filler. The initial

Northern sluice, Marib Dam.

Silting became a problem

height of the dam was about 4m but silt settling behind at an estimated rate of 0.7cm per year was a major problem, which could only be solved by raising the dam height to 7m by 500 BC and 14m by 250 BC. The thick deposits of silt can still be seen behind where the dam wall was.

It is not surprising that there came a time when the dam could no longer be safely raised and simply maintaining it became a major undertaking. Combined with the declining fortunes of the Sabaeans, these problems led to neglect and the dam burst several times around 100 BC. The final collapse around 570 AD is said to have been a retribution from Allah for the locals' pagan ways.

At its peak, the water was diverted along two primary canals from each end to irrigate land as much as 20km away. The irrigated area in this northern and southern 'oasis' is estimated at 9,600 hectares, which yielded two crops per year. It is thought that all the basic foodstuffs were grown, and up to 40,000 people could be supported.

Inhabitants left the region completely

During the decline, many of the inhabitants not only deserted Marib, but left southern Arabia altogether, to escape the warring Ethiopians, Himyars and Persians. It is from this time that many families in Syria, Kuwait and the United Arab Emirates can trace their Yemeni names.

Close inspection of the **northern sluice** shows how well the stones were shaped and fitted, and several have

Impressive remains

inscriptions carved into the face. What you are actually looking at are the sluice gates which directed the water around the side of the dam into the correct channels for supplying the areas to be irrigated. The highest part of the structure is a recently built guardhouse, from where you can clearly see the line of the primary canal that diverted water from the dam to the regulator sluice.

Carved blocks re-used in sluice gates, Marib Dam.

The sheer size is impressive, even if the actual use to which each wall, support and run-off was put is not altogether clear. It is easy to see where the structure has been repaired and in some places the outer facing has been removed showing the material used in the lining. Missing blocks were stolen for house building. The north gate was the scene of heavy fighting between rival tribes as recently as April 1989.

Recent confrontation

The ends of the dam are about 600m apart and the extent of the channel sections can be seen in context by climbing a short way up Jebel Balaq al-Qibli, directly behind the northern sluice. It was an incredible engineering project for the time, and justifies its fame across Europe and Asia.

To get to the **southern gate,** cross the tarred road and drop down to drive across the wadi bed. Direct access is restricted, depending on the amount of water that is being allowed through the new dam via a small 'river', but it is possible to wade or drive through. The solid curved towers and channels are even more impressive in quality than at the northern gate, as they have been incorporated and cut into the rock at the base of Jebel Balaq al-Awsat. An inscription credits some construction work to Yath'amar bin Sama Ali, who is thought to have ruled about a century after the Queen of Sheba, but much of this is still guesswork.

Other ancient constructions uncovered

Make sure to follow the flow of the stream down for a few hundred metres until you arrive at a smaller dam which was used to regulate and divert the flow into smaller conduits. Unlike the main sluices, only the lower levels of this symmetrical structure remain, built onto bedrock with some fine rounded abutments. About 2km further around the base of the mountain is another complex of stone pillars, outlets and channels, part of the system leading to the southern oasis.

The New Dam

A lifeline for the future ...

The modern dam can be seen about 3km upstream, like a flat hill placed in the wadi – a smaller version of the Egyptian Aswan Dam. After a nominal checkpoint, vehicles are now allowed to drive onto the dam itself, which saves the walk up. The canopied viewpoint at the far end is a good place for a picnic, with a view to distant houses across the lake, abandoned to the rising waters. Before the new tarred road to Sana'a the old route via Sirwah came up this wadi. The dam is 38m high and 763m long with a catchment area of almost 10,000 sq km and a capacity of 400 million cubic metres. Waters flowing from it can irrigate land up to 35km downstream. For most people, five minutes will be enough to take it all in. An interesting fact about it is that it was paid for by

... from a connection with the past

Sheikh Zayid, ruler of Abu Dhabi, who can trace his ancestry back to those who fled after the original dam collapsed. The construction work was carried out by a Turkish company, to Swiss designs. It took two years to build and was officially opened on 21 December 1986.

Temple Sites

Returning from the dams, turn right at the junction checking to see if the camel-driven sesame mill is in operation on the other side of the road. These camels are usually blindfolded to stop them becoming dizzy as they walk round and round. Some *qat* is grown here but the quality is considered poor. Fifteen kilometres from Marib a new road runs south to Harib (see Marib–Seiyun), but for the temples turn left, following a signpost to Safer.

A short way down is a road to the left signposted to Bilqis Palace. The five slender symmetrical pillars rising

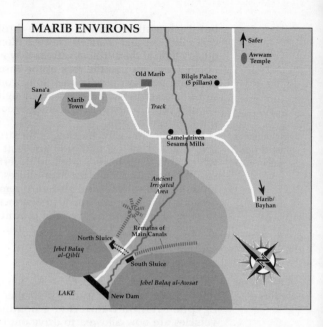

MARIB ENVIRONS

Safer

Awwam Temple

Sana'a

Old Marib

Bilqis Palace (5 pillars)

Marib Town

Track

Camel-driven Sesame Mills

Ancient Irrigated Area

Harib/ Bayhan

Remains of Main Canals

North Sluice

Jebel Balaq al-Qibli

South Sluice

Jebel Balaq al-Awsat

LAKE

New Dam

Ancient sites hidden in the sand

out of the ground are now the subject of a Dutch archaeological dig. The fences and 'Keep Out' signs are intended to stop people defacing and removing the stones. Even though the site is now not very photogenic, there are at least some walls, a marble altar and steps visible that have been buried for over 1,000 years.

This site is sometimes known as the **Almaqah** or **Moon Temple,** also referred to as Arsh Bilqis, meaning the throne of the Queen of Sheba. Much more research is required before such a claim can be substantiated.

Within sight but across the road are other similar columns that belong to the **Mahram Bilqis** or **Bilqis Temple.** It is thought to have originally been called the Awwam Temple, a place where all inside could take refuge. The vast site was partially uncovered in the early 1950s by the Wendell Phillips team and some objects made it to the National Museum in Sana'a. Unfortunately many were left unattended when the team was hurriedly forced out by tribal hostility.

Hasty exit

Much of what they achieved can only be seen in the photographs taken at the time, now on show at the Sana'a Museum. Today there are just a few pillars of a hall poking out of the sand, with fittings for roof sections. An elliptical inscribed wall made from well-cut stone, 4m thick and descending 9m into the sand is thought to be an assembly court, with the remains of a small mausoleum on the far (eastern) side. It is possible that the sites have something to do with Bilqis, the Queen of Sheba, from an earlier age but the inscriptions lead us to believe that it was Yada il-Dharih, ruling hundreds of years later, who constructed these monuments. German research recently called this the Sun temple.

Unfortunately there is little of exceptional quality to be seen at the Marib sites, but it will be fascinating to see how the emerging historical evidence fits in with folklore. There is no doubt that there are some amazing finds to be uncovered. In the meantime enjoy the peace and quiet, and think of what lies below. It might not be too long before an expensive entrance ticket includes a *son et lumiere* show and a visit to the Queen of Sheba Audio-Visual Experience.

Sirwah

An earlier capital

The first capital of the Sabaeans was where Wadi al-Malah runs off Jebel Marthad and joins Wadi Adhana about 50km upstream from Marib. Because the new dam blocked the old road, the route from Marib is now longer, branching off the road to Harib. Surrounded by mountains the site contains a ruined moon god temple to Almaqah and huge curved inscribed walls. It is not known when the capital moved to Marib, but it could well have been at the time of the great dam construction.

Film crew taken hostage

Access to the area is restricted and it is virtually impossible to get there. Even those people who do get special permission have not had the best of receptions. In the late 1980s two BBC film makers were kidnapped attempting to reach Sirwah to do some reconnaissance for a programme on the civilisations of southern Arabia for the *Chronicle* series. They were held for 48 hours while negotiations were conducted into the payment of *diyah* ('blood money') for the deaths of three locals. The tribesmen also wanted a water supply pipe and a school, all of which had been promised but never supplied. Fortunately all ended well, but it is not surprising that the government do not want a repeat of such actions and keep the area out of bounds. The film was never made.

Some maps show a 4x4 route that continues west of Sirwah to reach Sana'a via Jihanah. This is a spectacular journey through stunning geological formations, but it is still subject to the same limitations as Sirwah. There is a smaller and even more difficult route from Sirwah that runs for 90km almost parallel to the tarred road, but on the southern side of the mountains. This goes through Beit as-Sayyid and drops down to the main road near Shibam al-Gharas, but you are unlikely to have the opportunity of travelling between Sana'a and Marib on anything but the tarred road.

Well-armed northern tribesman in Harib.

Hotels
**** Bilqis Marib. Tel: 302371-8.
70 rooms, all air-conditioned with TV, telephone etc. Built in 1987. A beautiful paradise in the oasis with a swimming pool and tennis courts.
** Al-Janattayn, PO Box 97566. Tel: 302310/1.
28 rooms, all with bath and telephone. Huge dining room. Beware of mosquitoes. Office for desert crossing to Seiyun; contact Mr Nasser al-Shareef on 302227.
* Brothers
Above the al-Hanra Tourist Restaurant. Basic hotel with shared facilities.

MARIB–SEIYUN

A tour around the country

Since unification it has been possible to take a 4x4 vehicle across the desert from Marib to the Hadramaut, or vice versa. The exact route varies according to time available local knowledge and conditions. This makes it possible to tour around the whole country returning via al-Bayda or Ta'iz, eliminating uncertain internal flights or the lengthy retracing of routes. It also means that you will be travelling over sections of the Gold and Incense Road.

A popular route is an adventurous blast across to Seiyun in one long day, through the endless sandy stretches of the **Rub al-Khali.** The desert is locally known here as Ramlat as-Sabatayn ('Sand of the two Sabas', which probably refers to the area between Marib and Shabwa, the two great Sabaean towns). This desert crossing is not to be undertaken lightly and should only be attempted with experienced drivers. Sometimes there are prior negotiations with the Bedouin for rights of passage and armed escort. You may also need to employ local drivers (there is an office at the Hotel al-Janattayn in Marib) to find a way through, carry the extra fuel needed and help in case of breakdown or bogdown. It may not be obvious, but most tourist vehicles would be well-armed for this journey of around 400km, as well as for many others in Yemen.

Paying the Bedouin for rights of passage

The route can be used year round, but especially in summer, leave Marib early with plenty of water. Follow the roadsigns towards Safer until a police checkpoint (44km). Just beyond this, the track heads left into the sand, when the drivers will let air out of the tyres. Initially the route is along undulating dunes past the village of Lakhman and then becomes fast and flat past twin volcanic hills, close to the unmarked Saudi border. The vehicles will need to be refilled from jerry cans near the prominent flat-topped mountain Jebel al-Abr (290 km) to the left. Wadi Hadramaut now acts as a giant funnel, channelling all routes into its mouth with distant mountains guiding you from both sides. Small settlements survive amongst the sparse vegetation, the largest of which is al-Wahad below the solitary Jebel ath-Thukmayn. Towards the end of the crossing, the huge Wadi al-Qasr enters from the south, with the old palace at al-Qa'udah clearly visible at the base of the cliffs where the two wadis meet. Several tracks cross over to the tarmac road from Mukalla, including the old cobbled road. I have measured this desert crossing to be just under 400km from Marib, the quickest having taken 7 hours. Several restaurants will relieve your thirst and hunger before the final 65 km to Seiyun along the main road.

Several options heading east

By taking a more southerly route and camping, it is possible to visit the ruins of Shabwa, camp overnight and continue to Seiyun the next day. A longer itinerary would be to include Timna, another interesting site, on the way to Shabwa. If the route from Timna to Shabwa is also to include Nisab and Ataq, then allow another day. I will describe the longer three-day route south through Harib, Timna, Nisab, Ataq, Shabwa and al-Qatn, which should cover most permutations.

Pass the old town of Marib and the road to the dams, turning right at a junction saying 'Harib 90km'. This good tarred road was built in 1989, and has little heavy traffic to ruin the surface. This corner of the Rub al-Khali is similar to Wadi Rum in Jordan, crossing a flat sandy plain surrounded by tremendous mountains from which huge weathered slabs have fallen. You pass Jubat al-Jadidah (45km), a small village with new medical facilities, just before the climb up the recently blasted mountain section of road to Harib. Ahead is the mass of Jebel Bel'an.

Spectacular desert scenery

Harib (87km) is something of a one-camel town which has only recently been opened up to travellers; it was previously closed because of its sensitive position on the YAR/PDRY border. It lies under a small fortress and is essentially a single road of shops with a *qat suq* at the end. The chicken and samosa restaurant has an upstairs section for *qat* and tobacco, with a small room if you are forced to spend the night, although it would be better to camp. Hans Helfritz had no choice in 1935, when he was arrested for entering without permission from the east. In his book *Land Without Shade* he describes June temperatures as being 'unbearably hot', before he was taken to Sana'a and thrown out of the country at Hodeidah. His journey into north Yemen was the first known entry from the east since two Jesuit fathers travelled 'by mistake' from Goa at the end of the sixteenth century (see Early Travellers). In ancient times Qatabanian coins were minted here.

An unintended journey

From Harib there is a track south through the settlement of Ramadah joining the al-Bayda–Rada'a road near as-Sawadiyah. It is a hard 4x4 journey of over 100km along the former border and I have never met anyone who has done it. The route to Bayhan runs due east from Harib by first heading south towards a rock face and **Across the** turning left. The fast hard track makes for a split in the **border** mountains guarded by a command post which formerly belonging to the Abdali Sultan. This is the old YAR/PDRY border point, and the deserted building is still accessible, giving fine views from the roof.

Beyond this are impressive sand dunes with the **Manawa Highlands** behind. Soft sand alternates with corrugated tracks as tamarisk and acacia grow in abundance down Wadi al-Mablaqah. Suddenly you enter Wadi Bayhan from the side and join the tarred road (136km from Marib), which runs in an arc from Bayhan al-Qasab to Nuqub and Ataq.

Bayhan

Turning right, it is 18km to the main town of Bayhan al-Qasab which has a small *suq*, a *fonduq* and an airfield, all scruffy. A road runs south up Wadi Bayhan for all of 135km to al-Bayda, parallel to, but better than the one south from Harib.

Bayhan has a small museum housing some of the lesser finds from Timna (most exhibits are in Aden), unfortunately it was not open on my visit (the hours are supposedly 08.30–12.30 daily except Friday!). As with many of the smaller museums in the former PDRY, one wonders whether it opens at all! Two rooms are said to contain good Timna relics, another documents the independence struggle against the British, while the fourth has an ethnographic display of local clothes, implements and handicrafts.

Nuqub

For Timna head north on the tarred road into Nuqub (22km from Bayhan), the site of the impressive former palace of the Sultan of Bayhan, Sherif Hussein al-Mahdi. Over to the left just before a wadi bridge and checkpoint **A grand palace** there are actually two palaces, the first being an old stone **in the desert** and brick tower house standing alone. The other, built in the 1950s, is now a local government office but it is possible the guards will let you look around. Be careful walking around the back as there are hundreds of used needles and syringes!

This small desert town has some eating places and many interesting houses of a style that will become familiar to you throughout the Hadramaut.

Timna

Turn left off the road just before the palace and pass behind some tea shops heading northwards down the wadi for 6km. Go towards a large concrete water tower surrounded by pleasant fields with flitting bee-eaters, hoopoes and doves. Just 1km further are a group of buildings recently taken over by the military. The site of Timna (or Hajjar Kuhlan) is over to the left but it can only be visited with permission from the commanding officer. It is in situations like these that a good tour agency driver is well worth the cost, as few of the military speak anything other than Yemeni Arabic.

Strategic position The ruins are all that is left of a thriving **kingdom** which lasted about 500 years, even though the city was founded much earlier and contributed to the well-organised caravan trade route. Timna and Baraqish were roughly the same distance either side of Marib, and both took the chance to free themselves and set up as independent states when Sabaean control diminished around 400 BC.

Timna became the capital of the Qataban Kingdom, which had its own direct link with Qana as well as via Shabwa. The entire trade route system was changed by the Himyars, however, leaving the desert centres to inter-tribal warfare and the ravages of time. By the second century AD Timna was deserted, but unlike Baraqish and Marib the site was never fully reoccupied.

In addition to uncovering the Awwam Temple at Marib, Wendell Phillips excavated here in 1950-1 and revealed a **temple** dedicated to Athar, the Morning Star, from about the third century BC (there is another temple to Athar at Ma'in in Wadi al-Jawf). During PDRY times Soviet archaeologists continued working on the site, which has provided many fine exhibits for the National Museum in Aden (and the one in Bayhan). The site has again been abandoned and partly covered with sand, leaving just a few walls and gateways standing about 3m high. Beside a rough football pitch are the foundations of the large temple with a base measuring about 40m x 30m. The stones are huge dark blocks some with Sabaean inscriptions, with sun and moon, and hand motifs.

Only a hint of the wealth to be uncovered The **southern gate** is the most impressive sight, a 5m wide entranceway between solid walls consisting of roughly hewn blocks but inscribed with beautiful smooth lines of Sabaean writing. Unfortunately many of these inscriptions have been deliberately broken for easier removal of the blocks by robbers, and chunks now lie scattered haphazardly in the sand. All around the site are mounds of buried houses with bits of mud-brick walls poking through. Many of the smaller stone blocks have been taken to construct the nearby modern houses and unfortunately the whole site seems neglected, grubby and unimportant.

A wealth of information is still buried in the sand. The military presence hopefully protects the site but it is not particularly tourist-friendly, with access and photography seemingly at the whim of the officer in charge.

Adventurous routes along old trading routes

From Timna it is a sandy 4x4 journey of about 160km to Shabwa with a choice of routes: via the old salt workings at Ayadim Ubaylat near the end of Wadi Dumays or down Wadi Jannah. The Wadi Jannah route threads through shifting dunes and is not easy, especially if the vehicle becomes bogged down in the soft sand. Alternatively the tarred road leads south-east to Nisab and Ataq, or you could try the more southerly 4x4 route, retracing the incredible journey of Wyman Bury a century ago down Wadi Markha.

Wadi Markha

Wadi Markha is thought to contain the capital of the Kingdom of Awsan and no doubt hides many fascinating sites from this and later Qatabanian times.

The Wadi Markha route along the YAR/PDRY border is for real adventurers and starts at the village of al-Hima, 4km beyond Nuqub. From here a rough track runs around the eastern mountains into Wadi Harum. The route then goes due south up Wadi Mafayir to a low pass through the mountains at Rahwat al-Ribah and then south-east to join Wadi Markha itself. This is another of the wadis that spawned the early settlements which were crucial to the development of the trading routes, with ancient sites along its course such as Hajjar am-Nab. The wadi heads north-east but there is a track directly east to Nisab.

Timna–Ataq

Along the tarred road it is 145km from Nuqub (Timna) to Nisab, which is shown on some maps as Ansab. The road twists around massive outcrops of rock and cuts across sandscapes of mobile dunes and eroded pillars of stone. There is a petrol station at the small desert community of Wasit (111 km) and another at Nisab, the former capital of the Upper Aulaqi Sultanate.

A desert of dunes and stones

Nisab is within easy reach of Ataq and some of the oil boom money has filtered through to boost the local economy so that there are many new breeze block buildings rising around the traditional mud-and-straw-brick houses. There are some small restaurants in the back streets and you may find the man with the key to let you see the Sidi Mohammed Mosque and its large graveyard.

Getting from Nisab to Ataq direct is easy but again there are more adventurous 4x4 alternatives south towards the Lawdar–al-Bayda road. A southern route from Wadi Markha, also journeyed by Wyman Bury, will take you through spectacular scenery up Wadi Khaurah through Maswarah and as-Sawma'ah to al-Bayda (about 200km). There is also a route directly south from Nisab through am-Silabah which swings south-west to drop down the escarpment into Lawdar (about 160km).

The oil boom

For the direct route, return the 2km to the main road and turn right along the fast tarred road for 36km to **Ataq,** the busy capital of the Shabwa Governorate. On this road you will see the changes that oil money brings. Many sections of land along the road are already marked out and sold to service industries.

Interest for the tourist is limited to observing this boom economy, but it is not all negative as there are some good local fast-food places. The **Shabwa Museum** is situated in a small building on the Habban road to the south of town and houses interesting finds from Shabwa and Timna. Another section gives an insight into local modern history with everyday household and decorative items. Since so few tourists come here, however, the main problem is finding who has the key to let you in.

Ataq is trying to cope with the boom, but private enterprise has long overtaken any form of local planning and it is every man for himself in this modern gold rush. The major oil companies have compounds around town for all the equipment they require to drill and extract the oil. The sites are often hundreds of kilometres away to the north and east, but at the moment Ataq is the nearest they can get by tarred road. The need for the rapid movement of personnel has led to the establishment of a scheduled flight from Sana'a, which could be useful in an emergency.

Ataq is only 36km from the main south coast road that swings up through Habban (see Aden–Bir Ali). But the main reason for anyone not associated with the oil industry coming to Ataq is to use it as a departure point for the drive north to Shabwa.

Shabwa

North to an ancient capital

Once you have found your way out of busy, rambling Ataq, a graded road strikes due north for what must be the most uninteresting 112km in the Yemen – flat, straight and dusty. The road ends at an airstrip at al-Uqlah, but a graded track, and another earlier one, turn east towards Shabwa, and eventually stretch into the wilds of Wadi Hadramaut and other remote compounds.

As the ancient capital of the Hadramaut Kingdom,

Dar Al-Hajjar (Rock Palace).

Al-Muhdhar Mosque, Tarim, Wadi Hadramaut.

Old City, Sana'a.

Shibam, Wadi Hadramaut.

A highly prized objective

Shabwa has always been a focus of interest for travellers, with added excitement provided by stories that it was surrounded by thousands of square kilometres of marauding bandits and Bedouins. The idea that it was forbidden territory for foreigners was enhanced by early visitors such as Hans Helfritz, who claimed to have been the first European into the town. He was immediately ejected and his books give no information about what he saw.

Its history starts much earlier than most of the other trade centres. French archaeologists think that there has been a settlement on the site for at least 8,000 years, based on the ready supply of salt. The population was supported by some form of irrigation system in neighbouring wadis.

Strange positioning

When the trade routes started it would have been natural to include this reasonably sized town, even though it was not in an ideal position and situated off the direct routes between other towns. The main route from Qana was north-west to Timna avoiding Shabwa, but the important factor in the town's development was that the main incense-growing regions were in Dhofar at the eastern end of Wadi Hadramaut. By bringing the goods up the wadi through Shibam to Shabwa and then on to Timna and Marib, the longer coastal route could be avoided, as well as the high taxes at Qana.

Much work still needs to be done to understand fully how and why Shabwa became so powerful. There are said to have been 60 temples inside the walls, but looking at the site today this hardly seems credible. However it has been estimated that the area was much larger than the site one sees today. The city walls themselves are said to have been 4.4km in length, but exactly where these were and what they protected is unclear.

The rise and fall of Shabwa

Shabwa gained its independence from Marib around 400 BC and became the capital of the Hadramaut, later extending its control by defeating the Qatabans of Timna around the middle of the second century AD. This action led to its ultimate downfall, as there was no longer a buffer zone between it and the Sabaeans and to the west the emerging Himyars. The Sabaeans retook Shabwa in the middle of the third century AD and plundered the city. The inhabitants fled south to Yashbum and east to Shibam.

Salt has continued to be mined and traded from this site, with villages rising and falling according to the vagaries of the economy, the climate and disease. The local Bedouins have always had a reputation for being some of the most lawless and unpleasant people in the region. After Helfritz's visit in 1932 there was a stream of

Habban town, Shabwa.

travellers almost every year who had tales to tell of trying, with mixed results, to reach Shabwa. For Rickards, Bury, Stark and Philby through the 1930s visiting this hidden place became an obsession.

The ruins of the city lie 20km east of al-Uqlah and are still almost impossible to find, lying as they do low down against a hill. It is therefore a good idea to take someone who knows the site as there are not many people around to ask. It lies near the junction of Wadi Irma and Wadi Atf and is spread over low hills hidden from the main track. The positioning of the city is curious, as it can hardly be said to command any route through the Hadramaut but apparently all the trade from the east came through here.

Limited knowledge
The only excavations have been done by the French, who uncovered the foundations of several important buildings. Their finds are now on show at the museums of Ataq and Aden. Unfortunately many of the shaped stone blocks have been taken over the centuries and used to build new houses on the site and elsewhere. The mud-built houses of the inhabitants have also long since been destroyed and washed away. So for the visitor today there is precious little to see, considering the effort required to get there, and the interest is more in what it was rather than what it is. The site is extensive and there are essentially three periods of buildings. Low heavy walls constructed from large stones and some steps are the remains of the ancient town. On top of these are the more recent mud and reused stone buildings of the three small abandoned villages of Maiwan, Hajar and al-Mathna. Finally there are some brand new stone huts used as storehouses, but apparently permanently locked.

The most interesting site of the ancient period is the base of the **temple** or **palace** at one of the city gates. The two beehive tombs are from later Islamic times and belong to Mohammed bin Buraik and his son Abdul Qadir from the al-Buraik family of local *welis* ('saints'). Around the tombs are large areas of closely packed graves that some experts believe indicate periods of fatal diseases.

Extraction of rock salt still continues
Local tribesmen still mine and trade the rock salt as they have done for thousands of years, not just near the site but at other places up the wadis and in the desert, many with the word *milh* ('salt') in the name, such as Milh Kharwah, 15km to the south-west and Milh Maqah, 20km to the north.

To the east is an intricate *wadi* **system** with evidence of numerous settlements, much more than the other *wadis* along this northern *jol* escarpment. Wadi Irma can be followed to the plateau where there are signs of an ancient route almost straight to the coast at Mukalla. At its mid-point this is the same mountain route from which the southerly tracks from Wadi Amd and Wadi Do'an join to reach Mukalla.

Shabwa–Seiyun

The route from Shabwa to Wadi Hadramaut goes through an area called **al-Karab** and requires a 4x4 vehicle driven by someone who knows how to drive in sand. Get back onto the hard graded track from al-Uqlah and head north until the track ends after about 30km.

A difficult route This is now real desert driving that alternates between hurtling across flat hard plains at 100 k.p.h. and engaging 4x4 to slide and swing through patches of soft sand heavily rutted by bigger and heavier vehicles.

The main track is marked by large white-painted tyres, try to keep within sight of these even when it is necessary at times to leave the track to avoid sandy trouble spots. Most of the names do not mean very much along this section but for most of the time you can see hazy mountains to the south, where there are some small Bedouin settlements. The tyres lead to a petrol station stuck in the middle of absolutely nowhere; it is called Bir Asakir and is reached after 80km. Imagine working here!

With passengers and vehicle suitably refreshed, the track becomes very difficult at times when the loose sand has drifted to form steep or high ridges so that the vehicle 'bottoms out'. A stony desert appears as does sparse vegetation. A few houses can be seen towards the southern edge of the wadi and even the odd one, way out in the sandy wastes.

Entering the Hadramaut The desert village of Hiswah is set back into the entrance of Wadi Rakhyah, but you are more likely to pass straight by without even noticing. On my journey we hit tar again 157km from Shabwa, but the surface was very bad. You will still be following the white tyres, but usually way over to the left. The mountains to the south get closer all the time. After a checkpoint the houses and farms increase in numbers until the road runs through what seems to be, and is, the courtyard of an old palace. This is the village of al-Qa'udah (178km) where Wadi al-Qasr comes up from the south to join Wadi Hadramaut.

There are many tracks leading across the mouth of the *wadi* to join the tarred road running up the eastern side from Mukalla. The restaurants you see before al-Ajlaniya are just the place for a well-earned drink and meal after a tough 187km. From here it is an easy 65km on tar to Seiyun (see Mukalla–Seiyun).

SOUTH OF SANA'A

SANA'A–DHAMAR

South to Ta'iz and Aden

The tarred road goes directly south through several former capitals and crosses some impressive passes. You can get all the way to Ta'iz in around five hours without sightseeing stops. The road can also be used as a useful feeder to get to other destinations in the east, south and west. From Ma'bar there is the road to Bajil in the Tihama. From Dhamar the new connection at Mukayras now gives access through al-Bayda to Lawdar and the short cut to Mukalla. South-east from Yarim is the road through Qatabah that is now the quickest link between Sana'a and Aden.

Sana'a–Ma'bar

The main road to the south leaves the city from the Bab al-Yemen and it takes some time to clear the sprawling suburbs that are expanding rapidly down roads like this. Even beyond the Ring Road there are new hotels springing up all the time to cater for travellers using this road. At the village of Dharsan (9km) a road turns off left for Jihanah (see Environs of Sana'a).

The villages of **Hizyaz** and **Wa'lan** (35km) are good examples of everyday places that exist on agriculture in the high fertile basins. Houses tend to be quite small and built totally out of stone quarried locally, in this case from Jebel Kanin, which rises to the left. Just to the south of Wa'lan is a large fortress house on the left, one of the former residences of Imam Hassan, one of Imam Ahmed's brothers. The road leaves the Sana'a basin by climbing up the 2,755m Yislah Pass (51km).

Impressive passes connect high plains

Above the road at the top of a hill is a fine solid Turkish fort dating from the second Ottoman period, which is still occupied by the military for its strategic position. Views south from here across the Ma'bar basin on a clear day are breathtaking. The downhill run is 4km to the base village of Qariat al-Nakiel. The road runs along a wide expanse of flat volcanic farmland, all intensively irrigated and cultivated using some of the most modern techniques and the centre of the Yemeni dairy industry.

Cows and volcanoes

The main town of the area is **Ma'bar** (72km), which has a hotch-potch of building styles and materials and a few roadside restaurants and teashops. One of the reasons for the mud, stone, brick and block buildings was the need to provide quick replacement housing for the locals who suffered in the earthquake of 1982.

197

Ma'bar–Bajil

A new road west

Just before Ma'bar (the name means 'meeting place') is a road off to the right which goes through Dawran and drops down to the Tihama at Bajil (the sign reads 'Madinet al-Sharq 50, Bajil 155, Hodeidah 219').

Disastrous earthquake

This good tarred road was built with help from the Koreans and opened in 1985. It crosses a flat well-cultivated volcanic plain to Dawran (15km), the epicentre of the earthquake of 13 December 1982, the effects of which are still felt. At 12.15 a 40-second tremor, registering 5.9 on the Richter scale destroyed 15,000 houses, killing 2,500 people and badly injuring 2,000 more. Some 27,000 houses were also seriously damaged, causing over 100,000 people to become homeless.

The relief operation sponsored by UNICEF and other international aid agencies was severely hampered by violent aftershocks, which lasted until March 1983. Tented camps were built until the restoration of ruined houses and the construction of new earthquake resistant ones was completed. The result was that Dawran, once one of the finest villages in the Yemen highlands and sometime refuge of the Zaidi imams of Dhamar, was reduced to heaps of rubble. It will still be many years before the effects are completely overcome.

The terrain slowly starts to break up until the road drops over the edge of the escarpment amidst a spectacular panorama of chaotic broken mountains. Towards the foot is a very rough dirt track off to the left leading 13km back up to **Hammam Ali,** a famous hot-water spa. The route crosses a dry rugged landscape and a 4x4 is needed to reach the town, a collection of stone huts for sleeping, changing and bathing.

Hot springs and baths

Hammam Ali is the middle of three main therapeutic spas associated with the hot sulphur water that flows from the volcanic region. The other two are Hammam Damt (on the Yarim–Aden road) and as-Sukhnah (near al-Mansuriyah in the Tihama). January and February are the most popular months for Yemenis to come to Hammam Ali, and all the huts will be occupied. For the rest of the year there is plenty of room for bathing in the many natural 'saunas', with overnight accommodation if you need it.

There is a more direct route to Hammam Ali from Dhamar (leaving the Sana'a road 11km to the north of Dhamar) through maize and *qat* terraces down the amazing Naqil al-Masna pass. This is part of the original 1930s road from Hodeidah to Dhamar, but it now needs a good 4x4 vehicle to handle the rough remains of the paving.

Returning to the Bajil road it is another 16km to the end of the descent of the village of Madinat ash-Shirq

A remote area

(60km from Ma'bar). Just before the town another track turns off, this time to the right, and crawls slowly north back up the escarpment through the village of al-Hatha to **al-Jumah** (22km from Madinat ash-Shirq). This is all 4x4 territory with a maze of criss-crossing tracks linking hundreds of mountain villages, virtually unknown and unvisited by tourists.

There is a Friday market for the region at al-Jumah, which looks like a normal hill village except that none of the buildings is more than one storey, a consequence of the earthquake. This is really spectacular countryside if you have the time and the vehicle. From al-Jumah there is a long but interesting track west to Samh, and thence by road to Ma'bar that requires at least three hours to cover 60km.

A slave town renamed

Formerly settled by immigrants from African countries across the Red Sea, **Madinat ash-Shirq** was known for centuries as Madinat al-Abid – 'town of the slaves'. This derogatory term was unacceptable in the mid 1970s and so President Ibrahim al-Hamdi personally visited the town and announced a change to the present name, which means 'town of the orient'.

It is strategically situated at the foot of the escarpment where Wadi Rima flows south-west between Jebel Raymah and Jebel ash-Shu'ub. The engineers, however, decided to take the road north-west down the wider and more cultivated Wadi Ja'irah. It is mainly flat and straight, and in excellent condition.

Descending onto the Tihama

Wadi Siham drains a huge area including the southern slopes of the highest peak Jebel Nabi Shu'ayb, and meets Wadi Ja'irah at a spectacular flat plain surrounded by high mountains. To the right is Jebel al-Urr, at 2,240m one of the highest peaks behind Manakha, and on the left is Jebel Bura, which separates this area from the Tihama. The only thing that spoils this scene is the row of modern electricity pylons carrying power into the highlands from the power station north of Hodeidah.

Beyond the rough looking village of Raboa Bani Kwawli (115km) the vista opens to the more familiar flat and sandy windswept expanses of the Tihama. Thatched roof huts start to replace the stone constructions of the mountains around Ubal village. The road runs on and eventually meets the main Sana'a–Hodeidah road after 155km (see Manakha–Hodeidah).

Ma'bar–Dhamar

From Ma'bar, the Dhamar road runs into the Dhamar basin – in fact a continuation of the same 2,500m plateau. After 92km a signpost showing 'Hammam Ali 28km' indicates the rough track to the spa resort (see above) just before a large industrial plant on the right that is the distribution centre for bottled gas.

The outskirts of Dhamar have seen many changes as a result of the earthquake, with many new, but disliked buildings erected to replace the damaged tower houses in the old city. The main thing to notice on arrival is the enormous graveyard to the left of the road. Local people regularly walk or ride across the site as a short cut but they sometimes take exception to tourists inspecting and photographing the headstones or the grander tombs of early imams. The centre of modern Dhamar is at the junction of the Ta'iz and al-Bayda roads.

Rights of way in a graveyard

Dhamar

Dhamar is an ancient town even though it does not look like one. The Himyar capital was situated not very far away (see below), and Dhamar developed as a result of the moving of the main northward trade route into these mountains to run up through Sana'a and Sadah. Its name is thought to come from the Himyar King Damar Alay Yuhabirr (better known as Dhamar Ali) whose large bronze statue greets you at the National Museum in Sana'a.

The town controlled a large area and became the capital of the Zaidi imams on and off between the fourteenth and sixteenth centuries. Being on a flat plain it was difficult to defend and the imams regularly had to retreat to their mountain strongholds. It was a centre of Zaidi learning and the religious university survived into this century. The area was also famous for the breeding of quality Arab stallions and many were kept especially for the imams' stables in Dhamar. Today the town is a provincial capital.

A tradition in horses

The old town is hidden from view 500m to the east of the road but most tourists will pass straight through or perhaps just stop for a drink. But do not judge Dhamar just on what you can see from the main highway. The old section of town is a fascinating, if grubby, place to wander around and even better if you have to spend the night there.

Local buses

There is a good system for getting around town, a fleet of Toyota Coaster buses which traverse a fixed route at minimal cost. The route includes the main highway, the old town and the graveyard, and is particularly busy on Wednesday, which is market day. Inside the old quarter are an amazing variety of house styles and materials, with some sections of the *suq* almost primeval. The lights shining through the coloured windows give a much better effect here than in Sana'a, as the living quarters tend to be near to street level.

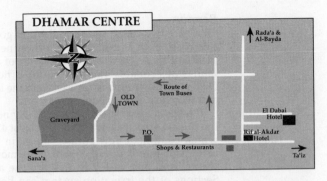

DHAMAR CENTRE

N

Rada'a & Al-Bayda

OLD TOWN

Route of Town Buses

Graveyard

P.O.

El Dabai Hotel

Rif al-Akdar Hotel

Shops & Restaurants

Sana'a

Ta'iz

Real life

For me, there is a real feeling of the Arabian Nights, more so than in any other Yemeni town that I have stayed the night in. It is an unspoilt, dirty, working town with friendly people, and just right for a quiet local evening. There are numerous good restaurants catering for the through traffic and a quiet hotel in the back streets.

West of Dhamar is Jebel Masna, the site of an ancient mountain-top town with cisterns, defensive walls and ditches. Possibly as old as 3,000 years, the site is notable as one of the few places with ancient burial chambers. It is not on the itinerary for most visitors as it requires a special permit into the area, which takes some time to arrange.

Hotels

** El Dabai. Tel: 501539.

12 rooms, all without bath. Difficult to find in the back streets. Start down the al-Bayda road and take the third right (yellow sign on the lamp-post). About 400m on the right is the hotel restaurant, immediately below an Arabic sign which says 'Tel: 501539'. A good, quiet place, quite modern.

* Rif Al-Akdar, Main road. Tel: 504951.

20 rooms. Above some restaurants near the al-Bayda turning. Good value and cleanish.

DHAMAR–LAWDAR

Connecting the mountains with the sea

The recent linking of the old YAR road to al-Bayda with the old PDRY road from Lawdar to Mukayras has opened up new possibilities for travelling around the country. The land between al-Bayda and Mukayras was formerly the border, but with these two linked it is now the fastest tarred road from Sana'a to Wadi Hadramaut. The Dhamar–Lawdar section is 228km, which can be covered in about three hours.

Baynun

There are two rough routes to Baynun going north from this road, both as bad as each other, needing 4x4 and plenty of time. There are tracks north of al-Isi and Jebel Isbil, but probably the best route is north-east from Dhamar itself. It runs north-east from the large graveyard and soon deteriorates into a poor track.

Ancient site in an ancient landscape

It takes at least three hours, probably nearer four, over the rugged volcanic terrain, to travel just 42km to the site, which contains a few ruins. The main interest is the man-made **tunnel** through the Baynun mountain to allow water from one valley to irrigate the adjoining one. Sections of the irrigation system can be seen and it is possible to use the tunnel as the local people do now, as a short cut through the mountain. It starts as a large cut in the mountain and then becomes a tunnel roughly 4m square. It is about 90m long and comes out onto a superb view of the surrounding land.

Very little is known of the site except that it was the Himyar capital at some point, but was totally destroyed by the invading Ethiopians around 525 AD. Himyar inscriptions can be seen, but it is the tunnel which attracts people. Unless you have ample time to spare it is debatable whether it is worth the time and effort to get here at the expense of another site. A large-scale excavation is needed but there are many problems with access to the site and there has always been trouble with the local tribes, which regularly used to attack Dhamar, another reason why you might decide not to visit.

Dhamar–Rada'a

The main road east out of Dhamar heads through the modern section of town and is fairly busy. Just outside is the new village of Bab al-Filak now resituated on the road; you can see the remains of the old town about 500m to the left – another victim of the earthquake.

Volcanic cones

Jebel al-Isi is the isolated mountain looming up on the left, topped by a telecommunications mast. A track leads directly to the base where it is possible to see the walls of the seventeenth century Ottoman fort. Unfortunately, because of the mast, the armed guards will not allow photographs or even too close an approach. This old volcano cone rises over 400m above the plain.

There are chambers for bathing in the hot steam, and it was because of the sulphur here, that the Imam's troops mined the raw material for the making of gunpowder, as mentioned by Niebuhr in 1776. The peak due north is Jebel Dhu Rakam beyond which is Baynun, reached by a poor track from here.

Back on the Rada'a road the remains of the town of al-

Kawlah (24km) stand on the rock to the left. Since 1982 the new housing has been sited at the base. From the village of Sanaban (32km) there is access by another poor track to the north, this time to **Jebel Isbil.**

Bathing in hot springs

Nine kilometres towards the mountain is Hammat Sulayman, a small village trading on the steam-bath visitors. Another 5km will bring you to a footpath at the base of the eastern slope. This is a tough climb of about 300m which gives access to the crater, where there are natural hot steam baths. Yemenis who wish to treat themselves in the health-giving atmosphere stay for anything up to a week, bringing all they need with them and camping in this giant sauna. Beyond the mountain the track continues north and one branch towards the left will also eventually take you to Baynun.

Rada'a

The road into Rada'a is distinguished beyond the village of al-Fugah by the vast fields of *qat*, each guarded by its own little watch tower. The town itself (55km) lies to the north of the road and was seldom visited by tourists until the connection to Lawdar was completed.

Short-lived golden period

Many pre-lslamic finds have been discovered here and there is certainly much more information to be gained from a proper excavation of the citadel, but this is still in the hands of the military. Rada'a's heyday was the period when it was capital of the **Tahirid Kingdom** (named after its founder at-Tahir from Lahej), which lasted for just 63 years until 1517. The Tahirids had defeated the Rasulids of Ta'iz and inherited the important towns of Zabid and Aden.

Their rule was never strong and they were soon swept aside by the Portuguese who had started to make their intentions clear as early as 1513 with the invasion of Aden. The Tahirids will be remembered not as fighters but as capable agriculturists who set up large irrigation schemes in the area, and as patrons of the arts. The mosque at Yifrus and the al-Ameriya Mosque here are fine examples of their unique blend of Indian, Persian and Yemeni architectural styles.

The town has avoided an excess of modern development by not being declared the provincial capital, a distinction that has fallen to nearby al-Bayda. The centre is approached down a busy road with several *fonduqs* on the left, at the end of which is the extensive *suq*. Many of the houses are naturally lighter in colour and appearance, owing to the light local mud used for building and also the preponderance of large windows, some of which still have the original alabaster sheets.

The town was once surrounded by a stone wall but

recent building has demolished much of it, leaving only a few sections including the eastern Bab as-Suq gate and the western Bab al-Mahjari. The **al-Ameriya Mosque** is to the left of the Maidan as-Suq – 'Suq Square' – which is broken up by a few eucalyptus trees.

Classical building style

The al-Ameriya is a superb building in a unique style which can only be compared to the Alwan Mosque at Yifrus; both were built by the last Tahirid Emir, Abdel Wahab bin Tahir, at the end of the fifteenth century. There is no minaret but a series of white domes on the roof break up the profile. There are similarities with the slightly older al-Ashrafiya Mosque in Ta'iz. It is officially closed, but if you can find the guardian you should be able to get inside for a small tip.

The mosque itself is essentially a two-storey building, the lower storey being used as a *madrasa* religious school and a women's praying area. Around the outside at ground level are a series of small shops built into the arches. Entrance to the upper floor is from the left, and leads into a small yard with ablution pool and chambers. The façade is more like an Italian villa with towers, steps and balcony. Inside there is an open courtyard surrounded by arched galleries and splendid thin carved columns, with stucco decoration everywhere.

Renovation of the highest quality

Restoration began in 1984 with financial help from the Dutch government and the Aga Khan Fund. Only traditional techniques and materials are being used, under the supervision of master stone mason Izzi Gasa'a. Some methods, such as the *qudad* protective coating and waterproofing plaster made from slaked lime and local volcanic ash, had to be relearned.

The balcony extends around the sides of the courtyard allowing good views into the Maidan as-Suq and across to the **citadel** (known as the *qala'a*) which dominates the town. Entry to the citadel is forbidden, but it is known that there are many inscriptions inside dating to Himyar times, together with cisterns, granaries and carved pillars. Between the *qala'a* and the *suq* is another fine domed mosque, ar-Rubbat, also dating from Tahirid times. The former local palace is nearby.

It is not easy to understand the layout of Rada'a especially as there are no vantage points to look over the town. Try to get onto the roof of the Arsh Bilqis *Fonduq*, an old-style Yemeni building dating from 1938 with fine *takhreem* windows. It can be found by turning left just before reaching the *suq*.

Most towns have trouble supporting one small hotel, but Rada'a has several reasonable places to spend the night. Most are on, or just off, the road to the centre. They are:

** **Brothers Tourist (Al-lkhwa),** PO Box 39117. Tel: 553466 or 551715.
20 rooms, two to each bathroom. Clean hotel, with friendly staff. Restaurant next door. The **Al-Ikhwa Jideed** (The New Brothers) Hotel is next door. There all rooms have bathrooms.
** **Al-Noor,** Near al-Aubaly. Tel: 551119.
18 rooms. A clean, local hotel, some rooms with bath. Amazingly dark, considering that the name means 'light'.
** **Arsh Bilqis Fonduq,** Tel: 551763
13 rooms. To the left of the main road. An old style Yemeni house, built in 1938 with good large rooms and fine *takhreem* windows. Reasonably clean. Good view from the roof. A good place for a few travellers to take over a large room.
** **Taj The Happy.** Tel: 551431 or 552819.
Beside the suq. 8 rooms, all sharing bathrooms. A good, clean local place.
* **Al-Salam.** Pretty basic.

Rada'a–al-Bayda

Crossing ancient trading routes

The first thing to note on this 125km journey is the right turn just beyond Rada'a. This is the start of a rough but spectacular 4x4 track south through Qarn al-Asad and the Jebel Mudir ad-Dar range to Juban (62km). This is the region from which the Tahirid rulers came.

From Juban the track drops down to cross Wadi Bana and then climb up to Qatabah after 30km (see below). The northerly continuation of this ancient route finally led to Marib, but today it meets the modern Marib–Harib road at Suq al-Jadidah.

The road to al-Bayda is mainly through a dry volcanic dust landscape with small villages every few kilometres. At Abbas (72km from Dhamar), a track angles across the lie of the mountains to run 92km north-east to Bayhan through al-Awafin and as-Sadr. As-Sawadiyah (111km) has a small *fonduq* and at-Taffah (139km) has fine three- and four-storey houses made out of local black and white stone blocks. The road undulates across a barren plateau dotted with a few houses and small fields.

Just before at-Taffah a track goes north through al-Quha and Ramadah to reach Harib, but this would be a very hard 4x4 journey. Tribal problems can be expected again in this region and it might be advisable not to go too far off the main road unless you have a good local driver.

Army town

A string of poor villages lead to al-Bayda (180km), the capital of the province, which still shows military evidence of its former importance as a border town.

Al-Bayda

Very little has been researched or written about al-Bayda ('the white') because for many years it was closed to tourists due to its sensitive position on the PDRY border. Even today there seems to be some sort of military installation on every hill. Opportunities for photographs are thus limited to the stone houses and *suq* area. Most of the town is experiencing a modern building boom.

There is no evidence of the town being on any of the trading routes and it does not have much in the way of Islamic architecture, as Rada'a was the main centre of the region. It is really only since the arrival of the British in Aden and the establishment of the border between Ottoman Yemen and the Aden Protectorate that it took on its importance as a strategic town.

North is south and south is north

It was something of an anomaly that al-Bayda was in North Yemen, whereas Bayhan, which lies 90km due north was in South Yemen. Today a good 142km road links the two towns and runs down the length of Wadi Bayhan.

There is little of tourist interest here compared to other towns the same size, but there are plenty of restaurants and some good *fonduqs* if you need to stay overnight. All the hotels are in the same area, near the centre.

Hotels

** **Adwa Al-Yemen,** PO Box 38138. Tel: 532783.

12 rooms sharing bathrooms. A good clean place, with a friendly and helpful manager. International direct dial telephone. Recommended.

* **Al-Salam. Tel:** 532787.

20 rooms, some with bath. Reasonable.

* **Al-Wahada.** Tel: 533335.

6 rooms. Basic.

Mukayras

A pleasant mountain retreat

The town on the other side of the old border is only 18km away, and there is nothing to indicate that the border ever existed. Similar in style to al-Bayda but with a bit more colour, Mukayras was a British army stronghold and a popular posting with its pleasant climate in contrast to the heat and humidity of Aden. The new road runs around the outside to am-Ma'dhan and it is possible to continue to Lawdar without even seeing the rather scruffy town.

Everything is relatively modern, and above the post office there is even a hotel – although it is currently closed owing to lack of interest. It was built in the early 1960s as the first hotel in the Protectorate and was used by the British residents of the coast escaping the summer heat. Because of the good climate the region was for many years an important supplier of fruit to the PDRY.

Mukayras is a good starting point for the ruined town of **am-Adiya** 12km to the north-east, which is reached by a terrible track. Am-Adiya has inscriptions to the effect that this Qatabanian town had a trading agreement for the transport of incense from Aden up to the capital Timna. It is also thought that it is built on the site of an earlier Awsanian Kingdom town which had links with Aden. The site has some precisely cut blocks in the remains of walls and steps.

Relics from the past

Nearby are the remains of an old stone road leading north. There are many tracks leading to the north and east from here, most of which would have been trading routes at some time: north down Wadi Bayhan to Timna and north-east down Wadi Markha towards Nisab.

Mukayras–Lawdar

One of the most thrilling 30km road journeys is up or down the 1,000m **Kaur al-Audhillah** escarpment, which runs like a solid wall of rock enclosing the town of Lawdar. Surrounded by lush fields Aryab and Barkan are the last typical Yemeni mountain villages that you will see before dropping over the edge of the plateau.

Feat of engineering

The road is one of those engineering feats that make you wonder how it was all done. The width, combined with the tight and steep bends, makes it exciting enough in a car let alone anything bigger. It took over 30 years to complete, the lower sections were first blasted out by British engineers in the late 1950s, but then the project was abandoned until unification, when it was completed by a Chinese team.

The views down onto Lawdar are magnificent. The descent is over 11km, ending at the checkpoint of Thirah, the village that gives its name to the pass. By now the heat of the plains has replaced the coolness of the plateau as the road runs flat and straight to the Lawdar turning. **Lawdar** itself is 2km to the left of the road and is reasonably unimpressive and probably best viewed from a distance as it lies at the base of the stunning escarpment.

If you do go into town, the hill-top palace of the Audhillah Sultan, whose capital was here, is a further 2km to the west. The town itself has a large *suq* and seems permanently busy; otherwise it is best described as being full of rubbish and wrecked cars, but it does have a small three-room *fonduq* if you are desperate.

Joining the main south coast road

The road runs 9km south from Lawdar across the flat farmland to meet the main south coast road (237km from Dhamar). The roads meet at am-Ayn village, 168km from Aden (see Aden–Bir Ali).

DHAMAR–IBB

Heading due south from Dhamar on the main road, you can easily cover in half an hour the 33km through a volcanic landscape to Beit al-Komani village, followed by the climb up to Yarim, the highest town in the country at 2,550m. Just before reaching Yarim the road enters the province of Ibb.

Yarim

A town recovers from natural disaster

Yarim was badly damaged in the 1982 earthquake and is now a purely functional modern town catering for the through traffic south to Ta'iz and south-east to Aden. The old town lies to the east of the road but many of the old style stone houses are still in ruins. The best day to visit is Sunday, the weekly market day. This is the town where Peter Forsskal, the 31 year old botanist on Carsten Niebuhr's expedition, died in 1763.

The town is noted for its good food and eating places and most of the public express buses to and from the south stop here for lunch. Interestingly, many of the new restaurants in the south which supply food to the oil workers have been set up by people from Yarim.

Yarim–Aden

The fast road to Aden

One of the best developments since unification has been the completion of the most direct route between Sana'a and Aden. The link is the 156km of new road from Yarim through Qatabah to Nawbat Dukaym, where it meets the old Ta'iz–Aden road. The total journey is now 385km.

The road leaves from the centre of Yarim and heads initially east through the pleasant stone villages of Khaw and Maris to ar-Radmah (29km from Yarim). This is where the road starts to follow Wadi an-Nasuq all the way to Hammam Damt (47km) through green volcanic landscapes. Just before the town Wadi Bana comes in from the right; the 4x4 track that runs beside it leads to an-Nadirah, Dhafar and Kitab (on the Ibb road). Wadi Bana eventually reaches the Indian Ocean at Zinjibar after almost 200km.

Hammam Damt

The first thing you see upon entering Hammam Damt from the north is the grand house of Imam Hassan (the brother of Imam Ahmed) on the left. The town is quite modern having recently developed with the new road, giving easier access for the health seekers.

Primeval settings

Above the town looms a large **volcano** looking rather like a leftover from the set of *Close Encounters of the Third Kind*, a real oddity in this land of surprises. The rim of the crater can be reached in five minutes up a series of rickety metal steps. The cone is an almost perfect circle with a path around the inner lip, surrounding a stagnant green lake that lies deep below. With no obvious way down, the plastic water bottles that have tumbled down seem destined to lie there forever.

Chaotic landscape From the top there are panoramic views across Wadi Bana, Damt and a chaotic landscape of other craters and volcanic upheaval. On the northern slopes of the volcano are small *hammams* that use the hot spring water to provide natural health spas. Some of the places are free to the public whilst others have a small charge levied to offer private hire facilities. The larger bath-houses cater for men in the morning and women in the afternoon. Note the water tank of the local mosque where people can ablute in warm water. The surface of this water occasionally erupts with dubiously 'healthy' fumes.

If you feel like a walk there are two craters on the other side of Wadi Bana and one more to the north. Damt is the village 4km to the east lying at the foot of a small hill, on top of which are pre-Islamic ruins.

Much of Hammam Damt's trade is from Yemenis visiting the spas for cures of almost every known ailment, giving rise to plenty of good hotels and restaurants.

Fonduqs ** **Fonduq Damt Tourist.** Tel: (04) 501708.
On a side road towards the crater. 15 rooms, all without a bath, but plenty of hot water, as you can imagine. A good, clean local hotel, well worth a stay. The restaurant at the back of the block serves good local food.
* **Fonduq Al-Rayyan.**
On the left of main road if going south. A small local place with few rooms, usually full.

Hammam Damt–Nawbat Dukaym

From Hammam Damt the road follows Wadi Bana down to Qatabah, including the long descent of Naqil Ash'ayb which starts at al-Jubara (70km). Qatabah (82km) is another nondescript old border town, but is surrounded **Tremendous mountain scenery** by tremendous mountain scenery. An interesting 4x4 road runs due west from here to Ibb (see Ibb–Ta'iz).

The YAR/PDRY border was drawn 3km south of Qatabah. The dominant mountain of the area, Jebel Jihaf, lies to the west of the road, which has already swung west from Wadi Bana and descends the upper reaches of Wadi Hardabah. Ad-Dhala (102km) is the corresponding border town for the south, definitely more interesting.

Ad-Dhala

Ad-Dhala is the former capital of the Emirate of Dhala, one of the states of the Western Aden Protectorate. Most confrontations between the British in the south and the Turks to the north were centred on this small town until 1902 when a meeting was convened and an agreement on **Southern** the border ratified. This is the centre of the southern *qat*- **qat-trade** growing industry from where, in earlier days, it was carried to Aden by camel. During PDRY times the government controlled its sale, so that it was only available to the public on Thursdays and Fridays. Now it can be bought on any day but has to compete with better quality *qat* from further north.

The climate of the town is good all year round, but especially in summer when many of the British community used to move up from Aden in the hottest months. Market day is Thursday.

The town has a basic *fonduq* with several eateries and a small **museum** in the town centre. There are some items from the ancient sites but the main theme is the action taken locally in the revolution and the expulsion of the British troops.

The road continues down some steep sections of Wadi Hardabah for 28km to **al-Habilayn** (ath-Thumeyr), the site of an RAF airfield. This was a region of great unrest during the 1950s and 1960s, when British soldiers were regularly ambushed. Guerrilla warfare ensued in the **First shots** mountainous Radfan region to the east. The first shots **against the** fired by the NLF against the British are said to have been **British** on 14 October 1963, which is now celebrated every year as the PDRY's National Day. The events of the War of Liberation are detailed in a museum in the town.

The same *wadi* now changes its name to Wadi am-Suhaybiyah, down the eastern side of which runs a track south-east to Zinjibar after a tough 100km. The main road goes south-west and drops down onto the coastal plain just before meeting the road from Ta'iz at the Nawbat Dukaym checkpoint (156km from Yarim). The road then heads flat and fast through Lahej to Aden (see Ta'iz–Aden).

Yarim–Ibb

An off-road Just 3km south of Yarim on the road to Ta'iz a track **option** branches right into the rough but spectacular mountains overlooking Wadi Sahul, which plunges down to the Tihama. It is 38km to the village of Rihab, where the main track then comes back 17km to the main road at al-Makhadir south of the Sumara Pass.

The main road, however, crosses the fertile southern Yarim basin to the town of Kitab (13km). The road to Ibb continues to climb the Sumara Pass, but from Kitab a dirt road goes left to the ancient Himyar capital of Dhafar.

Dhafar

From Kitab follow the track signposted 'al-Nadirah 30km' and at ar-Rabad (5km) take the left fork – it requires a 4x4. While crossing the rough fields, the ultimate destination, Beit al-Aswal, can be seen in the distance at the top of the hill just left of a pyramid shaped mountain. Always try to head for this village.

Minkat village (9km) is off to the left and you can see the minaret of the mosque that contains some inscribed blocks taken from the Dhafar site. Beyond this is a green carpet of smooth grass (a possible campsite) on the right after passing a large hill. The rocks have been eroded into **Naturally** strange shapes and colours: red, white and black, almost **coloured rocks** like the national flag! The final climb to the small village of Beit al-Aswal (15km) takes you to the top of the hill and the site of Dhafar (or Zafar), once the most powerful city in southern Arabia and the capital of the Himyarite Kingdom.

It is generally agreed that the **Himyar** period began in 115 BC, the year when the leader proclaimed himself to **Ancient capital** be King of Saba and Dhu Raidan (Raidan being the **now a village** mountain on which their new capital was situated). Before this time events are a bit hazy, but it is thought that the Himyars split away from the Qataban Kingdom, (with its capital at Timna) after a civil war, and then moved west into the mountains. As the Himyarites expanded their power, they came into conflict with the other great power Saba.

Several external factors affected the power of the southern Arabian kingdoms. The mystery of the monsoon winds had been solved, and this allowed the Roman traders to transport the precious goods from India and Africa by sea back to the Mediterranean, thus cutting out the overland route. The silk road was developing through Asia, avoiding the peninsula, and the spread of Christianity decreased the demand for burning incense in pagan worship. Until the end of the first century AD the Himyars were contemporaries of the Nabataeans who controlled the northern end of the Gold and Incense Road from their capital Petra.

Important Using the new port of Muza (to the north of **centre for trade** Mokha) the Himyarites imported goods from Africa and brought them up to Dhafar. Here they were repacked with items from Aden and Qana before being sent north on a new trading route through the mountains to Sana'a and Sadah to rejoin the older desert route at Najran. By 275 AD the Himyars were powerful enough to defeat the Sabaeans, take Marib and the Hadramaut and extend their control over all southern Arabia (the whole of present day Yemen and Oman). The conquered city of Marib was maintained as the principal capital of the Empire, but Dhafar remained as the focal centre of Himyar activity.

A great deal of Himyar script has been found, so we have a good idea of who ruled and when. **Samar Yuharis** was the charismatic leader at the end of the third century AD, and many poems and songs were written about him.

Adopting Christianity

Early in the fourth century an Ethiopian invasion spread **Christianity** through the kingdom, mainly through a Byzantine emissary named Theophilus Indus, who established a bishopric at Dhafar. It is thought that it was at this time that the early churches were built in Aden, Muza, Dhafar and Najran.

Marib was retaken in an upsurge of Sabaean power, but not for long. By the middle of the fourth century the great king **Damar Alay Yuhabirr** had regained all the lost land. He was succeeded by his son Tharan, and it is their giant statues that are restored at the entrance of the National Museum in Sana'a.

Under the leadership of **Abu Karrib Asad,** known as Asad al-Kamil – the perfect one – the Himyarites drove the Ethiopians back across the Red Sea and waged war on the city of Yathrib (now Medina in Saudi Arabia). Some experts claim that Abu Karrib Asad followed the Jewish faith but this is not certain. He made good use of horses, as the cavalry allowed his troops to raid successfully as far away as southern Iraq, and he is also credited with building a road from Dhafar to Mecca. In Dhafar Museum an inscribed block tells us that Sarahbi'il Yafur, his son, repaired the Marib dam in about 447 AD.

Himyar power declines

By the sixth century the region was in turmoil as Persia and Byzantium fought for superiority, the Ethiopians tried to return and Christianity and Judaism jostled for religious supremacy. As a defiant stand against the powerful Byzantine Empire in Constantinople, King Ash'ar Yathar (better known as Dhu Nuwas – 'flowing locks') converted the Himyar Kingdom to the Jewish faith in about 518, and carried out atrocities against the Christians in Najran. This provoked the Christians to attack from Ethiopia under the leadership of Abraha, the Axumite ruler, who defeated the last of the Himyars around 525.

Thus ended the last of the great southern Arabian kingdoms which rose and fell on the trading routes which they controlled for over 3,000 years. The links between the modern Yemen and the Himyarites are strong. Many stories, songs and poems popularise the mighty rulers even today, and if you ask any local about ancient inscriptions, they will reply that they are Himyar regardless of where they are and which kingdom they actually belonged to.

Proud descendants

The traditions of the Himyar kings stretched into this century as **Imam Yahya** claimed descent from them and would smear his letters with green powder (in Arabic, 'green' is *ahmar*, which comes from the same root as 'Himyar'). He also claimed direct descent from the Prophet Mohammed through Ali, although these two are incompatible as the Himyar were Qatanid (southern) Arabs whilst Mohammed was an Adnanid (northern) Arab.

There is very little to be seen of the site, as most of what is left is integrated into the modern houses of the village of **Beit al-Aswal,** scattered across the hillside. In many cases there are old inscribed blocks which have been used in the walls and the local children will gladly show you them – for a price of course. Carvings of wild goats, bulls and trees occasionally brighten up the plain walls.

Looking around Dhafar

At the end of the village are caves and cisterns sunk into the ground. Some of these were for early human habitation but were then reused at a later time as stables for horses. Small holes in the walls were used to tether the animals and feeding troughs were cut into the walls. There is a hole sunk vertically into the rock which is said to have been a prison into which people were dropped. Many other caves can be seen dug into the hillside and on the summit of the adjacent hill are the remains of the gigantic blocks of the citadel and sections of old city walls.

Well worth a visit

At the start of the village is the small **Dhafar museum** which houses some good finds. It will always be locked but the children will go and fetch the guardian, who deserves a tip for keeping it all protected.

The rooms are small but packed with objects from the ruined city, with explanations and diagrams. There are fine carvings of blocks, pillars and columns depicting bulls' heads, lions and various other animals. Other reliefs show classical and early Christian influences such as grape vines and birds; warriors fighting a lion; and a hand delicately holding a flower.

Dhafar–Ibb

The only route out is to return to ar-Rabad. From here, most people will return to Kitab, but the track continues east along a picturesque and seldom-used route to an-Nadirah and eventually arrives at Hammam Damt (54km).

South of Kitab the main road climbs up the 2,800m **Sumara Pass** from where there are beautiful views over the hundreds of metres of terracing which tumble down the mountainside. This has traditionally been the boundary between the northern Zaidis and the southern Shafi'is, as can be seen by the ruined Qala Sumara, a Turkish fort built in a commanding position.

Ibb, the green province

The area to the south has the best climate in the whole peninsula, with ample rainfall, and as many as four crops can be grown per year. Ibb is often called the green province and it is easy to see why in this high altitude region.

At the foot of the descent is al-Makhadir (41km) and 4km further on there is a turn across Wadi Sahul to Zulmah village (13km from the road) on the northern slopes of Jebel Nu'man. This is a beautiful area of mountain villages and verdant terracing. The Jebel Nu'man massif is bordered by Wadi Sahul to the east, Wadi Zabid to the north, Sa'ilat Armah (another *wadi*) to the west and the al-Udayn road to the south.

WALKING IN IBB PROVINCE

There are tremendous possibilities for walking around the central region of Ibb province. The area between Hajjah and Manakha has traditionally been the trekking centre, owing to better *fonduqs* and its access from Sana'a. It is true to say that the Heraz region around Manakha is much more spectacularly rugged, while the mountains of Ibb are more gentle. But it is the permanent greenness of the cultivated terraces and the lush natural vegetation that makes this region so appealing. The treks are not as steep or tough, the people are friendly, and the area is perfectly safe for tourists. Long or short walks can be taken from Ibb, Jibla, al-Udayn and Zulmah, and many other places are easily accessible.

Just before Ibb city is the market town of Suq as-Sebt – Saturday market – (53km), followed by a steady climb up to the city itself, lying under and surrounded by glorious mountains.

IBB

A modern by-pass sends traffic west around Ibb, which is built on Jebel Shemahi (ar-Rushi). The even higher massif behind is Jebel Ba'adan. As provincial capital, it has expanded rapidly over recent years, with buildings spilling down into the valley and along the main roads.

Highest rainfall in Arabia

The province receives the highest annual rainfall in the peninsula, about 1.5m annually, mainly between June and September but also throughout the year. This allows it to provide much of the produce of the country all year round.

The combination of rainfall, sunshine and altitude means that it is possible to see all the activities of the farming year occurring on a single day. Ploughing,

Agricultural activity

harrowing, rolling, planting and harvesting can take place concurrently. Donkeys and zebus (humpbacked oxen) do the majority of the work. The harrow is reversible: one side is studded with spikes, used to break up clods of earth, and the other is smooth and acts as a roller.

Little is known of the **history** of Ibb, except that it replaced Jibla as the main centre of the area relatively recently. Niebuhr reached Ta'iz in 1763 from the Tihama by coming through Jibla the main town at that time. Jibla lies in a virtual dead-end of a wadi running east-west and so the main route between north and south ran around it and was the stimulus for the development of Ibb.

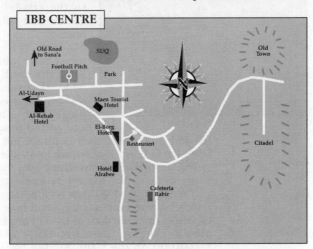

The **old town** is a classic Yemeni mountain village, but unlike smaller towns it has been almost suffocated by the modern developments outside of the walls – as recently as the 1930s there were few buildings outside. Water channels supplied running water from the mountain, and these can still be seen on the lower slopes behind the old town on the road to Mirarah.

Walking on the slopes behind Ibb is quiet, relaxing and thoroughly recommended. It is unclear whether Husn Hab, the fortress on the top, is out of bounds, but it would take several hours to find out.

No-nonsense working town

Stone-built tower houses are crammed together with only the occasional breathing room for a mosque or two, including the fine Grand Mosque. The small warren of *suq* shops are clustered around the southern edge of the walls. Do not expect a walled town like Amran or Sana'a, as this is more like a large version of al-Hajjarah or Thulla. The bleak dark stones of the

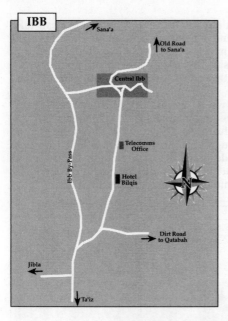

buildings add an eerie atmosphere to the place, especially around dusk.

Getting lost is one of the fascinations of delving into this intriguing place, but it is easy to walk around the outside from wherever you emerge. But be warned; the hills are steep and it is easy to get out of breath at 2,000m. Opposite the entrance to the old town is a wide street that climbs another spur. This leads to the citadel which is now government offices and closed to tourists.

Modern Ibb is a bit of a messy place with no real centre. From the north you will arrive beside the football stadium, with a short street containing a few rough hotels. The modern shops and central square are up to the left and strings of shops run up the hill to the old town. From the El-Borg Hotel (which looks like the *Marie Celeste* sailing down the high street) one long road runs downhill to the south for 3km to meet the by-pass.

There is a good teashop with a panoramic viewpoint which I can recommend for a half-hour wander. Across the street from the door of the El-Borg Hotel is a narrow alley angling up to the left. Halfway along is a good restaurant on the right, hidden behind some metal ladders. At the end of the alley climb the steps into the street and turn right into a busy road of gold and silver merchants. Turn first right up a steep hill and the road swings steeply upwards to the left, and would eventually bring you to the old town. Instead you should turn first right again onto a flat road and after 100m, Cafeteria Rabir is on the right. They do tea and kebabs and offer a fine view over the western section. Two amusement arcades across the street give you the chance to be beaten at pool, table tennis or table football by the local children. Avoided by many tourists, Ibb has friendly people, even though a wander around the old town will make you feel more alien than almost any other place.

Panoramic views

Hotels
*** Bilquis, Main St. Tel: 402630 or 410105.
18 rooms, all with bathroom and telephone. A new, good hotel with restaurant next door.

** **El Borg,** Town centre. Tel: 403586 or 401437.
23 rooms, half with bathroom, TV and telephone.
Threadbare but fair.
** **Al Aqsa,** Main St. Tel: 403432.
7 rooms, all sharing facilities. Built in 1992. Reasonable
but always full.
** **Al Rehab (Arhab Hotel Garden),** Al-Udain St. Tel:
403953/5.
20 rooms, all with TV, some with bathroom. Reasonable.
** **Maen Tourist,** Centre. Tel: 404623.
20 rooms, some with bathroom. A clean local place.

There are some *fonduqs* if you are really stuck:
Alrabee
A communal place.
De Luks
The same.
Sha'ab
Up the narrowest spiral steps ever built.

Jibla

To get to Jibla, take the long straight road down from the
El-Borg Hotel to rejoin the by-pass after 3km. Turn left for
500m and then right in the centre of al-Akamah village.
Ad-Dhithath is the halfway point on the 5km tarred road
to Jibla. The scenery is always of green fields and lush
crops in a series of fields and terracing that covers the
hillsides. Another track comes straight up the wadi bed.

Walking to a former capital — Alternatively there is a good **walk** to reach Jibla
through the fields, taking about an hour. Drive past the
Jibla turning at al-Akamah and start to climb up the Ta'iz
road. 5km past al-Akamah the road does a sharp U-bend
to the left, and there is an electricity pylon nearby on the
right. The track goes from here.

Initially it rises for a short way but otherwise it is all
downhill through an amazing landscape of *dhurra* millet
fields and *qat* terracing. Always follow the vehicle path; if
in doubt there are plenty of farmers and children to show
the way. The track winds down the mountainside
through trees and past all kinds of plants and exotic
flowers, offering views down on Jibla.

Within 500m of the town, do not start to climb up the
track to the left but descend a path between some houses
to get to the football pitch or the American Baptist
Hospital *(mustashfa)*. The Baptist medical team initially
set up their hospital in Ta'iz in 1964, but moved here a
year later to offer high-quality medical facilities.

The story of how Jibla became capital of the Sulayhid
state begins in Manakha where **Ali as-Sulayhi** started the
Sulayhid dynasty (see Manakha). After his death around

217

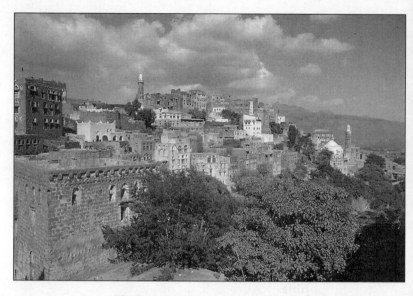

Jibla Town.

**A queen of
the people**

1067 he was succeeded by his son Mukarram, who continued to rule from Sana'a but was in poor health and was possibly a cripple. His wife Queen as-Sayyydah bint Ahmed (better known as **Arwa)** ruled on his behalf until the death of his mother Asma in 1084. After this Queen Arwa took control and moved the capital to Jibla in 1087 to distance herself from the awkward Zaidi tribes of the north. The territory that she controlled was probably the same as the Himyarite Kingdom almost a thousand years earlier, including Aden which paid a substantial annual revenue.

Jibla had been founded only a few years earlier as a seat of local government by Ali as-Sulayhi, but it was Queen Arwa who transformed it into a rich and fertile area. This was done by spending much of the annual revenue on the improvement of communications and agricultural land. She is remembered as a beneficent ruler who always had the interests of her people at heart. The entire Sulayhid period is in fact now remembered mainly as the life and deeds of Queen Arwa in Jibla.

After the death of Mukarram, she ruled through various male officials, many of whom sought to marry her in order to become rulers themselves. But she remained a widow throughout her reign of over half a century. One of her officials is said to have moved all the Sulayhid treasure to the fort at the top of Jebel al-Takar, just south of the town, for safekeeping.

The second Queen of Sheba

The Fatimid caliph in Cairo was doubtful of the Queen's power and sent an adviser called Najib al-Dawlah to help her. Based in nearby al-Janad, he tried to wrest control from her, claiming that she was unfit to rule. Her supporters captured him and he was sent back to Cairo in a cage. This glorious period of 'the second Queen Bilqis' ended with her death, aged about 90, in 1138. Without suitable successors, the dynasty ended abruptly, and the kingdom was swallowed up again by the Najirids, the Zurayids of Aden and the emerging Hamdanid sultans of Sana'a.

Picturesque collection of brick buildings

Jibla is built on a spur of hillside between two small *wadis*. The modern road runs past some new restaurants and it is a good idea to stop at the old stone bridge on the left rather than drive uphill. This footbridge over the *wadi* gets you to the base of the hill on which the town sits and it is all upwards from here. Steps lead to a small tree-covered square, to the left of which is the basic *fonduq*.

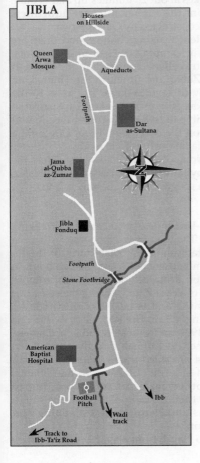

Do not turn left but continue up the steeper hill until it narrows past a superb example of a burnt-brick mosque low down to the left. This is the Turkish **Jama al-Qubba az-Zumar**, resplendent with an ornately decorated white dome and incredibly fine brick minaret in brown, white and green. From here or just further up the path it is possible to look across the *wadi* to see the Great Mosque of Queen Arwa at the other end of town.

Continue up the wide track, not cutting down any of the narrow alley-ways, and you will arrive at the remains of a large palace building on the right, the Dar al-Izz, or **Dar as-Sultana**. This is not the original Queen Arwa Palace but it might well be on the same site. The small mosque built into its base is the as-Sunna Mosque, probably dating from the sixteenth century, with another finely worked brick minaret. Carry straight ahead past the small workshops and drop down into the multi-level, twisting *suq* area. **The Great Mosque** rises up majestically in front and can be reached by climbing the steps to the left above the Turkish baths.

219

The Arwa Mosque

Even though it is still very difficult, this mosque is the one that you will have the best chance of getting into, but only if you avoid prayer times. Take your shoes off and step into the central courtyard beneath the two unidentical minarets. The right hand white minaret (nearest the hill) is the only one which has survived intact from the eleventh century. If you are lucky, you might be allowed into the prayer hall to see the **tomb of Queen Arwa** herself, decorated with texts from the Koran, in the far left hand corner. If you are even luckier you might be invited to the Imam's room on the roof above the tomb, with superb views over the mosque, town, *wadi* and countryside. The mosque is still a working *madrasa*.

The *suq* is an interesting place to wander around for half an hour, or if you are feeling fit, you might want to climb up the steep paths between the houses and get above the town. It takes about 20 minutes up and is quite tiring. Running from the higher hills are aqueducts supplying the town, constructed by Queen Arwa.

A centre for trekking?

This area is excellent walking country, and there are good opportunities for camping treks of more than one day. There are old travellers' routes that go west and descend into Wadi Zabid and down to the Tihama, an adventurous journey of several days. The mass to the south is Jebel al-Takar (site of the **Sulayhi treasure**) at 3230m and it is possible to trek west around the summit to Dhi Sufal village on the other side. From Dhi Sufal a track goes to al-Qa'ida on the Ibb–Ta'iz road.

An epic journey would be to the south-west across the mountains to Mudhaykhirah village via Gauala al-Hafar, from where there is a rough track all the way to Ta'iz.

Al-Udayn

The small town of al-Udayn is a good centre for trekking and mountain travel. The road leaves Ibb westwards from below the football stadium about 500m north of the El-Borg Hotel. The 30km journey takes less than an hour on a tarred road, and you drop into the town, which looks down the tributaries of Wadi Zabid. Facing the coast this area gets ample rainfall and is heavily cultivated. An earthquake measuring 4.5 on the Richter scale hit this region in November 1991 but fortunately did little damage.

Mountain routes seldom visited

North-east from here is Zulmah directly across Jebel Nu'man. To the west are steep tracks that descend into Wadi Zabid to reach al-Jarrahi or Zabid in the Tihama. Southwards is another series of tracks leading to Mudhaykhirah and then to Ta'iz. All these are tough walking expeditions and require good planning and provisions (see Trekking).

Like the journey to Hajjah from Amran it is the scenery

en route that makes this journey worthwhile, and the round trip can be completed in less than two hours.

Ibb–Qatabah

This is a little-used route that links the two main roads to the south. The surface is bad and needs a 4x4 vehicle, but it goes through wild verdant countryside with many species of birds, trees, plants and creepers. It will take over three hours to travel just 78km.

An obscure easterly track

Leave Ibb down the road from the El-Borg Hotel and after 2km turn left at the bottom onto a dirt track. The road crawls up a splendid rockface to **Najd al-Juma'i** (21km) where there is another Arwa style mosque about 350 years old. This would be a good place for totally unique walking, even if only for the day. From here a track goes north to ar-Rada'i on the higher slopes of Jebel Manar. The trees are full of weaver-bird nests and whole hillsides are smothered in small euphorbias. Beyond Mahawa (36km) are weird rock formations.

The final section is not as interesting as the first half, especially as the track is atrocious and it takes a very long time to cover the final few kilometres to Qatabah.

IBB–TA'IZ

South to Ta'iz

This final stretch of the road south from Sana'a leaves Ibb province to reach the foot of **Jebel Sabr.** From Ibb continue south past the Jibla turning and climb up the Naqil as-Sayyani pass through Najd al-Ahmar village (14km from Ibb) just below the summit at 2,337m.

Remains of old roads

From several look-out points by the roadside there are sweeping views to the south across rugged terracing bordering Wadi Duba. If it is clear it is possible to see the mass of Jebel Sabr due south. You can clearly see the old paved track said to have been built during Queen Arwa's time to link Jibla with Aden. Sections of this stone road – in flights of steps in steeper places – go across the *wadi* to the right as it climbs up the western side. Close to an old stone bridge is the almost circular roofed construction of an old wayside stop. This is the route taken by Hugh Scott in 1937-8 and described in his excellent book *In the High Yemen.*

While descending the pass to the south look back at the mountain summit to see the remains of a ruined fort on the very top, which controlled the route in Ottoman times. At the foot of the pass is al-Qa'ida (39km), an old trading town, with another track going north for 10km to Dhi Sufal village to the east of the pass. After the greenness of Ibb this area now starts to look very dusty and scrubby. The main airport serving Ta'iz is some distance to the north of the city and you pass it on the left (49km).

Al-Janad

The junction for al-Janad is 4km further on and is called Mafraq Mawiyah (the road continues past al-Janad to Mawiyah), a collection of busy shops and taxis. Turn left into the countryside and follow the road for 5km until it curves round some houses to the right. This is all that remains of the once important town of Janadiya. Take the road sharp right into the car park of the mosque immediately in front.

The **mosque of al-Janad** is a very plain building on simple lines and extremely effective, especially when surrounded by such a shabby modern village. In Arabic it means 'the garden', a far cry from the rubbish-strewn expanse that usually surrounds it.

An important mosque

It is one of the earliest mosques, and as you can imagine, there are many more stories and legends than there are solid facts. Its construction is attributed to Muad bin Jabal, a local governor sent by the Prophet Mohammed to establish the religion in al-Janad. 1,400 years ago Janadiya was the main town of the region, but it later lost its importance to Ta'iz, which developed quickly in the twelfth century to become capital of the Rasulid Empire.

THE SUNKEN MOSQUE

The mosque of al-Janad lies about 4m below ground level. An interesting but far-fetched Arab story explains why.

During the Prophet's lifetime, the Archangel Gabriel came to help in its construction, but was suddenly called back to heaven. As he ascended upwards many of the local people wanted to go with him, and the mosque physically rose up towards heaven. Gabriel restored the mosque to the ground, but inadvertently pushed it down a bit too hard. Thus the mosque remains to this day, a testament to the power of Islam!

Often damaged and rebuilt

Despite its status as one of the oldest and most sacred mosques in the country, al-Janad has been badly damaged in tribal wars throughout the centuries. Rebuilding took place regularly in the tenth and eleventh centuries and extensively in the early twelfth century by Queen Arwa. In 1973 it was again heavily restored. Archaeologists are furious at the current rebuilding using modern materials.

The layout is similar to the original Great Mosque in Sana'a, which is not surprising since experts now think that they were built within a few months of each other during 628 (four years before the death of the Prophet Mohammed). Three arched colonnades run around the central courtyard with the prayer hall to the north. In the centre of the open space is a gnomon, a stone pillar acting as a basic sundial to indicate prayer times, and

*Al-Janad
Mosque.*

copied from the Prophet's own garden. The tall slender octagonal minaret is in the rear corner and together with the ablution building outside is thought to be the oldest section. Several old inscribed blocks are incorporated into the walls.

Entering the mosque

The mosque also serves as a *madrassa,* a Koranic school of religious learning for the local children, which could explain the mass of children who are always hanging around. There is some uncertainty about access to the mosque for visitors. Sometimes I have been allowed inside and given a personal tour and on other occasions I have been refused entry, but it does seem that you can enter the doorway and remain with your shoes on inside the small archway without actually stepping into the courtyard. Friday is the worst day to visit.

The tarred road can be seen to continue across the brown landscape eastwards to Mawiyah. Beyond this a poor track runs to Musaymir to join the Ta'iz–Aden road at Aqqan (see Ta'iz–Aden Direct). There is also another seldom-used track that runs from here north-east to Adamat around the northern slopes of Jebel Sawraq. This rough 4x4 route runs for 78km to Qatabah, the final 13km on the route due east from Ibb (see Ibb–Qatabah).

Continuing to Ta'iz

Back on the main road to Ta'iz (53km from Ibb), there is a light industrial complex to the right that manufactures, amongst other things, most of the biscuits you are ever likely to eat in the Yemen. At ar-Rahida (59km) there is a left turn to Aden. The large expanse of formal trees and gardens on the right is the Luna Park amusement centre, popular with local families on Thursdays and Fridays.

There are several routes into the centre of Ta'iz, one as complicated as another. Try to stick to the main Sana'a road and you will arrive on Gamal Abdul Nasser Street (70km), the main thoroughfare.

Lakamat al-Ghadi village near Manakha.

WEST OF SANA'A

SANA'A–MANAKHA

The road from Sana'a to Hodeidah is the continuation of az-Zubeiry Street, which goes due west into the mountains. The building of this Chinese road is commemorated by the mausoleum and graves of those workers who died during its construction. Nearby is the larger monument to the Egyptian soldiers who died in the civil war.

Highest point in Arabia

This is the highest region in the country, with **Jebel Ayban** on the left at 3,260m and **Jebel Nabi Shu'ayb** at 3,660m the highest peak on the Arabian peninsula. Being so close reduces the impression of scale, and these peaks look better when viewed long distance from, say al-Hoteib near Manakha, or around Shibam-Kawkaban.

Just before Matnah village (40km from Sana'a) notice the huge boulder on the left, which has incredibly been turned into a house. A doorway has been cut into the rock to provide shelter; this was not done by some ancient cave-dwelling people, but by Chinese labourers building the road in the 1960s! From Matnah (43km) there are several tracks off to the right which pass through mountain settlements, and it is possible to drive a 4x4 vehicle to the top of Jebel Nabi Shu'ayb.

Into the mountains

From Bowa'an village an impressive road twists for 18km to the village of al-Urr on the western slopes. Beyond the Maima Pass the road descends to Khamis Madhyul (55km) offering spectacular views over hillsides covered in ancient and modern terracing. It is said that the practice of terracing spread from the Yemen as far away as the French province of the Ardeche at the time of the Moorish invasions.

The armoured vehicle wrecks around **al-Mafhaq** (65km) are not the result of any battles, but were abandoned by the Egyptian army as they could not make it up such steep hills from the coast! This was part of a giant military convoy sent prior to the revolution in 1962, under the pretence of helping the Yemenis celebrate the tenth anniversary of the Egyptian revolution!

The halfway point of the journey is al-Maghraba (85km) where there is a good trade in *qat*. From here the main road plunges down the western *wadis* to the coast, but another small road doubles back and climbs the 6km up to Manakha.

MANAKHA

This has always been an important town, owing to its strategic position at 2,250m in the centre of the Heraz mountains. The old Turkish road actually went through

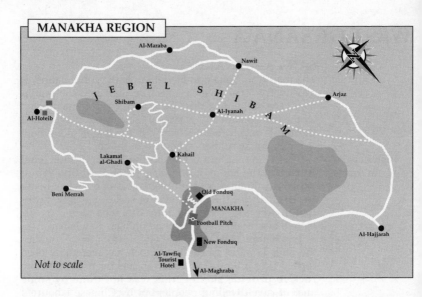

MANAKHA REGION

Al-Maraba

Nawit

Arjaz

J E B E L   S H I B A M

Shibam

Al-Iyanah

Al-Hoteib

Lakamat
al-Ghadi

Kahail

Beni Merrah

Old Fonduq

MANAKHA

Al-Hajjarah

Football Pitch

New Fonduq

Al-Tawfiq
Tourist
Hotel

Al-Maghraba

Not to scale

Manakha, and you can still see sections of it on either side of town, but the Chinese engineers decided to by-pass it. The town dates back to Himyar times as an important staging post to the coast, when the trade routes took to the mountains.

Queen Arwa's father-in-law founds the Sulayhids

One of the great periods of Yemeni history has its roots in Manakha, when Ali bin Mohammed as-Sulayhi, the founder of the **Sulayhid** dynasty began his Ismaili religious conquest of the country from here during the eleventh century. As the son of the regional judge he was well educated but had also been taught particular doctrines of the Fatimid branch of Islam by the local *da'i* ('religious head') Sulayman al-Zawahi.

Convinced that this was the true faith, Ali led the *Haj* pilgrimage to Mecca for 15 years until he had enough followers to proclaim his leadership, backed by the Fatimid caliph in Egypt. In 1046 he raised an army that took the Tihama from the Najahids of Zabid, and Sana'a from the Zaidis of the north, killing the Imam in battle in 1052. This was a low point for the Zaidis, who could find no suitably strong candidate for the imamate for almost a century. By 1063 Ali was given authority over Mecca and Medina and was in control of the whole country plus the Hijaz, except for the Zaidi mountain strongholds. He chose Sana'a as his capital.

Little is known of his later years except that he was probably murdered some time between 1066 and 1080, perhaps leading another *Haj*, during which time his wife Queen Asma was taken hostage in Zabid. Ali's death initially enabled the tribes to regain their lost land, but his son Mukarram rescued Asma and set about consolidating Sulayhid territory. Mukarram was in poor health, and he soon left affairs of state to his wife Queen as-Sayydah bint Ahmed, better known as Queen Arwa. One of her first actions was to move the capital from Sana'a to Jibla (see Ibb).

Strategic mountain town

Manakha was important to the Turks, who also took advantage of its position and built a fort overlooking the town from the north, where unfortunately there is still a military presence today. There are more Ottoman forts on the peaks of other mountains nearby, but all seem to be in the hands of the army. For centuries Manakha was also a centre for Jewish artisans, becoming one of their major communities, along with Sana'a, Ta'iz and Mokha, but by 1950 all Jews had left to go to Israel.

The town is quite a bustling community, which acts as the regional and agricultural centre of the Heraz mountains. The football pitch tends to be the focus of attention even when there is no game, for it is here that the Sunday weekly market sets up its stalls. The colourful trading on this mountain plateau in the clear early morning air is truly unforgettable. Modern shops backed by old *suq* hovels continue the trade through the rest of the week.

Mountain markets

The tower houses are fine examples of local stone being used to best effect. Sandstone and basalt blocks are shaped and fitted to create colourful natural designs highlighted by white *guss* paintwork. All *fonduqs* have dormitory style rooms of different sizes for up to 15 people sleeping on the floors on mattresses. Typical family food is usually served to guests.

Fonduqs

Old Fonduq

A tall stone-built tower house which houses the family and a few tourists. Rooms are small, and toilet and washing facilities are quite basic but acceptable. It is about 200m past the football pitch, to the left of the track to al-Hajjarah.

New Fonduq. Tel: 0722-5000.

Five dormitory-style rooms. Good value and clean. There is a kitchen and small dining room downstairs. It has larger rooms and better facilities than the old *fonduq*. Sometimes there is live music in the evenings. It is on the right, 200m before reaching the football pitch.

Al-Tawfiq Tourist Hotel

Almost the same as the new fonduq. It is on the left, one of the first buildings you come to on entering the town.

Terracing in the Heraz Mountains near Manakha.

The Heraz region is a stronghold of Ismaili tradition, and the shrine at al-Hoteib is a place of pilgrimage for followers world-wide. Some tourist groups stop at one of the *fonduqs* just for lunch, but for others, the attraction of mountain walking will mean staying overnight for one or two days, even more.

A centre for trekking

This is the main centre for trekking, offering a wide variety of routes, but always remember to take the basic essentials (see Trekking). Also look out for sudden changes in the weather – within minutes, a bright warm afternoon can become an icy cold wipe-out of thick mist.

If you are sleeping in Manakha there is a choice of walks: to al-Hajjarah and beyond, to al-Hoteib, to Kahail and to Shibam. Unfortunately these mountains are often covered in mist and cloud, but through the day the sun breaks through to give some spectacular and eerie views.

Agriculture

Depending on the season, there is often a great deal of agricultural work taking place. During harvest time (primarily October) you might observe animals threshing the grain by dragging around a large block of stone called a *madjar*. All parts of the stalk are used the roots and lower stem are burnt for fuel and the remainder is used as animal fodder.

The usual routes for tourists not wanting to walk anywhere at all are the 4x4 drives to al-Hajjarah and al-Hoteib, which can be included in a lunchtime stop between Sana'a and Hodeidah.

Al-Hajjarah

The most popular walk is around to al-Hajjarah using a vehicle track that rises and falls but does not include any serious climbing. This will take about an hour each way plus one hour to look around. Allow more time if it is wet. Continue along the main road past the football pitch and out through the other side of town.

The archetypal mountain village

Al-Hajjarah cannot be seen from Manakha as it lies just beyond the headland to the west, but always take the main vehicle track, or ask the many locals. It is the most impressive and perfectly built example of a heavily walled fortified village in the highlands and is still home to about 400 inhabitants. Many more now live outside in newer accommodation close to the modern school. There is just one narrow entrance gate leading to the incredible tower houses heavily decorated with *guss* whitewash.

The whole village, which was founded during the turbulent rise of the Sulayhids in the eleventh century, gives an impression of strength, unity and independence. Tourists are sometimes invited (for a small price of course) to the rooftops of the taller houses for breathtaking views across the mountains.

Going even further

For the more adventurous, the main track continues slightly uphill beyond al-Hajjarah, around the western slopes of Jebel Shibam to **Arjaz.** This village is about two hours' walk beyond al-Hajjarah and has basic shops for food and water.

Hagara Tourist Hotel. Tel: (033) 61183/4 (in Manakha). Seven large dorm style rooms. Built in 1993. A good, clean, friendly place.

Al-Hajjarah near Manakha.

Kahail in mist near Manakha.

Kahail

The next most popular trek is a bit tougher, and involves a climb of almost 300m to Kahail, a village perched directly above Manakha. There are two routes: one is a mule track up the western side, the other a 4x4 vehicle road that zigzags up the more open eastern face. Personally I prefer to walk up the mule track and descend by the vehicle road which can also include a visit to the lower village of Lakamat al-Ghadi.

Above Manakha

Walking up the mule track you need to keep just to the right of the spur of rock on which Kahail stands, so that you always look down into the valley to the right (west) of Manakha, high above the track to al-Hajjarah. Take the steep paths up between the houses from the end of the shops past the football pitch. The locals are usually quite helpful in showing you the way. Most of the track is on worn stone steps and takes about an hour.

Stupendous views

Enter the gate of the fortified village into a medieval setting that cannot have changed much for centuries. Go left inside the walls to reach the back of the houses and climb the look-out hill for incredible views over distant villages, *wadis* and peaks. The massif directly opposite contains Jebel Nabi Shu'ayb about 40km away. If it is misty, wait for half an hour, as it often clears. A second fortified gateway opens out towards Shibam.

From Kahail head up the vehicle track in front of the village and after about 500m take the track down to the left (straight on will lead to Shibam). The track descends in a series of long hairpin bends towards another village perched on top of a smaller peak. This is **Lakamat al-Ghadi** which can be entered by the single gateway on the far side. Through the day the village only seems to contain women and children, the men are in Manakha.

A hillside of villages

From Lakamat al-Ghadi another vehicle track goes right and descends onto the good Manakha–al-Hoteib track. However, if you take the footpath down directly in front of the gateway this will lead along the terraced fields to drop into Manakha from the east. This whole walk will take about four hours at an easy pace, but if you feel fit you could extend it to include the higher village of Shibam or the lower village of Beni Merrah (see below).

Al-Hoteib

Ismaili shrine

This is a shrine of particular importance to followers of the Ismaili Taiyibi sect of Shi'a Islam and a direct legacy of the Sulayhid state almost a thousand years ago. It is thought there are around 5,000 Bohras (named after their *da'i* – religious head – who lives in India) in the Yemen. Unlike mainstream Ismailis, the Bohras do not respect the Aga Khan as their leader. Today they live in relative harmony with their Zaidi neighbours, but this was not always the case as they gathered in these unconquerable mountains to escape the persecution of the imams.

The day of the annual pilgrimage to al-Hoteib is 16 Muharram (the first month of the Islamic year), when a small temporary village grows up around the site. The tomb that they visit belongs to *da'i* Hatem bin Ibrahim al-Hamdani, an Ismaili preacher of the sixteenth century (his father Said al-Hatem is reputed to be buried in a

Visitors from the sub-continent

mosque above Wadi Dhahr). Many of the pilgrims come from the Indian subcontinent (Bombay is the centre of the Bohra sect). The two other pilgrimage sites are Yifrus south of Ta'iz and Shibam al-Gharas near Sana'a on the Marib road. Traditionally pilgrims should walk between these sites, but today this is unusual, and most transfer by bus.

It is 5km from Manakha to al-Hoteib. The well-used track starts from just above the football pitch and swings around the *suq*. There are three possible short walks: stop above the village of Beni Merrah and walk down there for a look around; drive up to al-Hoteib and walk back (about one hour's walk); drive up and walk back via Kahail (keep to the flat terracing to Kahail at roughly the same altitude and then come down the mule track – about two and a half hours).

The **tomb** at al-Hoteib is the lower white building, and is usually forbidden to non-Muslims. The building to the right of the road is the new hotel for pilgrims, who visit all year, not just during Muharram. Above the tomb is the old house and mosque used by *da'i* al-Hamdani, on top of a pinnacle of rock. There are good steps leading up to the right, but take care if you suffer from a fear of heights as the steps are quite exposed around the back. Enter a stone gateway into a riot of cactus plants. Needless to say, the views are stunning.

Shibam

Even higher

As Kahail is above Manakha, so Jebel Shibam is above Kahail. A 3km vehicle track joins the two but it takes a tortuous route around the mountainside and it is often easier to cut corners using footpaths. If you are walking from al-Hoteib to Kahail, there is no need to go into Kahail, but turn left as soon as you can see the mountain top Shibam village high above to the left. It takes about 45 minutes to get from Kahail to Shibam (or one hour from al-Hoteib).

This place is an even better example of a medieval highland fortified village than Kahail. Not many foreigners get up here and the locals (plus dogs!) are not very friendly, so be careful where you point your camera. The village is small and compact with the houses surrounding a water cistern.

Even though there are footpaths that continue above Shibam, you should refrain from going any higher. The

Trekking in the Manakha region.

peak has a military installation on top, which is out of bounds and guarded. The vehicle road which goes up has

signs forbidding entry and photographs, but obviously you miss these if you take the footpaths. I once spent a long time explaining my mistake to a soldier who still wanted the film from my camera.

From Shibam you can descend to al-Hoteib or Kahail, and even plan a walk round to al-Hajjarah via al-Iyanah.

Walking Circuits

A walk to suit everyone

Instead of going to and from Manakha, there are some routes which avoid the town but can still be done in a day: Al-Hoteib–Shibam–al-Iyanah–al-Hajjarah (six hours); or al-Hoteib–Nawit–Arjaz–al-Hajjarah (seven hours). Longer routes can use Manakha as a start point. It is possible to trek north to ar-Rujum, between Mahweet and at-Tawila in about two long days: go through al-Maghraba, along Wadi Dayan, across Wadi Surdud and up Wadi Ashwal. The trek south to meet the Korean-built Ma'bar–Bajil road also takes two days by heading south towards Jebel al-Urr and then west through al-Hajjaylah and Ubal.

MANAKHA–HODEIDAH

Descending from the mountains

This 135km journey will take you from one extreme to the other: from the dizzy mountain fortresses of the cool tribal highlands to the humid flatlands of the Red Sea coast. The road returns to al-Maghraba (6km), rejoins the main road and swings around from one valley to another before entering a narrow gorge, leading to al-Gadem. Fed by a permanent water supply, the gorge is lush with wild trees and flowers such as *as-Shir*, *ilb* cactus and bottle tree.

Waterfall

A few vehicles are always parked at a narrow section of the gorge, from where it is easy to walk under the road and up a small *wadi* to see a waterfall under large shady trees. When the water is flowing during the rainy season, the locals enjoy swimming in the small pools. If the water is stagnant, beware of the bilharzia threat (see Health). The village of **Khamis Bani Sa'd** (48km) is preceded by lush plantations of banana and papaya. The village, which has a good Thursday market, has grown up where two *wadis* meet the main road and can offer local food and drinks.

With a 4x4 vehicle and enough time, you can drive across the stream of Wadi Surdud and head up Wadi Hufash (Wadi Sara). This is where the route from Mahweet emerges, and it is well worth going even a short way up the *wadi* just to see the small fields of vegetables and maize hemmed in by towering cliffs. There is a wide variety of birdlife in these wadis, especially weaver birds (see Flora and Fauna).

The final barrier before crossing the Tihama is known locally as **Bab al-Naga** (the 'camel gate'), but the imagination has to be stretched somewhat to agree that the outline is like a camel lying down. The road coming in from the left is the new highway from Ma'bar.

Cement city The cement factory town of **Bajil** (78km) is not the best introduction to the delights of the Tihama. It is a noisy and busy modern centre, where everyone seems to own a Suzuki motorbike. The main through road is normally just a mass of traffic, with many heavy trucks starting their journeys from Hodeidah. There are numerous local eating places serving good fast food. The main general *suq* area is set behind the roadside buildings to the right. If you find it too quiet, try visiting it on a Wednesday morning, when every animal in the Tihama seems to be on sale.

A local market food stall in Bajil, north Yemen.

Across the On the outskirts of Bajil is an old Turkish fort, which is
Tihama still in use, with some of the Saudi returnees living rough at its base. If the northern Tihama is your destination, a dirt road goes north from Bajil through al-Mighlaf and reaches al-Qanawis after 56km. It is 100km further by tarred road via Hodeidah.

Green fields alternate with a few encroaching sand dunes in this dry region, which has to rely totally on the water regulation system that starts many kilometres away in the highlands. The style of local housing is now typified by small reed-covered huts that show more than a hint of African influence (see The Tihama). The large *wadi* coming in from the left is Wadi Siham, which carries rainwater all the way from Wa'lan and Ma'bar in the rainy season. The town of al-Marawi'ah (110km) stands on a slight rise to the left above Wadi Siham, and has a Monday market.

Modern port and city Approaching Hodeidah, there is a more businesslike approach to land management for both agriculture and manufacturing. Factories produce soft drinks, cigarettes and flour. The Soviet-built road from Ta'iz joins your route at 121km. The final 15km into Hodeidah is a busy and noisy stretch – the airport is in the distance on the left. The road enters the city on Sana'a Street, the main thoroughfare.

Old wooden carved door, al-Luhayyah, Tihama.

THE TIHAMA

INTRODUCTION

This coastal strip, which runs between the foothills of the mountains and the Red Sea, is yet another fascinating aspect of the Yemen. It would be a mistake just to visit Hodeidah, Beit al-Faqih and Zabid, with possibly Mokha and al-Khawkhah tagged on. Certainly the climate for most of the year makes it a rather uncomfortable visit, but if you can put up with the heat and humidity, the Tihama has a lot more to offer.

Intense agriculture

The importance of the Tihama to the Yemen economy cannot be overstated. About half of all agricultural produce comes from here, sustaining 30 per cent of the population. The water which flows from the mountains brings rich deposits, which are ideal for crop-growing in the continuous sunshine. Salt is mined and exported; oil is piped to the coast; Hodeidah is booming as the country develops; even forgotten Mokha is starting to wake up.

IRRIGATION

The Tihama should be a coastal wasteland, dry for almost all the year, and capable of sustaining nothing more than a few hardy shrubs. It is only through a highly developed irrigation system that anything can be grown at all. Over the millennia, a process has evolved whereby each farmer takes enough water for his land, and then allows the rich silt to flow down to his lower neighbour. Such a system is easily open to abuse and it requires a powerful 'water master' to oversee the fair use and distribution of the waters. In this way, floods have been controlled and agricultural production increased.

Unfortunately, several factors have combined to put this age-old system in jeopardy. Deforestation and poor terrace management in the mountains has allowed topsoil to flow down to the Tihama, clogging up existing distribution channels. The answer has been to replace or renew the expensive channels which can get wrecked again – or simply to pump water from below ground. The resulting drop in ground-water level have left wells dry or allowed sea water to seep in.

Of all the regions that are considered safe for tourists, this is the one that still has most restrictions. Many places are out of bounds because of their strategic importance. They range from the Saudi border area to the Bab al-Mandab, and from as-Salif to Ras al-Kateeb just outside Hodeidah.

Un-used and un-developed

Having said that, there are still huge areas open for tourism which are seldom visited. The potential for developing this coastline is phenomenal. But one word of warning: beware of mosquitoes; malaria is still a problem.

TIHAMA HUTS

Climatic and environmental conditions around the country dictated how buildings were constructed. The rectangular and circular huts in the Tihama are very simple, but show a great deal of craftsmanship, in many different varieties. They are built around a wooden frame, onto which are tied reed bundles for the roof. The walls are usually made from packed mud or reeds. There are no partitions inside the hut, and several huts will be used by one family. The bedroom hut will contain wooden beds made of string, known locally as *ga'dah* but around the rest of the Yemen as *sarir*. The kitchen hut is always a hive of activity, with the smoke seeping out through the steep-angled reed roofing – a very African scene. Shelves are built into the walls during construction and all huts are colourfully decorated inside, including painting the mud walls with murals and hanging plates and decorations. Every tourist wants a photograph of a straw hut, but the inhabitants of villages close to the main roads are now reluctant to have their photographs taken.

HODEIDAH

Plenty to do   It is sometimes said of Hodeidah that there is nothing for tourists to see here, but I find the place a refreshing diversion from the gun-toting tribal areas, with a lively modern *suq*, a fascinating old Turkish section and the best fish market in the country. Swimming is best done away from the city – possibly along the Ras al-Kateeb sand spit – although many locals do take a dip off the Corniche.

Invariably you will be staying somewhere along Sana'a Street, at the western end of which is the large triangular **Hadiqat ash-Shaab** ('People's Park'). This is the place where the locals gather in the pleasant warm evenings to play and chat or watch the illuminated fountain. The grandly named Corniche runs along the coast for the full length of the city, and is another destination for evening strollers.

The Tourism Corporation office is not exactly designed to be user-friendly. It takes ages to find, and even when you do, it has no maps or information. However, you will need to visit the office in order to obtain written permission if you intend going to as-Salif. From the corner of Tahrir Square, go towards the Corniche and enter the busy building on the left. The office is on the fourth floor and should be open 8.00-13.00 daily except Fridays.

History

Recent history   This modern port has risen to be the county's second largest city after the capital. One of the advantages of its position is that it has plenty of room to expand, compared to Mukalla and even Aden. The city as we see it now, only took shape in the 1960s, when the modern port was built using Soviet aid. Before that, it had served through the centuries as the main Turkish port during Ottoman occupation

Important Red Sea port

It was first mentioned in 1455 as a small settlement of the **Tahirid** Sultans based in Aden, and by 1515 it had become caught up in the conflict for Red Sea supremacy between the Portuguese and the Mamelukes. The **Ottoman Turks** chose it as a garrison town, as it allowed easy access to the important Tihama trading town of Beit al-Faqih and the religious centre of Zabid, but they never really settled and were ousted in 1636. By this time, the booming export of coffee was centred on Mokha, which had a better harbour.

The town suffered at the hands of the warring northern tribes throughout the first half of the nineteenth century but then grew under the Turks, who returned in 1849, to rival Aden. Both ports benefited from the collapse of Mokha's coffee trade, and Hodeidah became the Ottoman Empire's greatest Red Sea port. It was

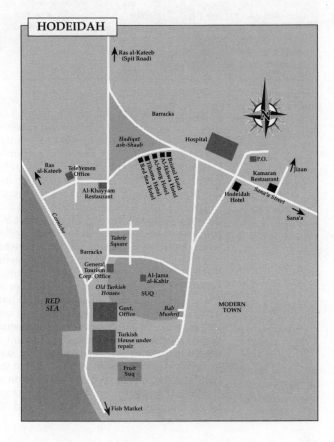

HODEIDAH

Ras al-Kateeb (Spit Road)

Barracks

Hadiqat ash-Shaab

Hospital

P.O.

Ras al-Kateeb

TeleYemen Office

Tihama Hotel
Red Sea Hotel
Al-Horg Hotel
Al-Ikhwa Hotel
Bristol Hotel

Jizan

Kamaran Restaurant

Al-Khayyam Restaurant

Hodeidah Hotel

Sana'a Street

Sana'a

Corniche

Tahrir Square

Barracks

General Tourism Corp. Office

Old Turkish Houses

Al-Jama al-Kabir

SUQ

RED SEA

Govt. Office

Bab Mushrif

MODERN TOWN

Turkish House under repair

Fruit Suq

Fish Market

during this time that most of the fine merchant and trading houses (the so-called Red Sea houses) were built. The importance of this region to distant Constantinople was highlighted by the Turks' ambitious railway plans.

RAILWAYS

Today, the Yemen has no railways, but that has not always been the case – a few kilometres of line did exist at one time. An ambitious plan was developed by the Turks at the beginning of this century to build a railway linking Ras al-Kateeb and Hodeidah with Sana'a. The initial idea was to cut a line through the mountains on a route similar to the present road from Bajil to Manakha. It was intended to continue it through Sana'a to Amran. But even the survey teams needed battalions of troops to protect them from the hostile tribesmen and the idea was scrapped.

Instead the Turks planned to run a line along the Tihama to Ta'iz and then go north to Sana'a. A contract was signed in 1911 for the French engineer Beneyton to commence work for the Ottoman Hodeidah–Sana'a and Branch Line Railway Company. Within a year the Italians were bombarding Hodeidah and the work stopped. The First World War not only ended the railway, but the Ottoman Empire itself. Altogether only about 7km of line was built from Ras al-Kateeb towards Hodeidah. The pitiful rusty remains of a locomotive and some carriages (only the bogies and wheels) now form the foundations of a military camp. You can just see them beside the road at the checkpoint on the spit road to Ras al-Kateeb.

Having signed the Treaty of Da'an with the Turks in 1911, by which they left Sana'a, Imam Yahya supported them through the First World War. This brought him into conflict with the British, who responded by backing **Idrisi** invaders from the Asir region to the north. Hodeidah was bombed and shelled until it fell to the British in 1917. They ceded it to the Idrisi in 1921. It was at this time that the British also took the Kamaran Islands.

The British arrive, but quickly leave

Imam Yahya took the opportunity of taking Hodeidah during a period of internal Idrisi conflict in 1923, but later conceded the Asir region to Saudi Arabia, a situation which has soured Yemeni-Saudi relationships ever since.

The isolationist policies followed by Imam Yahya meant that Hodeidah port was the only real contact with the outside world. Traders from all over the Arab world as well as Jews, Greeks, Italians, Russians and Indians were based here. As late as the 1930s slavery was one of the main trades, with East Africa as the main source. Hodeidah played its part in the overthrow of Imam Ahmed as student demonstrations were continually staged here, and he finally died as a result of being shot at the city's Soviet-built hospital, one of several assassination attempts.

Since the revolution, Hodeidah has grown rapidly, being the only modern port in the old YAR. It will be

Booming Hodeidah

interesting to see which city wins the battle to become the main port in the unified country. To compensate the former PDRY for making Sana'a the capital of the new republic, Aden was designated as the economic capital, with plans to make it a free zone. However, looking at the two, Hodeidah continues to boom, while Aden limps along, a cause of much of the recent southern unrest and fighting.

Walking Tour of Hodeidah

Orientation

This is a short one-hour walk around the main central sights starting and finishing at Hadiqat ash-Shaab.

To reach the **Corniche** from Hadiqat ash-Shaab, turn up the side street with the al-Khayyam Restaurant on the corner, and pass a tasty cake and pastry shop. At the cross-roads go straight ahead past the Yemen International Telecommunications office and turn left at the coast. This stretch of the Corniche has a few boulders on the beach and is not exactly attractive (it is more pleasant to walk on the sea wall amid semi-formal gardens just to the north).

Fish Market, Hodeidah.

Beautiful carvings

At the place where the old harbour wall juts into the sea, look across the road towards the crumbling buildings. Many of these fine **Turkish houses** with ornate decorations have recently been demolished – a great loss. To the right of the government office is a unique building which is fortunately being renovated; it has a central dome on the upper front room.

Quick, before they disappear It is well worth spending ten minutes wandering around the narrow back streets of other Turkish buildings. Many are derelict and are just waiting to be bulldozed, as in other Red Sea ports like Jeddah and Aqaba. Inspect the skilful carvings on the painted wooden door lintels and supports, or peep through cracks into the old houses to see the decorative plaster work on the walls while you still have the opportunity.

From the domed building it is about 2km along the coast to the fish market, but it is pointless to visit it after midday.

FISH MARKET

The best fish market in the Yemen is about 2km to the south of the centre of Hodeidah. An early morning walk there before breakfast is recommended! Most harbours and ports in the country are considered to be of strategic importance, but fortunately that does not seem to apply here. The main market hall is at the far end and usually crowded to bursting point with fishermen, merchants, traders and members of the public, all looking for bargains. Get there early to see the impressive sharks and tuna before they are cut and sold.

You will see wooden dhows or *sambooks*, known in the Yemen as *za'ima*, in various states of construction in the open-sided sheds. The men sitting cross legged mending the nets are usually happy to pose for photographs, but remember always to ask their permission. The harbour itself is full of brightly coloured fishing boats which also make good pictures. Apart from a *qat* market, this will probably be the busiest area you will visit.

A user-friendly town Turn left alongside the domed building away from the sea. Immediately to the left is the **Youth and Sports Club,** which will give you a warm welcome. Across the road on the right is the **fruit and vegetable market,** which is also much livelier in the mornings. The street slowly rises until it swings left and becomes the bustling market centre, with traders covering both pavement and road. In the evening this is a good place to buy some of the day's catch, with many varieties of grilled and cooked fish to be eaten on the move.

The large entranceway on the left is **Bab Mushrif,** now a police station, through which you can enter the modern *suq*. By veering towards the right, you should end up at the main mosque **al-Jama al-Kabir,** which has recently been rebuilt on two levels. Some money-changers have small shops around here offering much the same rate as in Sana'a. You might even pick up a Maria Theresa coin at a good price. Beyond the mosque you emerge into **Tahrir Square**, another pleasant formal garden, from where it is five minutes back to Hadiqat ash-Shaab.

Alternatively, from the *suq* you can go back to Bab Mushrif, and turn left down the main trading street for about ten minutes until you reach Sana'a Street, 500m east of Hadiqat ash-Shaab.

Hotels

All the major hotels are along Sana'a Street. The 'group of five' hotels (Bristol, al-Borg, al-Ikhwa, Red Sea and Tihama) are all next to each other where Sana'a Street curves around Hadiqat ash-Shaab.

*** Ambassador, PO Box 3491. Tel: 231247/9. Fax: 231028. 51 rooms. The first hotel on the road from Sana'a, about 1km from Hadiqat ash-Shaab. The best hotel in the city. Used by government officials and UN staff. All rooms air-conditioned, with bathroom, TV and telephone. Restaurant, bar and disco.

*** Bristol, PO Box 4205. Tel: 239197/58. Fax: 239760. 50 rooms. Overlooks Hadiqat ash-Shaab. A good hotel with all facilities. Restaurant on fourth floor and bar.

*** Al-Borg, PO Box 3254. Tel: 239336/279. 40 rooms. All facilities including air-conditioning and bar. Clean and friendly with a good value restaurant on the top floor. Good views from the balcony overlooking Hadiqat ash-Shaab, superb for a beer at sunset.

** Al-Ikhwa, PO Box 3389. Tel: 239432/779. All rooms air-conditioned. Has a local clientele. Reasonable.

** Red Sea. Tel: 239430/090. A clean, well-used hotel, popular with local businessmen. 20 rooms, some air-conditioned, not all with bathrooms.

** Tihama. Tel: 239558/9. All rooms air-conditioned and with bathroom. Reasonable.

** Hodeidah, PO Box 3712. Tel: 239100/1. 32 rooms, some without air-conditioning and bathroom. A good, clean local place.

* Al-Rawdha. Tel: 238619. 44 rooms, all air-conditioned and with a bathroom. A local place. A bit noisy if you are in a room at the front.

Restaurants

A walk down Sana'a Street will offer you many types of restaurants to choose from. Here are some suggestions.

Al-Khayyam. Tel: 217279. Used to be the restaurant which every visitor ate in, but now there are many other places at better value. Near Hadiqat ash-Shaab.

Deluxe
Good chicken.

Andlus
Good food, spotlessly clean.

Al-Nassim
Good shish-kebab.

Ras al-Kateeb

The best way to reach Ras al-Kateeb is to go north along the Corniche and turn right at the end. Turn left at the cross-roads onto Spit Road, passing the Naval School on the left. Anti-aircraft batteries protect the port, so be careful about taking photographs. There are small open beach huts for bathers and picnickers on the long stretch of beach. The waters near the port are not very clear, and you might find the odd blob of oil.

Long stretch of sand

Spit Road carries on for 11km, with wonderful birdlife, including pelicans and cormorants. The main reason for going to the military checkpoint is to see the remains of the ill-fated Turkish railway. At present, tourists cannot go on to Ras al-Kateeb, where there may well be other relics. Because of the military installation, the soldiers at the checkpoint will not even allow a quick inspection of the rusted rolling stock, and certainly no photographs.

THE NORTHERN TIHAMA

Towards Saudi

This area is usually neglected by tourists or occasionally used as a short cut from Hodeidah to Hajjah. For the more adventurous, there are some beautiful coastal stretches on the way to as-Salif and the delights of the seldom visited al-Luhayyah.

Although several of the old maps show a **coastal route** heading north, it would be hard off-road driving, with

Suq at al-Ma'aras, a typical Tihama scene.

the added problem of certain sections being out of bounds for security reasons. Most places are thus reached from the straight and fast main highway to Saudi Arabia. This road was built by the South Koreans, backed by Saudi finance, at the end of the 1970s.

Conflict with Saudi

The Saudis took much of this region in the 1934 war, showing how ill-prepared the troops of Imam Yahya were. The Treaty of Ta'if pushed the invaders back to the present border. Some of the 1990 returnees expelled from Saudi Arabia during the Gulf War are still stuck here in transit camps, surviving as best they can.

The main road north (Jizan Road) starts halfway along Sana'a Street (the Kamaran Restaurant is on the corner). It takes some time to get out of Hodeidah as every type of truck seems to be parked in and around the port and its attendant shanty town. You only ever get distant views of the cranes and warehouses of the port; the ships themselves have to negotiate a well-guarded 5km canal before reaching the open sea. The road eventually breaks free of the sprawl and a sign informs you that it is 255km to Jizan, in Saudi Arabia.

As-Salif

Special permission

The Tourism Corporation office in Hodeidah is not the place to call in for a chat about hotel rates, but it might be useful to get them to give you permission to go to as-Salif, an **old salt port** on the Ras Kharfa headland. The office will insist that you do not need permission, but that is not what they tell you at the as-Salif checkpoint. The exact position is unclear, as the authorities are not keen to encourage tourism along the coastline opposite Kamaran Island, an area of military camps! But if you can make it, the route to as-Salif is interesting.

Twenty-seven kilometres from Hodeidah there is a track going left to 'Ras Kathneeb'. Follow this to the electricity generating station and then on to a fast compacted track to the fishing village of **Urj**, which has a modern mosque (25km from the main highway). The peculiar grey sand beach is full of fishing boats, with men and boys sorting out the catch under sunshades. A 4x4 vehicle is needed as the dirt track runs along the beach and crosses Wadi Surdud (36km). Minor salt workings appear as white smudges in a surreal landscape of vast mud-flats and black sand dunes. A track to the left goes to Ras Issa, the marine terminal of the 431km oil export pipeline from Marib (out of bounds).

Fifty-six kilometres from the highway is the checkpoint, manned by guards who take great delight in turning away Westerners who do not have a permit. If you do manage to get through, then you will find as-Salif

245

on the headland, overlooking the island of Kamaran. It is still the main producer of high quality rock salt, an important mineral export.

Returning to the highway, you could try to cut across to al-Munirah and az-Zaydiyah from a point where you first reach the sea on the right, but you are likely to become bogged down and lost.

The Highway North

New tarmac highway

Most of this road runs across flat desert scrubland which alternates between small rolling sand dunes and acacia covered *wadis*. Many tracks criss-cross, with dirt roads leading right to Bajil and al-Mighlaf. The latter has a good Saturday market specialising in trading dromedaries.

Just before the small Monday market town of **ad-Dahi** (55km), you cross Wadi Surdud. Around the large *wadis* in this area, the water table is never far below the surface and water pumps throb day and night irrigating the large fields. Modern settlements have grown up along this important highway and you will often see a village of huts on either side of the road, set back about 500m. The older towns tend to be larger and they have dictated the zigzag course of the road as it links them together. For centuries ad-Dahi was one of the main cotton producing centres, a trade which all but vanished after the revolution.

Sights and sounds of 'Africa'

Az-Zaydiyah (71km) is the first main town. It is a collection of small buildings dominated by the sturdy brick Turkish fort, which is still occupied by the military. Tuesday is market day, but every morning the small *suq* is alive with the 'African' colour of the Tihama. This is the main town where the *thuma* is made, the gently curving *jambia* reserved for religious teachers, descendants of the Prophet. Beyond camel-driven sesame mills is the mosque in gleaming white with its many cupolas and a six-sided minaret. If you continue west through the town there is a 4x4 track which leads to al-Munirah and the coastal track to as-Salif.

The next town is **Al-Qanawis** (95km), which apart from the Friday market and some nearby salt mines is a bit disappointing. It is a modern place with a small *suq* and ruined brick buildings of some minor Turkish importance. Just beyond town, a rough track leads south-east to Bajil and an even rougher one heads due east into the mountains to al-Mirwah and Mahweet (see Sana'a–Mahweet). The track going north-west to al-Zuhrah is a 34km short cut to the al-Luhayyah route and is worth considering if that is your destination. A very rough 4x4 route also goes due west down Wadi Ayyan to reach the coast at al-Khawbah.

Two kilometres beyond the bridge over Wadi Ayyan is the right turn at Khushm (114km) for Hajjah (see Amran–Hajjah–Tihama). This area is more arid, and the wind and dust blow constantly around the African-style reed huts, of which the village of **Qureish** is a fine example.

A large bridge crosses Wadi Mawr and 2km beyond that is the turning for **al-Ma'aras** (120km). This is the start of the main track west to al-Luhayyah (see below), and al-Ma'aras itself is famous for its large Saturday market, the major livestock centre of the area.

North to the Border

Fields and fast cars

Few tourists venture beyond the turnings to Hajjah or al-Luhayyah. There are more hut villages, both old and new, on either side of the highway, surrounded by vast irrigated fields of *dhurra* millet. **Suq al-Khamis** – 'Thursday market' – (144km) consists of some roadside restaurants which have developed where the road crosses Wadi Bani Nashar. Sha'afar is full of wrecked cars, offering a foretaste of the abandoned armoured vehicles and military hardware littering the road into **Abs** (162km), a modern regional centre with an airport but not much else. A 40km track heads east from Abs to al-Mahabishah (see Amran–Hajjah–Tihama).

Harad (212km), in Wadi Sulayman, is the last town before the border post. Sightseeing is not encouraged in this area and you might well be stopped at one of the checkpoints. The wadi takes its name from a dynasty of Hasani sharifs, the Sulaymanids, who occupied the region after leaving Mecca in the middle of the eleventh century. They were heavily involved in the Najahid-Sulayhid conflict and were finally overrun by the invading Turanshah at the start of the Ayyubid period.

A through-route to Sadah?

A rough 30km track runs to Midi on the coast, with another heading east into the mountains, eventually arriving at Sadah through either Haydan or Suq ath-Thaluth. For many years a new road has been planned to link Harad and Huth, over 100km to the east through the mountains, but as yet it has not materialised.

Al-Luhayyah

Running west from al-Ma'aras, a bumpy track leads to the coast. **Al-Zuhrah** (21km from the main highway) has many large Turkish brick buildings in various states of collapse. Beyond this are large fields and healthy trees fed by the waters of Wadi Mawr. Straw huts scattered around the flat landscape could easily be mistaken for northern Kenya, or even central India.

Jebel al-Milh 'Salt Hill' – (52km), is a range of low

peaks visible from some distance, each topped by a small nineteenth-century Turkish fort. The huts of the salt miners who still work here are scattered around the base. In earlier times, salt was carried by camel the short distance to the coast.

The raised track crosses an expanse of mud-flats which are subject to tidal floods, but it is still possible to see large numbers of camels wandering around this barren, scorching wilderness. Al-Luhayyah literally means 'the end of the world' and travelling over these flood plains, it is easy to see why.

The end of the world

Overlooking al-Luhayyah is another Turkish building, also still used by the army. The road into town has a few shops selling essentials, and then runs through a section of dilapidated houses down to the old harbour. The low white mosque and tomb of the port's fifteenth-century founder is to the left, surrounded by a chaotic graveyard. Most local people refer to the founder as Sheikh Ahmed ibn Alwan, but others call him Sheikh Saleh!

Over the centuries, many pilgrims have landed here to start their *Haj* to Mecca. The town had a brief but colourful spell as one of the two coffee-exporting ports, which placed it on the maps of all European traders. Carsten Niebuhr's group visited it during their eighteenth century expedition.

The view from the beach is restricted by the thick banks of mangrove trees – a haven for seabirds and waterfowl. The harbour is now silted up and choked by the swamp, and only a few small fishing boats are capable of reaching the open sea. Despite its remote position, *qat* still arrives regularly each day from the mountains and the climax of the day's activity is the buying and selling of this substance.

A crumbling Turkish possession

Most of the **houses** are in a poor state, and little attempt is being made to maintain them. But unlike Hodeidah, it is at least the climate and natural weathering that is slowly wrecking them rather than men in bulldozers.

One of the highlights of this excursion is to wander around these old Turkish merchants' homes and warehouses, built with stone carried from the mountains or local coral blocks. Some of the wooden beams, shutters and friezes are finely carved, especially in the properties of the wealthy. Wooden door carvings need closer examination to reveal bunches of grapes dangling from vines, or intricate swirling patterns. Two of the houses of the Abdul Adud family are linked by a dangerously decayed wooden bridge which is about to crash down onto the street. If war-torn Beirut were a village, it would surely look like this.

Hundreds of **coral islands** lie just off this coast including al-Murk, Jezirat Antufish and the Uqbans – a scuba diver's paradise. Unfortunately only official visits are allowed, but you can learn more by reading the book *Motoring with Mohammed*..

Retracing the route

A coastal track goes north and south from al-Luhayyah, and it would be amazing to go the 80km or so north through Buhays to Midi, but it would be very unwise, both for practical and military reasons. One can, however, take the 4x4 route south from Jebal al-Milh to al-Khawbah, a small fishing village below Ras Haram. Before reaching Ibn Abbas, which looks out over the as-Salif headland, you will probably be forced well inland to rejoin the main highway near az-Zaydiyah.

Otherwise the return route from al-Luhayyah goes back to az-Zuhrah, where you could reach the main road by taking a more southerly track through the village of Mawr.

HODEIDAH–ZABID

Two choices

Two possible routes leave Hodeidah heading south: the main road, or the 4x4 track around the back of the airport. This track goes along the coast for 20km until opposite the island of Jezirat al-Mujamalah, where it turns inland to **ad-Durayhimi** (30km), one of the few towns where traditional Tihama weaving is still done commercially. Carsten Niebuhr mentioned the weaving in 1762, but nowadays chemical dyes are used rather than indigo. The track then roughly follows Wadi Rumman for another 30km to meet the main road just south of al-Mansuriyah.

But the main road is the route everyone takes. Leave Hodeidah as though heading for Sana'a, but then turn right after 15km onto the Soviet-built road towards Ta'iz. It is a bit of a roller coaster, dipping into every *wadi*, surrounded by large-scale cultivation. The crops help bind the sandy soil together, and stop it blowing away.

Al-Mansuriyah (44km) is a large and uninteresting conurbation on the left. The only reason to enter the town would be to take the dirt track north-east into the foothills, leading 20km to **as-Sukhnah** at the base of Jebel Bura. The final stretch is an extremely pleasant journey leading to the health spa which has grown up around the hot water springs. The agreeable winter climate persuaded the Imam to build a palace there, which is now ruined. Five kilometres before reaching the resort, another track goes right and climbs for 31km up to al-Jabin on the slopes of Jebel Raymah. This 4x4 track continues down the other side to meet the Ma'bar-Bajil road where it crosses Wadi Siham.

An unknown
region

The **Jebel Raymah** region is picturesque and remote; it has still to be discovered by tourist groups. There is superb walking through fields of wheat, barley and sorghum for those who do not fancy the heady heights of Manakha but still want good views. The high peaks are topped by houses, but singly rather than in small villages. **Jebel Bura,** to the north of as-Sukhnah, is unique in having the only remnants of a juniper forest with troops of baboons. The whole area is popular with natural history enthusiasts. In the early morning, it is even possible to see beyond the Tihama and the Red Sea islands, all the way to the Ethiopian coast.

Beit al-Faqih

Back on the Ta'iz road, 15 minutes beyond al-Mansuriyah is the turning for Beit al-Faqih (62km). Some of the modern town has spread along the main road, but the old town is over to the left. Follow the connecting road until it narrows into a small square.

House of the
Wise Man

The original town was started in the late thirteenth century by Ahmed bin Musa bin Ujayl and his followers. He was a respected scholar who had travelled widely around Arabia and passed his wisdom on to those who appreciated his spiritual knowledge and guidance. After his death, the settlement was given the name Beit al-Faqih, 'the house of the wise man'. The reason for it's fame and history might not be obvious, until you look at a map of the Yemen in the seventeenth or eighteenth century.

Coffee was being exported from the two main ports of Mokha and al-Luhayyah, with the capital Sana'a in control and growing rich. Exactly in the centre of this triangle and equidistant from all three was Beit al-Faqih. It became the centre through which all coffee, and much of the tobacco, was traded. During the time of Niebuhr's expedition in 1763 there were merchants and coffee dealers here from Hejaz, Egypt, Syria, Turkey, Morocco, Persia and India. Camels were used to transport the coffee beans, and donkeys carried the tobacco on these new trade routes through the Tihama. But there is little to see of this great wealth today.

Best market
in Yemen?

For six days a week the town slumbers in the heat and dust of the Tihama, until Friday, when the prosperous trading times return for one of the best weekly **markets** in the country. The importance of this market grew as the trade in coffee declined towards the end of the eighteenth century. Textiles, handicrafts and pottery are all produced locally and find eager buyers amongst the livestock traders. Stalls are crammed into the central *suq*

The mother of all *suqs*

and spill out up the lanes, engulfing any patch of open ground. This is Istanbul and Damascus gone 'over the top' with a manic intensity scarcely believable in the heat. Because it is so large, this is one market that usually keeps going well into the afternoon.

Away from market day, there are other things to see. In the morning the permanent stalls in the covered *suq* are always pretty lively, but it tends to look a bit grubby and only half interesting. Leather handicrafts and pottery are always available, and make good souvenirs if you can carry them. Hats, ropes and baskets are woven using the *doum* palm. In the Tihama, and here in particular, you will notice that the women have much more freedom than in mountain areas, and they can often be seen trading unaccompanied in the *suq*.

Producing local material

On the outskirts of town, especially to the south, you can find huge **handlooms** erected in open spaces, which are used to weave the long cloths. Smaller ones also make *futahs*, the short wrap-around cloths worn by men, although most are now imported. Buying direct from the weaver might get you a good price, but as always, bargain hard.

Abandoned fortress

Also on this south-eastern side of town is the Turkish citadel known as **Husn Uthman,** built on a small hill. This is well worth a visit at any time, and can be found by asking any of the children, who are generally friendly and helpful. It is an impressive, sturdy building with ramps and turrets. The guardians are usually asleep and do not seem to mind tourists wandering around, which is quite an opportunity as most Turkish forts are still occupied by the military. On a rampart is a fine British cannon with a VR insignia, dating from 1892. The stables are still used, as is the mosque in the corner beside a very deep well, but it is all gloriously ramshackle. Some of the rooms on the first and second floors of the main block are living quarters; others are abandoned, and most of the stairways lead to bat-infested towers. Old cannon barrels lie abandoned both inside and out.

When Niebuhr's expedition left Beit al-Faqih in 1763, their route to Ta'iz was through al-Udayn and Jibla. In the 1990s your route will be due south, down the fast tarred road towards Zabid. Al-Husayniyah (82km) is another modern-looking town, but it was an important centre during Ottoman rule in the nineteenth century.

Wadi Rima can be followed upstream by an easterly 4x4 track from town. Al-Mishrafah is 30km into the foothills. This *wadi* could be followed as it climbs between Jebel Raymah and Jebel ash-Shu'ub all the way to Madinat ash-Shirq on the Ma'bar–Bajil road. All these major *wadis* have carried water and soil onto the Tihama for millennia, creating a rich agricultural area, ideal for *dhurra* millet, papaya and bananas. Contrast this with the more southerly semi-desert with a few acacia trees and low scrub.

ZABID

Early focus of Islam

Wadi Zabid flows across the Tihama just to the south of Zabid town, and has no doubt been cultivated for millennia. In the seventh century it was home to the *Asha'ir* tribe, whose leader Sheikh Abu Musa bin Ash'ari visited the Prophet Mohammed in Medina. He returned to build a mosque at the site of the present town. This al-Asha'ria mosque became a Koranic school and a centre of learning for the Hanafi code of Sunni Islam.

A revolt by the inhabitants against the ruling Abbasids in Sana'a caused the Caliph to send Mohammed ibn Ziad to Zabid in 819 This highly educated man not only restored order, but formed the basis of the world's oldest **university.** With him he brought Sunni Shafi'i religious teachers who excelled in all forms of education, and gradually replaced the Hanafi code. Zabid's fame spread and attracted intellectuals from around the Arab world, all paid for by the *waqf* religious tax. The Arabic words for university, *jami'a,* and mosque, *jami,* are taken from the same root. Zabid highlighted the fact that a mosque is not just a place of prayer, but also a seat of learning.

Great centre of learning

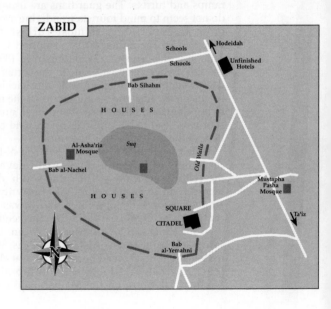

ZABID

Schools
Schools
Hodeidah
Unfinished Hotels
Bab Sihahm
HOUSES
Suq
Al-Asha'ria Mosque
Old Walls
Bab al-Nachel
HOUSES
Mustapha Pasha Mosque
Ta'iz
SQUARE
CITADEL
Bab al-Yemahni
N

It became a centre of Sunni teaching and many of the teachers who started the al-Ahzar University in Cairo came from here. As well as the religious aspects of law and history, the town was famous for poetry, grammar and mathematics. It is thought that the scholar al-Jaladi invented a mathematical system called *al-Jabr*, from which we get the word algebra.

Algebra invented here

Ziad's dynasty lasted for over two centuries, but control fell to the dark-skinned Najahids until halfway through the twelfth century when the Bani Mahdi took over and ruled for 20 years. In 1174 Saladin's brother, Turanshah, took the Tihama and set about expanding Zabid. Within 50 years, however, the **Rasulids** had taken control and during the following 230 years made the al-Asha'ria university the educational centre of Arabia, attracting 5,000 students to the 250 schools and mosques. The searing heat of the Tihama forced the Rasulid rulers to spend the summer in Ta'iz, but Zabid was always the winter capital.

Tahirid rule and the subsequent Ottoman invasion were not kind to Zabid, which slid back into relative obscurity. Finance and stability were required for the centre to continue, but the Tihama has had little of either in the last 500 years (even Saudi patrols probed this far in 1934 in their drive against the Imam's forces). As Mokha grew, so Zabid died, and the rise to power of the northern Zaidis further restricted its Sunni teachings. The al-Asha'ria mosque remains, but a wander around this small town gives no indication of its former greatness.

Remains of an impressive citadel

You enter the town through many large gateways, and you can immediately see the old brick constructions used for channelling water – and in fact almost everything seems to be constructed from fired bricks. The unusually large town square is bordered by the impressive **al-Nasser Citadel** and the Iskander Mosque.

Inside the S-shaped citadel gateway, the modern buildings on the right are local government offices and courthouse, Zabid is now a municipal centre. The citadel itself is named after the Rasulid ruler Nasser Ahmed who built the fortress at the beginning of the fifteenth century. A team from the Royal Ontario Museum has been excavating the area since 1982 and has created a small dusty museum containing small dusty relics. For a nominal fee, someone might find the door key and let you see examples of local and imported pottery, cannon balls and wooden friezes. Of particular interest in the single room is a plan of the citadel and a map of Zabid naming many of the mosques.

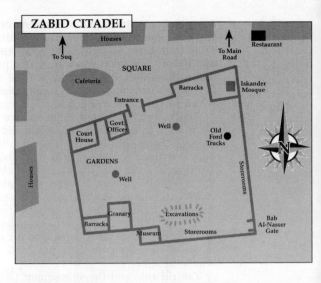

ZABID CITADEL

The rest of the fortress contains barracks dating from the turn of the century, a granary and a couple of rusted chassis of 1926 Canadian Ford trucks. The white-domed **Iskander Mosque** was named after the sixteenth century local governor, but probably built much earlier. It lies in a quiet corner with its slender minaret (built in 1530-6) piercing the blue midday sky. Hope for some white puffy clouds to make a polarized photograph an absolute stunner. The best overall views are from the south walls and roofs which can be climbed in several places.

The *suq* and most of the houses lie across the square, and are reached by wandering down confusing dim and narrow covered alleyways. High walls hide many fine houses, which give no clue to their wealth, decoration or construction. Occasionally you can catch a glimpse through a doorway before it is politely closed. The *suq* is rather like the one at Beit al-Faqih, but much smaller and very tiring to walk around in the heat.

An important old mosque The midday slumber might give you the opportunity of getting into the famous **al-Asha'ria Mosque;** it is worth a try. It lies on the western edge of town and is quite unassuming from outside, with low proportions. The purification basins are just inside the entrance which leads to a central courtyard surrounded by thick columned galleries. With a squat minaret, it has a heavy overall appearance which is lifted by its basic simplicity and brilliant whiteness. This old Arabian style is different from the majority of mosques in the region, which tend to show Egyptian or Turkish influences.

**A port
for the town**

A track from the Bab al-Nachel ('Palm Gate') leads west from the town to at-Tuhaytah, but then becomes bogged down in the lower reaches of Wadi Zabid. It reaches the sea at **al-Fazzah**, the twelfth century port of Zabid, which is now badly silted up. The Ontario team started excavations here, but the inhospitable conditions forced them back to concentrate on the citadel.

The **Mustapha Pasha Mosque** lies on the other side of the main road and should be viewed when coming to or from Ta'iz. It can be seen clearly set back slightly from the road and is reached down a dirt track (beware of the crazy dogs!). Initially in the town centre, but now isolated, it is another thick-set building, with a curious half-finished minaret surrounded by white cupolas and domes. Named after the Turkish governor it was built around 1540, later than the Iskander Mosque.

CAMELS

Dromedaries are more common in the Tihama than in the mountains, and are generally better suited to the hot dry desert conditions. You will often see camels used as beasts of burden, carrying large bundles of reeds and stalks and gently swaying across the flat landscape. Very occasionally they are used as farm animals to pull a plough or some other piece of equipment across the fields. They tend to be unsure of their footing when climbing and are replaced by donkeys for the steep inclines of highland travel. They are more delicate animals than donkeys, and certainly less profitable – but far more prestigious.

In the mountain regions they are more often seen in the cramped conditions of the sesame or mustard seed mill. The animal walks around a central press which slowly grinds the small seeds. Young children are given the task of keeping it moving, and it is blindfolded to stop dizziness. Over to the east on the edge of the desert, camels fulfil many of the farming and transport tasks on level land.

ZABID–TA'IZ

**Typical
Tihama
towns**

Just south of Zabid is the fertile Wadi Zabid with remnants of old dams and water channels plainly visible in the fields to the right. **Al-Jarrahi** (113km from Hodeidah), which lies just beyond Wadi al-Ayn, is a modern roadside halt with many restaurants and stalls. Arguably the best weekly market to be seen is 2km to the east of the main road on Tuesdays. A good road starts from here to al-Mabraz in the foothills, a major junction of superb tracks into the mountains. These eventually lead east to al-Udayn and Ibb, south to ar-Rawnah and Ta'iz and west to Hays.

RUBBISH

Many visitors remark on the amount of rubbish to be seen in every town and village. In the Tihama the level reaches new heights as the constant winds blow all types of detritus across the flat expanses. Even areas well away from villages are littered with paper and plastic. Some of the trees which are covered in plastic bags have been described as 'glowing like magical flowers'. There comes a point when it is difficult to find anything positive in such inherently dirty areas. The question is why there is so much about.

For thousands of years the Yemem approach to rubbish has been to throw it out of the window and wait for it to go away. Until the 1960s this was what happened, as most packaging was organic matter which was eaten by livestock or slowly degraded. Unfortunately, progress has introduced plastic and metal packaging, which does not disappear so easily. It is not a lack of standards of health and cleanliness that we see, but the result of rapid development, before the necessary shift in understanding.

Pots for the country

You cross Wadi Nakhla just before **Hays** (134km). The town is off the main road, and is a bit like a small version of Zabid, but not so interesting. It is famous for its glazed pottery, which is found all over the country. Heaps of fired clay pots and garish coloured censers lie around even when it is not Monday, market day. These are good locally made souvenirs, but they are easily broken and very heavy.

Just south of Hays is the dirt track which goes to the coast, so you have a choice of tar to Mafraq or a 4x4 track to al-Khawkhah and Mokha. The main road reaches Mafraq through a semi-desert landscape that becomes increasingly arid after al-Sayyif.

Al-Khawkhah

A north Yemen coastal retreat

This large fishing village lies 29km from the main road. Most vehicles can get here, but 4x4 is needed for any journey along the coast. There are some local eating places (the al-Whda does excellent *siyadia* – whole grilled fish) and the inhabitants are used to individual tourists spending a few days relaxing. Rather than use the accommodation in the village, it would be preferable to stay in a straw hut under palm trees, or even sleep on the beach. Most of the tour agencies have set up small camps along the beach to make the area more attractive to tourists. They consist of small thatched huts with a kitchen, a drinks supply and fresh water. The guardian of the site keeps things ticking over until a group arrives. But, if mosquitoes and heat are a problem in the huts, you can stay at the new air conditioned **al-Khawkhah Tourist Village,** some 7km to the north, or you might prefer just to camp by the sea. North of al-Khawkhah there are clumps of palm trees which provide good shade for

Camel-cart in Crater, Aden.

Bab al-Yemen Suq in Old City, Sana'a.

Spices in Ta'iz Suq.

Interior of al-Airdrus Mosque, Crater, Aden.

campers. The Tourist Village, which was built in 1991, has 24 clean rooms, all with air-conditioning. It is on a pleasant sandy beach surrounded by palm trees.

Just beyond an inland lagoon is Abu Zeh settlement, with a mosque and graveyard, and past the Tourist Village is the tiny fishing settlement of Qatabah, which is near a military camp.

BOATS AND FISHING

Many different types of boat are used today, but there are two main designs which have been used for inshore fishing for centuries. The *huri* is the most common fishing boat, and has been described by many travellers to these shores. It is fairly high and narrow, and cuts through the swell with amazing efficiency. As many as ten fishermen will go to sea in the larger versions, which are traditionally made from wood, although modern plastic hulls are now imported. Around Mokha and Hodeidah the authorities are not keen for tourists to take to the sea, but outside these centres the situation is more relaxed. Around al-Khawkhah, local boatmen sometimes offer trips in their *huris*, but be prepared for a soaking, as they are inherently unstable. There is nothing particular to look at or visit, and from experience, I would advise against such a trip. If you do go, check your insurance carefully.

In the poorer fishing villages you might see some wooden beams or tree trunks bound together to create a large raft, with the ends slightly raised. This is known as a *ramass* and is used by one or two fishermen, mainly to fix fish traps. The maximum distance they go from shore is about 5km, but even large fish can be caught from them.

Red Sea islands

It is good to see another aspect of the country, and in the clear morning light it is an impressive sight across to the mountainous islands of Hanish al-Kabir and Jebel Zuqar, halfway to Ethiopia, but to spend more than one night here would be too much, with little to do but sweat in the shade during the day. Since unification, all the southern beaches have become accessible, and they are generally preferable. Swimming and snorkelling are not as good here, as the wind stirs up the sand, reducing visibility, and there is no defined reef to drop onto.

Al-Khawkhah–Mokha

The two-and-a-half-hour coastal drive south to Mokha is featured on many organised tours, but it needs a 4x4 vehicle on the soft beach sand. Ten kilometres from al-Khawkhah is the new YATA camp on the beach, with the village of Mawshij (locally known as Moshi) to the south.

A lost port

The cove along the shore is thought by many experts to be the site of ancient Muza, the forgotten port of the Himyarite Kingdom.

Slightly inland is the domed **Qubbat Ali Abu Taleb Mosque** (said to have been built by the Prophet's son-in law Ali Abu Taleb) on the site of a pre-Islamic place of worship with cult worship pillars. Such places were the object of pilgrimages which coincided until recently with a local tradition of celebrating 15 Shaban (the month before Ramadan), as a feastday.

The track is sometimes along the beach

It is possible to walk along stretches of beach and meet your vehicle further down, passing isolated fishing huts and boats, but beware of unfriendly dogs. Depending on the season, you might have to go inland to avoid treacherous mud on the shore, especially around Wadi Rasyan. Most of the shoreline tends to be deserted apart from prolific bird life, with villages such as Zohary and al-Gufran just inland.

Yakhtul village (51km) is 500m inland because of the salt workings along the coast, and it is one of the main smuggling points for restricted goods crossing the Red Sea. The track then runs along the beach, past some old abandoned lighters and work camps. You might see the

A fish called Wizuf

locals drying *wizuf*, a very small silver fish added to other dishes for taste, or fed to cattle. When dried, they are about 80 per cent protein with almost no oil at all. Sackfuls can be found in most *suqs*. In the evenings, the baskets tend to heave with insects having a free meal!

From the electricity generating station there is a tarred road which joins the road from Mafraq. Turn right and go into Mokha (67km).

Mokha

Whenever the Yemen or Southern Arabia is mentioned in the accounts of early travellers, Mokha is usually among their first impressions. John Jourdain, a sailor from Lyme Regis, recalled in 1609 that it was a city of great trading for tin, iron, lead, cloth and sword blades. It held a large market every day of the week, where one could buy enough fish for three pence to feed ten men.

Origins of coffee

Many stories are told of how the locally grown **coffee** came to be adopted as one of the world's favourite drinks. It probably came via early Portuguese sailors returning home from the Indies, or through Constantinople during the first period of Ottoman occupation, popularising Turkish coffee.

Sir Henry Middleton of the British East India Company stopped in Mokha in 1610, and eight of his crew were killed and most of his cargo looted. He was arrested and held in chains until he was forced to march to Sana'a in winter. There he received an apology from the Pasha. Upon returning to Mokha, he was thrown into jail again by the Governor, a renegade Greek pirate. Middleton escaped to his ship in a barrel and trained his guns on the port, demanding the return of his goods. Not wholly satisfied, he then partook of a little piracy himself before continuing to the Indies.

Non-Muslims were always treated with suspicion, as many Arabs believed that they were looking for a route into the Holy Cities, but by 1620 there were both Dutch and British traders established here, and a few even survived the battles to expel the Turks in the 1630s.

The new Imam, based in Sana'a, was keen to make as much money out of coffee as possible, and by the end of the seventeenth century, coffee grown in the Yemen highlands and traded in Beit al-Faqih was shipped through Mokha to an eager world market. Coffee shops sprang up across Europe and the emerging North America, creating an unprecedented demand that made a fortune for all those involved in its supply.

An international drink

The Dutch, French and English capitalised on their East India trade links during this brief rush in order to secure the best prices. In the boom years between 1720 and 1740 merchants from all over the world grew wealthy, building grand villas around Mokha. But the mystery surrounding the cultivation of coffee could not remain unexplained forever, and in the eighteenth century young plants were smuggled out to find new homes in Ceylon and south-east Asia. With the monopoly broken, Arab traders quickly lost out, as other more influential powers took control. The coffee trade went into decline, and local merchants were eager to leave the horrendous climate of the Tihama.

Mokha's decline

Carsten Niebuhr's expedition into the interior started and finished here, and one of its members – Professor Friedrich von Haven – was buried in the European graveyard to the north of the port. In 1763, Niebuhr described Mokha as trading in gold, ivory, myrrh, frankincense and mother of pearl.

Towards the end of the eighteenth century Mokha became important to the British as a staging post *en route* to India, and many stories reached England about the strange ways of Arabia, in the process enriching our language. For example, a certain Major Rooke describes the horrific process involved in a local bath-house where the victim was smothered in soap and then rubbed and pinched with great violence, known locally as *champooing*. And in 1795 Prof. Hugh Cleghorn described local fishermen killing sharks from a native boat called a *catamaran*.

As the size of ships increased, Mokha's harbour became increasingly inadequate and suffered silting problems. With the trade gone, local Jewish traders switched to the opportunities offered by the recently captured British port of Aden. After 200 years of renown, Mokha quickly declined into a ruined ghost town, leaving only its name to be remembered.

THE COFFEE PLANT

Coffee arabica is a bush with rich, green leaves which can grow to several metres in height. It is cultivated between 1,000m and 2,000m along the full length of the western facing slopes from Razih in the north to Ta'iz. The red coffee beans are hand-picked between April and June in various stages of maturity, and left to dry on the flat roofs. The coffee beans *(bunn)* are separated from their husks and sacked up. The husks *(qishr)* are themselves used to produce a pleasant local drink, often infused with cinnamon, cardamom and ginger.

Production has slumped badly as farmers find it easier, and much more profitable, to grow *qat* instead of coffee.

By the late 1980s Mokha was growing again, with new port facilities handling oil industry equipment. In the 1990s the town appears to be buzzing again, with trucks transporting a variety of goods which arrive in the harbour, from Australian sheep to light bulbs.

The skeleton coast
As you enter town, the main area of interest is on the right. There are derelict merchants' houses almost every 100m. They are in a poor state and dangerous, but you do have the opportunity of seeing some of the interior design and structure. There is a tremendous combination of construction materials – brick, stone, wood and coral – all covered with mud and then painted. There are some fine stucco reliefs on protected walls, as well as richly coloured designs and carvings on some of the remaining wooden shelves and partitions.

In solitary splendour a single minaret, sometimes mistakenly called the **lighthouse tower,** also has some good designs, but has been badly weathered. Close by, the **al-Shadli Mosque** thrusts a tiered but tilting minaret out of its sandblasted white cupolas and domes. It dates from the end of the fifteenth century and is named after the patron saint of the port, Ali ibn Omar al-Shadli.

Closer to the *harbour* (no photographs please) are the remains of single-storey warehouses and customs sheds dating from the eighteenth century. In the centre are several Turkish-style balconied houses, some of which have been restored, but generally it is a bit of a mishmash of styles from various periods. To the left is the main harbour. The best beach is to the right, but do not go too near the military checkpoint.

Coffee break
Some small food halls serve local fare, including excellent grilled fish. One or two teahouses do serve coffee, but don't be surprised if it's instant!

Mokha–Ta'iz

A coastal 4x4 track runs south from Mokha for almost 100 km, to the headland of the Bab al-Mandab straits. It should be possible to reach the village of Dhubab (50 km from Mokha) but there are military areas beyond this. A track turns inland from Dhubab across Wadi Samadah to Mawza, but this is tough driving territory.

The American-financed road to Mafraq is a fast straight highway of 46km, and the only diversion is the dirt track across to **Mawza.** The track is signposted after 35km and runs south across Wadi Mawza.

Jewish enclave The Jews of Sana'a were expelled to this desolate place in 1679, after Imam al-Mahdi failed to convert them to Islam. This expulsion is known by the Jews as the *Galut Mawza* – 'exile in Mawza'. A small number went to Mokha to trade, but the majority were soon allowed back to the capital, when their expertise in making and repairing tools, utensils and jewellery was sorely missed.

Buying booze **Mafraq,** which means "junction', connects Mokha to the main road, and is an outlet for illegal goods smuggled across the Red Sea. Driving along the road, especially just to the north, you will see dubious-looking characters lounging in the shade, waiting for customers. Most foreigners wanting to buy beer or spirits for personal consumption will be brought here. Whisky, gin and vodka are usually available, as well as cans of imported beer, but be sure to check the 'sell by' date. If you do not fancy this type of deal, you can normally buy the same at hotels in Ta'iz, Sana'a and Hodeidah at much higher prices. Tougher crackdowns by the fundamentalists could halt this trade.

From Mafraq the road turns east and climbs into the hills through **al-Barh,** where there always seem to be more Pariah kites than people. It appears to be the oil changing centre of the country, and has some old camel-powered sesame and mustard seed mills. The produce of these mills is used for cooking oil and in the cosmetics and leather industries. Just beyond the new cement factory, a track to the left leads to Maqbanah in the Jebel Ghurrat Shamir range and eventually trundles down into Hays. One of the mountain villages near Maqbanah is **Asube,** which was the scene of one of the few newspaper stories, apart from the earthquake, to come out of the YAR in the 1980s. It concerned the two sisters born and brought up in Birmingham, who were persuaded to come here on holiday, only to find that marriages had been arranged for them (see Further Reading).

International newspaper story

As the road climbs through good scenery to Hajda village look out for grey hornbills in the trees. Another track to the north-west also goes to Hays and has an impressive initial climb.

The gorge narrows up Wadi ar-Ramadah to Karba and Beer Basha (261 km), which was a separate village but is now caught up in the expansion of Ta'iz only 5km away. The road to the right goes to at-Turbah (see Ta'iz–Aden via at-Turbah).

The centre of Ta'iz can be reached by two roads. To the right is 26 September Street, which leads direct to the *suq;* the dual carriageway which goes left is Gamal Abdul Nasser Street, which threads through the new centre towards most of the hotels.

TA'IZ

INTRODUCTION

Bustling and noisy city

Every time I visit Ta'iz it seems to have grown in size, noise and business. Without a proper ring road there are now too many vehicles trying to squeeze through the narrow streets and it sometimes gets close to gridlock. Two new footbridges over Gamal Abdul Nasser Street are very popular – not for crossing the road, but to enjoy a better view of the traffic chaos!

The city lies at the foot of Jebel Sabr and spreads itself over several smaller hills on the edge of a broad valley. It is an interesting city in which to spend at least a day, and two if you want to visit Ibb, Jibla and al-Janad as well.

History

Ancient trade centre

The hilltops around Ta'iz reveal evidence that the area was inhabited in pre-Islamic times and that it possibly acted as a small station on an unimportant trading route from Ocel's, the ancient port on the mainland at the entrance to the Red Sea near Perim Island, to the Himyar capital at Dhafar. The steep pinnacle overlooking the town has always been the key to the route there and seems to have had some form of defences on it from early times. It is now topped by the impressive al-Qahira fortress or citadel.

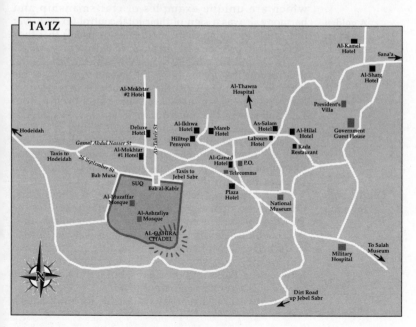

263

Ta'iz becomes capital

The main development of the town occurred around the end of the twelfth century. Until then al-Janad had been the main centre, but a reversal of fortunes began when the **Ayyubid** invaders chose Ta'iz as their capital in 1174 to avoid the debilitating heat of the Tihama. They were led by Turanshah al-Ayyubi, the brother of Saladin, and invaded the Tihama on the pretext of restoring Sunni doctrines over Fatimid Ismaili rule. This was the first real invasion by a powerful foreign army that stayed to rule, but it was by no means the last – it happened again many times during Yemen's history. The Ayyubid troops took Zabid and then most of the south from the smaller states that had arisen after the death of Queen Arwa. Ta'iz developed as a place where goods from the emerging port of Mokha joined those from Aden to be sent to the markets in the north.

Turanshah was succeeded by his brother Tughtakin and then by a further four sultans of Turkoman descent until after 55 years, Ayyubid rule came to an end, and power shifted to the **Rasulids** who claimed descent from early Yemenis who had emigrated to Syria in the third century AD.

A golden age of art

This was a golden period in Yemeni history. For two centuries a succession of rulers encouraged literature, architecture, medicine and other major disciplines. They expanded and developed the university in Zabid and undertook the construction of large mosques, many of which are unique examples of craftsmanship and harmony. It was a sign of their total control (except over the Zaidis in the northern mountains as usual) that they were able to patronise the arts to such a degree.

The second ruler of the dynasty was al-Muzaffar, who was responsible for building the mosque that bears his name towards the end of the thirteenth century. He was followed by his son al-Ashraf who ruled briefly from 1295 and started the construction of his own mosque. The dynasty came to an end with the twelfth ruler, al-Ashraf IV, who lost several territories including Aden and whose rule was marked by internal fighting and severe plague throughout the land. His rule ended in 1441 and within 13 years the **Tahirids** had taken control.

Conflict with the north

Tahirid rule was never strong and ended with the first **Ottoman** occupation in 1517. Ta'iz was taken by the Turks in 1546 and used as a defensive stronghold against the rebellious Zaidis to the north. Jews settled here to trade between Mokha and Sana'a, forming their own community. For the next 400 years control swung between the Turks and the Zaidis, but it did not become capital of the Yemen again until 1948.

In that year, as a reprisal against the forces of Sana'a

which had been responsible for the assassination of Imam Yahya, his son and successor **Imam Ahmed** burned and looted the old capital before establishing himself in Ta'iz. So once again the southern city took centre stage, for the final years of the imamate.

In March 1961 three gunmen tried to shoot Imam Ahmed at the hospital in Hodeidah. He was badly wounded but survived to return back to Ta'iz where he spent the last 18 months of his life as a virtual invalid, permanently on drugs. Mohammed Alolufie, Abdullah Allukayah and Alhanswan Besidthemare were beheaded for the shooting, and Ahmed eventually died on 26 September 1962. His son Badr proclaimed himself the new Imam and within a week the revolution had started.

The end of Imamic rule

Fortunately for many of the unique buildings there was little fighting in Ta'iz itself. Sana'a replaced it as capital, and Hodeidah slowly overtook it as a commercial centre. Lt Col Ali Abdullah Saleh was Governor of Ta'iz before he took over as president of the YAR. With unification it has suffered another blow by having to contend with Aden as the major city in the south.

A natural crossroad

Ta'iz is an industrial city and its future could depend on several factors. Its proximity to Aden could be an advantage when the free zone starts to operate, and the new cement factory down the road at Mafraq will boost the local economy, as will the resurging trade coming through Mokha port. The town is not directly involved in the oil and gas industry as such, but as an industrial centre it can manufacture many of the goods and supplies required. Judging from the bustle in the streets, Ta'iz certainly seems to have a bright future.

Al-Ashrafiya Mosque

A fine example

This gleaming white building with twin minarets is the peak of Rasulid religious architecture, and is visible from almost every part of the city. It was constructed in two periods, at the end of the thirteenth and fourteenth centuries. The prayer hall is backed by identical minarets, and above it are eight small cupolas surrounding one large dome. Inside the enclosed courtyard are the tombs of the rulers who constructed it.

The building, which was also a religious school, was neglected for years and is currently undergoing some restoration work. The restoration is a bonus for the visitor as it usually means that access will be granted by the guardian for a small tip, even on a Friday.

The mosque can be approached from above or below. If you are coming along the road which goes around the back of al-Qahira stop at a point that overlooks it, with good views of sections of the massive city walls. If you are coming from the *suq* the approach is not quite so grand.

At the top of the steps an open gallery runs along the side of the building. The guardian is usually to be found in one of the rear rooms. The gloomy **courtyard** is half mausoleum, half building site, and fairly dusty. The tombs are separated by ornate carved wooden screens, and the guardian acts as unofficial guide and indicates which belongs to which member of the family.

Going inside

Remove your shoes here and enter the peaceful **prayer hall** but be careful not step over the white line close to the *mihrab*, or over anyone sleeping on the floor. The room is richly decorated, with verses from the Koran on the walls and ceiling, and fine plaster designs throughout. The dome is covered in colourful motifs with more Koranic texts. If you are struggling to get the right photograph of the dome design, the guardian can indicate the exact spot on the carpet for a dead-centre shot.

A muezzin's view

From the back of the building there is an entrance to the steps going up inside the **minaret.** It is worth the effort of climbing them, as you get excellent views over both the mosque and the city. Each minaret has two narrow balconies at the top. Access to the eastern one is from roof level. From here you can look down on the other great Rasulid mosque of al-Muzaffar, which is distinguished by its three large white domes and single white minaret.

Al-Muzaffar Mosque

This is the oldest of all the local mosques, and was built some time before 1295. Its patron, al-Muzaffar Yusuf bin Umar, was one of the great early Rasulid sultans. He ruled for 46 years and was the father of al-Ashraf I. Entry is not allowed but you can sometimes see through the side door that it is a long thin mosque. The interior decoration is similar to that of the al-Ashrafiya.

At the far end is the new minaret, built in the 1980s to replace the one destroyed earlier this century. Until 1990 it was of red brick with white designs, but it has now been completely whitewashed. Views of the mosque can be obtained by looking over the graveyard wall to the north.

Other Mosques

There are four other distinguished mosques in the back streets of the same suburb within the old city walls. These run down the hillside in a straight line just to the west of the two more famous mosques detailed above. The higher one is al-Mutabiya, which is similar in style and age to al-Ashrafiya. Then come Abdul al-Hadi, al-Taquiya and Qubbat al-Husseini, the last being the tomb of the Ottoman ruler Hussein Pasha, built in 1899.

National Museum

You must try to see this museum, which is open 8.00-12.00 every day except Friday. It is not so much a museum, more an insight into the life of the imams and their insular world. It is inside the Imam Abdullah Imam al-Buder Palace, and has been kept just as it was in September 1962 when Imam Ahmed died. There are many things here that will surprise you, and others that will remind you of things that you had totally forgotten.

The museum is at the top of 26 September Street, past the main post office and the Plaza Hotel, and is reached by turning left at the roundabout. At first the building is hidden behind some government and military blocks with a lot of soldiers around. A sign welcoming you to the 'National Museum in Salah' would be slightly more appropriate 5km out of town at the Salah Museum itself, as this is the National Museum in Ta'iz!

It is one of the few places where you will have to buy an entrance ticket, and the ticket area is a gruesome reminder of what people had to endure under the rule of the imams, with photographs showing public beheadings in slightly out of focus detail. There is even the sword that used to do the work. However this is not a true reflection of what is inside, which is a great deal less disturbing. No cameras or bags are allowed.

Entering the first room is rather like stepping into the Imam's living room with all the favourite possessions and souvenirs on show. There are hundreds of identical bottles of eau de cologne, Old Spice and Christian Dior, an electronic bed, a child's KLM handbag, projectors, films, guns, ammunition and swords. There are also more personal items such as passports, personalised Swiss watches and blood-stained clothes. One of my favourites is a strange pair of periscopic binoculars. There is also a yellowing United Arab Republic calendar for 1959.

It is an amazing collection of purchases and gifts from all over the world, some of which must be worth a fortune, but displayed with all the skill of a jumble sale – which is half its charm. There are also bits of information about pre-revolution days, including the pictures and guns of the three martyrs who were beheaded for that assassination attempt in Hodeidah. A large picture of Ahmed's brother Abdullah is displayed in memory of the part he played in the attempted *Coup d'état* of April 1955. Imam Ahmed subsequently killed him.

The three levels of rooms provide a fascinating view of something that you almost feel you should not look at.

Instead of going straight out, go through the door beside the ticket desk. Out in the courtyard is a small teashop and a collection of local animals, usually baboons which still roam wild in the surrounding mountains. Their conditions here, however, are pretty grim.

Al-Qahira

Even on the sunniest days, the citadel of al-Qahira on the 180m peak behind the city looks dark and gloomy. A modern road runs around the back of the fortress, and that is the closest view you can get, as it is in the hands of the army. Massive walls run across and along the hillside interspersed by heavy towers.

Gruesome reminders

The fortress has been an easily defended residence from before the time of the Rasulids. It was also one of the prisons where the imams kept their young hostages (sons or relatives of governors and tribal leaders), to ensure that there was no resistance to their rule. The whole site is classified as a historic monument, but that does not mean the military has to leave it. It is still used as a barracks, but there have been interesting recent finds of early weapons and objects. Underground passageways and secret tunnels are said to honeycomb the sombre hillside.

City Walls, Gates and Suqs

The square outside **Bab al-Kabir** (the 'big gate') is the usual entry point for the *suq* and the old town. It is at the end of the main shopping street, at-Tahrir, which runs between Gamal Abdul Nasser Street and 26 September Street. The gateway itself is a solid stone construction dating from only the 1950s.

Compact commerce

Inside the square, long lanes of traders spread away from the gate. To the right are local cheeses and every type of spice imaginable – buckets full of multicoloured conical heaps. A narrow pedestrian entranceway leads through the wall to 26 September Street.

Straight ahead are hundreds of fabric retailers selling every type of material in a blaze of swirling colour. This street also leads past the makers of *jambia* belts to Bab Musa at the far end of the *suq*. To the left of Bab al-Kabir are some food shops, fresh produce sellers, bakers and some newly established souvenir shops. This street bears right at he end to climb up to the al-Ashrafiya Mosque. Most of the gold and silver shops are good value, but are now situated outside the old *suq* and can be found in the streets just outside Bab al-Kabir.

The walls cannot be walked, although they encompass large sections of the lower slopes of the hill and can be clearly seen around al-Qahira.

**Watching
the world**

If there is enough time, why not just take it easy and sit in the *suq* with a glass of *chai*, watching the traders, dealers and punters going about their hectic daily business. Many of the women here are unveiled and wear colourful dresses and head scarves, something unique to the countless villages on the slopes of Jebel Sabr.

A Jambia belt maker in Ta'iz Suq.

Jebel al-Dabua

This hill, on which the old hotels of Ta'iz are situated, is in a very prominent position overlooking the city. Both the Mareb and al-Ikhwa Hotels are past their prime, but it is worth climbing the hill on which they stand to get to the Park Restaurant. This is more like a small coffee shop, and belongs to the al-Ikhwa. There can be few better places to sip a Nescafe or *chai*. Prices are higher than normal but the views across the old city to al-Qahira and Jebel Sabr are just stunning, day or night.

**A different
perspective**

It can be found by turning left at the roundabout which is at the top of Gamal Abdul Nasser Street as it climbs away from the old city. This street is steep with a tight bend at the top, the Mareb Hotel is on the right, the al-Ikhwa on the left. Do not go into the al-Ikhwa but walk through the construction site of the new extension to the Park terrace. Any taxi will take you there from the centre.

Jebel Sabr

Colourful unveiled women

A journey up the slopes of Jebel Sabr will give you panoramic views of the city. You will also see some of the unveiled women in the local villages. The road out of the suburbs is a bit tricky to find, but it climbs up between the National Museum and al-Qahira. All the agency drivers know the road, or you can ask a taxi driver for the village of al-Arus (near the summit) and point up the mountain.

There is a good light on al-Qahira in the early morning, so try to stop for a photograph before you get too high, otherwise the fortress will be lost in the general panorama. Do not worry if you miss it, because you have to take the same route down. The dirt track has simply been hacked out of the mountain face, swinging around some weird eroded rocks up to a new building called **Muntazah** (9km and about half an hour from the centre). This is a new government rest house only for official visitors, but there are many modern mansions built here by the wealthy. Just around the corner is a row of shops, the normal destination for tourists.

The track continues up the mountain, but you would need about another two hours to tackle the steeper, rougher and narrower track, as well as permission. It is feasible to trek back down at any point, either on the road or down one of the winding footpaths, but unfortunately some of the local children have taken to throwing stones at tourist vehicles. This is one reason why drivers do not like going beyond Muntazah.

The track eventually reaches a high valley packed tight with lush, green terracing interrupted by sections of ancient aqueducts. The Sabr women wear colourful clothing when they work in the corn and *qat* fields or collect wild herbs and plants.

Even when Ta'iz is enjoying sunshine, the summit is often cold, windy and covered in mist. This restricts the views but when it clears, you can see that the ridges and spurs of Jebel Sabr are covered in hundreds of villages and houses – almost a hidden world. This is the only place where I have seen a *fokhakh*, a chameleon; they are normally killed by locals because they eat *qat*.

Reaching the top

After a painful, lurching 27km the track arrives at a restricted zone around the TV mast on the summit at 3,006m, about 1,600m above Ta'iz. There are said to be the ruins of a Himyarite castle within the military area. Many other tracks run around the peak and it is possible with care to by-pass the summit and drop down the south face to reach the main track running from the at-Turbah road through al-Misrakh village onto the Aden road.

Salah Museum

On the outskirts This is another former royal residence turned into a museum, but it is not frequented by tourists as much as the National Museum. It is located beyond the Military Hospital at the end of Salah Road, 5km from the centre of Ta'iz.

It is laid out on more traditional lines, with good displays of coins, stamps and pre-Islamic carvings. There are some valuable examples of manuscripts drawn on animal hides, including sections of the Jewish Torah on goat skin. Some of the more interesting items are the large aerial photographs of towns, many of which have expanded rapidly since they were taken in the 1970s. Shots of the Marib excavation show what the archaeologists uncovered before the sand reclaimed the site.

The museum also has a small zoo attached which falls far short of Western standards of animal welfare. Having **The Imam's** said that, the lions especially look to be in good **lions survive** condition. They are the descendants of a gift of lions from Haile Selassie, Emperor of Ethiopia. During my last visit there were six males, eight females and two cubs. The cages are incredibly small, and the locals tend to poke them with sticks to get them moving.

The lions are permanent residents but other cages keep animals that are occasionally caught in the surrounding mountains. At various times there are honey badgers and striped hyenas, which incredibly still exist in the wild (see Flora and Fauna).

Yifrus

This Ismaili village and mosque is a good half-day excursion, about 30km on a tarred road from Ta'iz. It involves travelling through Wadi al-Dhabab (good for its Sunday market) and along the side of Jebel Habashi with views over to the western slopes of Jebel Sabr. With more time the visit could also include at-Turbah (see Ta'iz–Aden via at-Turbah).

Off the Leave the main road to at-Turbah at a few roadside **main road** huts called Mafraq Yifrus (29km), and turn right on a dirt track for 5km to arrive at the rather scruffy and unattractive stone village of Yifrus. To visit the splendid mosque of the local saint, Ahmed bin Alwan, you unfortunately have to run the gauntlet of the entire village asking for *baksheesh*. Ahmed bin Alwan was a religious scribe during Rasulid rule in Ta'iz who established a Sufi school in order to oppose the Zaidi teachings of the north and the wasteful practices of the Rasulids themselves. Much venerated by the populace, he wrote books on religion, law, agriculture and astronomy. His sixteenth century mosque was built by Amer bin

Abdul Wahab, one of Ahmed bin Alwan's pupils and the last king of the Beni Tahar dynasty centred on Rada'a (he also built the al-Ameriya Mosque).

Ismaili pilgrim site

This is one of the holiest places in the Yemen, and religious festivals are held here, including the practice of self flagellation. With al-Hoteib and Shibam al-Gharas this is one of the most important centres for Ismaili Taiyibi sect worship.

The famous aqueduct that brings water 3 km from the mountains is supported by arches as it approaches the mosque. If you are allowed inside the mosque, climb the steps under the final arch and enter the simple white courtyard with the ablution pool. You can leave via the rear doorway.

Access to the village used to be through a tunnel beneath the mosque. Turn left before the final arch to enter the tunnel. Vents in the roof from the courtyard floor allow some light but not much. It is possible to leave the tunnel where it joins the steps at the back of the mosque. Notice where the overflow channel flows down from the pool halfway down. If you walk up into the village it is possible to take a track east through the fields and drop down onto the dirt road. The walk takes about 20 minutes and there are more than enough children willing to show you the way for a small fee. There are also many villages higher up the slope of Jebel Habashi, which provides excellent scenic and unspoilt walking opportunities.

Hotels

*** **Mareb,** Jebel al-Dabua, PO Box 5285. Tel: 210352 or 525150. Fax: 212122.
52 rooms, all with TV and bathroom, some with air-conditioning. There is sometimes water in the swimming pool. Formerly the top hotel in town, but standards and quality have fallen, unlike the prices. Better value elsewhere.

*** **Plaza,** 26 September St, PO Box 5166. Tel: 220224/6 or 221369.
25 rooms, all with bathroom and fan. Good restaurant and bar. Usefully opposite the International Telecommunications Telephone office. Much better value than the Mareb.

*** **Yazan,** Beer Basha. Tel: 217999/8.
On the outskirts of town, 4km from the centre on the road to Hodeidah. 40 rooms, all with bathroom, telephone, TV and fan. Sometimes water in the pool. Good, clean, modern hotel, built in 1990.

** **Al Mokhtar #1,** Ossaifira St, PO Box 55602. Tel: 222492 or 214717. Fax: 214718.

21 rooms, all with bathroom, telephone, TV and fan. A good clean hotel in an excellent central location. There is also the ****Al Mokhtar #2,** further out of the town centre on the same street, with 42 rooms and the same good value, built 1993.

** **Al-Ikhwa,** Jebel al-Dabua, PO Box 5413. Tel: 210364/5/97.

25 rooms, all with air-conditioning, fan, telephone, bathroom and TV. A musty 30 year old place on the same hill as the Mareb, but with better views. A new extension will have 80 rooms, but this has been in a skeletal state for several years. Expensive for what you get, but superb views across the city from the Park terrace tea bar outside.

** **Deluxe,** Off Gamal Abdul Nasser St, PO Box 5476. Tel: 226251/2.

70 rooms, half with bathroom. A large rambling place with plenty of escape routes! Near Al Mokhtar #1. Good value.

** **Burg El-Tahreer,** At-Tahrir St, PO Box 6390. Tel: 221488/3 Fax: 221482.

48 rooms, all with bathroom, fan and TV. Good value if you can get in; it tends to be full. Very central and there is a good restaurant next door.

** **Al Kamel.** Tel: 224501.

In Suq al-Gumrah suburb, off Sana'a Road about 3km from the centre. 24 rooms, all with bathroom, telephone and fan. Good, new, clean and good value for money. Spoilt by being difficult to get to (left at the Al-Sharg).

** **Al-Sharg,** Sana'a Road. Tel: 224307.

About 2km out of town. 25 rooms, some with fans. Two rooms per bathroom. Opened 1992. Another good, clean place. Good value for money.

** **Al-Ganad,** Off 26 September St. Tel: 210529/8.

Between the Plaza Hotel and the post office. 34 rooms. A good old-style place. Quiet, considering its good location.

* **Bilqis,** Off at-Tahrir St. Tel: 230056.

9 rooms, all with fans. Very central but basic and noisy.

* **Hotel Hadramaut,** At-Tahrir St. Tel: 219720.

21 rooms. Three blocks closer than Al Mokhtar #2, built 1990. OK.

* **Hilltop Pensyon,** Jebel al-Dabua. Tel: 213836.

Just before Al-Ikhwa and Mareb Hotels on the hill. 10 rooms, all with bathroom, but threadbare and basic.

* **El Whda**, 26 September St.

Near Bab al-Kabir. A very local place in the town centre. There are several basic hotels to the east of the centre, where the buses and taxis drop people from Sana'a.

* **As-Salaam**, Tel: 210110

On a noisy main road. 30 rooms.

* **Habib,** Tel: 210260.
Reasonable local place.
* **Himyar.**
Basic.
* **Al-Hillal,** Tel: 216626.
16 rooms. Rough.
* **Labours.**
Qat commune.
* **Sheba Palace.**
Reasonable.
* **Al-Mansoori.**
Basic.
* **Shahbain.**
Rough.
* **Al-Gohaymi.**
Basic.
* **An-Naham.**
Very basic!
* **Golden Beach.**
An optimistically named basic *fonduq* on the outskirts.

Restaurants

There are many local places around the *suq*. The better places tend to be slightly out of the centre.

Al-Boustan (Lebanese Restaurant)

At the eastern end of Gamal Abdul Nasser Street. The front section is for sweets and take-away food. The main eating place is at the back. Lebanese specialities are on offer at lunchtimes. In the evenings it is generally fish and meat. A speciality is *sanbouseks* – cheese or meat mini-pasties. Good quality.

Arabian Night Broast (Layl al-Arabi)

Near al-Thawra Hospital. Good local dishes in non-tourist area. Good value if all you want is grilled chicken or *kofta*.

Arabia Felix

Very central, where Gamal Abdul Nasser Street crosses at-Tahrir Street. Good value local food on the first floor.

Yemen Modern

Close to the Arabia Felix. The usual fare, but it varies with the staff on duty.

Rada'a

Beyond the start of Sana'a Road. Good local food – not all meat. Good potato and okra curry.

TA'IZ–ADEN DIRECT

Ta'iz–Aden

The quickest way to Aden is down the fast main road; it takes a couple of hours to cover the 160km. The first 11km are the same as if you were heading north to Sana'a (see Ibb–Ta'iz), until the road to the south turns right just past the Luna Park amusement centre. The road rolls around the eastern slopes of **Jebel Sabr** and then descends through the *wadi* system towards the Indian Ocean. This stretch is usually quiet, as the majority of the traffic now uses the new road from Aden through Qatabah to Sana'a.

Skirting around Jebel Sabr

From ad-Dimnah (34km from Ta'iz) there is a turning to the right signposted to as-Solw, which crawls up and over the southern ridge of Jebel Sabr and eventually drops into Wadi Bani Khawlan near al-Misrakh. A marvellous one-day 4x4 journey would be to circumnavigate Jebel Sabr and its off-shoots along this route. This was one of the first areas designated as being of special interest to tourists, but nobody comes here. Jebel Mansurah gives its name to a castle on the slopes.

Every few kilometres there are small settlements beside the road to tend the cultivated areas in the *wadi*, all overshadowed by the peak rising up on the right, Jebel Sami (2640m). Sixteen kilometres along the road, at **ar-Rahida,** there is another track up into the mountains, to the village of Hayfan. This 14km route via Naqil Hamra Pass offers spectacular views over the former border area with a few hilltop defences. It is possible to return to ar-Rahida by a different track further to the east.

Across the old border

Ash-Shoraija (69km) and **Kirsh** (77km) were right on the YAR/PDRY border. They now have a few roadside cafes for *chai*, with no indication of their previous strategic significance. The two large *wadis* that are crossed in quick succession are Aqqan and Tuban, and the small village of **Aqqan** appears at 93km.

Aqqan–al-Janad

Qat trade to Aden

At Aqqan, a minor road north follows Wadi Tuban to **Musaymir,** a rough looking place today, but a former state capital. Here are remnants of the powerful Sultan of the Haushabi tribe who grew rich from the *qat* trade which passed through Wadi Tuban to get to Aden. He charged 1 rial per camel, compared with the 2 rials paid to the Imam in the north and 3 to the Sultan of Lahej further south.

In the centre of Musaymir, on the left, is his former palace, now converted into a private house and clinic. The big house slightly to the north used to belong to his mother and the similar one on the hill to the east was his brother's. The striking peak to the north is **Jebel Warwah,** described by Ameen Rihani who travelled this route in 1930 as looking like the profile of the pontiff, wearing his tiara, sitting upon his throne (see Further Reading).

This road is old and subject to frequent closure because of landslips during the wet season, which sometimes take months to repair. The former border point of ad-Duraijah is 20km further on and gives a good view of the five needles of rock standing on Jebel Humar. Mawiyah is another 20km further on, and is reached by travelling down Wadi Lusab. From here the road goes north then west for a further 27km to the al-Janad Mosque (see Ibb–Ta'iz) to meet the Sana'a–Ta'iz road.

Aqqan–Aden

Join the main highway

Sixteen kilometres beyond Aqqan, on the main Aden road, is **Nawbat Dukaym,** the major junction and checkpoint for the main Aden–Sana'a direct road. The combined road heads south down Wadi Tuban, with the volcanic mountains of the Qarn az-Zabi massif across to the left.

The *wadi* splits in two, the branches diverting water into different regions of the coastal strip on either side of Aden. Wadi as-Sagir ('little *wadi*') heads eastwards, whereas the main road tends to follow Wadi al-Kabir ('big *wadi*') down towards Lahej. The vastness of the dunes and jagged peaks provides some unique views, which make a tremendous contrast with the fertility of Lahej province. Together with Abyan, this province is the major cotton growing region.

An important ruler

Lahej (138km) is the former capital of the Abdali tribal region, whose sultan was the most powerful in the south. As the rulers of the Aden Peninsula it was with the Abdalis that the British negotiated for its use, until they decided that invasion and total control would suit them better. The Sultan of Lahej then became the premier Arab ruler in the Western Protectorate and it was through his good services that many of the peace treaties with other tribes were arranged.

The town is now a provincial capital and consequently most of the interesting buildings, such as the Sultan's Palace are now used as government offices or schools. If you turn off the main road into town (and many visitors do not) you can find a busy market street with the former palace over to the east. Beyond is the old mosque with its white cupola. The new mosque, built in the 1970s is to be found to the west down one of the side streets. If you have plenty of time to spare, then Lahej is worth a quick look. If not, you will not miss much by keeping to the main road and pressing on to the village of Sabir, where the rough road from at-Turbah comes in from the west.

Approaching
Aden

The main road gets busier as you get closer to **Aden,** and long queues of traffic can build up at the checkpoint just before the suburbs of Sheikh Othman and al-Mansurah, both badly damaged in the 1994 battle for Aden. The main Aden bus station is to the right of the Sheikh Othman roundabout, after which is the start of the causeway across the shallows of Aden harbour. Smallscale salt extraction takes place here, the remains of older workings. Just before the airport, far over to the left, are some equally spaced towers. These are the derelict windmill towers which pumped sea water into the shallow evaporating salt-beds. This is a good area for seeing the more exotic coastal birds, such as flamingos and pelicans (see Flora and Fauna). At the end is the Aden Movenpick Hotel and the choice of going to Crater straight ahead or Ma'alla and Steamer Point to the right.

TAIZ–ADEN via AT-TURBAH

The road to at-Turbah is tarred but beyond at-Turbah 4x4 is needed, and a very good driver.

After ten minutes on the road to Mokha, just past the Yazan Hotel, turn left at Beer Basha (5km). Descend into **Wadi al-Dhabab,** a pleasant and green valley with a permanent stream, large trees and weaver bird nests. If you are lucky enough to be here on a Sunday, there is a large lively market that attracts traders from all the mountain villages, the women looking colourful and active. Look out for the women in this area who smear their faces with a yellow mixture of egg yolk and curcuma, a type of turmeric root powder, which gives them an ashen, ghoulish appearance but protects them from the sun. The distant high peak over to the right is Jebel Habashi, which overlooks Yifrus.

Ghoulish
women

The road climbs out of the *wadi*, giving good views of Jebel Sabr to the left. Descend into **Wadi Bani Khawlan** (23km), a beautiful valley surrounded by towering peaks, surely one of the best examples of 'Arabia Felix'. A track runs left to the Thursday market village of al-Misrakh, hemmed in by the mountains. This track continues up the southern slopes of Jebel Sabr and eventually joins the main Taiz–Aden road at ad-Dimnah.

At Mafraq Yifrus (29km) a dirt road leads up to the nearby village of Yifrus (see Ta'iz), but the white mosque can only be seen about 500m beyond the junction. After the village of Najd an-Nashamah (37km) the road crosses a low pass and enters another rich, verdant valley. From this point there is almost continuous habitation and cultivation crossing Wadi al-Fujayhah. Beyond Asafiah (54km) the mass of Jebel Dafar rises to the right, with one

The largest tree   of the largest trees in the Yemen just off to the right before As-Samsarah village (59km). The local name for the tree means 'tree of the stranger'. Climb up the mountain amid weird euphorbia candelabra plants onto the Hujjariya plateau to reach at-Turbah (80km).

AT-TURBAH

The stone built town of at-Turbah is not particularly interesting to wander around in itself, although it does have a bustling daily market. Its main attraction for tourists is as a centre for the many viewpoints looking down from 1,800m southwards onto the baked desert surrounding Aden. In some places the escarpment is several kilometres from the town, so a vehicle is necessary. Until recently it was impossible to go south from here because of the border and the lack of suitable track. A new route has now been blasted out of the Maqatirah plateau, but it should only be attempted by a 4x4 vehicle in the hands of a very competent driver.

Hair-raising drops   Head east out of at-Turbah on a dirt track to Beni Razi (83km), through a small village with a petrol station (87km) and over a very rough track of former frontier territory. The villages have a similar 'feel' to Kawkaban, especially **Beit al-Ghaylan** (90km) where a cleft in the rock invites you to walk down and after about 3km rejoin the 4x4 track, which plunges over the edge giving spectacular views of hidden *wadis* and mountains. A new track is being prepared, but the old one threads around ruined fortress houses on narrow ledges above 1,000m drops that are not for the faint hearted.

Volcanic activity is indicated by the black outcrops that run across the landscape. The track drops into Wadi Uboy (103km), which leads to the small village of **ar-Rubuwah Sharq Makartarah** (107km). As you can imagine after such a journey, few visitors come here. The locals are extremely friendly and inquisitive and it is a good place to enjoy *chai* and *qat*. The village looks like one of the Berber villages on the southern Anti-Atlas range in Morocco; stone houses perch above ravines, with steep-sided twisting *wadis* covered in wispy tamarisk, acacia and the small-leafed *ilb* trees.

The coastal plain   The *wadi* opens out, and the road becomes straight and fast. Jebelayn means 'two mountains' and it is easy to see the two distant jagged peaks on the right, which appear out of the barren desert (138km). Wadi am-Rija joins from the left, from where it is just possible to see the mountains above Imran on the coast. Further around are the peaks above Little Aden and Crater. Cross Wadi al-Kabir (204km) and join the main Ta'iz–Aden road at Sabir (209km) just south of Lahej.

ADEN

INTRODUCTION: THE FORMER PDRY

The former PDRY consists of six governorates whose total area is about twice that of the former YAR. Unlike the north only about 2 per cent of the land is suitable for cultivation and terracing is only practised in the mountains along the former border.

The wide coastal plain runs from the Bab al-Mandab entrance of the Red Sea all the way to the Omani border. In some places the coast is scarred by lava flows (Bir Ali), volcanic outcrops (Aden) and steep mountains (al-Mahra). To the north-west the land rises up to join the Yemeni mountains with the central section being a huge barren plateau called the *jol*. This plateau is split by a tremendous *wadi* system that forms Wadi Hadramaut. To the north of this the land disappears into the wastes of the Rub al-Khali.

Confusion with money

One difference between this area and the north is that fewer men carry *jambias* and chew *qat*, but both are on the increase. There are also differences in the currency, as Yemeni dinars continue to be handled, although the term 'shillings' is often used (see Money). It might be worth collecting some of the old PDRY coins, especially those from before 1967, which are inscribed 'South Arabia'.

The brewery in Aden no longer produces Seera beer because of fundamentalist objections. Generally, however, alcohol is more freely available than in northern cities.

HISTORY

Ancient trading port

Aden is mentioned in the Bible (Ezekiel 27: 21-23) as being a trading partner of the Mediterranean port of Tyre and was probably the main harbour of the **Awsan Kingdom** around the sixth century BC. Its vast natural harbour and defences have always made it a prize to be fought over by those trading between East Africa and the Indies. The **Sabaeans** conquered the Awsanians and used Aden as an important trade link between Africa and their inland Gold and Incense Route via Dhafar and Marib.

By Roman times the port was known as Eudaemon Arabia and was famous for trading in ivory, cotton, indigo, diamonds, sapphires, wine, spices and incense. It was added to the kingdom of **Ali as-Sulayhi** in the eleventh century and it is known that when Arwa bint Ahmed married his son Mukarram, she received 100,000 gold dinars as an annual dowry from the port (see Ibb). In the twelfth century, Aden, like the rest of the Yemen, fell under **Ayyubid** control, but trade continued. Marco Polo and Ibn Battuta called in on their epic journeys in

**Prized by
the Europeans**

the thirteenth and fourteenth centuries respectively.

In 1497 the **Portuguese** sailor Vasco da Gama found the route to India around the Cape of Good Hope, which gave a new importance to Aden as a port *en route* to the Indies, but this time its importance was to the rapidly expanding Europeans. In 1513 the Portuguese under Affonso d'Albuquerque tried to take the port for themselves but were defeated by the Bani Tahir, who had their capital at Rada'a. Concerned by the Portuguese presence in the Red Sea, Egyptian Mamelukes took control of the Tihama, but they also failed to gain Aden. The dissolving Bani Tahir empire finally collapsed in 1538, and Aden fell to Pasha al-Khadim, the commander of the fleet for Suleiman the Magnificent. This is the year that saw the start of **Ottoman** occupation of the whole of the Yemen.

As we have seen, the Yemen was a difficult place for the Turks and their control was at best tenuous. This lack of authority had the effect of reducing Aden from one of the most powerful cities in the Middle East to little more than a fishing village within 200 years. By 1735 control was in the hands of the nearby Sultan of Lahej. **British** interest started as early as 1799, as an effort to contain French expansion in the region after Napoleon had taken Egypt the previous year. They occupied Perim Island, but a shortage of water forced them to try to purchase Socotra from the Sultan instead.

**A British
possession**

The East India Company was established on Socotra by 1834, but dealings with the Sultan ceased after the Indian vessel *Driadolt* flying the British flag, was plundered near Aden in 1837. A British force from Bombay under the command of Captain Stafford Bettesworth Haines of the Indian Navy, attacked and captured Aden on 16 January 1839. Thus the first territorial acquisition in the reign of Queen Victoria started the period of British control in southern Arabia.

Unlike its other colonies, Britain's aim was not to rule the region but simply to keep a foothold in Aden. Surrounded and protected from the Turkish-controlled north by 'loyal' Sultans in protectorates, Aden became a bunkering station as sail gave way to steam, and was known as the 'coal hole of the East'. The coal and oil were imported, but it was the discovery of artesian wells at Sheikh Othman – at that time the only fresh water supply within 1000km – which made Aden the most important port between Europe and the East.

Two Anglo-Turkish agreements were broken during the First World War, when the Turks fought their way south, intent on taking Aden, and actually got within sight of the city. Even their defeat in the war did not solve Britain's problems however; the newly independent

Imam then claimed Aden for himself.

Coal-fired ships became oil powered and Aden, with its strategic location on the edge of the Persian oilfields, again became a vital link. Until 1932 it was still part of the Bombay Presidency, but was finally separated from India in 1937 to become a **Crown Colony.** Indian independence in 1947 had little effect on Aden's trade, as by then it was well established as an international port. In the 1950s a quarter of a million passengers from 6,000 ships stopped at Aden for refuelling each year, making it second only to New York as a port. The revenue from these visitors in tax-free goods was the fourth largest in the world.

Rapid decline   Many books have been written about the nationalist uprisings of the 1950s and 1960s. Many factors affected the situation including Britain's role in the Suez crisis in 1956, her support of the North Yemeni royalists in the 1962 revolution and subsequent civil war, and the 1967 Six Day war. Bitter fighting broke out between British troops and the two nationalist groups FLOSY and the NLF. Events overtook Britain's sluggish attempts at granting independence and the last troops hurriedly left Aden in late 1967. The **People's Republic of South Yemen** came into being on 30 November 1967 and with the approval of the NLF, Qahtan al-Shaabi became its first president (see Politics).

Aden's economic strength had depended on the British presence; with this removed and ships avoiding the port because of the fighting, the city declined. Aden suffered greatly as a result of internal power struggles and the closure of the Suez canal. Economic support came from Communist countries looking for a Middle Eastern base.

Communist   By June 1969 the government had moved to the left, **take-over**   with its so-called **Corrective Movement.** Al-Shaabi resigned to be replaced by Salem Rubayi Ali, and the country became the only Marxist Arab state. Relying totally on help from Eastern bloc countries the country became the **People's Democratic Republic of Yemen.** All industry was nationalised except for the BP oil refinery in Little Aden.

The 1970s and 1980s saw **border disputes** with both the YAR and Oman, with each country intent on destabilising the other's government. Support for terrorist groups further harmed the PDRY's position in the world. Internal tension developed into a full scale civil war in Aden during January 1986, which ended only when the main protagonists were either killed or expelled. Haidar Abu Bakr al-Attas became the new president, still following pro-Soviet doctrines. Within three years however, the Soviet system itself was collapsing, leaving the PDRY virtually bankrupt and with few friends.

Refinancing a natural harbour

After unification Aden became the new economic capital of the Republic of Yemen. In 1993 the YFZPA (Yemen Free Zones Public Authority) completed a 25 year master plan, requiring direct investment of $5.8 billion. The fierce offensive by northern troops to take Aden in 1994 has devastated the city, with many sites badly damaged or destroyed (see p.80).

SITES

Throughout its chequered history Aden has managed to hang on to various influences. Not only is it the place where Britain met India, but also where the Eastern bloc met East Africa. The whole place appears to be caught in a time warp of the mid-1960s, but it is slowly awakening.

It was only after several visits that I became fully orientated in and around Aden. It is fairly obvious when you are actually in Crater, but outside it is difficult to know exactly where you are and the names do not really help.

At its thinnest point the neck of the peninsula is only about 1km wide, with the Aden Movenpick Hotel on the inner harbour. From the hotel roundabout roads lead north to Khormaksar (sometimes shown as K-Sar); to Sheikh Othman across the causeway; south to Crater (along the east coast); and to Ma'alla (see map p.289). Signs dotted about the seashore of the harbour forbid parking, fishing and photography.

Crater

Inside the crater

On old maps (is there anything else?) Crater is referred to as the Native Town and occupies only about 10 per cent of the peninsula. Nowadays, there are two entry points for vehicles. The first is the **Aden Gateway,** where the road from Ma'alla rises over the rim of the crater and drops in from the north.

Old pictures show the British stone arch that connected the walls and ramparts on either side, but this was removed in order to widen the road. A model of the Gateway has been built in the middle of the roundabout above Ma'alla. The second route is the newer coast road that swings in along the eastern edge from Khormaksar.

Local town

Most of the central shops within the Indian-style **Bazaar** are laid out on a grid pattern which is easy to follow. The Bohra Bazaar takes its name from the Ismaili sect that has its spiritual home in India but has important pilgrimage sites in Manakha, Yifrus and near Sana'a. Around the outside of the Bazaar area are the larger buildings of banks etc., with one side open to the sea, the other rising up the lava cliffs.

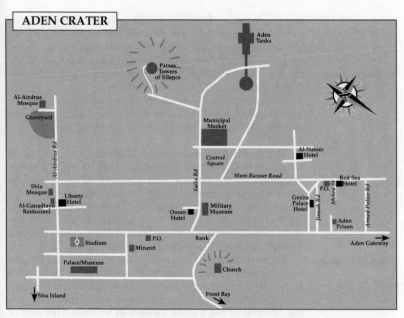

ADEN CRATER

Aden Tanks

Parsee Towers of Silence

Al-Airdrus Mosque

Graveyard

Al-Airdrus Rd

Municipal Market

Al-Nasser Hotel

Central Square

Main Bazaar Road

Saila Rd

Red Sea Hotel

P.O.

Mehra St

Shia Mosque

Liberty Hotel

Al-Ganadtayn Restaurant

Gezira Palace Hotel

Jinnah Rd

Armed Police Rd

Ousan Hotel

Military Museum

Aden Prison

Stadium

P.O.

Minaret

Bank

Aden Gateway

Palace/Museum

Church

Sira Island

Front Bay

Aden's Patron Saint	On the edge of town is the **al-Airdrus Mosque,** built on a slight hill and dating from the fourteenth century, but rebuilt in the 1850s. It contains the body of the patron saint of Aden, Sayyid Abdullah al-Airdrus who originally came from the centre of religious teaching in Tarim. He and his family are laid in finely carved wooden tombs, decorated with colourful banners.

Legend says that the original builders were at a loss what to do about the doors, until ready-carved doors floated onto the shore all the way from India! Renovations are being carried out and it is possible to gain entry to see the rich colours of the religious banners and covers in the tomb. Next door is the new mosque.

From the mosque look upwards towards the Tawila Tanks and you can see the crumbling white walls of the Parsee Towers of Silence on a small hilltop.

'These tanks'   The **Aden Tanks** or the Cisterns of Tawila are about 500m from the mosque, hidden up a fissure cut into the crater wall, however, the entrance is frequently locked. At many sites in the country you will have seen rock-cut cisterns to collect rainwater, but this is the ultimate system: a series of 18 interlinked chambers that possibly date back to the Himyar period and are capable of holding up to 100 million litres. A plaque of 1899 entitled 'These Tanks' explains how they were discovered under rubbish by Lt Playfair in 1854 and subsequently cleared and repaired. The collected water was sold by auction to the local Arabs. There is a sinister belief that when the tanks become full, there will be three deaths by drowning! They are set within British formal gardens, and do not usually hold any water – but they are filling **Recent flooding** up again with rubbish. Some of the disastrous flooding in 1993 began when the tanks overflowed.

At the higher level are steps up to the top tanks and a giant banyan tree. The steps up the mountain to the left eventually lead to the Parsee Towers of Silence (see below).

The small **Ethnographical Museum** named 'Aden Museum 1930' is usually shut, but there are some inscribed blocks outside and a couple of cannons. The Tank gates are usually closed, but you can gain entry by tipping the guardian. If you cannot get inside, go back to the narrow road between high walls and look over the wall away from the gardens and at least you will get a view of the giant lower pool called the Playfair Tank.

Zarathustrism A great trading centre like Aden had to cater for a wide variety of religions. With such strong links with India it is no surprise that religions from the subcontinent are represented here. Here, on the slopes of the crater, are the remains of the **Parsee Towers of Silence.** This sect of Zarathustrism is centred in Bombay and Parsees are known to be extremely good businessmen, hence their presence in Aden. Towers of Silence is the name given to any Parsee funeral site where the bodies of the dead are left to rot in the atmosphere and be eaten by scavengers.

It takes about 20 minutes to climb up to the site by two paths. Turn left just past the Market Hall on the road up to the Tanks, or take the steps up to the left from the higher level in the Tank area itself. A circuit based on the Tanks and Towers will take about an hour.

The gleaming tiered tower known as the **Salama Minaret** is thought to have been built around 1770. It is all that remains of an earlier mosque, possibly dating from the Turkish occupation in the reign of Suleiman the Magnificent in the sixteenth century. Near the post office, a sign on a house indicates it to be the former residence of French poet Rimbaud.

The Sultan's The **National Archaeological Museum** has recently
Palace been relocated in the former palace of the Sultan of Lahej, close to the Aden Minaret, between the football stadium and the sea. It is open 08.00-12.00 (and possibly some afternoons) every day except Friday, and entrance is free.

Inside the ground floor museum are most of the finest pieces from the southern cities of the great ancient kingdoms. A bronze statue of a woman from Timna and an alabaster statue of a woman set on a plaque in the pose of Dhat Hamim (Goddess of Good Fortune) rival anything on show in Sana'a. From the Awsan Kingdom there are alabaster statues of three kings. The alabaster bulls head is exquisite. Qataban jewellery from Timna, with seals and coins, are also among the highlights.

The place is a bit chaotic, even the opening times seem uncertain.

On the first floor is a separate exhibition depicting memorabilia from the days of the Sultan. Clothing, coins, pottery, handicrafts, guns and musical instruments are well displayed. There are some interesting old photographs of Aden during British rule.

The struggle for Independence

Heading back towards the *suq* is the **Military Museum** dedicated to the War of Liberation, which opens 08.30-13.30 and 15.00-19.00 daily except Thursday. No bags or cameras are allowed. Through a series of halls, each covering a different aspect, the struggle for independence unfolds. Understandably much of the story is anti-British, with a formidable array of guns, bombs and bullets from all sides. The story ends in the 13 January Hall, referring to 1986 when the civil war erupted. Being so recent, there are some interesting photographs of Aden, taken at the time, including the blasted Aden Hotel.

From the Military Story Hall on the ground floor, make sure to look out of the windows to see the giant bronze statue of Queen Victoria in the car park. This used to stand on the hill above the Church of St Francis in Tawahi and has reportedly been the subject of a recent enquiry by the British government.

Sira Island

From the National Museum, access to the offshore island of **Sira** is along a causeway which separates the more northerly Front Bay from Holkat Bay, where the British landed in 1839. In the late afternoon this is a lively place where locals come to buy fresh fish, chew *qat* and watch the sunset.

It is well worth climbing the hill up the paved path which starts from the end of the road on the left. Halfway up are large gun enplacements and on top a small but impressive bastion with rooms and terraces. This strategic position has always been important and improvements were carried out by every occupying force. Notice how old cannons have been used as modern gun bases.

Highest point

Jebel Shamsan is the highest peak overlooking Aden, at a height of 560m. A paved path winds up to the summit on the inside of the crater, starting to the west of Crater *suq*. Standing on the edge of the crater there are superb views over the different sections of the city, across the harbour to Little Aden and north beyond the airport. It is also the only place where you will get a good view of Sawayih, the old slave island which is now used for beaching old ships. Sections of the defensive wall and

285

look-outs are also incorporated on the crater rim.

The walk will take between one and a half and two hours each way, but be sure not to stay on the summit for sunset, as I did. The path is in a poor state and dangerous in the dark, and packs of wild dogs roam the hillsides at night. There is a rough track that drops down the outside of the crater towards Gold Mohur, which comes out near the tunnel entrance, but it is difficult in some places.

Ma'alla

Development The road to Ma'alla hugs the inner harbour coastline opposite Sawayih and emerges after some small shops and light industry. The road climbing up to the left leads to the Aden Gateway and Crater. Just before the Gateway is a look-out point on the left with good views over the inner harbour. The giant key symbolises the gateway as the key to the city. Directly below is a Muslim cemetery; the one beyond the small roundabout is the old Jewish one.

Modern Ma'alla is essentially two long lines of British built flats and shops split by a road. Old Ma'alla is along the coast behind the flats. This has always been the seafaring quarter of Aden, where all sections of the sailing vessels were shaped and fitted. Traditional dhows have reputedly been made here since the days of the Queen of Sheba, but there is little to support such a claim.

Somalipura is not to be found on modern maps, but it is the area at the end of the flats. As the name suggests, this was where sailors from the Horn of Africa worked on their lateen sails. It was also the end of the line for the **Old railway** narrow-gauge railway which the British built to link the salt-pans to the docks, the wagons being pulled by camel. Further up the slope towards Jebel Shamsan is a redevelopment area that was formerly occupied by huge oil tanks.

Tawahi

Colonial centre If you go left at the roundabout beyond the Ma'alla flats, you will pass a housing area and go through the tunnel to Gold Mohur Bay. But straight ahead is Tawahi district (formerly Steamer Point) and the Crescent. This is the start of colonial Aden, typified by the **Rock Hotel** (now 26 September Hotel) on the left of the main highway, where nothing has changed since the mid-1960s. It is worth going to the bar and restaurant on the eight floor for good views of Tawahi and examples of swinging sixties mod decor. Lumps of inscribed blocks from Marib and Shabwa, which I am assured are real, are cemented into the wall.

The Crescent Hotel is in a similar state on the right,

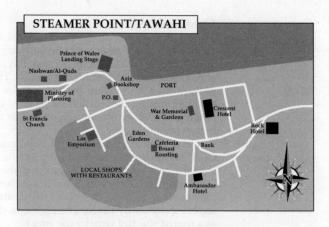

STEAMER POINT/TAWAHI

Prince of Wales Landing Stage

Nashwan/Al-Quds

Ministry of Planning

P.O.

Aziz Bookshop

PORT

St Francis Church

War Memorial & Gardens

Crescent Hotel

Rock Hotel

Lax Emporium

Eden Gardens

Cafeteria Broast Roasting

Bank

LOCAL SHOPS WITH RESTAURANTS

Ambassador Hotel

N

Half-forgotten shops

opposite a war memorial. The Crescent itself runs around **Aden Gardens,** a favourite night-spot for locals visiting the Cafeteria Broast Roasting. Behind this are a number of small lanes with shops and local restaurants. One of the most bizarre shops is just behind the post office. Known as **Lax Emporium,** it is like an annexe to the National Museum in Ta'iz, except that here everything is for sale. From a stuffed turtle to an old pram, from new-ish Soviet hair curlers to a few thousand Ugandan bank notes, this is the place for those less predictable souvenirs.

Back on the front is **Aziz Bookshop,** a great institution amidst the derelict shops with dusty signs still offering Rolex and Elizabeth Arden products. Aziz has the pictorial history of Aden in his postcard selection and sets of old Protectorate stamps with dated scenes of the Hadramaut. Just across the road is the Prince of Wales Landing Stage, where all the transit passengers first set foot in Arabia, before rushing around the duty-free shops. The road now enters a one-way system running around the Ministry of Planning building.

All aboard for Arabia

Along the shoreline on the right are two Palestinian restaurants in the same complex, Al-Quds and Nashwan, with pleasant views across the harbour. To the left above the Sheikh Ahmed Mosque is the small clock tower, a replica of Big Ben.

The Catholic Church of St Francis, built in the early 1950s, seems slightly lost in its present situation. Beyond here the area becomes military, but you can follow the road around to Gold Mohur (pronounced 'more') about one hour's walk away. The army uses much the same area as the British and you can see some of the old wooden barracks and officers' bungalows on the slopes.

Gold Mohur

The road emerges at the coast almost opposite Little Aden, with good views over the entrance to the harbour, and then proceeds around Sapper Bay, Telegraph Bay and through a tunnel into Gold Mohur. This is a safe and pleasant beach to swim, but the hotel is actually in the next bay around Elephant Point. The reason for the name of the point will be obvious if you look at it from the hotel in the morning light.

A quiet
backwater

The sectioned off beach is for hotel guests (the Yemen Club) and further down is the Diplomatic Club. Continue over the headland past the entrance to the lighthouse and into **Conquest Bay,** which has a beached assault craft. This relic of the 1986 civil war totally ruins an otherwise superb quiet sandy beach. The plan is to develop this bay as a tourist site and remove the wreck.

You can return from Gold Mohur by heading directly inland towards Jebel Shamsan. The road enters Ma'alla through another tunnel, and the rough track up to Shamsan peak leaves the road just before the tunnel entrance, through some building works.

ADEN RAILWAY

In his book *Arabian Peak and Desert*, Ameen Rihani describes his journey from Aden to Sana'a and Hodeidah during the 1920s. The first section was by rail, from Aden to Lahej, and covered 20 miles (32km). An old 1930s map I have seen shows a railway running from Somalipura to Lahej with stops at Ma'alla, Khormaksar, Sheikh Othman and Dar al-Amir. It was built mainly to transport the dried salt from the salt-pans around Khormaksar. Some reports at the time describe small wagons being pulled by camels to the wharves at Somalipura. As far as I know, there are no remains to be seen of this system.

North of Aden

Towards the
Causeway

Two roads head north from the Aden Movenpick Hotel. To the right is the road to Khormaksar, which passes along the old military parade ground towards the international airport, with access to the coastal road that heads north to Zinjibar. Just past the row of shops behind the Aden Movenpick Hotel is the Victory Duty-Free Shop for all the imported goods you need including beer and spirits. Payment is in hard currency only.

The left-hand road is the 8km causeway which cuts across the salt flats straight to Sheikh Othman. About 500m past the Aden Movenpick Hotel a road to the left

Slave Island

leads to Sawayih Island where slaves were kept after their journey from East and Central Africa. The southern end is packed with the rusting hulks of every type of craft, but it is under the control of the Fisheries Department and thus

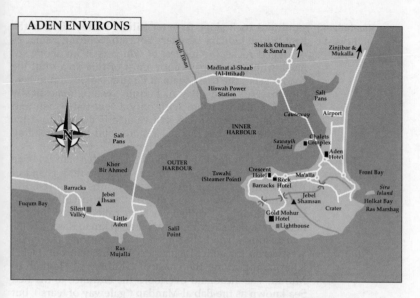

ADEN ENVIRONS

out of bounds. The Chalets Complex Hotel has a bar and veranda overlooking the lagoon.

Back on the causeway the road swings around the end of the airport runway and passes over several lagoons which fill and empty according to the tides. There are old salt-pans further over to the east, and always good numbers of interesting birds in this area including pelicans, flamingos and herons.

Main centres of population

From the roundabout at the end (8km from the Aden Movenpick Hotel), turn right for **Sheikh Othman** (10km), the devastated Aden suburb which housed much of the population. From here there is a good bus and taxi network spreading out to the rest of the country.

West of Aden
Little Aden (al-Burayka)

The westerly road from the causeway roundabout is signposted 'Little Aden' and passes the massive power station built between 1985 and 1989 by the Soviet Union. To the right is the new centre of Madinat al-Shaab, formerly Al-Ittihad, the South Arabian federal capital under British rule.

Just beyond the salt workings at Khor Bir Ahmed inlet is Little Aden (27km). Beyond the bus graveyard to the left are the refineries, but straight ahead past some shops and houses, is the wide curve of a good beach, with a mosque, an abandoned mosque and some boat building.

East of here, beyond the headland, is a small scruffy local fishing village, but to the west the road climbs a

**Reminders
of the past**

sand and rock slope to enter **Silent Valley.** This is the neat British military cemetery beneath towering pinnacles of jagged rocks, the highest of which is 375m above sea level. Military camps occupy most of this area until the road reaches the coast again at **Fuqum** (44km). From here the peaceful sandy Bay of Fuqum sweeps majestically west for almost 10km with only a few fishermen and seabirds for company. A 4x4 vehicle is needed to drive along the coast, but there is a more solid track threading through the dunes behind the beach.

**Remote
coastal areas**

The distant headland to the west of Aden stands above the tiny fishing village of **Imran,** with the little island of Abu Shamleh and a few Muslim tombs just offshore. Around the back of the village is an odd collection of craft, including a Scottish car ferry called *Largs!* Beyond here Imran Bay stretches for another 40 km to Ras Qa'wah.

There is a road that goes roughly along the coast westwards, through Mushirah to Am Jumar, around Jebel Kharaz and along the coast of Ghubbat al-Haykah to Murad. This headland overlooks the entrance to the Red Sea known as the Bab al-Mandab ('gateway of tears'), but because of its strategic position it is out of bounds to tourists. Perim Island (also called Miyun Island) stands in the middle of these straits and is large enough to have an airport. For centuries it has been a military base, but at times also a centre for the fishing industry (see Perim). The coast of Djibouti and Ethiopia is only 30km from the Yemeni mainland at this point.

Hotels
(subject to many changes following 1994 conflict)
***** **Aden Movenpick,** Khormaksar, PO Box 6111. Tel: 32911. Fax: 32947.
182 rooms. By far the best hotel in the south. All facilities, including swimming pool and floodlit tennis courts. CNN and videos. International-standard restaurants and bars. Music and entertainment. Almost always full.
*** **Hotel Gold Mohur,** Abdul Qawee Othman Ali, Tawahi. Tel: 24171-9. Fax: 41721.
120 rooms. A Bulgarian concrete slab built in the late 1970s, situated on beautiful beach and bay. Good food in the restaurants, good views from sea facing rooms. Many improvements since new management took over. The Yemeni Panorama Club on the beach has live music, bar and restaurant.
*** **Chalets Complex,** Sawayih Island. Tel: 31301.
55 rooms in lagoonside chalets, all with air-conditioning and bathroom. Within sight of the Aden Movenpick Hotel. Bar. Quiet, with few tourists.
** **Crescent Hotel,** Tawahi, PO Box 1364. Tel: 23471/2/3.

72 rooms, some in an annexe along the road. All rooms have fan and bathroom. An old British hotel with a seedy appearance. Interesting local bar.
* 26 September, Tawahi. Tel: 22266/7.
Just along the road from the Crescent Hotel. 65 rooms. Old British hotel, but now very rough. Excellent view of the harbour from the restaurant and bar on the top floor.
* Ambassador, Tawahi. Tel: 24403/4.
28 rooms, all with bathroom, fan and air-conditioning. Bar and restaurant. A basic local hotel.

Expect some new beachside hotels and complexes to be built on the coast towards Abyan.
There are also several local hotels located in Crater.
* Ousan, Off Saila Road. Tel: 53357.
12 rooms, some with air-conditioning, others with fan. Basic. Situated near the *suq* and the Military Museum.
* Al-Hurreya (Liberty), Al-Airdrus Road. No telephone.
24 rooms, some with fan, others with air-conditioning. Well situated near the stadium.
* Gezira Palace, Jinnah Road. No telephone.
15 rooms, some with air-conditioning, some with fans. Shared bathrooms.
* Al-Nasser. Tel: 51311.
5 rooms. A central local hotel in a former private house. Larger rooms (5 beds) with air-conditioning or with fans.
* Red Sea
6 rooms, all with fans. Basic accommodation connected to a local restaurant.

Restaurants
Outside Crater
Ching Sing, Ma'alla.
Good Chinese food.
Candles (Ash'moh), Khormaksar.
Good Yemeni and Lebanese food behind Aden Movenpick Hotel.
Nashwan Al-Quds Center, Tawahi.
Two restaurants in one, offering good Palestinian food. Night-club (smart dress required) and floorshow. Bar and patio overlooking the harbour.
Mermaid Club (Military Club), Tawahi.
Difficult to find in the military district.
Inside Crater
There are many local places serving good food, including:
Tanzania
Tasty and central. Note the interesting picture of a rhino goring a child!
Red Sea Restaurant. Good food.
Aftah Ya Sam-Sam. Good food.

Looking west from Husn al-Ghurab, Bir Ali.

THE SOUTH COAST

Rich variety

It is a long journey of 625km along the south coast to Mukalla, but fortunately the scenery changes about every hour to make it a fascinating way to get to the Hadramaut. Public buses and taxis do the journey in a single day, but this is by blasting along the road hour after hour, with no stops for sightseeing or photographs. Many tours break up the journey by having an overnight stop, usually camping at Bir Ali, or miss out Aden altogether and drop down from the north through Lawdar and al-Bayda.

ADEN–BIR ALI

Aden–Habban

Travelling along the coast

The route from Aden is along the eastern coastal road, which was built with help from the Chinese in the 1970s, and runs parallel to the beach for over 50km. Beyond Khormaksar you pass the international airport on the left, and the remains of **windmill towers** which until the 1950s were used to pump water on the salt-pans. Along the road are some oil company compounds, which provide facilities for the workers in the uncramped coastal areas well outside Aden itself. The potential for beach and leisure complexes along this stretch is phenomenal, and this will no doubt develop as Aden starts to pick itself up.

The road makes its way across coastal scrub until the village of **al-Koud** (52km from the Aden Movenpick Hotel). This swampy but fertile region of palms and papayas, corn and cotton, indicates the outflow of Wadi Bana, draining water from as far away as Hammam Damt and Rada'a. The British established this area as the centre of the southern cotton-growing industry; it is famous for a high-quality strand known as Abyan Long. During Communist rule a ginnery was set up to process the cotton. The Cotton Producers' Associations were some of the PDRY successes.

'Black man's earth'

There is a bridge over a *wadi* just before the town of **Zinjibar** (58km), the capital of Abyan province – most often referred to nowadays simply as Abyan. The name Zinjibar comes from the same Arabic root as the more famous Zanzibar in East Africa, which has ancient trading links with this entire coastline. Both mean black man's earth. It was the capital of the Fadhli Sultanate (one of the major states in the Western Aden Protectorate), and was a prosperous town about 7km inland, with a distinct

Remote tracks to the hinterland

African flavour both in the people and the buildings. Heavy fighting took place here during the 1994 conflict.

A road goes directly inland from here up Wadi Bana to Ja'ar, the old capital of the Lower Yafa Sultinate, and **al-Hisn** (22km), where several tracks spread up different wadis: up Wadi am-Suhaybiyah to al-Habilayn on the new Aden–Sana'a highway (97km); continuing up Wadi Bana through Batays to al-Askariyah (68km), from where a track runs direct to al-Bayda through Labus; or north-east on an old trade route to Timna up Wadi Hassan to as-Sawad and ar-Rawdah (83km), the former base of the Sultan of Yeramis, a feudal lord of the Fadhli Sultan.

The road eastwards from Zinjibar soon returns to the coast, but then runs about 500m inland from the beaches, which are deserted except for the odd local fisherman. The fishing potential of this whole coastline is virtually unlimited, but at present it is only exploited on an individual basis. The road bounces up and down concrete *wadi* ramps, which tend to perform better in flood periods than bridges. In the winter months you may well see migratory beekeepers with their lines of hives beside the road. The final town on the coast before the road swings inland is Shuqra (100km), a weary-looking collection of buildings, but one that can at least provide food and drink.

BEEKEEPING

There has been a tradition of beekeeping in the Yemen for well over 2,000 years, and you are likely to see hives by the roadside at some point in your journey. The timing of the moving of the bees is determined by rainfall and the subsequent flowering of natural vegetation, unlike in Europe and North America where apiculture depends more on agricultural crops.

After the spring and autumn rains, the lowland acacia are in flower, and you can see long lines of hives in the Tihama and in Lahej and Abyan provinces during April and December. The hives were traditionally hollow logs, blocked at one end and standing on short metal legs to protect them from ants. Wooden boxes with bolted doors are now also used. In most villages around the southern highlands there will be at least one beekeeper, who tend to go unprotected, as the small local bees *Apis mellifera yemenitica* are particularly gentle.

The honeycomb is hand-squeezed into a suitable container, quite often still with pollen particles and dead bees in it, and this local *baladi* ('country') honey is very expensive and highly prized as a gift. Types of honey are classified from the species of tree in flower, the *ilb* being the best known. Honey from the euphorbias in the highlands has a distinctive chilli aftertaste.

Shuqra was the earlier Fadhli capital, but was in continual conflict with the neighbouring sultanates, especially the Lower Yafa, over the Nazi'a canal built by the British between 1840 and 1850 to irrigate the Abyan lowlands. Two kilometres beyond the town the main road forks left to climb up into the lava fields and despite what you may see on some maps, it is the only practical way to Bir Ali and Mukalla.

The **coastal road** is just possible, but local drivers will not use it. It continues from here until it becomes a poor 4x4 track beyond Muqaybirah (45km from Shuqra) and eventually reaches Ahwar (137km), below a small hill which rises out of the Wadi Ahwar delta 10km inland. Ahwar was the old capital of the Lower Aulaqi Sultanate. From here it is more like an expedition than a journey along the coast to ar-Ragah, before you rejoin the main road where it hits the coast below Azzan. A geologically fascinating, but tough route from Ahwar runs north-wards up Wadi Ahwar and then Wadi Dayqah to reach the main road just before al-Mahfidh.

"... like an ant climbing over the cinders of a boiler room."

The **main road** leaves the coastal plain shortly after Shuqra, and climbs up and over a fascinating collection of perfect volcano cones amid a black jagged lunarscape dotted with some lava tunnels and a few hardy acacias. The top of the 1,000m climb is marked by some disused onion farm buildings followed by a long run down onto the Lawdar Plain, a vast wasteland with a few termite hills, the only place in the Yemen where they can be found.

Just beyond the village of am-Ayn (168km), the road to Lawdar turns off left (see Dhamar–Lawdar). Continuing eastwards the road runs parallel to the huge escarpment of Kaur al-Audhillah, which reaches 2,500m and hides Wadi ar-Ruqub, which joins Wadi Hatib, an ancient trade route to Timna.

A vast wasteland

This area, known as the **Dathinah** region, is well culti-vated among the broken outcrops of the escarpment, and is fed by Wadi al-Jahr, which eventually flows down Wadi Ahwar to the sea. After 20km the impressive sugar-loaf peak of Jebel Wa'ban can be seen way off on the right. **Mudiyah** (197km) is a good place to stop for *chai*.

The road winds through narrow gorges around great lumps of rock, some folded into almost vertical strata by the nearby volcanic activity. There are hot springs at al-Hami and lava flows to the north. Life becomes tough again for the locals around here and is mainly limited to goat herding and subsistence farming.

The Masharah Pass lies at the top of the climb up Wadi Marya, and beyond it is al-Mahfidh (288km), a one-Toyota-town with some small restaurants overlooked by a mountain top telecommunications tower. Another small town, Sahilah (301km) lies in Wadi Makraban, and marks the start of mud houses. After this the whole vista

The Rockies opens up, with scenery not dissimilar to that of Arizona and Colorado. This area is awesome in its size and beauty, and for me it is one of the real surprises of the Yemen.

Al-Aram (320km) is roughly halfway between Aden and Mukalla, and has therefore established itself as the lunchtime stop for most of the daily traffic. There are several restaurants and petrol stations, picturesquely slumbering beneath a magnificent 'science-fiction' mountain called Jebel Suqaymah. If you are caught here at nightfall, it is possible to spend a rough night on top of one of these buildings.

We have now crossed the watershed into a tremendous landscape, and also passed from Abyan province into Shabwa. The run down Wadi Habban starts where a new road turns north to Ataq from Naqaba. The signpost says 'Aden 334km, Mukalla 289km, Ataq 36km'. The road to Ataq mainly serves the oil companies drilling in Shabwa province, but it can also be used to reach as-Said and Yashbum. There is also a minor route direct to **Naqaba** Yashbum from Naqaba, which follows the original **junction** incense road up from Qana, and can be negotiated by 4x4. It starts at the bridge over Wadi Yashbum just before the signpost.

Wadi Yashbum

The road to Ataq climbs steeply for a few kilometres before giving you a stunning view down on Wadi Habban. After 16km there is a left turn towards **as-Said** **Hidden for** at a petrol station, while the Ataq road carries straight on. **protection** It is 18km up this turning to as-Said, which was the former capital of the Upper Aulaqi Sheikhdom, and has some very fine mud tower houses. It is the major town in the picturesque Wadi Yashbum and has the best constructed houses in the region.

The village of **Yashbum** is a further 5km along a rough track from here, back in the direction of Naqaba. A good off-road vehicle is required to reach Yashbum, and the town is difficult to find.

Yashbum and Shibam in Wadi Hadramaut were both founded by the fleeing inhabitants of Shabwa after the invading Sabaeans from Marib had defeated them in the third century AD. Yashbum would thus have been established only towards the end of the incense trade, and has little to show from this period.

As-Sufal is the third centre in Wadi Yashbum, about halfway from Yashbum on the direct track to Naqaba.

If you have plenty of time, it is worth going to as-Said and if you also have the right vehicle, it is also fascinating to go further down the *wadi*. But for most people the fine mud houses on the road to Habban will be sufficient.

Habban Town.

Habban

Four kilometres past Naqaba you get your first views across the *wadi* to Habban (338km), an amazing collection of tall grey mud houses, some painted white, contrasting with the lush green of the *wadi* and the barren mountain backdrop. To reach it, go another kilometre past the town, and then cut back right along the *wadi* on a dusty track. The town has houses of many different shapes and sizes punctuated by the occasional old style mosque.

Habban has seen its fortunes fluctuate wildly over recent years. Until the late 1940s it was a prosperous centre for silverwork and had the largest concentration of Jews in the south. Most of these left for Israel, and the muslim silversmiths have since moved to Ataq. Irregular rainfall and poor crops further dispersed the population, as the town could hardly support itself. This dispersal coincided with the recruitment of Yemenis to work in the oil-rich countries.

A rich town for rich people It is a region famous for exporting shrewd businessmen, especially in the field of banking. As in the Hadramaut, all the locals who left planned to return home at some time – a process which was speeded by events during the 1990 Gulf War. Many of these returnees have built impressive houses in and around Habban, mostly in the traditional style. You should start to notice the horns of the *w'il* (ibex) set into the outer walls, a common practice throughout Shabwa and the Hadramaut to ward off evil spirits.

It looks as though Habban is growing again, with the whole region set to prosper from the oil and gas fields in Shabwa. You can be sure that where there is a business deal to be made, a modern trader from Habban will not be far away. It is likely that you will arrive at Habban **A quiet welcome** about midday or early afternoon, when the entire *wadi* tends to sleep, so there will be little to observe in the town, and no shops open. Externally the houses and buildings give a hint of their wealth with intricate decorations. Outsiders are tolerated but not entertained.

Beyond Habban there is an air of opulence and importance to the houses, which rise up majestically along the roadside. Unlike the northern walled towns, here each house is a fortress in itself, with very small windows on the ground and first floors, if any at all. This is compensated for by having an enormous number of windows on the upper floors, usually covered by traditional blue shutters.

The route follows almost exactly the route taken at the start of the Gold and Incense Road from Qana up to Timna. Descending Wadi Habban the vastness of the landscape adds to the surreal shapes of the buildings, trees and rocks, before the road climbs a short ridge and drops down into Wadi Amaqin. There are several small **The 'casbah'** villages that have the look and feel of the *casbah* towns of **route** southern Morocco, particularly **al-Amarter** (380km) with its concentrated palm groves, tall fortress houses and towering mountain surrounds.

The approach to **Azzan** (392km) is marked on either side of the road by sections of land created by speculators. Their hope is that Azzan will become a busy centre on the way to the oil fields. Here the panorama opens up to the wide Wadi Mayfa'ah. Like Habban, Azzan has seen prosperity and decay, but its history stretches much further back, and there are some interesting stories associated with it (see 'The Three Wise Men').

Ancient myths Azzan was a stronghold of the Wahidi tribe, which formed one of the sultanates in the Eastern Aden Protectorate during British rule. Nowadays it is a large village spread on either side of the main road, with the old town to the east. The finest and most dominant mud houses date from Wahidi times.

Four kilometres south of Azzan are the ruins of **Naqab al-Hajar,** the ancient **Mayfa'ah**, which can be seen from the road. They are about 1km over to the right, lying on an island which rises out of Wadi Mayfa'ah. The easiest route is to turn right at a white mosque on the main road, or about 500m beyond a fine four-storey house on the

Finding Mayfa'ah right with about 100 blue coloured windows, and to head straight to the *wadi*. You should only attempt to cross the wadi with a 4x4 vehicle, and do not make the mistake of asking the locals for Mayfa'ah, which is a dilapidated modern village of rough houses about 10km away.

THE THREE WISE MEN

Azzan was an important town on the gold and incense road in the centuries before Christianity, and traded widely in gold, frankincense and myrrh.

According to St Matthew (2:1-12) wise men came from the east bearing gifts for the Christ-child. The number of Magi – a Persian priestly class of astrologers – is not given, but the tradition is that there were three, one for each gift. Elevated to kings, they also represent the three ages of man, and the three races of mankind. Some scholars claim that Azzan was the starting point for the black African Balthazar (carrying frankincense), who met with Melchior and Caspar at Golgotha, before going to Bethlehem.

To escape detection by King Herod, they returned home by 'different routes', but their bodies are said to have been discovered by the Empress Helena (born around 255 in Colchester, Essex) who was keen to preserve as many relics of Christ's life as she could find. Some bones were taken from Sessania Adrumetorium (a Roman named town, thought to be Azzan) to Constantinople, where they were buried in a marble coffin. This coffin was removed to Milan where it rested until 1164, when it was taken to Cologne Cathedral, where it remains to this day.

In some respects the site of Mayfa'ah, the capital of Lower Hadramaut is similar in size and appearance to Baraqish, but it is not so complete. Like Shabwa, the capital of Upper Hadramaut, the town is built on a slight rise which consists of two small hills, in the bed of the *wadi*. It could thus control all the trade up and down the *wadi* and became the most important station between Qana and Timna. Most of the surrounding wall still exists, with evidence of repair work, and bastions at regular intervals.

Around the impressive southern entrance is an inscription, whilst other inscribed blocks are in Bombay Museum. Many of the huge cut stones were used for repairs or to build nearby houses, but there are still the outlines of ramparts and houses to be seen, as well as a large building near the northern gate (possibly a temple), a tower and a well. To the south of the site are the remains of the water channels used to irrigate the surrounding land to provide food for the inhabitants.

Back to the coast It is another 50km before the sea appears in the form of the huge bay **known as Ghubbat al-Ain,** where Wadi Mayfa'ah reaches the coast. The scenery is like the Sahel in Africa, with huge impressive dunes that sometimes drift across the road. The area is called the Jol al-Sarih.

Ain al-Juwairi (460km) is a small oasis in the sandscape with local restaurants and traders selling fish and excellent red dates in season. It is also the last place to load up with food, bottled and tap water if you are camping at Bir Ali.

The road now runs roughly parallel to the coast, but some way inland, allowing only distant views of Balhaf and its peculiar tower far over to the right, where lava fields reappear on their way to the sea. The headland is called **Ras al-Usaydah** and was a place of piracy into the 1950s. The pilot charts at the time gave the following information: 'Caution. The coast between Maquatain and Wadi Mayfa'ah is inhabited by tribes with murderous and piratical habits.'

'Here be pirates'

The pure white sand lying around the black lava creates a weird monochromatic effect, as the looming fortress of Husn al-Ghurab indicates that you have reached the ancient site of Qana (503km).

Bir Ali

Where it all started

The volcanic bulk of Husn al-Ghurab ('crow fortress') rises out of the turquoise sea, and it is easy to see why such an easily defensible position was chosen to control the start of the great overland trading route. The bay itself was the best natural harbour between Aden and Oman in which to unload the shipments of frankincense from Dhofar and Socotra and escape the ravages of the monsoon. Here, all the luxurious items for the early Mediterranean civilisations – gold, frankincense, silk, spices, rare woods and other valuable raw materials – were reassembled and packed onto camels for the two month journey northwards.

The village of Bir Ali survives now on small-scale fishing in the shallow waters among the offshore islands. A police checkpoint on the main road uses the old fort, but presumably not the British cannon which is engraved VR. There are some small shops, but essentially you should bring everything needed for camping on the beach.

Camping on the beach

Without 4x4 it would be easier to enter the village, pass the cemetery and swing left past the semi-derelict buildings and fishermen's huts to camp further around the bay, making sure that you have gone far enough away from the crazy dogs that fiercely defend the hut area. The **beach** is fine, with good views across the bay to the fortress. It is sometimes used for minor boat building.

A much better idea, however, is to make for the beautiful sandy bay that lies just to the west, immediately beyond the fortress. If you intend to climb the Husn you will need to come here anyway, or face a long walk along the curving beach from Bir Ali. This route can be made without 4x4, as long as you stick to the hard tracks.

If you are coming from Aden, turn right off the main road about 500m before the checkpoint, and about 50m beyond a solitary building on the left. Follow the compacted track to the right of the fortress, always taking the right-hand track, unless it obviously leads back to the road. Never drive directly towards the fortress, as seawater coming in from the left regularly forms inland **Don't get stuck** lagoons on soft wet sand. If you are unsure, send someone ahead to check the route, but it is always better to head too far to the right of the fortress and get stuck in dry sand, than it is to get bogged down in wet sand on the left. With the fortress now to the left, you will soon make out five small breeze block buildings, used as windbreaks for cooking food and basic shelter stretching along the beach ahead.

There always seems to be a wind blowing along this coast, but usually the water is fine for swimming, as long as you don't stand on the irregular patches of coral. If you are lucky you can see, and maybe even swim with, one of the many schools of dolphins that regularly pass **Phosphorescent** through the warm shallow waters between the beach and **glow** the small island of **Hillaniya.** In calm conditions, the night phosphorescence of the sea is truly magical – the waves unfurl like green neon strip lights, and a swim disturbs the water into a million glowing flashes of colourful sparks. The later you stay up – the better it gets!

Qana and Husn al-Ghurab

Only if you climb Husn al-Ghurab can you see where the buildings are on the ancient site of Qana. A leisurely climb up, a wander around and the descent will take about one and a half hours. Looking at the fortress from the breeze block buildings to the west, do not make the mistake of following the well-worn sandy track that angles up the slope from the left. This is not a path to the summit; it is more likely to land you in hospital, as it **Taking the** ends in sheer volcanic cliffs. Better to use the remains of a **Citadel** paved route which zigzags up the north (inland) face. Walk around the base to the left, just past a small tunnel that burrows into the foot of the mountain, until you are due north. Just opposite the remains of a small building are the walls of a path that lead upwards.

It is an easy path to follow coming down, but easy to stray from on the way up. Eventually you will reach a narrow ledge, on the left of which are two inscriptions the smaller one telling us that the 'defender of Qana has written an inscription on **Urr Mawiyat** [the old name of Husn al-Ghurab]'. This is dated 640 years into the Himyar period, and thus corresponds to 525 AD, as it is known that the Himyars conquered the site in 115 BC. There is also a more recent carving, left by the Chinese engineers building the modern road.

History laid out   From the northern edge of the summit, it is possible to discern the outlines of many buildings in the sand below. The site of Qana is the area below the fortress at the western edge of the main bay. Over to the left, somewhat separated from the rest, are the black volcanic block foundations of a large structure 64m x 44m, possibly a temple.

As the overland trade route disintegrated, Qana continued to be the main port for the luxury goods, where they were repackaged and then sent by ship up the Red Sea, well after the secrets of the monsoons had been discovered.

It is another ten-minute climb to the highest point, and well worth the struggle, for the **stunning views** over the entire coastline. There are the remains of another temple at this point, possibly a religious sanctuary from an earlier period.

Observing sea-life   It is a good idea to continue round the summit for good views down onto coral outcrops. With binoculars I have observed dolphins, turtles and barracuda in the clear waters from here. Take care not to walk too close to the edge, however, as this volcanic rock has a tendency to create dangerous overhangs. Looking out to sea, the nearby island to the right is Hillaniya, the distant one straight out is Sikha, and the larger one to the left is Ghadarain.

There are a total of four water cisterns cut out of the rock on the summit, all designed to retain as much run-off rainwater as possible. The one at the north-eastern corner is unusual in that it bends around a natural curve in the shallow valley. Take plenty of water and sun cover, and this will be a pleasant excursion, and so far one of the few places in the Yemen free of litter – let us try to keep it that way.

BIR ALI–MUKALLA

A volcano full of sea   A few kilometres beyond Bir Ali, high up to the right, is a large crater known as **Kharif Sharan.** Inside is a sea water lake with mangroves growing along the edge. The climb up is relatively easy.

Two bays further along is the headland of **Ras Majdahah,** with the impressive island of Barraqah just off the coast. Past the lava flows, an extensive stretch of small dunes reach the coast; it is an idyllic spot with thousands of seabirds. The road runs straight through the dunes until it bears inland again at a small beach-side fishing village, where, depending on the time of day, it is possible to see some of the large sharks and barracuda that they catch. Pieces of agate can be found on the beach which leads one to think that there must be some interesting layers in the nearby mountains.

Arabia's only permanent river to the sea

Inland from Ras al-Kalb the road runs through a cultivated area around **as-Sufal** (547km), where there is a continuous flow of water down Wadi Hajar provided by springs higher up on the south-western *jol*. This was a popular route to Hajjarain and the western Hadramaut for many of the travellers earlier this century. The village has a small teashop on the left, and the remains of a Soviet camp to the right, and it is also the point where the province of Shabwa becomes the province of Hadramaut.

The road now regularly dips down to the coast and then skirts back around volcanic outcrops. Watch out for the crazy tracks made by turtles coming ashore at night to lay their eggs along all the beaches that punctuate this rugged shore. Also try to spot the black and turquoise flashes of the Abyssinian roller, a bird common to the area.

Turtles

After crossing Wadi al-Ghabar, the road climbs spectacularly around the headland of Ras Husaysah before dropping down into **Burum** (595km), which is becoming a quiet retreat away from the chaos of Mukalla. Many beach and roadside areas are earmarked for future expansion, but for the time being it is still a small fishing village in a beautiful bay, and a good place to buy locally produced henna. Five kilometres later, on the left, is a row of *nuras* lime kilns which burn palm wood to produce the basic white powder used in the decoration and weatherproofing of mud houses throughout the Hadramaut.

Expansion around Mukalla

The distant headland of Mukalla can now be seen beyond the beautiful beaches. The economic development of the port has recently spread far south to encompass the once sleepy RAF landing ground at **Fuwwa** (609km). This whole area is now a huge housing and industrial complex supporting the oil and gas industry, and attracts large numbers of mobile workers from all over the Yemen and overseas. As Mukalla is hemmed in by mountains which severely restrict any expansion, many of the new premises are in Fuwwa, and the town now offers a good choice of restaurants at low prices. Tourist and leisure resorts are also planned along this coastline.

There is a buzz of activity and excitement in the areas of modern industry that lead into Mukalla, which is good to see as a contrast to the somewhat 'laid-back' way of doing business in the Yemen. On the way into Mukalla you will see the shanty-town housing of visiting labourers attracted by the work prospects, and then the bridge across the *wadi* to bring you into the town proper.

Almost all the travellers earlier this century wrote of the distant beauty of Mukalla when first seen from the sea. Freya Stark wrote. 'Anything more picturesque than its approach you cannot imagine' *(The Coast of Incense)* and Harold Ingrams said: 'To me modern Aden is almost undiluted ugliness, but Mukalla has a real beauty of its own' *(Arabia and the Isles)*. I think they might describe it slightly differently these days if they arrived along the *wadi* bridge.

MUKALLA

A relatively
recent port

This provincial capital and gateway to the Hadramaut can be divided into two parts; the old town around the headland and sea front; and the new town which has sprouted up along the road to Riyan. Compared to other towns and ports, Mukalla has a relatively recent history, with no ancient sites of interest. The port is mentioned as far back as early Christian times, when it was used as a mainland connection to the island of Socotra, 500km out in the Indian Ocean (see Socotra). But generally it seems to have been overlooked in antiquity, as the ports of Aden, Qana, esh-Shihr and Seihut had much better harbours or easier access to the interior or both.

The city is said to have been founded in 1625 by **Ahmed bin Medyem al-Kesadi,** a local Yafa sultan. The opening up of the sea route to the Indies in the seventeenth century gave the Hadramis the opportunity of leaving their poor homeland, and many found employment in new countries. Most journeys started and finished at Mukalla, which expanded throughout the eighteenth century to become the South's second port. **Bedouin** tribesmen managed to take control during a period of chaos, but it was then taken by the Seiyun based Sultan **Ghalib bin Mohsin al-Kathiri** in 1866.

Kathiri/Qaiti
conflict

Control changed from the Kathiris to local **Qaitis** (a tribe of the Yafa) and these two powerful ruling families were at war with each other, particularly in Wadi Hadramaut, until the Ingrams Peace Treaty of 1937.

At this time many local products were exported, including gums, hides and henna, while imports included cotton, metals and crockery from India, dates and dried fruits from Muscat, coffee from Aden, and sheep and frankincense from Africa.

The heads of the Qaiti dynasty were the Sultans of esh-Shihr and Mukalla, who spent much of their time looking after their overseas interests, particularly in Hyderabad, India, where many Hadramis (an estimated 13,000) had gone to work as officers and men in the service of the Nizam of Hyderabad's Arabian Regiment. Qaiti tribal

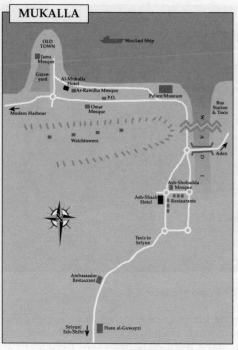

lands were split into five provinces: Esh-Shihr, Mukalla, Do'an, Hajar and Shibam, each ruled by a local governor.

To ensure the safety of the Mukalla *suq*, all visiting Bedouins had to deposit their rifles and cartridge belts at the city gate before they were allowed inside to trade and buy the basic commodities they required such as flour, rice and dried fish (usually small sharks).

Qaiti rule lasted until 1967 and the establishment of the **PDRY**. Even in recent times, however, it has not been easy to reach Mukalla, owing to the tough overland conditions and the usually hostile tribes that inhabit the vast wastelands around it. Until the Chinese road was built from Aden, most visitors had to arrive by boat, or occasionally fly to the Riyan airstrip.

Mukalla in the twentieth century has been written about a great deal, as every traveller in the 1930s and 1940s spent time here making arrangements for the interior, and there are some very good accounts (see Further Reading).

You will reach Mukalla by passing down either side of the *wadi*, which has recently become a large open sewer, seldom flushed by floodwaters from the *jol*. Fierce fighting took place here as Mukalla became one of the last southern strongholds repelling northern troops during the summer of 1994

Old Mukalla

The Palace Museum
Swinging on to the front, the impressive building set back on the right is the **museum,** converted from the Sultan's Indian-style palace.

Known as Qasr al-Mu'in, it was built in the late 1920s by Sultan Omar bin Awadh al-Qaiti on some reclaimed land opposite the old palace in an area called Bara as-Sida. Two large entranceways lead into a forecourt with the tree-fronted palace extending slightly beyond the new breakwater.

Ash-Shohadda Mosque at sunset, Mukalla.

On the ground floor are a few finds from some of the ancient sites in Wadi Hadramaut, notably Shabwa and Husn al-Urr, and a room dedicated to the freedom fight against the British-supported sultan. The upper floor is dedicated to the life and times of the sultans, including a unique silver throne made in India. Articles of everyday use and symbols of the sultans' rule under the British, are displayed. The museum should be open daily except Friday, 08.30-12.00, but the hours seem rather flexible. There are good views of the coast and harbour from the balconies if the guardian will open them up for you.

Natural defences
The old town is spread along the sea front guarded by 300m cliffs called **Qarat al-Mukalla,** with the remains of four watchtowers spaced along the top. Good natural defences meant that there needed to be only a short section of wall near the present-day museum to protect the town completely. The wall has now been removed, and the limits of the old town are set by Bara as-Sida in the west and the small but modern port of al-Khalf to the east.

The headland cemetery
From the museum, the road drops down onto the newly reclaimed seafront and runs to the famous ar-Rawdha Mosque, just before the stubby headland which lies between two bays. Most of this small peninsula is taken up by the Muslim cemetery of *al-Muqbara*, with the large *qubba* tomb of Yacub, patron saint of the town, on the highest ground.

The western side of the graveyard is an unusual two-storeyed colonnaded terrace which looks as if it has been lifted straight from India. Upstairs at the far left end is the **Mukalla Sports Club,** where the local youth gather in the evenings to pass time and play *carob,* a cross between snooker and Subbuteo, played with draughts pieces.

Carob

Because of the high walls, not much can be seen of the cemetery from street level; the best view is from high up in the nearby al-Mukalla Hotel. From here you can also get a good view down into the amazing marbled courtyard of the **ar-Rawdha Mosque** next door, with its Hadrami-style minaret in white, green and brown. This minaret tends to be repainted regularly, and can be seen in blue and white in older pictures. There are several small eateries in this area serving fresh grilled fish.

It is worthwhile walking to the headland through the narrow alleys between the four- and five-storey buildings of the former **Indian Quarter.** These are the old merchants' houses, some with wooden balconies, in an area called al-Bilad where the customs posts used to be. Before 1988, the alleys led straight to the sea, but now the huge concrete breakwater protects all building along the front and also allows some expansion. The locals are none too pleased by such modernisation, as they can no longer moor their small boats directly outside the back door, nor dangle fishing lines out of the windows! Some Bedouin women can be seen in colourful clothing and Arabian Gulf type face masks.

An unwanted development

Looking west you can see an old cargo vessel aground in the bay; it does not look too bad until you notice the giant hole in the hull. In the late afternoon the view from the Jama Mosque, across the fishing boats in the eastern bay to the white houses against the mountain backdrop is just beautiful.

Main harbour

Continuing around this bay is a small *sambook* and fishing boat harbour, with the larger oil tank terminal beyond, and old quarantine sheds. Be careful taking photographs, however, as this is a sensitive area. The road continues along the coast, past **Ras Mukalla** and some new tourist and oil company resort compounds, before eventually rejoining the Riyan road after about 10kms.

The main road through town is one-way and runs from the small roundabout behind the al-Mukalla Hotel (note the old red British pillar box) back down to the museum. There is a good system of local buses operating here, starting from the end of the cemetery, where there is also an old map of routes painted on the wall. In the early afternoon this street is almost deserted, usually because the heat and humidity combine to create an oppressive lunchtime atmosphere.

Halfway down on the right is the glaring white **Omar Mosque,** built at the same time as the palace. The turrets and arches give this building more than a passing resemblance to a church, especially the stocky tower-like minaret. In a small square beside it there are fast-food vendors with bread, cakes and *fool,* and behind it, in the **Haft al-Hara** district, there are many interesting alleyways and houses. Running parallel to the main road are some streets with gold and silver merchants. Just before the hospital and clinic on the right is the small **Ba-Zura Mosque,** in an area that was formerly the black slaves' quarter outside the town wall.

Quiet back streets

Musicians at a wedding in Mukalla.

The New Town

Heading back up the smelly *wadi,* the road passes the bridge to Aden and enters another one-way system that leads to the **main square,** with the ash-Shaab Hotel and the new ash-Shohadda ('martyrs') Mosque. This is the centre of activity for the new oil money, and good restaurants and shops have sprouted up within a couple of years to serve the transient population.

The view from the roof of the ash-Shaab at sunset is superb, across the Mosque to the *wadi* and the distant mountains. The road past the ash-Shaab runs down to the busy junction, where every person and vehicle seems to be on their way to Wadi Hadramaut. From here it is about ten minutes' walk up the Riyan road to **Husn al-Guwayzi,** past the Ambassador Restaurant on the right and over the small hill.

The surfing house

At first sight, it looks as though Husn al-Guwayzi is surfing on a petrified wave. It is a fortress, named after the al-Guwayzi family, and was the customs point controlling all traffic in and out of Mukalla to the north and east. On the opposite side of the road is its ruined twin.

The building only dates from the end of the last century, but it has been well preserved as an example of Yemeni architecture taken to the extreme. It is possible to enter the fenced area to get the best possible angle for photographs, and to inspect the 1917 George V cannon. There were plans at one time to make it a small museum, but nothing seems to have materialised. The road continues out of Mukalla in the direction of Riyan.

Hotels

Both the established hotels are run by the Public Corporation for Tourism and hence lack the interest and investment of private enterprise. The sooner they have competition, the better.

** Al-Mukalla. Tel: 2650.

In the old town, on the sea front next to the ar-Rawdha Mosque. 24 rooms. Under chaotic management. Bar and restaurant. Good views from some rooms.

* Ash-Shaab. Tel: 52646 or 52345.

In the new town, opposite ash-Shohadda Mosque. 33 rooms, each with a key to its own toilet/shower. Pretty rough. Bar and restaurant on the ground floor. Usually booked up solid for months. Good views from the roof.

A brand new hotel has just been opened by the Universal tour agency at the far eastern end of the harbour.

A great many good restaurants have recently opened to cater for the boom in temporary workers. The better ones tend not to be on the sea front, but in the new part of town around the ash-Shaab Hotel. Halfway to Husn al-Guwayzi is the good Ambassador Restaurant on the right-hand side of the main road.

MUKALLA–OMAN

Heading east

The roads to Wadi Hadramaut and Ghail Ba Wazir split off from the coastal road which runs up to Seihut and eventually the Omani border. Simply getting information for this end of the country is difficult enough, and is not helped by the fact that even the most useful maps stop in the vicinity of Mukalla.

Leave Mukalla through the new town and pass Husn al-Guwayzi on the left. Every piece of usable ground along the roadside seems to be busy with compounds full of oil workers, mechanics and repair shops, stretching almost all the way to the Wadi Hadramaut turning, 28km from old Mukalla (see Mukalla–Wadi al-Ain).

Old airport

Just beyond this major turning is the old Riyan military airstrip on the left, dotted with a few old Mig fighter planes and other Soviet hardware. The new Riyan airport is a bit further along to the right, and is Mukalla's international link with neighbouring countries. The road bounces down a concrete ramp across Wadi Huwairah into the small town of **Shuhair** (40km). Turning first left will take you through town, whereas second left will send you around the outside, but both meet up to head towards Ghail Ba Wazir.

Ghail Ba Wazir

10kms inland

The tarred road climbs up from Shuhair for 10km until it joins a street of wealthy houses and villas. Large amounts of money have been invested by wealthy Hadramis in this pleasant distant suburb of Mukalla. If you plan to stay at the summer palace it is better to ring first or reserve a room through the ash-Shaab Hotel in Mukalla (good luck!). It is not easy to find, but at least when you do you will have seen most of the town.

At the end of the wealthy street is a main square and football pitch, with some good restaurants nearby. Turn left and first right. A youth club on the right serves reasonable set menu food. After the youth club the road becomes a dirt track (although 4x4 is not needed), with the power station also on the right. Swing left past a cemetery and after 500m enter the old town via a small one-way system, notice the carved wooden doors. Straight in front are some teashops, with the main *suq* area and mosques to the left, as well as some good and lively food places. Turn right and the **summer palace** is about 500m on the right behind some metal gates, just as you enter a narrow country lane.

Sultan's Summer Palace

The palace is less than 100 years old, and was the summer residence of the Qaiti sultans based in Mukalla. The driveway leads past thick trees and semi-formal gardens to a raised swimming pool, which on every one of my visits has been either dry or full of dirty green water! The thought of staying in a summer palace is probably much better than the reality, as it is rather like staying in a youth hostel with six dormitories. In summer the heat is unbearable, although there are working fans, and you are kept up all night by the shrieking giant fruit bats battling it out in the palm trees. Mosquitoes are a problem all year round. There is no food – you have to eat out or cook for yourself.

Local tobacco

The whole area has been famous for over a century for growing good quality **tobacco,** called *hamumi* (named after the local tribal federation), which you can see in fields around town between August and December. The locals seem to like it, and they smoke home-made water pipes, mainly in the late afternoon. The pipes are made from a tin can, half a coconut shell, and a hollow stick. The pipe is passed round the group, each member of which has his own removable mouthpiece.

If you are staying here, and have ample time, it is worth trying to find the nearby springs of **al-Homa** to the east – the reason why this area is so well watered. Instead of turning left at the end of the 'wealthy road' from Shuhair, turn right past a petrol station and a school on the left. Branch left at a sign to al-Garh and al-Homa, then carry on until you reach some houses; turn left there onto a cobbled track. Follow this round towards a large water tower in the distance. On the left is a small sink hole with perfect cool water among pleasant trees, ideal for swimming.

Sink holes　　There is another sink hole further along the track to the right, but the water has a habit of disappearing below ground, especially towards the end of the dry season. With 4x4 you could head westwards and join the track that works its way back to Ghail Ba Wazir past the palace. The track through this richly cultivated oasis (it is also famous for growing henna) has many ruined villas.

Esh-Shihr

Back on the flat coastal desert road, esh-Shihr is 27km beyond Shuhair. The entire area is on the verge of rapid expansion as a pleasant overspill zone for Mukalla. A new by-pass diverts traffic inland around this busy modern town, but it is definitely worth calling in for a look at the old port.

Your first sight is the restored western gateway, called **Bab al-Khor** which now acts as a small roundabout. The city wall and gates were intact until about 60 years ago, but with so much building and expansion it is almost impossible to imagine how it looked. You can climb inside the Bab, but everything is uncared for; even the recently restored paintwork is peeling away badly in the difficult climate, and the two cannons are looking decidedly weary.

A former　　Esh-Shihr is mentioned by early travellers, the most
major port　　renowned being Marco Polo, who saw it on his way to China in the early thirteenth century, and described it as being an important harbour of the Rasulids based in Ta'iz. It was undoubtedly used for millennia before this, as a departure point for Socotra and a port for ships sailing down the coast from Dhofar to Qana. It is also known that frankincense was exported from here until quite recently.

The harbour is not particularly useful; it is only suitable for shallow boats. The port therefore declined as Mukalla rose to prominence. The Qaitis continued to use the town well into this century, and for many years the main route to the eastern Wadi Hadramaut led from here direct to Wadi Idim and Tarim. After years of inactivity under PDRY rule, the town is awakening to the new opportunities offered by the Mukalla/Shabwa oil boom.

The town square beside the sea is open and impressive. A solid fort, **Qasr bin Ayash,** looks out along the coast, backed by the century-old Qaiti Sultan's palace known as **Dar Nasir.** Between these two, in the centre of the square, is a giant muscular statue dedicated to the defenders against the Portuguese.

As you can imagine, the neighbouring *suq* area is a display of every type of fish imaginable, from hammerhead sharks to the small fish that are dried and ploughed into the land as fertiliser. There are excellent grilled fish meals to be had in the very local eateries around.

Shipbuilding and repairs are still carried out on the beach using traditional tools and materials. Bits of the end sections of the town wall can be seen reaching the sea, and it is pleasant to wander around. The town is also famous for weaving bright coloured cloth on handlooms.

Impressive gateway
The route out is via the northern **Bab al-Airdrus,** a three-storey gateway much larger and impressive than the Bab al-Khor. The huge wooden doors with protruding metal spikes are open to pedestrians, and the arch provides good shade for sleepy locals in the afternoon. The whitewashed gateway stands in splendid isolation with a couple of large 3.5m cannons lying on the ground, one crowned and dated 1796.

To the eastern side is a section of old mud wall that backs onto some dilapidated inner-city housing, a fascinating district to walk around. This extensive area of ruined houses, many with beautiful carved wooden doors, leads down to the sea front past numerous *qubbas* (domed tombs) and cemeteries. Near the gate is the large old mosque of al-Airdrus. Outside both gateways and around the square are several teashops and food places.

Environs of Esh-Shihr

Before the new highway was built along the coast from Mukalla, the road headed inland through Ghail Ba Wazir and across to Tabala before dropping south to esh-Shihr.

Inland sites
It is still possible to retrace this route for 15km to **Tabala,** an oasis of spring water which is good for swimming. Water channels lead from here to irrigate the surrounding fertile area of palms and vegetables.

Taking the route west from Tabala you will arrive at the remains of the old town, dominated by the ruined fortress of **Husn al-Sheikh Ali,** now just a hollow shell of a building. Continuing west on the old road to Ghail Ba Wazir are the abandoned stone-walled houses of **Shiklinza,** lying at the foot of the greatly dissected mountain chain. This town was established by the inhabitants of esh-Shihr when they fled an early Portuguese invasion, but was deserted after two centuries because of the failing water supply. Nearer to Ghail Ba Wazir are the ruins of the solid al-Suda fort, built completely from mud brick.

Old route to Wadi Hadramaut

From Tabala, the old paved road towards Tarim goes north up Wadi Ma'adi to the village of **Ma'adi,** the territory of the Ba Hasani tribe, where betel nut and pepper vine are grown. The habit of chewing the nut and leaf was brought from India, and you can still see little packets of them being prepared by hand in Aden and Mukalla. There is a distinctive smell as red globules of spit are deposited by adherents sporting red-stained teeth.

The continuation of this route north is currently out of bounds because of fears for the safety of tourists, but there are some interesting sights *en route* (see Seiyun–Tarim).

Esh-Shihr–Seihut

Rejoining the new road around esh-Shihr and heading east, you will see a marker stone indicating Seihut 204km, Aden 678km. This is followed by similar posts every 2km. **Al-Hami** (25km from esh-Shihr) is a small fishing village, where you can see just how many of the shaped native fishing boats are now made of fibre glass rather than wood.

The road rises above the coastal plain and goes inland to the amazingly lush **Addis Sharqiah** (48km), a small town lying in an oasis *wadi* surrounded by thick palms running to the sea.

Beyond a lava flow, the road rejoins the coast just before **Qusaier** (94km), another small fishing village heavily influenced by Far Eastern architecture. A long single street of old houses with carved doors joins the main road to the almost deserted pristine beach. A few boats, a few fishermen and a mosque overlook the beach, – a quiet, relaxed place.

A little way past the small town of al-Ridah (112km) the road crosses a totally flat expanse of wilderness, interrupted only by the meanderings of a lone camel or the black streak of an old lava flow. This is where Hadramaut province becomes **al-Mahra**, a tough place to survive where water, vegetation, settlements, animals and people are all sparsely scattered.

Into the wild east

Today it is a relatively unimportant corner of the Yemen, but it used to be an essential link in the trading of frankincense. Not only was the bush grown in the near-perfect conditions on the mountain slopes, but the coastline was a series of ports used by the flimsy frond and reed boats which carried the goods from Dhofar in Oman. Ancient chroniclers describe frankincense as 'lying in heaps all over the country', with control so good that nobody would dare steal any of the valuable grains.

From the ports to the east, frankincense was brought to Seihut where, depending upon conditions, it was either bundled up to go overland up Wadi Masilah to **Incense country** Shabwa, or taken by sea to the main port of Qana and inland from there. There are still some isolated frankincense trees *(Boswellia sacra)* to be found growing in the region, but climatic and economic changes means that Dhofar, further east, is now the main producer.

Despite such a rich history, no famous sites or ancient cities have been discovered in al-Mahra, and even the Tourism Ministry in charge of the south cannot suggest any places worth seeing. The region is dominated by vast expanses of desert that drift into the Empty Quarter of Saudi Arabia and Dhofar Province in Oman. On the coast people rely on fishing. There is limited farming in the hills, but there are still nomadic Bedouins who tend herds of camels and live in cave dwellings and rough tents.

During Communist rule, this area was out of bounds because of frequent border disputes and even serious fighting with the Omanis, who were very anti-Communist.

The natives of al-Mahra are separated from the rest of the Yemen by vast distances and differences in culture. They have a strong regional identity with their own style of clothes and decoration, and even their own language **An ancient** quite unlike Arabic.

route into the Just past the town of al-Aiss there is some vegetation, **Hadramaut** where a large bridge crosses **Wadi Masilah** (186km), the remote extension of Wadi Hadramaut as it finds it's way to the sea. This has been used as a trade route into the interior at some point in history, as you can see from the ruins of forts on either side of the *wadi* entrance. It is possible to penetrate the *wadi* from this point to reach the towns of the Hadramaut in a four- or five-day expedition (see Tarim–Qabr Hud).

Owing to the lack of heavy traffic, the tarred road surface is still excellent all the way to **Seihut** (204km), the largest town in this frankincense-producing region. Along the desolate stony beach there are a few fishing boats, with the main centre to the left. A cemetery with two large *qubbas* to local saints, and a fish market greet the visitor, but the main shops are a couple of blocks further in. At one end of the main street is a small modern *suq* with restaurants, and at the other a *fonduq*, which is closed at present owing to lack of custom. The manager said he needed a week's notice to put anybody up, but without a phone that does seem a little difficult!

Towards the back of the town is a newly constructed mosque, replacing the 350-year-old Bakariyat Mosque which is ten minutes' walk away across Wadi Seihut. This single-storey white building is presently being repaired after being damaged by a severe flood that swept down the *wadi*.

Tough going

Seihut is where the tar finishes, and if you want to go on to al-Ghaydah, it will take you at least twelve hours on bad tracks that do not always stick to the coast, but do sometimes run along the beach, needing 4x4. In some places impressive green mountains, split by deep ravines reach right to the coast.

One of the benefits of unification has been the agreement by the Yemeni and Omani governments on their border, which allows normal border crossings. Road building should be a priority in the area, but any foreigner venturing past Seihut will be taken for an oil worker. This whole stretch of coastline, all the way from Mukalla, is one of the largest oil concessions – over 35,000 sq km, currently being worked by Canadian Occidental.

Beyond Itab (264km) is Ras Sharwayn and **Qishn** port, an important anchorage which once exported frankincense, and now has an airport. Huswayn (345km) lies just before the headland of Ras Fartak, on the other side of which is **Nishtun,** where a new port with facilities for processing and storing fish was built by international development agencies in 1984. Nishtun is strategically placed in the huge Qamr Bay, and almost everyone in the area is dependent on the plentiful fishing season from

Remote regions

October to June.

Inland from here are the rugged mountains of the **Jebel Qamr** range which rise to 1,400m, and are often covered in fog and mist, created by the onshore winds. With the rainfall it is possible to successfully grow millet in these mountains.

The whole of this bay and the land up to 50km inland are part of the 8,500 sq km oil block run by Namir, the Saudi-backed oil company whose controlling Bin Mahfouz family originally came from the Hadramaut.

Finally you reach **al-Ghaydah.** This is such a remote area that very few Yemenis have been here, even those from the neighbouring Hadramaut, although there are scheduled flights from Riyan. If you do manage to make it, there is sure to be a welcome for you at the town's

To the border

fonduq – which does not require a week's notice. From al-Ghaydah it is a tough 140km to the border, through al-Fidaymi, Damqawt and Hawf.

The remote end of Wadi Hadramaut.

HADRAMAUT

MUKALLA–WADI HADRAMAUT

Any overland journey to Wadi Hadramaut, whether from Marib, Ataq or Mukalla, will show just how inaccessible it is, separated from the outside world by vast areas of wilderness. From the south coast the route climbs onto the *jol* plateau, runs across and drops into Wadi al-Ain, a feeder of Wadi Hadramaut. The exact route is difficult to follow on any of the older maps, as the new road creates its own course between many of the established tracks.

The *jol* plateau

Mukalla–Wadi al-Ain

The tarred road strikes north from the coastal road (see Mukalla–Oman) just before the old military airstrip (28km from Old Mukalla), and crosses a scrubby plain dotted with oil company compounds and equipment. At the foot of the escarpment it swings around a water eroded rockscape until it arrives at the ramshackle village of **Abdullah Gharib** (63km), conveniently named after the pass that towers above it. In these few basic market stalls you can buy all you need for the journey, and even try some fresh coconut milk.

Access by *aqaba*

Passes up and down the *jol* are known locally as *aqabas*, and there are hundreds of them, but only a few can take vehicles. The Aqaba Abdullah Gharib has been widened and improved recently to allow people to pass the painfully slow trucks on the very steep sections. When the road reaches the top of the major climb and heads inland, there are excellent views from the right looking down on the zigzags, but take care of the overhangs at the edge.

There is still more climbing to do over the next 30km, giving huge vistas over raw rolling plains, across which the road sweeps in almost every direction except north. It climbs from one plateau to the next, with only a few bushes and ravines to break up the landscape. Onshore winds carry enough moisture to allow a variety of hardy plants and shrubs to grow, but even these disappear towards the interior, leaving as inhospitable and desolate a place as you could imagine.

Classic travel

Hurtling across this wilderness in the comfort of a modern vehicle, it is impossible to imagine the hardships endured by the early travellers, not hundreds but only tens of years ago. Journeys by camel, donkey and even foot used to take between six and ten days in some of the harshest conditions on earth. There are some enthralling descriptions of these journeys, and of encounters with tribesmen, in the books of Stark, Ingrams, van der Meulen and Helfritz (see Further Reading).

Many ancient tracks wander across this area and it is never too far over to the old route from esh-Shihr to Tarim, down Wadi Idim to the east. The more traditional routes are certainly longer, but they were chosen because the *wadis* were well protected from the marauding bands of Bedouin tribesmen which inhabit the *jol*.

The work must go on

There are certain surprises, such as the **Total Oil Company base camp** (105km) for their East Shabwa concession, complete with temporary village and airstrip. You can still see the occasional settlement around a few fields, and many beehives are brought up here in the summer rains, but they will soon be back on the littoral, as the land quickly dries out. You might see the odd camel wandering around, or the even odder person.

Into the feeder wadis

The new road surface has already succumbed to the ravages of temperature, water action and heavy oil industry trucks, with some sections reduced to pot-holes and seriously undermined. Towards the far end of the plateau, roughly halfway to Seiyun, are some roadside teashops. As the *jol* itself starts to break up, steep-sided *wadis* tumble down to right and left, until the road itself finally tips over the edge of a gully and drops into Wadi al-Ain (207km).

Wadi al-Ain–Adab

After the endless light brown scenery, the *wadi* looks like a flowering green paradise, with strips of palm trees meandering downstream. Almost immediately you come to the first village, **Sharj ash-Sharif,** followed by a continuous ribbon conurbation of picturesque houses and small settlements, all nestling at the foot of dramatic vertical walls of rock.

Fish for lunch

As the new road across the plateau was never part of an established track, it is only now, back on the ancient route in the *wadi*, that you will regularly start to see the essential small white *siqayas* (see box). Beyond Bourgat village (226km) there is a nominal checkpoint and a few village eateries selling delicious grilled fish at lunchtimes. To the right notice the layers of loess, thick sediment, in the *wadi* bed.

The *wadi* opens wide at the point where the larger Wadi Hajjarain enters from the left. At the small village of **Adab** (246km) a dirt track doubles back left to run up to al-Mashad and Hajjarain town. If you pass a tyre service on the left followed by a pillared house, you have gone too far.

One of the main features of the extensive system of caravan routes is the numerous *siqayas* – water tanks – by the wayside, built to provide water for thirsty travellers. They are small roofed cisterns, painted white to reflect the heat, with small holes in the walls through which cups or tins can be inserted. Their construction is paid for by a rich benefactor, and a sum of money is regularly paid to someone in the nearest village to bring water and keep them filled. For centuries travellers have relied on these *siqayas*, and it is a serious matter if they are dry, causing annoyance to travellers and disgrace to the tribe in whose area it is. Close by there are sometimes small safe overnight rest houses for both people and animals, known here as *murabba'as*.

Wadi Hajjarain and Wadi Do'an

Important routes

This side track will take you back up one of the main routes used to enter Wadi Hadramaut over the last few hundred years, and described by many of the great adventurers. Unless the wadi is in flood, most vehicles can make it to Hajjarain. Through 1993 a new road was being constructed up the wadi.

Wadi Hajjarain is the name of the lower part of Wadi Do'an, and both contain many interesting ancient sites.

Tomb of a holy man

The tiny village of **al-Mashad** (6km from the main road), also known as Mashad Ali, can be seen across Wadi al-Ain, with some modern houses on the right, and white tombs nestling at the base of cliffs to the left. These tombs make Mashad Ali one of the holiest places in the Hadramaut, with people coming from as far away as Sana'a in the pilgrimage month of Rabi al-Awal, the third month of the Islamic year. During this time a huge temporary village of market traders, bakers and water sellers is erected to cater for the pilgrims, some of whom rent the otherwise empty houses of the town. It is like a small version of the greater pilgrimage to Qabr Hud at the other end of Wadi Hadramaut.

The white beehive tombs, dating from the 1830s, are fairly compact and usually open for visitors to look around, but they come with the usual gaggle of local children.

Inside the dark dusty room of the main tomb is a large wooden casing, beautifully carved, containing the body of Sayyid Ali Hassan al-Attas, a famous religious mediator between warring tribes. As a *sayyid* he claimed descent from the Prophet Mohammed through Fatima and Ali, and as such he could not be harmed, even in these areas of fierce intertribal fighting. His devout behaviour and peacemaking greatly influenced the local Bedouin, who elevated him after his death to the level of

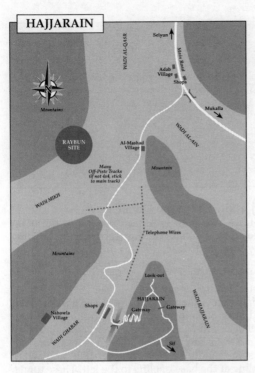

HAJJARAIN

weli ('saint'), and his tomb became a place of worship. Other graves inside are those of members of his family. Just outside are later additions, the larger white grave by the roadside being that of his son Hassan Ali Hassan al-Attas.

Continuing south the road drops down into a maze of tracks at the bottom of thick deposits of mud, the result of an early dam built across the *wadi* to enable the area to be cultivated in pre-Islamic times. The town that developed here was known as **Raybun**, and its extensive ruins are situated towards the western side of the *wadi*. From this track it is just possible to make out some excavated walls protected by temporary roofing.

Raybun was strategically

Ancient sites placed at the mouth of a cultivable *wadi*. As at Marib, the dam was not intended to store water, but simply to allow the water height to rise so that it could be then distributed along gravity-fed channels to land that needed irrigating. The town also controlled the minor trade that came up Wadi Do'an from the coast, before joining the main route to Shabwa.

The buildings whose remains can be seen on the higher ground are thought to have been important temples dating from 1000 BC to 300 AD. Some of the sites are protected, and are not at all easy to identify, let alone reach. Even if you do reach them, most are little more than **Limited** bumps in the ground, years of British and Soviet excava-**archaeology** tion work having now been covered again with sand.

It is still possible to find mosaic sections, inscriptions, small slivers of obsidian, flint and alabaster, the off-cuts of implements and other objects made here in ancient times. Most of the important finds are in the archaeological section of Seiyun Museum, along with good aerial photographs, plans, maps and excellent paintings of the buildings as they would have looked at the time. Some of the pieces have now been dated to the Neolithic period.

Fish market, Hodeidah.

'Takhreem' fan-light windows in tower house.

Bottle tree (Adenium obesum) *near At-Tur.*

Mukalla seafront.

Village 'Qat' chew near Lahej.

Local handicraft worker, Seiyun market.

Making bread in Tihama.

The track winds through the bottom of the loess deposits towards the mountain that splits Wadi Hajjarain from Wadi Mikh, which enters from the south-west. Very occasionally troops of baboons are seen scampering across the *wadi* floors. It swings left to cut up to **Hajjarain** which can be seen on top of a flat mountain, the mud houses looking as though they are built on top of one another. Follow the telephone wires until you arrive at 'Lower' Hajjarain (16km), a row of shops on either side of the track. The main town is high above to the left, and is reached by a series of well constructed cobbled zigzag paths with no access to the upper parts for vehicles.

Hajjarain means 'two rocks' and features widely in the accounts of travellers up and down Wadi Do'an. It is one of the few towns in the Hadramaut that is not situated in the bed of a *wadi*, and from its dominating position on top of an outcrop it guards both Wadi Hajjarain and Wadi Ghabar. Early chroniclers described it as a very prosperous city, based on trade and taxes. An old cistern above the town indicates that there was a pre-Islamic settlement of some sort here.

Walking up through Hajjarain

One way up starts beyond a dry water channel, usually full of rubbish. Another flight of steps is just to the north. Certainly it is the situation of the town that is the attraction, rather than the hygiene; even as early as 1934 Harold Ingrams wrote about the place being 'indescribably filthy'. Access to the upper town is through a gateway. The path is always steep and narrow as it passes between the towering houses.

The only way to get more than the odd glimpse down into the *wadis* is to keep climbing upwards through the small *suq* square and get above the houses. The old cisterns are amongst the houses to the left. The final rock climb is quite difficult, but the views are superb, stretching for kilometres up the *wadis*, and across to the village of Nahowla on the other side of Wadi Ghabar.

Early cave settlement

About 7km up Wadi Ghabar is the site of **al-Ghuza,** an early cave settlement, photographs of which can be seen in Seiyun Museum.

Hajjarain is reputedly close to the site of **Dammun** (now a suburb of the town?), the old capital of the Kinda tribe, and once ruled by a Christian called Amir al-Qeis al-Kinda, mentioned by the chronicler al-Hamdani.

You can go down the other side of Hajjarain through a modern concrete gateway into Wadi Hajjarain, a fertile palm and 'lake' area that has been settled for thousands of years. The route up it and Wadi Do'an is still used, but far less than before the modern road was built.

**Travelling up
Wadi Do'an**

Just before the town of Sif (42km), Wadi Qaidun enters from the right creating a pleasantly fertile area called **Qaidun**, the site of the tomb of Amud ad-Din, leader of the Amudi tribe whose capital is 10km further up the *wadi* at Budah. A pilgrimage takes place to his tomb on 27 of Rajab, the seventh month of the Islamic calendar.

Sif had a poor reputation for hospitality among early writers, but it can now at least offer visitors a small restaurant. Many of the houses are recently constructed by returning overseas workers and are painted in a unique and colourful style. This is the start of Wadi Do'an, where there is a great tradition of men going to work in Red Sea countries such as Egypt, the Sudan, Ethiopia and, more recently, Saudi Arabia.

At **Tafilah** (47km) a large *wadi* comes in from the south-east through which there is an old route to the coast or up onto the *jol* to join the new road. Continuing up Wadi Do'an there are many villages including **Budah** (52km), the capital of the Amudi tribe, all in a lush area of wheat fields and date palms.

Hudun (60km) is an old settlement said to be named after the son of the Prophet Hud (see Tarim–Qabr Hud). **Masna'a** (70km) is now a small village, but in ancient times was an important place. There are many tombs, cisterns and remains of fortresses on the clifftops around it.

The largest town in the area is **al-Khuraybah** (74km), at the head of Wadi Do'an, formed by several smaller wadis coming together. If you need accommodation there is a small and basic *fonduq* here, and it is roughly halfway between Seiyun and Mukalla.

**Ancient routes
to the sea**

A tough 4x4 track runs south-east up a series of *wadis* onto the *jol*, and then over the highlands through Qamram, passing just south of Kor Seiban, the highest mountain in the Hadramaut. The track then drops off the *jol* into Mukalla from the north.

An easier route from al-Khuraybah is to return north to Rihab near Hudun, and head east onto the *jol* to meet the main road after about four hours. All these slow and bumpy routes are off the usual tourist trail, and may be out of bounds, so do check.

Adab–Sadbeh

Back on the main road to Wadi Hadramaut (246km from Mukalla), the enlarged watercourse is now called Wadi al-Qasr. The road runs through the villages of Keraan, Ard Bozaed and Sadbeh, at the foot of the eastern wall, sometimes 3km from the opposite bank.

Many of the new villages are built at the base of small mounds on which there are the remains of old mud

Internal unrest

houses and palaces, which were destroyed over many years of tribal fighting, a consistent feature of the area until halfway through this century.

Just past Sadbeh (254km) is the paved road left to Wadi Amd, another through route and the last great *wadi* to link up before the whole system enters Wadi Hadramaut.

Wadi el-Khun, Wadi Hadramaut.

Wadi Amd

An early important town

The road crosses Wadi al-Qasr and enters Wadi Amd beyond a bluff. Almost immediately on the right is the small village of Lakhum (9km), behind which are the ruins of **Andal** on the slopes of the western cliffs. The place crops up in many of the accounts of wars and trade and was known as the 'first town of the Hadramaut'. Today it is a site of little importance, where beads, jewels and pottery are sometimes dug up by the locals, but it will become famous again when there is a proper archaeological dig.

The road clings to the base of the eastern wall, and after 14km there is evidence of defences high on the top of Jebel Ghumdan. Among the ruins is the famous **Bir Ghumdan,** a subterranean passage said to lead all the way to Bir Ali on the coast, 170km due south! The dry vertical shaft is about 30m deep with a horizontal passageway at the base, and was first tentatively explored by van der Meulen's expedition team in the early 1930s.

Hureidah (18km) can now be seen lying at the base of the dramatic Jebel Jahran, with Wadi Amd going south-west. The first thing you notice is the large white and green mosque at the foot of the village, with the houses climbing slowly up the lower slopes to another large mosque, the Great Mosque. Once in amongst the tightly packed houses, some with great carved wooden doors, it is difficult to appreciate the Great Mosque, as you are always too close. It is also in white and green, but has an interesting octagonal minaret. It is also a library and centre of learning.

Centre of learning

The first mosque in the town is said to have been built by Sayyid Omar Abderahman al-Attas in the middle of the seventeenth century. One of his sons was Ali Hassan al-Attas, who settled in al-Mashad and has his tomb there. All the al-Attas family can trace their history back through Sayyid Omar to Ahmed bin Isa, the original Sayyid from Basra (see Seiyun–Tarim). One of the most famous people to carry the name was the first vice-president of the unified republic, Haidar Abu Bakr al-Attas.

The town itself is quite small and compact, with many new colourful houses being built on the outskirts amongst palm groves. There is a lot of Far Eastern influence, especially from India, Java and Singapore. To the east of town, about 2km away, is a small spring with the ruined buildings of the ancient town of Khureidah, thought to be the original name and site of the settlement. Beyond this is a cluster of houses called Sherj, above which, high up in the mountains about 8km away, is a permanent pool of water known locally as al-Bahr ('the sea').

Ancient **Madhab,** which probably thrived for about 300 years from around the fifth century BC, is now just a collection of hillocks about 3km across Wadi Amd towards the western cliffs. The site was excavated by the intrepid Gertrude Caton-Thompson in the late 1930s and extensively written about by the even more intrepid Freya Stark at about the same time in *A Winter in Arabia*. Today there is nothing to see from ground level of the 12m x 10m raised 'Sin Temple' that was excavated (Sin being pre-Islamic Hadramaut's principal deity). It has been retaken by the sand. As you look out over the gently rolling sandy wastes, the entire *wadi* looks as though it holds ruined buildings just below the surface. Several tombs were excavated at the same time. Some of these holes can be seen dug into the scree slopes at the base of the cliff.

Freya Stark's accounts

It is about an hour and a half's journey by 4x4 continuing up Wadi Amd through Nafhun to Anaq, which is said to have the deepest wells in the region, a staggering

200m. Twelve kilometres further on is Amd itself. It is the main town in the *wadi*, and has some fine tall houses, beyond which are a series of minor *wadis* offering different expeditionary possibilities to the coast. Freya Stark's route, described in *A Winter in Arabia* went west through Damhan, across the *jol* via Rakhiya and came out near Azzan. Van der Meulen's route went initially south-east over the *jol* and reached the coast along Wadi Hajar.

As with the Wadi Do'an routes to the sea, most of these areas are unsafe and out of bounds.

Sadbeh–Wadi Hadramaut

Rejoining the main road, you almost immediately come to the main town of Haura (256km). However, the towns here are not as lively as those elsewhere in the Yemen, and even 'main towns' seem almost deserted, as does
Tribal villages   Haura. Three kilometres further on is the village Ard al-Mukhashen *(ard* meaning 'land of' followed by the name of the tribe). The ruined buildings to be seen on the right after another 6km are the remains of al-Mukhainiq village, a victim of tribal fighting.

The road swings to the right around a bluff and past a string of three roadside restaurants, one called the Shabwah, which serves good local lunchtime food for travellers. A kilometre later is **al-Ajlaniya** (266km), formerly a major town but now reduced to a village. One of the most famous South Arabian traditional dances and pieces of music originates here.
Entering Wadi   To the left many tracks head across the *wadi* bed to the
Hadramaut   opposite side, from where the 4x4 track strikes off into the wilderness towards Shabwa. The whole *wadi* system expands on a grand scale as the north-flowing Wadi al-Qasr finally enters the huge eastward draining depression. The name Wadi Hadramaut tends to be used eastwards from here, all the way to the main towns of al-Qatn, Shibam, Seiyun and Tarim.

WADI HADRAMAUT

If any geographical name conjures up an image of distant mysterious lands hidden in a swirl of exotic history, then it is Wadi Hadramaut. Outside the country the name Hadramaut has tended to refer just to the *wadi*, but in the Yemen, Wadi Hadramaut is just one part (albeit the major part) of the large governorate of the Hadramaut, which stretches to the coast.

Wadi Hadramaut has a giant catchment area which stretches from the edges of the Rub al-Khali, to halfway to the coast, with many accessible *wadis* feeding into it.
Eroded layers   Unlike the volcanic action closer to the coast, the layers here are perfectly flat, not folded or deformed in any

way. These alternate soft and hard layers have been uplifted to form the *jol*, but then spectacularly weathered and dissected by the fierce action of water to the east of the Yemen mountains, as it searches for a way to the sea.

The average annual **rainfall,** which falls principally in April and July/August, is only 5cm, but it has allowed the *wadi* to support large numbers of inhabitants by the use of dams and water channels. Sometimes the floods are violent and they have in the past caused severe damage to towns such as Shibam.

Occasional flooding

The eastern limit of the *wadi is* the Ramlat as-Sabatayn. Wadi Hadramaut proper extends from where the distant edges close in near Hainin to where it becomes known as Wadi Masilah beyond Tarim. Of course these names are merely human inventions; the whole system, flowing some 500 km from the edge of the desert to the sea, should really be treated as Wadi Hadramaut.

History

Much of the early history of the area is linked with the rise and decline of the trade route (see The Gold and Incense Road). However, if the historians are correct, the *wadi* is one of the oldest recorded centres of human existence. Hadrami tribesmen believe implicitly that they are linked through their land to the dawn of creation. It was a place inhabited by a race of giants, the tribe of **Ad,** who lived for hundreds of years and had thousands of children. The stories live on today, and there are several giant grave sites, especially along the north of the *wadi.* To the east is the famous grave of Hud (the prophet of the Ad tribe) at Qabr Hud.

A tribe of giants

Much of the detail is lost in the mists of time, but there are many traditions, both locally and through religious books, that associate the place with Noah's descendants and the book of Genesis. **Hazarmaveth** is an old name for the *wadi* and derives from the name of one of the sons of Qahtan, himself a fifth-generation descendant of Noah, from whom all Hadramis (and southern 'true' Arabs) claim descent. Hazarmaveth means 'death is present' and reflects the troubled times even then. As Harold Ingrams says 'In the Hadramaut you are living in Genesis.'

'Walking through Genesis'

During the time of the incense trade, the **Kingdom of Hadramaut** had its capital far over to the west at Shabwa, the main city on the Qana–Marib route. Towns became wealthy on the taxes levied and some experts say that many of these old cities can be identified nowadays by their name endings: they all end in -un – Raybun, Qaidun and Dammun in Wadi Hajjarain, Nafhun in Wadi Amd. But this remote region, purposely kept secret by the traders to hide the exact origins of the products, has left us with few details of historical events, especially after the decline of trade around the third century AD.

The **Himyar Kingdom** took control from the Sabaeans, but as they in turn declined, the local **Kinda** tribe ruled from their capital Dammun near Hajjarain. They worshipped a god called Haslad until the arrival of Islam.

The local rulers fell away from the true religious course during turbulent times of the middle of the eighth century. The **Abbasids** under Ma'n bin Zaida invaded, killed 15,000 men in a battle at Furt al-Hussein near al-Qatn, and restored Islam in 758 AD.

A religious leader arrives

The greatest religious event in the *wadi* occurred in the middle of the ninth century with the arrival from Iraq of **Ahmed bin Isa al-Muhajir,** a *sayyid* who brought with him the concept of non-violence, and who never carried weapons. In a land that had rarely known anything but violence, this was a great step in spreading peace. All *sada* (plural of *sayyid)* in Wadi Hadramaut claim descent from him and thus in turn from the Prophet Mohammed. He was responsible for bringing orthodox Sunni Shafi'i Islam to the region, and many people make a pilgrimage to his tomb just east of Seiyun.

The **Rasulids,** based in Ta'iz, were the next to incorporate the *wadi* into their territories, during the thirteenth century. Towards the end of the fifteenth century the more recent tribes began to establish themselves. From Sana'a a force of soldiers under Badr bin Tuwairiq conquered the *wadi* and started the **Kathiri Sultanate,** which survived on and off until 1967. To help repel attacks by the Portuguese along the coast, Badr enlisted the help of mercenaries from many other tribes, who ultimately rose up against him. The prime movers were the Qaitis, a Yafa tribe which took control of towns at the western end of the *wadi.*

In the middle of the seventeenth century there was an incursion into the region by the troops of the imams of the Yemen, keen to extend their territory after their success in ending the first Turkish occupation in the highlands, but control from such a distance lasted only 20 years. The warring Kathiris and Qaitis did their best to wreck the entire infrastructure of the region, and almost every minor tribe was continually fighting its neighbours. This made it impossible to carry on any agricultural work and many men left the *wadi* to find work overseas, a tradition that has lasted over 300 years.

Warring neighbours

Tribes from what is now Saudi Arabia added to the chaos by looting towns in the early nineteenth century, in a form of religious purge by the Wahhabi sect. The splitting of Kathiri-ruled Shibam into two halves led to much bloodshed until the Qaitis took total control and

Local women on a cart in Wadi Hadramaut.

established the new border a few hundred metres to the west of town.

This was the chaotic and troublesome situation that the **British** found when they arrived in Aden in 1839, and it was one they were keen to leave well alone.

The Hadramaut formed part of the East Aden Protectorate, but it was of only nominal interest to the British, who entered into protective treaty relations with the Qaiti Sultan of Mukalla in 1888 and the Kathiris in 1918. In an attempt to impose some sort of authority in the region, Harold Ingrams travelled the area to consult hundreds of sultans, sheikhs and minor rulers, eventually concluding the Ingrams Peace Treaty, which required 1,200 signatures. Some 'persuasion' was occasionally necessary, and RAF planes were sent to bomb certain villages or tribes which were accused of breaking the new rules. But generally the treaty was effective in giving Aden a buffer zone and stopping the tribes from fighting amongst themselves.

The 'Ingrams Peace'

Wadi Hadramaut was somewhat excluded, by distance and attitude, from the independence upheavals in the 1960s, and already much of the workforce had left to work in other countries. Moreover, there has been minimal investment in the *wadi* over the last 20 years. However, there will now hopefully be a more vigorous attempt to profit from the oil extraction and the tremendous tourist potential.

Current stability

AL-AJLANIYA–SEIYUN
Al-Ajlaniya–Shibam

From al-Ajlaniya (266km from Mukalla), where the road strikes east down Wadi Hadramaut, many things suddenly change. The panorama extends to a wide-angle view of dramatic scenery, and the drab colour of the *jol* and side *wadis* gives way to a lush greenery. There also seems to be a bit more urgency about the way of life here, and people appear more active and mobile.

Women's hats
One of the greatest sights, peculiar to this area, is the *mathalla*, the strange wide-brimmed conical straw hats of the women. The sight of three or four women wearing these hats whilst riding on a cart from the fields is something never to be forgotten. However, the women here are very against having their photographs taken, and the only way to do so without causing offence would be to snap quickly while driving past. If you thought the women of the northern highlands were well covered, then they go even further here, covering almost every piece of skin, even sometimes the bridge of the nose between the eyes.

Remote northern areas
Tracks over to the left lead to the town of **Hainin**, which you can see at the base of the northern wall known as Jebel Qamran, guarding the entrance to Wadi Hainin. The sands drift up the open Wadi Hadramaut mouth, causing severe problems around the town. Directly due north of Hainin up a short side *wadi* is Mazar al-Sayyid Ahmed (8km) the site of a pre-Islamic Bedouin sanctuary, renamed to bring it into line with Islam.

Wadi Hainin is the traditional route leading 60km north-west to the Raydat as-Sayar region and its desert town of Markaz al-Hajar. Together with al-Abr (a further 60km due east), it controls the main tracks heading north into the Rub al-Khali and Saudi Arabia.

Qaiti capital
Continuing on the tarred road, the villages come in quick succession for most of the next 100km. **Al-Qatn** is signposted at 282km, even though the town centre is not for another 5km. It is the former capital of the Qaiti tribe in the *wadi*, and still retains some of this importance, although not as much as when Freya Stark was here in the late 1930s.

Unlike the other three main towns, al-Qatn is usually by-passed to allow more time elsewhere, as it is rather an uninteresting place. Modern expansion has led to the disappearance of the town walls, and there is little of interest left for the visitor other than a quick tea and wander around. If you need to stay the night, there are three hotels to choose from:

* **Ar-Rawdhah Tourist Hotel.** Tel: 57380.
A new tourist hotel on the left of the road to Shibam,

500m from the town centre. Dorm style rooms without bathrooms, but reasonable.

* Red Line Hotel. Tel: 57953.

Pretty rough, only to be used in an extreme emergency! On the second floor above a restaurant opposite the central roundabout.

* Al Qutn Rest House

4 rooms. On the right of the road towards Seiyun. Seems to be government-run. Rough and basic.

Ribbon conurbation   At the roundabout in the centre of the town, turn left and carry on through no less than ten named villages in less than 25km to Shibam. Evidence of the effects of tribal wars and general neglect can be seen in the hundreds of abandoned mud houses, some quite substantial, which sometimes outnumber the occupied ones.

The area is well cultivated with countless varieties of fruit and vegetables, all growing under shady clumps of palms producing good-quality dates. Sometimes all you can see of the women working in the fields is a row of the tall straw hats slowly moving around.

Giant grave sites to the north   From the village of Dar ar-Rak (302km) a track runs through the sand dunes in the middle of the *wadi* across the other side to the entrance of Wadi Serr, a major tributary. Up this *wadi* and in many of the side branches are historic giant graves, such as that at **Qabr al-Nabi Salih** in Wadi Khaunab. This is the 20m tomb of the prophet Salih, reckoned to be the father of the prophet Hud. Further north in Wadi Sudaf is the long grave of **Nabi Mawla Sudaf.**

As this area is sometimes considered unsafe, the best you can do is read about it in the accounts of Harold Ingrams, who travelled up here with his wife 60 years ago. They are to be found in his excellent book *Arabia and The Isles*. Excavations began in 1990 at an ancient site known as Jujah, which controlled the entrance to Wadi Serr.

Shibam can now be seen through the trees, far off to the right. Around the checkpoint before Shibam you will see gypsum sellers, who make up the material to order in small sheds splattered in white paste from the slaking process. Beyond the checkpoint, stop to get a distant view of Shibam.

Shibam

Chicago of the desert   It is often said that Shibam is to the south what the old city of Sana'a is to the north, and indeed there are many similarities. Both are unique examples of a specific style of southern Arabian architecture which has survived through the centuries in a very compact area. A lot of

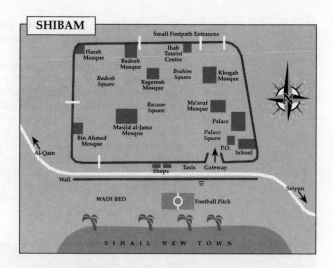

time and money is required to protect these towns, and both have been afforded the distinction of being declared World Heritage sites by UNESCO.

Some people think that tall buildings like these were first constructed at Shabwa, possibly as early as the fifth century BC. When Shabwa was attacked and destroyed by the Himyarites in the third century AD, the inhabitants retreated further up the trade routes to settle at Yashbum (see Aden–Bir Ali) and Shibam, which became the new **capital of the Hadramaut Kingdom.** A small island in the *wadi* bed was chosen as the site of Shibam (a name meaning 'height' in Himyar), unlike all the other settlements in the area, which were built at the foot of the cliff walls. This meant that the site was always prone to flooding, and the town has almost been destroyed many times over the centuries.

Founded by fleeing from Shabwa

Shibam was always important as an **agricultural** and **trade centre** and was the largest city in the *wadi* through the fourteenth century; it was sometimes known as the 'eye of the Hadramaut'. From the fifteenth century it was a **Kathiri outpost,** halfway between the Qaiti capital al-Qatn and the Kathiri capital Seiyun. Around 1830 the Kathiri ruler Sultan Mansur raised much-needed money by selling half of Shibam to the rival Qaiti family, part of the Yafa tribe. An uneasy peace over the split town was broken when Mansur killed all the Yafa residents during the feast of Id al-Fitr at the end of Ramadan.

Kathiri/Qaiti confrontation

Revenge had to wait, because the Kathiris were too strong, and so the Qaitis enlisted the assistance of Omar bin Awadh in India. He sent his three sons with soldiers to besiege Shibam, which they did for 16 years. The stalemate was broken by arbitration, when the Qaitis regained their lost half of the town, which was once again divided in 1858.

Kathiri expansion

Sultan Mansur then arranged a feast to which many Yafa tribesmen were invited, including the three brothers, with the intention of blowing them up. On hearing of this cunning plan, the brothers arrived separately, ate quickly and left. Mansur got his just desserts when he and all other Kathiris were murdered at a return banquet, leaving Shibam under the total control of the Qaitis.

The brothers went on to build up the Qaiti empire as they ruled separately from al-Qatn, esh-Shihr and Ghail Ba Wazir. The second brother, Awadh, became the first Sultan of esh-Shihr and Mukalla, and signed the initial peace agreement with the British in 1888.

Shibam, Wadi Hadramaut.

Multi-storey mud brick houses

All the **houses** in Shibam are constructed in the same way, with mud-brick walls and wooden struts for supports and beams, all on a stone foundation. Most of them have four or five storeys, but some rise to nine, and appear to have even more, owing to the small sets of windows which are set between floors. Most of the tower houses are around 200-300 years old, but some sections date back to the fifteenth century.

There is only one entrance to the town for vehicles, through the imposing white gateway at the far south-eastern corner after the road has passed along the southern side of town. This gateway is similar to the two at esh-Shihr on the coast, and leads immediately into the main square of the town, known as **Palace Square** because of the old Sultan's palace on the right. Also in the square are some small shops, a post office, a school and, directly in front, the Ma'aruf Mosque with its round Hadrami minaret.

A concentration of housing

When you enter the town through the impressive gateway, take the time to inspect the old spiked wooden doors and cannon lying against the wall to the right. There are seven mosques inside the old town, the most important being **Masjid al-Jama,** the Great or Friday mosque, which is found by walking due west from the far left-hand corner of Palace Square. The open space in front of the mosque allows you to stand back and observe, an unusual treat in an area with narrow alleys and cramped housing.

One always seems to be able to hear the pleasant sound of **birds,** not from those flying overhead but from pigeons and hens which are kept in converted tin boxes and hung on the sides of houses. With no gardens, this is the only way for the inhabitants to keep poultry and birds.

Wandering around, you can see fine carved wooden doors and gaze up at amazing buildings, some of which are starting to look a bit cracked and dangerous. Many properties are empty, as the houses are too unstable for families to live in, yet the owners do not have the finances to repair them. This is where UNESCO funds can help to maintain the buildings before they get beyond help, as did the house at the south-western corner, which collapsed completely in 1992. Underground tunnels link many of the houses, but almost all of them are now disused and blocked up.

Tourist development

The locals are quickly adapting to the new tourist boom, with more and more inhabitants opening small **souvenir shops** selling unique items, like the local wooden door locks, with keys that look more like giant brushes. The Ihab Tourist Centre, with more souvenirs, can be found on the northern side. Unfortunately the children have also acquired the habit of throwing stones at visitors, which is common in the north but unusual in the south. Just outside the town gate to the east is the new Shibam Guest House offering meals and drinks. Along the northern side there are three small pedestrian **passageways** leading to the outer wall, and thence into the lower fields outside. Even if your visit is short, try to get away from the town to get a better view, by walking down into the *wadi*, which is normally a football pitch with strolling camels. At the far side are some palm trees which add greatly to any long shot of the town.

**Views from
across the wadi**

This is now the edge of new Shibam, **Sihail,** the 'garden city'. If you go past these smaller, more modern, mud houses, it is possible to climb up the scree slope to the base of the Jebel Khibbah cliff for stunning views over the town and *wadi*. It is a tough scramble up loose stones, but from here the concentration of houses in such a small space can really be appreciated. The brown mud walls are topped by white gypsum for protection from the rain and then sometimes painted green – absolutely stunning. Directly across the *wadi* is the entrance to two other large wadis that come from the north, Wadi al-Na'am from the north-west and Wadi Ju'aimah from the north-east.

The main problem for the authorities at the moment is to work out how to protect Shibam. Investigations are being carried out by experts from around the world to decide what should be done, not only to repair ruined houses, but also to stop further damage occurring from water action. A large concrete dam to the west which will divert flood water around the town is one possible solution which UNESCO experts are considering.

Shibam–Seiyun

**The
Kathiri/Qaiti
border**

Within a minute of leaving Shibam, a concrete ramp across the *wadi* bed shows you how close the dangerous flood waters come to the town. After the Qaiti take-over of Shibam, the border between them and their Kathiri enemies was set for over a century at **al-Hazm,** just 1km to the east. There are two identical customs posts guarded by fences standing beside the road on the right.

The Qaiti/Kathiri territorial problem was extremely complex, with Qaiti-controlled land spreading up from the coast to Wadi Hadramaut and the Kathiri area coming down from the north. The border was not a neat line but a series of huge curves (and even isolated pockets) up and down the *wadi*. Smaller tribes allied themselves to one or the other in varying degrees at different times.

**More routes
to the coast**

The main road continues east to Seiyun, but al-Hazm is also the place where two *wadis* meet and enter Wadi Hadramaut. The smaller Wadi al-Haryah comes from the south-west and is the site of Husn al-Atam (8km from al-Hazm). The larger is **Wadi Bin Ali,** which stretches way into the *jol*, ascending it by Aqabat Suwaighirah. This southern end almost links up with Wadi al-Ain near Sharj ash-Sharif on the main road from Mukalla. There is evidence of a well-worn ancient paved path passing along the *wadi*, which Freya Stark reckoned was an old trade route from the coast direct to Shibam. The best, albeit brief, description of the route was by van der Meulen in 1939 in his *Aden to the Hadramaut*.

Four kilometres to the east of al-Hazm is the straggling

town of Hawta (314km), which signals the build-up of housing almost all the way to Seiyun. The road sticks to the southern side of the *wadi* to **al-Ghurfa** (322km), where it runs straight through an unwalled cemetery containing the white sixteenth century mosque of Ba'bath on the right, beside which is his large *qubba* tomb.

This town was the scene of many prolonged wars between rival tribes, not just the usual Qaiti-Kathiri battles, but even wars between two Kathiri tribes, the al-Umar and the al-Amr. An elaborate system of trenches allowed people to move between fields and houses

Destruction and war without being shot. As if the conditions here were not tough enough, one popular method of attacking your enemy was to pour paraffin on the base of his palm trees and set fire to them, thus destroying the roots!

The town of Taris is now almost a suburb of Seiyun, one of the old gateways of which can be seen over to the right, as the road starts to swing left around the town. The new by-pass avoids the town centre and runs past the airport to the left. Almost all the traffic, however, heads for Seiyun (328km from Mukalla) by turning right to run into the town centre.

SEIYUN

Kathiri capital of Wadi Hadramaut If there were a designated capital of Wadi Hadramaut, it would undoubtedly be Seiyun. Centrally located along the *wadi*, this large town with a fairly modern airport is the only place where tourists' problems can be resolved. Every tourist comes here, and all the main tour agencies have offices or representatives to make any necessary arrangements.

Even in **pre-Islamic times,** the town was on the trade route up Wadi Masilah from the coast. In those early days small amounts of frankincense were also grown locally. Seiyun is built in a commanding position at the foot of Jebel Ayyub, in the centre of a fertile area providing ample food supplies. After the trade had gone, its influence seems to have been mainly religious.

The greatest change came at the end of the fifteenth century with its invasion by the troops of Badr bin Tuwairiq from Sana'a. They started the **Kathiri** dynasty with Seiyun as their capital, a dynasty which lasted until Sultan Hussein bin Ali fled to Saudi Arabia in 1967.

The town is nowadays well spread out along the main *wadi*, and also down the short but wide Wadi Jathmah which runs south. Since unification, businessmen from both Aden and Sana'a have seen the opportunities for developing Wadi Hadramaut and are using Seiyun as their centre of operations. The return of government seized property since 1990 has also added to the building

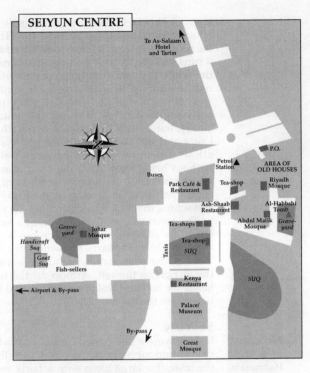

SEIYUN CENTRE

To As-Salaam Hotel and Tarim

P.O.

AREA OF OLD HOUSES

Petrol Station

Buses

Park Café & Restaurant

Tea-shop

Riyadh Mosque

Ash-Shaab Restaurant

Al-Habbshi Tomb

Abdul Malik Mosque

Grave-yard

Grave-yard

Johar Mosque

Tea-shops

Handicraft Suq

Goat Suq

Fish-sellers

Taxis

Tea-shop

SUQ

Kenya Restaurant

SUQ

← Airport & By-pass

Palace/ Museum

By-pass

Great Mosque

and development boom that Seiyun is experiencing.

Almost everything is accessible from the central square, which is dominated by the incredible gleaming Sultan's palace, now converted into the regional museum.

The Museum

Impressive building

Most of the rooms are clean and well looked after by a couple of guardians, who might have to open up the rooms for you; it depends on the time of year. The museum is free and open 08.30-12.00 (maybe 13.00) every day except Friday and certain local, national and religious holidays.

The **customs and weapons** section is a fascinating collection of objects from colonial days, including the flags of all the relevant tribal rulers. Passports, coins, old guns, spears, saddles and local musical instruments all date back to Kathiri control.

In the **marriage, birth, costumes and jewellery** section there are fine examples of women's dresses embroidered with silk, sequins and shells. The black dress belonged to a Bedouin, the purple one to a town dweller. Among the gold and silver jewellery there is a strange petrol-powered fan belonging to the Sultan.

For practical everyday objects, the **handicraft goods and tools** room has an interesting collection of lamps, baskets, ornate carved wooden doors and locks, old coffee- and tea-making equipment, leather drinking vessels and more instruments.

The smaller **agricultural** section has wooden ploughs, old water-well gear, farming tools and examples of women's hats, which can still be seen in the fields. Note the carved wooden pillar in the centre of the room.

In the **cooking utensils** section there are pots, pans, plates, grinding stones and jars. The Liberation War Section and manuscripts library are sometimes closed to the public.

From the higher rooms try to find a stairway that will give access to the roof for superb views over the *suq*, the town centre and the general area; it may not be possible, as the doors are sometimes locked.

Good archaeology room

Before you leave make sure you take the right stairs to get to the new **archaeological** section (or more correctly The Yemeni Centre for Cultural Research, Archaeological Excavations and Museums). There is also an entrance to the right of the courtyard. This section has some very good maps and aerial views that you cannot find anywhere else. Most of the main room is dedicated to finds from Raybun (1000 BC-300 AD) in Wadi Hajjarain, with good artifacts and an explanatory text in Arabic and English. Drawings, plans and photographs further help to locate and describe the site. There are pictures of the cave dwellings of early man, Himyaritic inscriptions, painted pottery, carvings and Bronze Age stone statues from Wadi Idim. In the rear room there are some larger objects, including two thirteenth century wooden *minbars* (a sort of pulpit) from mosques in Wadi Do'an.

The Town

If you cannot get onto the roof of the Palace, see if you can make it onto the roof of the small stage facing the courtyard via the steps at the rear. From here there are good views down onto the *suq* below.

The local *suq*

The *suq* has both an indoor and an outdoor section, and retains much of its local character, despite the number of tourists passing through. There are general trade items here, and also at the handicrafts *suq*, a little to the north.

Go down the main road with the *suq* to the right (the Palace is over to the left), straight over the roundabout and the next cross-roads. Traders will be selling dusty chunks of dried fish on the ground immediately in front of the Johar Mosque and cemetery on the right. Turn right up a dirt road and past an interesting goat market

*Seiyun town,
Wadi
Hadramaut.*

under shady palms in a small compound on the left. Turn left through a charcoal dump and the **handicraft compound** is on the left.

**Locally
manufactured
goods**

Inside is every conceivable type of material shaped, wrapped, tied or carved by local craftsmen, and the closest you will get to a Yemeni home improvement centre. Wooden doors, windows, tables and beds are piled up alongside palm-frond baskets, mats, trays and conical hats. Goatskin water containers hang above stacks of samovars and piles of pots, and even if you are not in the market for a bedroom cabinet this place is well worth a visit. 300m east of here on a parallel road is one of the two remaining town gateways.

West of the Palace, up the slight hill and set back to the right is the large central mosque, recently repaired, with its square minaret. Beyond is a large section of three- and four-storey **housing.** It is amazing to think that they are all made of mud. I particularly like the system of preventing damage to the fragile corners of the buildings by embedding any suitably sized piece of old vehicle chassis in the ground. Going west among these buildings you will eventually arrive at the other town gate near the main road to Shibam, but it is not that easy to find in the maze of narrow streets.

To the east of the square there are many **teashops,** also serving good local fast food dishes, and it is interesting to watch what is going on, over a *fool* and *chai*, before the place becomes too modernised. On the right, and above the general dust level is the excellent first floor Ash-Shaab Restaurant, which does a good grilled chicken. Diagonally opposite is the Park Cafe and Restaurant, a local eatery in the public park.

Behind the Ash-Shaab are some interesting mosques and tombs, including the fine green dome of the **al-Habbshi tomb.** This respected local holy man died at the beginning of this century, and his death is still celebrated by pilgrimages lasting ten days every year. The small mosque across the lane just to the north of this graveyard is the modest **Abdul Malik Mosque.** The square, stubby white minaret with a palm tree behind, provide a very simple but effective photograph against the dramatic blue sky, even more so if you have a polarising filter.

Continuing along the alley there are some good examples of old houses with carved wooden doors, and then the large white **Riyadh Mosque** with its circular Hadrami-style minaret in white and green. This is a fascinating area of large old villas, some now abandoned, with wooden shutters, archways and narrow alleys. This alley comes out at the main post office on the sunken *wadi* road. You can reach the As-Salaam Hotel by crossing the *wadi* road and heading east for about 2km. You will see it on the right.

Residential centre

Local eateries

Picturesque local mosques

ARTISTIC SEIYUN

With the number of instruments on display at the museum, it will come as no surprise to hear that Seiyun is a centre of the arts in Wadi Hadramaut. The locals are proud of the tradition and honour musicians, singers, writers and painters. There are two large paintings of poets in public places, Hamedi outside the Palace, and Merzoog near the Park. Hadrami singers are well respected, and are backed by skilful drumming and bass notes. To hear the best examples, call in at one of the many cassette shops in town and get a copy of something you like the sound of.

Protected dates in Seiyun.

Local produce

If you have some free time, I can recommend walking into the **fields and plantations** which surround Seiyun. Very few visitors do this, but it is a good way to see everyday life, and the farmers and their families are usually very welcoming. You will notice that almost every piece of land is used for growing something, no matter how small or difficult it may be. Chillies are a popular local crop, as are the regular millets and vegetables. Ripening dates are kept on the palms until required, and are protected from birds and insects by frond matting placed around the bunches.

National connections

The **airport** is just 1km north of the town centre, on the by-pass road, and is served by both al-Yemda and Yemenia, giving direct flights to Aden and Sana'a. Most of these flights use Dash 7 aircraft with fewer than 50 seats, but occasionally the demand for seats is so great that a 737 will be put on for the service to Sana'a. If you are flying out, try to find out from which side Shibam can be seen. Once up high the *jol* looks like a series of giant fern leaves, each vein linking to a larger water run-off before meeting the main wadi. If you are flying to Sana'a the dam at Marib can easily be seen to the right.

Hotels and Restaurants
As with all tourist sites in the former PDRY except Aden, there is a chronic shortage of accommodation in Seiyun.

Tourist development

For years the As-Salaam Hotel could handle the well-regulated numbers, but since unification demand has far outstripped supply, and some groups have been put up in chalet complexes on the outskirts of town. If you are travelling independently and without reservations, it is now possible to find small privately run hotels and *fonduqs* all over town. These are generally good value and brand new. Several high-grade hotels are being built to cater for the group tourist boom, many of them linked to the tour operators from Sana'a, and these will hopefully ease the shortage. A luxury hotel has been built by the YATA agency overlooking the town. Try the new ones for cleanliness and eager service.

*** As-Salaam. PO Box 9030. Tel: 3181/3208/3366.

40 rooms, most with air-conditioning. This is the old hotel which everybody had to stay in during PDRY times. It has a pool, usually OK. When the hotel is full (as it is all the time!), there are chalets in the annexe about 3km to the south. Meals can be taken at the hotel if required.

The town tourist office is here, under the friendly control of Hassan Ali Sheikh Bahumaid. Tel: 4222 (office) or 2401 (home). Office hours: 08.00-14.00. He is very helpful, and speaks good English.

** Bin Safi. Tel: 3216 or 3411.

6 rooms. A new establishment on the road to the As-Salaam Hotel. Clean and good value.

SEIYUN–TARIM

This is an interesting journey of 36km, during which the *wadi* bed becomes narrower further downstream, and almost every hillock is topped by a ruined mud fortress. The road is tarred all the way, with sections of the old paved road visible alongside. The road going east past the As-Salaam Hotel meets up with the by-pass road just at the end of the airport runway.

Beyond the ruins of **Maryamah** (5km) is the site of an unusual tomb belonging to a respected religious woman

Unusual tomb

known as Sheikha Sultana, a Suri dignitary who died in the middle of the fifteenth century. Her village, Hauta as-Sultana (8km), is over to the right at the cliff base, where the village mosque and her green-domed tomb can be seen.

Tomb of Ahmed Bin Isa

Important site of pilgrimage

Probably the most famous site on this road is the tomb of Ahmed bin Isa al-Muhajir (12km), which stands out as a tiered set of white buildings to the right. He is the man credited with bringing the line of *sada* (plural of *sayyid*) into the Hadramaut in the ninth century. Originally from

Basra in Iraq, he made the *Haj* pilgrimage to Mecca, and continued south to spread the Sunni orthodox branch of Islam *(Muhajir* means 'migrator'). From his full name you can work out that Ahmed was a seventh generation descendant of Ali, the Prophet Mohammed's cousin and son-in-law: Ahmed bin Isa bin Ali al-Uredi bin Jafar as-Sadiq bin Mohammed al-Baqr bin Za'in al-Abidin bin Hussein bin Ali bin Abu Taleb (Abu Taleb was Prophet Mohammed's uncle).

What's in a name?

Working initially in Wadi Hajjarain, he converted the locals by force back onto the true path. It was his teachings and the setting up of the privileged class of *sada* that created a class system unique in the Muslim world, stretching through sheikhs and tribesmen to traders and slaves. The site of his death is now a tomb, which attracts many pilgrims, especially women wanting to be blessed with a child.

The tombs are best approached by going past them a short way down the road and turning back on a dirt track. Many of the mud walls have been painted white, giving the site a well-kept appearance. At ground level is a mosque and ablutions room, alongside which is the domed tomb. Clean white steps then lead up the lower slopes to another collection of tombs and graves, those of members of his family. Stuck to the inside of the tomb wall and ceiling are hundreds of little balls of thread, placed by pilgrims hoping to be blessed with good luck.

On the northern edge

Back at the main road, a track angles off across to the opposite side of the *wadi,* leading after 2km to the village of Bor. To the right of the houses is the **Abdullah Mosque,** reckoned to be possibly the oldest mosque in the *wadi,* now restored and looking resplendent in white and green.

Giant graves

Five kilometres back upstream, on a track from Bor, is the entrance to Wadi Madar, and another site of **giant graves.** The prophet Handal and his son Handalah are said to be buried in the two long graves (20m and 25m) at the base of the small hill to the west of the *wadi* entrance. They are along the edge of a large cemetery close to a mud house. By tradition, the longer the grave, the more important the person. This is a tradition which is spread sparingly throughout ancient Arabia, the most famous being that at Qabr Hud further down the *wadi.* It is possible that these were initially multiple graves dedicated to the leader or prophet.

Back along the southern edge, on the tarred road past the Ahmed bin Isa tomb is the town of **Tariba** (22km), just beyond the entrance of Wadi Tariba. If you turn right just after the football pitch, you can visit the old ruined town among the new buildings. For many years Tariba was a village under Bedouin protection, independent of Seiyun and a constant problem for the Kathiris.

Building the old road   From here, look across to the opposite side of the *wadi* and notice an old track that angles up the side of the cliff face. This was a rough road built by the Kathiri sultans of Tarim so that their new and extensive fleet of motor cars could avoid the troublesome wadi bed area of Tariba during localised warring in the 1930s. The track climbs 200m onto the top of the plateau, drops into Wadi Dhahab and then rises up and over a similar climb before entering Tarim from the back. A nightmare journey along this mountain track is described by Harold Ingrams in *Arabia and the Isles* (see Further Reading).

TREKKING ON THE OLD ROAD TO TARIM

To reach the starting point of the old road, travel along the northern wall of the *wadi* for about 3km east of Bor, or try to find a track across the *wadi* bed from Tariba. If you are walking from the main road near Tariba, allow 40 minutes to reach the start. The badly scarred track begins to the left of a small hillock and climbs steadily to the *wadi* rim in 45 minutes. There are excellent views up and down the *wadi*, and also down into the fertile Wadi Dhahab. The descent is easy and obvious, taking about 30 minutes. Look across and right to the other side of Wadi Dhahab to see where the track climbs out.

It takes about half an hour to walk through the fields and across the *wadi* bed to the start of the next climb. If you get tired or short of water, you could take the track down Wadi Dhahab and get quickly around to Tarim. The second climb will also take about 45 minutes to get to a cutting in the cliff wall, from where the Qubba resthouse can be seen in the fields and gardens of south west Tarim, another 45 minute walk away. Allow a total of 4 hours and take plenty of water.

Ancient and modern settlements   **Al-Ghuraf** (26km and not to be confused with al-Ghurfa on the other side of Seiyun) contains the ruined site of Qaret as-Senehiye at the foot of the southern escarpment. A mixture of inhabited and ruined houses lower down, the central hill is covered in the remains of an extensive mud-built village containing a crumbling fortress and a mosque, with shards of broken pottery everywhere. The site was extensively excavated in the early 1980s, and some pieces are in Seiyun Museum. It is an interesting place to wander around, and to get good views across the *wadi*.

In the centre of the *wadi is* the site of the British landing strip for the area, and the main airport for the wadi until the new one at Seiyun was built in 1985. All that remain are the abandoned and isolated white buildings over to the left, looking more like a desert railway station.

Wadi Idim

The original route to the coast

Al-Masilah (27km) is at the confluence of the large Wadi Idim, where Wadi Hadramaut turns 90° to the north. The first paved road to link with the coast was built along Wadi Idim following an ancient route travelled for thousands of years, and used by many Europeans arriving in the 1930s from esh-Shihr. There are famous and interesting sites due south, but due to trouble in the area it is usually out of bounds to tourists.

The track is in a bad condition requiring 4x4. Many small villages survive in this fertile *wadi* now that the threat of tribal warfare has diminished. There are the ruins of a large pre-Islamic house at **Masga,** just before ruins of an old dam. This dam once stretched across the *wadi* just beyond er-Rudud (10km from al-Masilah) with the ruined town of Sunah (the site of a 1978 excavation) a couple of kilometres further on the left – a site similar to the bumpy ground at Raybun in Wadi Hajjarain.

Ghail Umar (40km) is a pleasant palm-tree oasis, with just outside it the tomb of Nabi Umar. Wadi Idim is one of the largest tributaries and it reaches far into the *jol*, the cliff edges sometimes lined with cairns of stones, especially south of Sah (50km). As the *wadi* becomes shallower and narrower it swings around in great curves, until you climb onto the *jol*, from where a route strikes westwards to join the new road. The continuation of the ancient route drops into Wadi Ma'di to reach esh-Shihr through Tabala, or by a side track to Ghail Ba Wazir.

The road to Tarim

If you turn left at the roundabout at al-Masilah, the road transfers to the northern wall, running around the sprawl of as-Suweyri town to the right. Built onto the slope of the *wadi* wall on the left is an impressive ruined fortress which formerly controlled the eastern Kathiri border, beyond which was Qaiti land, except for the walled and well protected town of Tarim. Wadi Dhahab enters from the left where the *wadi* widens again, becoming more fertile and cultivated as Tarim is approached. The road continues past the town, but a link road turns left into the centre.

Tarim

The road arrives at the shady central park and taxi rank on the edge of the town centre, and about 1½ km from the resthouse.

Centre of learning

Shibam has the architecture, Seiyun is the political and artistic centre, but Tarim (pronounced 'Treem') is the **religious centre** of the Hadramaut. Like the other main towns it used to be a trade centre on the route to Shabwa. The downturn in trade was closely followed by the rise of Islam, and Tarim became the centre for the Sunni branch.

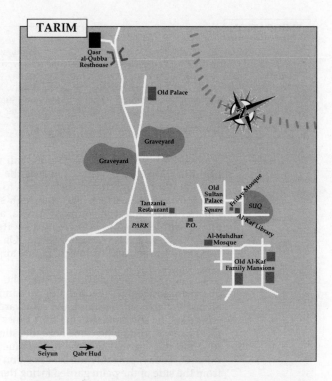

TARIM

Qasr al-Qubba Resthouse

Old Palace

Graveyard

Graveyard

Tanzania Restaurant

PARK

P.O.

Old Sultan Palace

Square

Friday Mosque

SUQ

Al-Kaf Library

Al-Muhdhar Mosque

Old Al-Kaf Family Mansions

← Seiyun   → Qabr Hud

Following the desertion of orthodox Islam by the powerful Kinda tribe of Hajjarain, the 'true' faith was restored after their surrender at Hujail, about 8km from Tarim towards Einat.

After that Tarim became a centre for religious teaching in southern Arabia, as important as Zabid, with school and mosque functions overlapping. Many *sada* leaders in the south trace their roots back here. The people are still very conservative and reserved, an attitude that some visitors take for unfriendliness.

A history of emigration

Over the last three centuries, the town's inhabitants have escaped the poverty and warring by travelling to the Far East, especially Singapore. where there were as many as 100,000 Hadramis, dealing mainly in property. The town's Kathiri rulers were the al-Kaf family, wealthy philantropists, who tried to bring peace to the region and improve local conditions. Sayyid Umar al-Kaf's wealth came from the splendid Europe Hotel in Singapore in the 1920s. He imported cars into the *wadi* before there were even any roads for them to run on! The vehicles were taken to bits, transported over the *jol* by camel, and then reassembled in Tarim. The road was then built from the interior to the coast, rather than the other way around.

EMIGRATION

Women never left the Hadramaut to travel with their husbands, who regularly married again abroad. However, their young half-caste sons were always sent back to the *wadi* to be taught Hadrami ways and religion. Money was sent back to buy land and houses for the immediate welfare of the family, and for when the man finally returned to his homeland. Thus Indian, Malay and Far Eastern architecture, language and blood have become integrated into the everyday life of Wadi Hadramaut.

Tallest minaret

Given a bit of space, the famous tall minaret of **al-Muhdhar Mosque** is visible towards the south-east. Its position is a bit unfortunate as it seems to be on a rather unimportant back street. The 50m high slender square minaret is the tallest in southern Arabia, and the stature of the whole mosque is increased by its resting on a raised base, which is reached by steps. On either side are two small towers, and the whole façade appears light and breezy.

I was once briefly allowed into the mosque by a guardian, and had just enough time to admire the series of arched galleries surrounding the courtyard, before being chased out by someone else. In PDRY times it was possible for the few tourists who came here (the slim ones at least) to climb the narrow staircase of the nineteenth century minaret. Today, probably the best position for a picture is from the side of the palm garden facing the mosque.

Decayed mansions show eastern influence

While you are in this part of town, continue past the mosque into a small square, where diagonally opposite to the right is the decaying **mansion of Sayyid Umar al-Kaf.** He was one of the ruler's wealthy cousins, who ran the municipal affairs of Tarim during the 1930s. This grand residence is now sectioned off inside and occupied by several families, but it still has an impressive, grandiose, Far Eastern style.

If you want to see more, go past the building and turn left. At the end of the street turn left again, and on the right is another former al-Kaf mansion, with yet another further along. All are very grand buildings, and though unmaintained, have an Indian feel of the British raj about them. From here you can bear left and thread through the narrow streets to the centre, or go to the es-Safa Mosque across the road, which continues back to the al-Muhdhar Mosque.

The **central square** can be approached from the taxi rank up the main street, with the good Tanzania Restaurant on the left and the post office on the right. The square is a scruffy area surrounded by half-interesting buildings. The government offices are in the former rulers' palace on the left with the side of the Friday

Important library

Mosque ahead. The **Al-Kaf Manuscripts Library** is situated beside this 120-year-old mosque, with steps climbing up the far side of the mosque from an alleyway.

Most of the 5,000 volumes in this library are kept in bookcases around the walls, and labelled according to subject matter: Islamic jurisprudence; mysticism or sufism; the Prophet Mohammed's sayings and deeds and commentaries on the Holy Koran. It is an extremely valuable collection of religious books, mostly hand written, from all over the Arab world. Some of the oldest and best examples are on show in a glass cabinet.

The manuscripts can be seen daily from 08.00-13.30 except Friday, and it might be advisable, if you are with a group, to arrive independently, as large numbers of non-Muslims have sometimes been turned away. Shoes must be removed just inside the door.

There is a small indoor *suq* behind the Friday Mosque, and many traders also sell goods from the roadside, especially dried fish. Even far from the sea this has been a basic food item for many years, simply because of the huge amount available on the coast and the ease with which it can be transported.

Viewing Tarim

After a few days in the *wadi* it is good to get above it and shed the oppressive feeling of being permanently hemmed in by the steep walls. For an overall view of Tarim head north through the town towards the cliffs of Jebel Ba Hussein, and after about ten minutes climb up to a ruined watchtower on a small hill. The view is superb but beware of the wild dogs that have taken over the ruin. Just to the north of Tarim at the mouth of the next wadi is a suburb known as Dammun, the probable site of the earlier ancient settlement.

Tarim is a dusty town – indeed it seems to manufacture dust – and despite the numerous gardens and shady palm trees, I can see why some visitors are disappointed. A religious centre seems somehow to imply solitude and cleanliness, words that don't immediately spring to mind when describing Tarim. But at least it has dignity, and I can always sense a feeling of superiority in the people.

A restful place

One of the most pleasant places to relax is the colourful **Qasr al-Qubba Tourist Resthouse,** a former summer palace, ten minutes walk to the west. From the taxi rank go between the two cemeteries and bear right into the one-way system. When you see another large mansion (now a school) to the right, turn left for 50m and then right and over a small bridge, and the Qasr al-Qubba is over to the left. It was built in the 1950s, in Far Eastern style, and has two swimming pools, male and female. It is very pleasant, but hot at night. Some rooms have no air-conditioning, so beware of mosquitoes. You need to book ahead for one of the 17 rooms and even a meal in the good restaurant. From August to January it is usually full with groups, but from February to July it is generally all right. Tel: 55221 (Manager 55488).

TARIM–QABR HUD

Following the pilgrims

It is less than 90km to Qabr Hud along the continuation of the *wadi*, but the journey needs a good strong vehicle, preferably 4x4, and it will take a full day to get there and back. It is well off the tourist route and there are no places to stay overnight. It is also a good idea to take plenty of bottled water as it might not be available in the villages. But if you have the time it is well worth the effort as there are interesting sights on the way to this holy place of pilgrimage.

Rejoin the main road outside Tarim and turn left to follow the tarred road, which soon gives way to the old stone highway with its many pot holes, landslides and broken bridges. For most of the route the road is on the northern side of the *wadi*, only switching to the south beyond Fughma. Just 4km from Tarim is an area of **gypsum kilns** similar to those on the south coast road near Burum. The workers heat the limestone in the kilns by burning huge amounts of palm fronds and trunks, and the slaking is carried out in open-ended huts. Nearby is the site of an old fortress named Husn Dhiban Masilah from where the name Wadi Masilah has come to identify the remainder of the route to the sea.

Town loses importance

Turn right after 20km, off the main road, and head for the town of **Einat**, formerly one of the largest and most famous in the *wadi*. Its decline is largely due to it's position furthest down the *wadi;* it thus receives the most powerful and destructive floods, which have gradually washed away crops, houses and small dams.

Young goat herders near Qabr Hud.

The white *qubbas* can be seen from some distance. They became a site of worship *en route* to Qabr Hud, as almost all pilgrims had to pass this way. The main tomb is that of Sheikh Abu Bakr bin Salim, and there are other beehive tombs of important *sada* close by, with hundreds of graves scattered around. All the tombs can be entered, but remember to take your shoes off. Some have a single grave inside while others are full of smaller graves clustered around a large carved wooden shrine. The headstones are finely inscribed, similar to but not as good as those at Sadah.

Ibex horns
The town has some pleasant houses, many with the horns of the *wi'l* (ibex) projecting from the roof to bring good luck.

The main road now heads due north, and there are many ruins to be seen to the left at the base of the cliff. For 5km there is an almost continuous string of abandoned houses and fortresses from Kut Beni Mani to ed-Dodi. Between these two are the extensive ruins of the town of **al-Mahriya** (24km) with its mud-built mosque and houses now used as animal pens.

The *wadi* bed has a mixture of sand dunes and thick deposits of silt on which grow a bush called *rak*, which is eaten by all the local animals but because of its laxative properties tends to give them diarrhoea.

Qasam (25km) is another formerly important town with grand houses which has now been reduced to village status through war and drought, and through many of the men traditionally going to work in East Africa. The town has a few mosques and other fine buildings but otherwise continues to slumber. Low down on the water course to the right you can see the remains of a dam that failed to stop the floods damaging this area. Such large floods occur every few years, but for the rest of the time agriculture can proceed as normal.

The *wadi* takes a huge bend to the south, and the ruins of Khwela village (29km) can be seen about 1km to the left low down at the foot of the weathered rock face. The amazing thing about **Wadi al-Khun,** which now enters from the left, is that it has a permanent water flow from a small oasis to the north called Suwedif. The deep water is used for irrigating a large productive area of crops, especially dates, as well as a swimming pool for all the local males. This wet lush area is in complete contrast to the rest of the dry and dusty *wadi*.

A watery surprise

Only 2km further is a rocky hill close to the road on the left. On the summit is the prehistoric site of **Qaret Kibdah,** a few clumps of stones forming vague walls, which is said to be associated with the tribe of Ad and the prophet Hud. As no excavation has been carried out at

Ancient sites retain their secrets

any of these sites there is still much to be uncovered and it might be worth the five minute climb to the top. However, I would suggest that it would be better to spend the time 4km further on, at the imposing Husn al-Urr (39km).

Husn al-Urr

An imposing fortress

Husn al-Urr is an ancient site perched on an isolated rock in the middle of the *wadi* a few hundred metres to the right of the road. If you do not have 4x4, leave your vehicle on the road and walk through the soft sand, remembering to take drinking water. The northern wall rises up dramatically above the surrounding plain. Access to the summit is up a clearly visible zigzag path facing the road, and on top are complete walls, chambers and floors with a tremendous view of the entire *wadi*.

Hints of the past

Water was provided by wells dug below the western entrance and on the summit, and in its prime this small but impressive fortress would have presented an awesome sight to the traders coming up the wadi. Some carvings and column sections found here are now in the Aden and Mukalla museums, and give some idea of southern Arabian art from the first century BC to the second century AD. For me this moody, remote pre-Islamic site captures the essence of the well-controlled trade route and I just wish that we knew more about the history of the route in general and this site in particular.

Traffic becomes lighter towards as-Som, where the *wadi* makes a 90° turn to the right. An ancient site on the outside of this huge curve is **Makaynun,** consisting of temple foundations, where unique glazed pots have been found. As-Som has many *wi'l* horns on the mud houses, a common sight around here.

Fughma (68km) is a small village with a cold drinks shop on the left. Surrounded by such a dry wilderness the owner has gone completely over the top by covering the walls in giant murals of beach scenes from the Seychelles! Just beyond the road dips down through the flowing stream and continues along the southern wall.

Many buildings and sites along here look to be of ancient origin; some of the rock-cut caves are now used as small gypsum kilns or animal barns.

Qabr Hud

The Bible and the giants

This is the most important site of pilgrimage in the Hadramaut. The prophet Nabi Allah Hud is thought to have been Eber of the Bible, the great great grandson of Noah and father of Qahtan, hence the father of all the true Qahtanid Arabs of the south. The story goes that Hud tried to convert the tribesmen of Ad to the true faith but ended up being chased by two infidel horsemen to this site. Being trapped, he asked for Allah's help. Allah responded by opening up the rock, and Hud disappeared inside. The rock closed, but not completely, leaving a crack to indicate where this miracle occurred. Hud's camel died nearby at the site of the lower mosque.

Hud disappears

Since those times (whenever they were), there has been a tradition of pilgrimage to this sanctuary of the old religion. It was treated as a secure area in which no person could be attacked even in the most violent times of war. To help reconcile this pagan worship with Islam the story of Hud is included in the Koran as the work of an early prophet.

Incorporated into Islam

When Ahmed bin Isa al-Muhajir came here from Basra in the ninth century he wanted to incorporate the local beliefs and so he ordered a *qubba* to be built over the site. The centre of the *qubba* is said to be above Hud's head and the huge grave stretches for over 30m up the hillside, its length possibly indicating his importance.

The pilgrimage takes place over three days in the middle of the month of Shaban, the eight month of the Islamic year and the one prior to Ramadan. During this time the town has a thriving market and people rent all the houses for living quarters, mostly provided by the al-Kaf family from Tarim.

When they arrive, the pilgrims go to the permanent river to make their ablutions before praying. Then follows two days of rituals under the leadership of a respected *sayyid*, while all the time there is a bustling fairground atmosphere, including Bedouin dancing. For the rest of the year it is a ghost town of just a few souls who guard the site and tend the adjoining land.

Visiting the deserted town

Cross the deep Wadi Barhut which runs to the west and drive through town to the base of the gleaming white steps. At the top of the steps, the lower building is the open-columned mosque built into and resting below a huge boulder, said to be the petrified remains of Hud's camel. A few steps above is the tomb itself. Inside, all the walls, columns and rock have been painted white except for the actual split in the rock, which is left untouched by paint, but made smooth by the millions of hands and lips honouring Hud. Oils and fumigants are used in the worship, and there are bottles of the stuff lying around. Stuck on the inside of the ceiling and walls are thousands of tiny blobs of material, each a physical reminder of a pilgrim's wish. Many of these are from women who want to be blessed with a child.

Unless you plan to camp for the night, it would be difficult to include much else during this visit. Your driver might also not want to leave the main course of the *wadi* unless he knows the area and the locals reasonably well.

Wadi Barhut is the deep *wadi* that wriggles due south and contains the infamous **Bir Barhut**, about 10km from Qabr Hud. There is a mass of ancient legends about this natural hole in the ground, stories of boiling mud, lava and explosions and tales describing it as the entrance to hell – in fact everything you would associate with a volcano.

The entrance to hell

The van der Meulen expedition of 1931 found the entrance to the cave 300m above the *wadi* bed in a narrow gorge. They claim to have penetrated it to a distance of about 3km, to a series of dead ends inhabited only by bats. They found a large 'cathedral' hall and some fossil shells, evidence which confirms that it is a limestone cave.

Return or continue?

It is almost impossible to travel any further, so it is appropriate that this site feels and looks like the end of the known world. All you can really do is retrace your route to Tarim.

Qabr Hud–Seihut

To the coast

It is just about feasible to organise a special expedition on to Seihut if you are feeling really adventurous. However, the only people known to have completed the trip since Harold Ingrams, whose account is included in *Arabia and The Isles*, were some long-term European workers based in Sana'a, who did so recently. All supplies would have to be carried with you, as there is no guarantee of food or water for the four or five days it would take. Before the establishment of the PDRY, the Qaitis controlled the route for about 100km, after which it entered Mahra territory for the final 150km to the sea. The route is littered with old dams and ruined settlements, some attributed to the ancient people of Ad, showing that the area was a lot more accessible then than it is today.

The main village of **Rahta** appears before a giant rugged lava flow and beyond is Teheir and the forest of Buzun. The *wadi* becomes as narrow as 80m between sheer 300m sides, where the flood water can be as much as 7m deep. The giant grave of **Mola al-Ain** is on the plateau of Samarma and is another site of ancient pilgrimage, this time not from Wadi Hadramaut but for seafarers coming up from the coast. Dhubeia is the last village before the *wadi* meets the new road bridge, beyond which are some old fortifications guarding the entrance to the sea (see esh-Shihr–Seihut).

More giant graves

THE ISLANDS OF YEMEN

As sea traders the southern Arabians have always valued the islands lying in the Red Sea and Indian Ocean. At one time they ruled over more than are currently possessed by the Yemen. Some have been lost to Saudi Arabia, Ethiopia and others handed over to the Sultanate of Oman. Perim Island, which guards the narrow entrance to the Red Sea, is extremely important and, in effect, controls the Suez Canal. The largest of the islands is Socotra.

SOCOTRA

Difficult access

No matter how far you travel, there are certain places which always seem unreachable, and this is particularly true of offshore islands: in India it is the Andaman Islands, in Italy the Lipari Islands. In the Yemen it is the 36,400sq km island of Socotra. There are over 750 species of plants, of which 250 are endemic.

The island itself is the largest of the archipelago which stretches from the Horn of Africa eastwards into the sea from Cape Guardafui, the easternmost point of Africa. Smaller islands appear in the chain such as Abd al-Kuri and a group of two known as the Brothers. Despite their proximity to Somalia they all belong to the Yemen, although the mainland is almost 400km away.

The island has a long history stretching back to the frankincense trade and the earliest sea-trading routes.

Early trading centre

Known originally as **Dioscorida,** it was garrisoned by the ancient Kingdom of the Hadramaut and sent goods on rafts and small boats to the main port of Qana about 500km to the north-west. Texts tell us that products included tortoise shell and cinnabar (red mercuric

Dragon's blood

sulphide, better known as dragon's blood), which were traded for Indian cloth, foodstuffs and female slaves. No mention is made of frankincense or aloes which are only recorded as coming from frankincense country (probably meaning Dhofar).

As the desert trade routes collapsed, the islanders exported the same materials to the **Himyarites,** but now via Muza on the Red Sea coast. The island faded into relative obscurity except for the sailors who continued to call in throughout the monsoon sailing months. The Bedouin tribesmen were converted to Christianity probably just before the arrival of Islam, but unlike their mainland counterparts they remained Christian right up to the present time.

The island features in the accounts of many seafarers who have already appeared in the histories of Aden and Mokha. The **Portuguese** under Affonso d'Albuquerque established a fort and church at Suq in 1507 but soon left when they could not manage to take Aden. John Jourdain stopped off in 1609 and traded some aloes. Socotra was used as a semi-official supply and postal depot for the Indian fleet during the seventeenth and eighteenth centuries.

British interest   Five years before the **British** took Aden they arranged to establish a coaling station on Socotra with the ruling Sultan of Qishn on the mainland. The island's fortunes during British rule were largely linked with Qishn and the al-Mahra region, but it suffered greatly from drought and disease. Because of its remoteness it seems to have escaped the general adventurous rush of early travellers, apart from the Bents (Theodore and Mabel) in 1897.

The island was the last piece of Aden Protectorate to remain under British rule; the forces of the NLF landed on the very day the last British troops left Aden. It then became a strategic Soviet Indian Ocean naval base and was out of bounds except for military personnel. With unification the Ministry of Culture has realised that there are special sites on the island and steps are being made to open it up to tourism. However there is a long way to go in every sense of the word.

The modern   **Facilities** are basic (camping only) and transport
visitor   almost non-existent, but there are certainly enough people willing to put up with such hardships. The **bird, plant, animal** and **sea life** are unique and of considerable interest to scholars and amateur enthusiasts. There are weekly scheduled flights from Aden via Riyan, but only from December to May, outside the monsoon and rainy periods. Permission must be obtained from the Ministry of the Interior in Aden, a formality which in theory should only take five minutes. The distance involved makes the cost of a return ticket quite high and would really only be justified by a long stay, rather than trying to tag Socotra onto a full Yemen tour.

The island is 113km long and 32km wide, and rises to a height of 1,500m. For the most part it is a layer of limestone punctured by the Hajhir Range of peaks which form the backbone of the island. The natural history is superb especially the plant life which features the strange dragon's blood tree (*Dracaena cinnabari*), which looks like a sort of inside-out umbrella. The bark of the tree is stripped off and then heated to produce glazed, decorated pots. The underwater life is also unique and virtually untouched.

Own language   It is estimated that there are about 30,000 inhabitants on the island. They still speak their own Socotri language, which is closer to Mahri than Arabic. The capital is Hadibu in the centre of the northern coastline.

PERIM

Controlling the
Bab al-Mandab

Unlike Socotra, there is at present no possibility of getting to Perim Island in the Bab al-Mandab straits. It lies halfway between Yemen and Djibouti and is still a military base. A pilgrimage takes place annually to the tomb of Sheikh Berqud, on the northern tip of the island.

The **British** established a coaling station here but it fared even worse than Aden. The Perim Coal Company employed a hundred Europeans and 2,000 locals at its peak, but closed down in 1936. A businessman called Jason Gurney who tried to set up a fishing industry towards the end of British rule described it as '... a desert island ... one of the most desolate islands in the world'. He described small water channels and cisterns similar to the Aden Tanks, which appear to date from similarly ancient times. His book *Sheba's Coast* describes the seasonal fishing industry of the area (see Further Reading).

KAMARAN

Red Sea Islands

Kamaran is an oddity, as it was taken by the British at the same time as Hodeidah in 1917, and administered from Aden. When Hodeidah was retaken by the Imam, the islands remained British and later became part of the PDRY. Logistics dictated that this was not an ideal situation; it was only 3km from the North Yemen peninsula of as-Salif, but 400km from Aden.

The name means 'two moons' and stems from a local tradition that at certain times the reflection of the moon can be seen on both sides of the island at the same time! The **Turks** held it for a long time, establishing a quarantine station for pilgrims travelling to Mecca. At the end of the First World War Britain inherited it. The Imams of North Yemen always wanted control (and nine other smaller islands in the same group), but never had any historical claim to it. Moreover the Sunni Muslim inhabitants were not keen to be taken over by the Zaidis.

The quarantine station closed in 1952. The local economy collapsed and only supplies from Britain kept the islanders going. In 1967 it became an outpost of the PDRY but caused serious problems for the YAR when as-Salif was designated as the new deep water port in preference to Hodeidah. It is now a heavily protected military base, and so out of bounds.

USEFUL WORDS AND PHRASES

NUMBERS

0	zifr
1	wahad
2	ithnain
3	telata
4	arrbaa
5	khamsa
6	sita
7	saba
8	tamania
9	tessaa
10	ashara
11	hudasha
12	itnasha
13	telatasha
14	arrbaatasha
15	khamastasha
16	sitasha
17	sabatasha
18	tamantasha
19	tessaatasha
20	ashareen
21	wahad wa ashareen
30	telateen
40	arrbaeen
50	khamseen
60	siteen
70	sabaeen
80	tamaneen
90	tesseen
100	miya
101	miya wa wahad
200	miten
300	toltomiya
400	robomiya
500	khamsamiya
600	sitamiya
700	sabamiya
800	tamnamiya
900	tessamiya
1,000	elf
2,000	elfain
1,000,000	milyon

USEFUL WORDS

First:	awal
Second:	tarni
Third:	talit
Fourth:	rabi
Fifth:	khamis
Once:	mara
Twice:	martain
Three times:	telaat marat
Half:	nuss
Quarter:	rub
One third:	tilt
Yes:	iowa
No:	la
What?:	aysh?
O.K.:	tammam
Please:	min fadlak
Tomorrow:	bukra
Today:	alyom
Day:	yom
Night:	layl
Big:	kabir
Small:	sagir
A little:	shwayya
Left:	shemal
Right:	yameen
Money:	feloos
Bread:	hubz
Rice:	ruz
Water:	ma (moya)
Salt:	milh
Pepper:	filfil
Bananas:	mohz
Chicken:	dijaj (frahk)
Fish:	samak
Liver:	khibda
Sugar:	sukker

USEFUL PHRASES

As-Salaam alaykum:	Peace be upon you (greeting or welcome)
Wa alaykum as-Salaam:	And peace be upon you (response)
Sabah al-Kheir:	Good morning (greeting)
Sabah an-Nur:	Good morning (response)
Mesa' al-Kheir:	Good evening (greeting)
Mesa' an-Nur:	Good evening (response)
Keyf halak?:	How are you?

Marhaba!:	Welcome!
Ma salama:	Goodbye
Bikam?:	How much?
Bikam hada:	How much is this?
Shukran:	Thank you
Afwan:	You're welcome (response)
Ana min Britania/Amrika:	I am from Britain/America
Al-Yemen balad jameel:	Yemen is a beautiful country

Common phrases which will be said to you include:

Inshallah:	God willing
Bukra inshallah:	tomorrow God willing
Al-humdililah:	thanks be to God
Fee...:	there is, there are
Mafeeh...:	there isn't, there aren't any
Tammam:	OK (good)
Ma'alesh	never mind
Aish tishti?:	what do you want?
Min fein inta?:	where are you from?

CALENDAR

There are twelve months in the Islamic year:

1. Muharram	2. Safar
3. Rabi al-Awal	4. Rabi al-Thani
5. Jumada al-Ula	6. Jumada al-Thania
7. Rajab	8. Shaban
9. Ramadan	10. Shauwal
11. Dhu al-Qada	12. Dhu al-Haj

The last day of Ramadan is the start of the feast of Id al-Fitr (Little Id). Id al-Kabir (Great Id) starts on 10 Dhu al-Haj, and always occurs 99 days after the first day of Ramadan. The Prophet Mohammed's birthday is celebrated on 12 Rabi al-Awal.

LOCAL TELEPHONE NUMBERS

All numbers are in Sana'a unless otherwise stated.

Enquiries:	118
International Operator:	155
Local Operator:	110
Police:	1111 or 270439
Yemenia:	
Head Office:	232381-9
Central Reservations:	250800/1
Az-Zubeiry St Office:	260834/5
Ali Abdul Mogni St Office:	274803/4
Aden Office:	Crater 53848
Al-Yemda Aden Office:	53966 or 52528
TeleYemen:	225594
DHL Couriers:	249878
Ministry of Tourism:	271970/2
Ministry of the Interior:	252701/7
Immigration Office:	250761
Customs Office:	260381/2

FURTHER READING

This is by no means an exhaustive list of books on the Yemen, but simply an indication of what is available from book shops and libraries.

EARLY TRAVELLERS

Robin Bidwell: *Travellers in Arabia* (Hamlyn 1976)
   A brief look at the pioneering journeys of famous travellers throughout Arabia.
David Hogarth: The *Penetration of Arabia* (Stoker 1904)
   A turn-of-the-century account of the very early travellers, updated by the author. Limited Yemen information.
Thorkild Hansen: *Arabia Felix* (Collins 1964)
   The story of the Danish expedition of 1761-7 led by Carsten Niebuhr. The first detailed journey into the North.
Ross E. Dunn: *The Adventures of Ibn Battuta* (Croom Helm 1986)
   Subtitled 'A Muslim Trader of the fourteenth century', this book chronicles Ibn Battuta's amazing journey around the known world. Only a small section deals with southern Arabia, and even then in hazy detail, but it is an interesting read.

GENERAL

Werner Daum (Editor): *Yemen: 3000 Years of Art and Civilisation in Arabia Felix* (Penguin-Verlag 1987)
   Exactly what it says – detailed historical information about many aspects of the country (written for the exhibition in Munich the same year).
Michael Jenner: *Yemen Rediscovered* (Longman 1983)
   An interesting collection, covering both Yemens through the eyes of the Yemen Tourism Company. Many photographs.
Pascal Marechaux: *Arabia Felix: The Yemen And Its People* (Thames and Hudson 1980)
   North Yemen through the camera lens. Superb photographs.
Pascal and Maria Marechaux: *Arabian Moons* (Concept Media 1988)
   More great images.
R.B. Serjeant and R. Lewcock: *Sana'a: An Arabian Islamic City* (Scorpion Press, London 1983)
   A superb definitive view of the city. Expensive.

BOOKS ABOUT WOMEN

Clara Makhlouf: *Changing Veils* (Croom Helm 1979)
   Women's society in Sana'a.
Eileen Macdonald: *Brides For Sale* (Mainstream 1988)
   The much publicised story of two British-born Yemeni girls taken from Britain for arranged marriages in the Yemen.

TRAVELOGUES

D. van der Meulen and H. von Wissman: *Hadramaut: Some Of Its Mysteries Unveiled* (Leiden 1932, reprinted Brill 1964)
D. van der Meulen: *Faces In Shem* (John Murray 1961)
D. van der Meulen: *Aden To The Hadramaut* (John Murray 1947)
   Exciting journeys, well described and still relevant today. Unreservedly recommended.
Harold Ingrams: *Arabia And The Isles* (John Murray 1942)
   High adventures during his 'Peace Treaty' travels. Recommended.
Harold Ingrams: *The Yemen: Imams, Rulers And Revolutions* (John Murray 1963)

A more scholarly tome of North Yemen.

Doreen Ingrams: *A Time In Arabia* (John Murray 1970)
Good accounts of the travels with her husband.

Freya Stark: *The Southern Gates Of Arabia*(John Murray 1936)

Freya Stark: *Seen In The Hadramaut* (John Murray 1939)

Freya Stark: *A Winter In Arabia* (John Murray]940)

Freya Stark: *The Coast Of Incense* (John Murray 1953)
Detailed accounts of everyday life between the World Wars by the queen of Arabian travel writing.

Hans Helfritz: *Land Without Shade* (Allen and Unwin 1934)

Hans Helfritz: *The Yemen: A Secret Journey* (Allen and Unwin 1958)
Adventurous travels without a political motive. Embroidered tales with hazy detail.

Ameen Rihani: *Arabian Peak And Desert* (Constable 1930)
Aden to Sana'a and Hodeidah in the 1920s. Rambling account, not very dynamic.

Peter Somerville-Large: *Tribes And Tribulations* (Hale 1967)
One of the first Westerners to travel through the north after the death of Imam Ahmed. Reasonably hard going.

NATURAL HISTORY

Michael McKinnon: *Arabia: Sand, Sea And Sky* (BBC 1990)
An excellent book which accompanied the television series looking at the nature of Arabia. Amazing photographs.

Hugh Scott: *In The High Yemen* (John Murray 1942)
Two members of the British Museum staff visited North Yemen in the 1930s, collecting information and specimens. An excellent account.

ANCIENT CIVILISATIONS

Brian Doe: *Monuments Of South Arabia* (Immel 1983)

Brian Doe: Socotra: *Island Of Tranquillity* (Immel 1992)
All the details currently available on the ancient sites.

Al-Hamdani: *The Antiquities Of South Arabia* (Milford reprint 1938)
Chronicles of the tenth century Yemeni historian.

Wendell Phillips: *Qataban And Sheba* (Gollancz 1955)
Digging at Timna and Marib in the early 1950s.

Harry St John Philby: *The Queen Of Sheba* (Quartet 1981)
The result of his travels and research into this mysterious character.

POLITICAL AND MILITARY

David Ledger: *Shifting Sands* (Immel 1983)
The background to British rule in and departure from Aden.

Robin Bidwell: *The Two Yemens* (Longman 1983)
Political background to the revolutions and beyond.

Fred Halliday: *Arabia Without Sultans* (Penguin 1974)
A detailed economic and political review of the Arabian peninsula countries, including the YAR and the PDRY. Heavy going!

Fred Halliday: *Arabs In Exile* (IB Tauris 1992)
An interesting account of Yemeni migrants in urban Britain.

Edgar O'Ballance: *The War In The Yemen* (Faber 1971)
The YAR revolution and civil war of the 1960s.

ADVENTURE

Eric Hansen: *Motoring With Mohammed* (Hamish Hamilton 1991)

An interesting modern-day adventure looking for lost 'treasure' - probably
more relevant after a visit to the Yemen.

Jason Gurney: *Sheba's Coast* (Robert Hale 1966)
A dated account of setting up a fishing business in British controlled Aden.
Good descriptions of the Gulf of Aden coastline.

Barbara Toy: *The Highway Of The Three Kings* (John Murray 1968)
The author's journey by Land-Rover along the full length of the incense road.
High adventure during the North Yemen revolution. General interest.

Lord Belhaven, formerly R.A.B. Hamilton: *The Kingdom Of Melchior* (John Murray
1949)
The subtitle sums it up: 'Adventure in South West Arabia'.

Timothy Morris: *The Despairing Developer* (Tauris 1991)
The everyday problems of an aid worker, specific to the Tihama.

THE RED SEA

Peter Vine: *The Red Sea* (Immel 1985)
The complete history of this important waterway.

Peter Vine: *Red Sea Safety* (Immel 1986)
Guide to dangerous marine animals.

John Randall: *Red Sea Reef Fishes* (Immel 1992)
All the details you need to spot and identify the fish, either underwater or
being wheeled around in Hodeidah fish market.

John Randall: *Sharks of Arabia* (Immel 1986)
All you need to know about the 44 species of shark around Arabia.

MAGAZINES

The following issues have articles on the Yemen (the older the date, the
more stylised the view of Arabia).

National Geographic

December 1909:	Arabia: the Desert of the Sea
August 1917:	The Flower of Paradise: *Qat*
March 1918:	Socotra: The Isle of Frankincense
October 1932:	Into Burning Hadramaut
December 1935:	The Rock of Aden
November 1947:	Yemen: Southern Arabia's Mountain Wonderland
November 1948:	Sailing with Sindbad's Sons
February 1952:	Yemen Opens the Door to Progress
February 1957:	Along the Storied Incense Roads of Aden
March 1964:	Behind the Veil of Troubled Yemen
August 1979:	North Yemen
October 1985:	Arabia's Frankincense Trail

Geographical Journal

Issue 3 (1894):	A journey in Hadramaut
Issue 4 (1894):	Expedition to the Hadramaut
Issue 6 (1895):	Exploration of the Frankincense country
Issue 12 (1898):	Exploration of the Yafai and Fadhli countries
Issue 19 (1902):	Expedition to South Arabia
Issue 28 (1906):	The new frontier of Aden Protectorate
Issue 43 (1914):	An account of the railway survey in Yemen
Issue 58 (1921):	Hodeidah before and after the war
Issue 62 (1923):	A visit to the Idrisi territory in Asir and Yemen
Issue 77 (1931):	An air reconnaissance of the Hadramaut

Issue 77 (1931):	Notes on the Hadramaut
Issue 85 (1935):	House building in the Hadramaut
Issue 87 (1936):	Two months in the Hadramaut
Issue 88 (1936):	Hadramaut: a journey to the Sei'ar country and through Wadi Maseila
Issue 92 (1938):	The Land of Sheba
Issue 92 (1938):	The Hadramaut: present and future
Issue 93 (1939):	A journey to the Yemen
Issue 93 (1939):	The use of *Qat*
Issue 93 (1939):	Climate, irrigation and early man in the Hadramaut
Issue 93 (1939):	An exploration in the Hadramaut and journey to the coast
Issue 98 (1941):	Excursion into the Hajr Province of Hadramaut
Issue 99 (1942):	Travels in the Yemen 70 years ago
Issue 100 (1942):	Six weeks in Shabwa
Issue 101 (1943):	Archaeological sites in the Western Aden Protectorate
Issue 102 (1943):	Halevy in the Yemen
Issue 105 (1945):	The Hadramaut in time of war
Issue 108 (1946):	A new journey in Southern Arabia
Issue 110 (1947):	A journey through the Tihama, the Asir and the Hijaz mountains
Issue 115 (1950):	A Journey by two Jesuits from Dhofar to Sana'a in 1590
Issue 121(1955):	The historical development of Aden's defences
Issue 124 (1958):	The Oxford University expedition to Socotra
Issue 129 (1963):	*Qat:* its production and trade in the Middle East
Issue 132 (1966):	Socotra: Island of Bliss

Geographical Magazine

Issue 8 (1938):	A journey to the Hadramaut
Issue 8 (1938):	People of the Hadramaut
Issue 14 (1942):	The dhows of Aden
Issue 15 (1942):	The mountain tribes of the Yemen
Issue 17 (1944):	Yemeni Arabs in Britain
Issue 21 (1949):	Wolves of the desert: the Sa'ar tribe at the watering place
Issue 27 (1954):	Through Sheba's Kingdom
Issue 31 (1958):	Aden in Retrospect
Issue 35 (1963):	A Journey through Yemen
Issue 37 (1964):	Aden: strategic cross-roads
Issue 39 (1966):	South of the Empty Quarter
Issue 51 (1979):	Perilous politics in two Yemen states
September 1990:	Recently United Yemen
March 1992:	Democracy in Yemen

GENERAL INDEX

PLACE NAMES INDEX